REMEMBERING AND FORGETTING IN *ACADIE*:
A HISTORIAN'S JOURNEY THROUGH PUBLIC MEMORY

In 2004 and 2005, Acadians observed two major anniversaries in their history: the 400th anniversary of the birth of *Acadie* and the 250th anniversary of their deportation at the hands of the British. Attending many of the commemorative activities that marked the anniversaries, Ronald Rudin has documented these events as an 'embedded historian.' Conducting interviews and collecting the opinions of Acadians, Anglophones, and First Nations, *Remembering and Forgetting in 'Acadie'* examines the variety of ways in which the past is publicly presented and remembered.

A profound and accessible study of the often-conflicting purposes of public history, Rudin details the contentious cultural, political, and historical issues that were prompted by these anniversaries. Offering an astounding collection of materials, *Remembering and Forgetting in 'Acadie'* is also accompanied by a website that provides access to films, audio clips, and photographs assembled on Rudin's journey through public memory (www.rememberingacadie.concordia.ca).

RONALD RUDIN is a professor in the Department of History at Concordia University.

Remembering and Forgetting in *Acadie*

A Historian's Journey through Public Memory

RONALD RUDIN

UNIVERSITY OF TORONTO PRESS
Toronto Buffalo London

© University of Toronto Press Incorporated 2009
Toronto Buffalo London
www.utppublishing.com
Printed in Canada

ISBN 978-0-8020-9950-1 (cloth)
ISBN 978-0-8020-9657-9 (paper)

Printed on acid-free paper

Library and Archives Canada Cataloguing in Publication

Rudin, Ronald
Remembering and forgetting in Acadie: a historian's journey
through public memory / Ronald Rudin.

Includes bibliographical references and index.
ISBN 978-0-8020-9950-1 (bound)   ISBN 978-0-8020-9657-9 (pbk.)

1. Public history – Maritime Provinces.   2. Collective memory –
Maritime Provinces.   3. Acadia – Anniversaries, etc.   4. Acadia –
Historiography.   5. Acadia – History.   6. Rudin, Ronald.   I. Title.

FC2041.R83 2009   971.6   C2009-900550-6

University of Toronto Press acknowledges the financial assistance to its publishing program of the Canada Council for the Arts and the Ontario Arts Council.

University of Toronto Press acknowledges the financial support for its publishing activities of the Government of Canada through the Book Publishing Industry Development Program (BPIDP).

This book has been published with the help of a grant from the Canadian Federation for the Humanities and Social Sciences, through the Aid to Scholarly Publications Program, using funds provided by the Social Sciences and Humanities Research Council of Canada.

To the memory of Belle Rudin

Contents

Not Alone on the Journey

This book is about the intersection of various journeys. It begins with the journey of the Acadians over the past four hundred years, and it takes in the journeys of the First Nations People who befriended them and the English-speakers who came to occupy the sites of their initial settlements. Ultimately, my own path crossed those of the subjects of the book because of my interest in the public presentation of the past. In the end, however, this book would not exist without the incredible support that I received from the people whom I met along the commemorative trail, some of whom literally opened their doors to me, putting documents at my disposal and sometimes feeding and housing me. The list is simply too long to produce here, but I hope that those whose stories are at the heart of this book know how grateful I am for their time, their thoughts, their hospitality, and in a few special cases – their friendship, which may be for me the most important legacy of this project.

Of course, from my perch in Montreal, I would never have met any of them without the financial support of the Social Sciences and Humanities Research Council of Canada which allowed me to travel across both Atlantic Canada and France to follow manifestations of Acadian memory. In addition, SSHRC's support made it possible for me to indulge my interest in telling a story about historical memory, not only through text but through the use of film as well. Having spent what feels like a lifetime working within a text-based environment, I wanted to explore the use of a different medium, in a sense mirroring the use of various media by the commemorative event organizers whom I encountered. However, my half-baked idea to create a film would have led nowhere had it not been for my partnership with the documentary film-maker, Leo Aristimuño. While he is now a professor at Rutgers University, at the time that this project was taking shape Leo was a colleague at Concordia who brought along some of his best students as fellow travellers, most notably Dino Conginidis and Emmanuel Hessler. In regard to the film project, I also owe a large debt to Geneviève Vallerand, who served first as my research assistant and was then made (with no increase in pay) production coordinator as the film crew took to the road.

The journey that brought this book to completion could not have taken place without the constant support of University of Toronto Press, and in particular of Len Husband, who provided guidance and encouragement at every step along the way. In addition to supporting the multimedia aspects of the project (described in greater detail in the 'Additional Resources' section, which follows), Len wisely advised me to translate all of the material originally in French, to allow an English readership to have access to the whole story being told. This is now the second project I have worked on with Len, and I can only hope there will be others.

Among my academic friends, I owe a special thanks to Margaret Conrad of the University of New Brunswick, who encouraged me to take the plunge into Atlantic waters when I was embarrassingly unprepared, and to Maurice Basque of the Université de Moncton, who not only participated in the film but also was an endless source of references to all matters *acadien*. Closer to home, I am grateful for the financial assistance made available by David Graham, at the time Concordia's Dean of Arts and Science, and for the support of my colleagues Mary Vipond, Shannon McSheffrey, Graham Carr, and Steve High, who provided both encouragement and careful critical eyes. Finally, closest to home, my wife Phyllis and son David did not make the journey, but always encouraged me to do what was necessary (as long as I returned home with gifts).

This book is dedicated to my mother, Belle Rudin, who died along the way and who never had the chance to brag that her son was a film producer. She always encouraged me to bite off more than I could chew, so I think she would have liked the *chutzpah* (to use an Acadian expression) needed to take this journey.

Additional Resources

Much like the maps and travel books that people take along on road trips, there are two additional resources available to enhance the reader's journey through this book. First, for those who want to see what the commemorative events of 2004 at Île Ste-Croix actually looked like, or what the individuals (Acadians, English-speakers, and Passamaquoddy) had to say in regard to them, there is the documentary film *Life After Île Ste-Croix* that I produced and Leo Aristimuño directed. The film is available on DVD from the National Film Board of Canada (www.nfb.ca).

In addition, however, there is footage that did not make the final cut, but which is pertinent to the issues being discussed in this book. Moreover, there is film acquired with other crews, photos taken at various events, and audio of interviews with some of the people with whom I spent time on the road. This material is accessible to the reader by means of the website (rememberingacadie.concordia.ca) that has been constructed, with the assistance of Ezequiel Gerszonowitz, to accompany this book. Within the text, I have included prompts (🖥) to draw attention to the fact that there is supplementary material available on the website. Were the reader to find a prompt on the page currently being perused, then it would only be necessary to go to rememberingacadie.concordia.ca/page/xi to consult the media in question. Readers can also go directly to the website and browse the media that have been organized by themes, or they can access material by keyword search.

Of course, readers have the final say in how to employ the film, photos, and audio, and so, in a sense, are also along for journeys of their own. Some may choose to employ these other media as illustrations for the book, some may access them independently of my text (perhaps even being encouraged to ignore the book), while still others will ignore the supplementary material altogether. Authors always need to understand that readers can subvert their grand designs by approaching a book as they wish, but in this case the choices are greater than in a 'normal' monograph. I can only hope that readers will find their own journeys as interesting as I found mine.

REMEMBERING AND FORGETTING IN *ACADIE*:
A HISTORIAN'S JOURNEY THROUGH PUBLIC MEMORY

Prologue:
Journeys

Acadian Journeys

Early on Labour Day morning 2005, I marched with forty other people across the back roads of Nova Scotia in a 250th anniversary procession that marked the reading of the order that would lead to the deportation of Acadians living in the vicinity of Grand-Pré. In 1713 the British had taken control of the French colony of *Acadie*, whose roots stretched back to 1604. The Acadians had professed their neutrality for decades, trying to avoid being embroiled in the battle for supremacy in North America between the French and British empires, but in 1755 the British decided that the neutral Acadians posed a threat, and ordered their deportation. Until the end of the Seven Years' War in 1763, a succession of expulsions resulted in the uprooting of the vast majority of the Acadians, in what has been described as the first modern example of ethnic cleansing.[1]

We marched on the edges of fields that were in the process of being cleared of their last crops by farmers whose mother tongue was English, itself a testament to the clearance of the Acadians. However, while *Acadie* was destroyed, the Acadian people lived on, and nearly everyone who walked with me that day had Acadian roots, made clear for all to see by the banners with their families' names that they carried. They had been scattered across three continents and on both sides of the Atlantic, but a significant number of them, including most of those with whom I spent Labour Day, ended up in communities that stretched along the eastern coast of what became New Brunswick, having escaped the grasp of the British, often with the aid of their Mi'kmaq allies. These were survivors who had achieved sufficient political power by the 1960s that they were able to achieve equality for their language in New Brunswick, currently the only officially bilingual province in Canada.

The Acadians' presence in this procession was a further manifestation of a people's rise from the ashes. While their ancestors in 1755 had walked from the parish church where the deportation order was read to the ships that awaited them three kilometres away, we walked in the opposite direction, reaffirming the survival of the Acadians who, in a sense, were reversing the process of deportation. At our starting point, there was a large cross that had originally been erected elsewhere in the vicinity of Grand-Pré in 1924 by tourist promoters eager to attract visitors who found something romantic about the story of the Acadians, popularized by the Longfellow poem *Evangeline*, which told the tragic tale of Evangeline and Gabriel. Separated by the deportation at Grand-Pré, the heroine wandered across North America to find her lover, only to have him die in her arms.[2] On the occasion of this anniversary of the deportation, Acadian leaders successfully lobbied to have the cross moved to the site where we began our march, so that it spoke directly to the Acadian experience and not to that of tourists. Our destination was a church reconstructed at the same location where one had stood in 1755, now part of a historic site managed by the Acadians so that their story might be told.

This story, as it was presented that day, mostly had to do with the deportation. Upon our arrival at the church, the leader of the procession, Jean Gaudet, a city councillor from Dieppe, the largely Acadian suburb of Moncton, read a proclamation. However, the words he read were not those that had been proclaimed in 1755, but rather much more recent ones, from a royal proclamation issued by the Canadian government in 2003, which recognized that the Acadians had been wronged. Some of the marchers grumbled a bit on the reading of these words, which did not indicate that anyone had been particularly responsible for the deportation; lawyers had sweated over the details of this document, which was by no means an apology. Others felt some sense of satisfaction that there had finally been, however tardy and however insufficient, some recognition of the deportation, and by extension of the Acadians as a people who had survived.

In addition, there were also other stories that were told that day that touched upon an *Acadie* that had just celebrated its quadricentenary. As we made our way through the fields, overlooking the Minas Basin from which the ships bearing the Acadians had once departed for sites far away, we stopped from time to time so that Jean Gaudet could read various texts about an *Acadie* whose roots stretched back to the early seventeenth century. There were fourteen stops along the route as Gaudet's procession imitated the Stations of the Cross, the Catholic devotional procession that recreates the last hours of Christ: from his being sentenced to death, to his crucifixion, and finally to his body being placed in its tomb.[3] Given the unmistakably Catholic form of the procession, some observers viewed us as objects of curiosity. After all, such a procession had become an oddity by the early twenty-first century, inspired as it was by certain traditions of public commemoration of the past that had largely disappeared from view. However, Gaudet wanted to stage an event that would allow Acadians to be active participants in their remembrance of the past, and not passive observers at carefully choreographed official ceremonies.

Although the story told in the Stations of the Cross ends before Christ's rising from the grave, the Christ-like rebirth of *Acadie* was central to the story told by the procession in which I marched. In essence, Gaudet described an *Acadie* with two distinct moments of birth. First, there was the one that began in 1604 when an expedition led by Pierre Dugua, Sieur de Mons, established the first permanent French settlement in the Americas. Dugua's small band of men, which included Samuel de Champlain, established itself on a tiny island that Dugua named Île Ste-Croix, which sits on the current border between New Brunswick and Maine.[4] A disastrous winter resulted in the death of half the men and their departure for Port-Royal, in present-day Nova Scotia, the following summer. It was in places such as Port-Royal and Grand-Pré that the Acadians planted deep roots, and some of Gaudet's texts spoke to that experience. Then came the deportation, followed by an Acadian rebirth, marked in the late nineteenth century by the creation of the various symbols of national identity: a flag, an anthem, and a holiday.

It was the deportation story that had drawn my fellow marchers that morning. After all, they were a part of the *nouvelle Acadie* that had been reborn. Their relationship to that first moment of birth, however, was not so clear. As I walked with those Acadians, I asked them whether they had participated in the commemorative events during the previous year, in 2004, that had marked the 400th anniversary of the arrival of Dugua and his comrades, but few had been on that journey. Some aspects of their past had been remembered, but others had been forgotten or pushed to the side. As for myself, this procession marked the end of a long journey that had begun years earlier, and Jean Gaudet recognized my perseverance by giving me a banner that bore Acadian colours and my decidedly non-Acadian name. So how did it come to pass that among the Melanson, Béliveau, Richard, and LeBlanc banners there was one that bore the name 'Rudin'?🖥

The Historian's Journey

Historians have written voluminously about why in the past some moments from an even earlier time were marked by spectacular celebrations while other moments were relegated to the shadows. Along the way, they have explored the different means used by commemorative organizers to bring the past to life for the public. I made my own contribution to this literature, having written about a series of commemorative events staged in Quebec City in the late-nineteenth and early-twentieth centuries to fete either Samuel de Champlain (the founder of Quebec City) or Mgr François de Laval (the first bishop of Quebec), in a sense the sacred and secular fathers of Quebec. In *Founding Fathers*, I discovered (as have other historians in other contexts) that there was nothing inevitable about which events would be thrust before the public and which would be accorded relatively little attention.[5] Leaders invested significant amounts of time, energy, and money in order to promote some events, with others left marginalized, but only after considerable debate that also touched on how to mark those moments chosen for public remembrance. The spectacles viewed by the public may have looked as if they could not have been organized any other way, but in fact they were usually the product of intense negotiation.

In order to discuss the actions of individuals who had their own reasons for presenting the past in a particular fashion, historians have been limited by the chance survival of documentation, mostly the accounts left behind by event organizers. As for what actually transpired at those events, they have had to rely largely on newspaper accounts. In my own case, when I was studying the spectacular events staged in 1908 to mark the tercentenary of Quebec City's founding, I frequently wished that I might have had the chance to talk to Earl Grey (the governor general who was the mastermind behind the Quebec tercentenary) to ask him precisely what he had had in mind; and I wished that I might have attended those events to see them for myself and to talk to those in attendance about what they took away from them.

In a sense, my wishes came true when I learned early in the new millennium that a series of commemorative events, all linked by an Acadian theme, was being organized for 2004–5. This commemorative cycle would begin with the quadricentenary in 2004 of the founding of the settlement on Île Ste-Croix, what Acadian leaders billed as '*le 400e anniversaire de l'Acadie*,' and would end in 2005 with the 250th anniversary of the start of the deportation of the Acadians, what they often refer to as the *Grand*

Dérangement (the Great Upheaval).[6] The procession on Labour Day 2005 was the last act in the cycle.

It was, of course, no great feat to discover commemorative events, which now occur with such regularity that one French observer has remarked that his country, and presumably other societies as well, suffer from 'an avalanche' of efforts to mark the past.[7] This proliferation of commemorative events is only one element in a process that has made the past more accessible to the public than ever before. Cable history channels report healthy ratings, documentary films on historical topics have a wide audience, and the number of museums dealing with the past has mushroomed.[8] Some have written about this process with a certain sense of scorn, bemoaning the corruption of history as it is marketed for the larger public. In this regard, David Lowenthal has remarked that such public representations of the past 'thrive on ignorance and error.'[9] Lowenthal placed history as practised by professionals on a pedestal, assuming that their work was somehow pure, as opposed to that of 'ordinary' people, which was invariably corrupted.

In the end, however, this study is not about whether the past that was presented by a wide range of individuals and organizations over the course of 2004-5 was 'good' or 'bad' history. Rather, I wanted to explore the stories that were told, along the way trying to understand why some aspects of the past were remembered while others were forgotten. Assuming that remembrance was not an entirely innocent act, I wanted to reflect upon the various uses of the past in the early twenty-first century. At the same time, I was interested in examining how these events were presented to the public, given the wide array of options that exist for marking moments from the past, ranging from intimate processions, such as the one led by Jean Gaudet, to large-scale, intricately choreographed spectacles. During my time on the road, I also saw history presented through statuary, museum exhibits, theatrical performances, and historical re-enactments.

By being in attendance at these events and by having the chance to talk with others who were there as well, I had the opportunity to get a sense of how the audience responded to these presentations, quite aside from what organizers may have hoped to be their impact, although as I would learn it was not always easy to engage with people in large crowds who were often at a commemorative event either to have a good time (frequently the case with 400th anniversary celebrations) or to reflect on a tragic past (in terms of moments to remember the deportation). It was much easier to spend time with the organizers, who were invariably willing to explain to me why they wanted to tell stories about the past and why they chose to tell them precisely as they did. Given the growing interest of historians in questions of public memory and the proliferation of commemorative events, when I began the project I expected to find other examples of historians observing the construction of such activities. However, as far as I know, this study is unique, at least in the Canadian context, for the way in which I played the role of the 'embedded' historian for several years along the Acadian commemorative trail.[10]

Nevertheless, no work is ever entirely original, and in this case I owe a significant debt to Roy Rosenzweig and David Thelen. In their fascinating *The Presence of the Past*, they set out to explore 'how people outside [historical] circles understood and used the past,' a goal they pursued through a massive telephone survey of Americans.[11] This survey revealed a widespread engagement with the past, so much so that they referred to their respondents as 'popular historymakers.' Breaking down the barriers that others such as Lowenthal imagined, Rosenzweig and Thelen observed: 'Like professional historians, these popular historymakers crafted their own narratives, albeit as dinner table conversations or family trees rather than scholarly monographs. They preferred constructing their own versions of the past to digesting those prepared by others, and they viewed other sources and narratives with sharply critical eyes.'[12]

While Rosenzweig and Thelen never got close to their popular historymakers, who remained at the other end of a telephone call, I set off to spend time with individuals who had a variety of stories to tell, grounded in the Acadian past. Starting several years before the events would begin, I took to the road, meeting with community organizers, government officials, and ordinary citizens, some of whom had been hard at work since the late 1990s, at various sites in Canada, the United States, and France. In the end, the best part of the project was the opportunity to become acquainted with people who were passionately engaged with the past in a way that is difficult for professional historians, trained as we are to provide the appearance of objectivity. Of course, the evidence I collected could not be taken at face value, and so I have tried to place the testimony of these commemorative organizers within the larger social, political, and economic contexts in which they found themselves, also taking into account how such moments from the past had been remembered by other organizers on the occasion of earlier anniversaries.

I also considered my evidence from the road in the context of representations of the Acadian past produced by such creators as writers, lyricists, and film-makers. From time to time in the text, I have made reference to how the public memory presented in 2004–5 was similar to, or departed from, the depictions presented by individuals whose work may have had a significant audience, but who were not involved with representing the past in public space. I make no claim that my treatment of literature, music, and film is in any way comprehensive, because what follows is primarily a study of the presentation of the stories of the Dugua expedition, on the one hand, and the deportation, on the other, through such means as organizing public ceremonies, constructing monuments, staging theatrical productions, and mounting museum exhibits.

Along the way, I reflected on these various public representations of the past in light of the documentation produced by event organizers, government agencies, and other interested parties including those, such as First Nations people, who had some difficulty in having their stories told. Some of this documentation was designed for public consumption, but in other cases I benefited from the kindness of organizers who allowed me to see their internal minutes, which provided glimpses into the construction of their events, with all of the twists and turns that are inevitable. In the case of the pertinent government agencies, I also benefited from various access-to-information programs that helped me to see how the 'official mind' viewed the various representations of the past. Even with this documentation, however, I often felt rudderless, a historian without his archival documents to lean on, left only with notebooks filled with observations, a digital camera filled with images, and cassettes of various types filled with audio and video evidence.

Three Peoples' Journeys

When I set off in 2002 for my first journey to *Acadie*, I was completely unprepared for the stories I would find.[13] In part, this was a product of my own education, or lack thereof. Quebec historians, such as myself, tend to equate the French Canadian experience with that of Quebecers, and so the Acadian past remains something of a mystery. I quickly became sensitized to the gross inaccuracy of the claim, trumpeted loudly at the Quebec tercentenary and still maintained by numerous federal and Quebec government officials whom I encountered, that Champlain's founding of the town in 1608 had marked the beginning of French Canada, if not Canada more broadly. While I came to the project with some understanding that Champlain had been involved with the establishment of a settlement at Port-Royal, in current-day Nova Scotia, in 1605, I knew nothing about the permanent settlement that had been set up on Île Ste-Croix a year earlier, marking the start of a permanent French presence in *Acadie*. This expedition (as well as the one to Port-Royal) included Champlain, but was led by Dugua, whose exploits have been obscured by the very large shadows cast by his cartographer.

Several years before the 400th anniversary of Dugua's arrival at Île Ste-Croix, the Société nationale de l'Acadie, the leading organization for the advancement of Acadian concerns, was busily promoting a series of activities that would draw attention to the moment at which *Acadie* had been born, in a sense to give Acadians a founding moment comparable to 1608 for the Québécois, as well as a founding father, Dugua, who might unseat Champlain. However, in the years that followed I found that this enthusiasm among Acadian leaders was not always shared by ordinary Acadians. This reticence was evident among my fellow marchers in that procession, who had not been engaged by the story of the settlement on Île Ste-Croix. The Dugua story could not compete with the story of the deportation, which had brought them out to walk three kilometres that September morning in 2005. They were far from unanimous about how to engage with the memory of the deportation, as was evident in their various reactions to Gaudet's reading of the royal proclamation, Nevertheless, there could be no escaping the fact that the memory of the deportation was far more powerful than that of their beginnings on Île Ste-Croix.

If the Acadians' attentions were not particularly focused upon Île Ste-Croix, or for that matter upon Port-Royal whose quadricentenary was marked in 2005, this was not the case for two other peoples, whose own journeys were even less known to me than those of the Acadians at the start of this project. With the deportation of the Acadians, these two sites of memory came to be occupied by English speakers. In towns such as St Stephen and St Andrews in New Brunswick, as well as Calais, Maine (in terms of Île Ste-Croix) or Annapolis Royal, Nova Scotia (in the case of Port-Royal), I found people who had been passionately engaged for some time in promoting the 400th anniversaries. However, their motivations for becoming involved with the past had little to do with any connection to the French regime. Rather, these organizers were interested in developing the economic potential of sites that might speak to tourists about a distant past. Norma Stewart, the executive director of the St Croix 2004 Organizing Committee, described St Croix Island (using the English version of the name) as a 'heritage resource ... Using that resource to further improve the prosperity of this region is very, very important.'[14]

At the outset, the English-speaking leaders of those small towns innocently prepared to 'celebrate' four hundred years of history. They soon learned, however, that there were those in their midst who felt there was nothing to celebrate, but much to remember. Stories about the arrival of the first Europeans to any site in the Americas inevitably lead to the question of the role played by the aboriginal inhabitants. In terms of both the Île Ste-Croix and Port-Royal settlements, the relationships forged between Dugua and his men, on the one hand, and the First Nations people, on the other, were generally positive, at least in the short term. In the former case, the Passamaquoddy provided assistance that prevented the consequences of that disastrous winter from being even worse than they were. In the latter, the Mi'kmaq were such trusted allies that when Dugua lost the charter in 1607 that had allowed him to maintain the settlement, he left the Mi'kmaq chief Membertou in charge.

Both the Passamaquoddy and the Mi'kmaq thought long and hard about the relative merits of participating in anniversaries of events that had had disastrous consequences for them over the long term. In the end, however, both agreed to participate only if the word 'celebrate' were changed to 'commemorate,' and beyond that, only if they would have an opportunity to tell their own stories. In the case of the Passamaquoddy, the story that they wanted to tell was grounded in the fact that they were a people divided by an international boundary, who lived on two reservations in Maine, but who existed in fact, if not in law, on the Canadian side of the border as far as the Canadian federal government was concerned. After much debate, the Passamaquoddy decided that the issue of securing their legal recognition in Canada trumped all other concerns, and they set out to influence the shape of the commemorative events so that their story might be told. As Donald Soctomah, the tribe's Historic Preservation Officer put it, 'We decided to become part of the event, making sure everybody realizes that this isn't a celebration for us; it's a chance for us to educate, it's a chance for us to remember.'[15] As for the Mi'kmaq of the Bear River First Nation, whose reserve is not far from Annapolis Royal, the stakes were different, as they chose to participate in order to tell a story from a newly constructed cultural centre that offered the prospect of tourist dollars for the reserve and an opportunity for constructive activity for its often troubled youth.

Mi'kmaq leaders appeared from time to time as the Acadians marked the anniversary of the deportation in 2005, as was only natural given the aboriginal assistance provided to the Acadians at the time of their dispersal. By contrast, the English speakers were not to be seen, lending some credence to the comments of Maurice Basque of the Université de Moncton. In an interview conducted just before the 400th anniversary of the settlement at Île Ste-Croix, he observed that there were anglophones 'lining up to mark the 400th anniversary of Acadie, because it is of interest, but also because there is much money available to organize these celebrations. But I don't see anybody lining up to commemorate [the deportation] in 2005.'[16] Basque's remarks reflected a certain resentment both that English speakers were attempting to profit from someone else's past and that they had conveniently remembered one anniversary while forgetting another. As we will see, such resentment over the ownership of the past and evidence of forgetfulness (alongside remembrance) frequently surfaced on the commemorative trail.

In the end, this book is largely built around the various experiences of Acadians, English speakers, and First Nations people as they negotiated the anniversaries of 2004–5. While its starting point was two Acadian anniversaries, it is not exclusively about Acadians. The four chapters of Part One deal with the involvement of these parties with the events to mark the quadricentenaries of the founding of the settlements at Île Ste-Croix and Port-Royal that signalled the first efforts to establish a 'permanent' French presence in *Acadie*. After an exploration in the next chapter of twentieth-century efforts to remember these settlements, the subsequent ones turn to the engagement of the three groups, along the way taking into account the role played by various levels of government in both Canada and the United States, whose financial support was crucial to public remembrance of the past in the early twenty-first century. Leading the way in this regard was the Canadian government, whose involvement was highly controversial given that it invested much more heavily in a series of commemorative projects in France than in those in Atlantic Canada. The two chapters of Part Two then shift the focus to public memory of the deportation, starting with an exploration of previous efforts to mark this moment of trauma, most notably the bicentenary events of 1955, before turning to the dynamics of marking the 250th anniversary. On this occasion, significant debates emerged within Acadian society as to whether it was more appropriate to remember this past, as was evident in Jean Gaudet's procession, or to push it to the side, or *tourner la page*, to employ the expression widely used in 2005.

The epilogue departs from the previous chapters, which are largely focused upon the stories told during 2004–5 and the reasons that three peoples had for advancing them, in the process marginalizing other tales that might have been told. Rather, in the epilogue I have tried to step back to reflect not only on the messages communicated, but also on the means used to tell them. While it is impossible to separate substance from form, I wondered why it was that some events seemed to have an effect on the audience and others left them cold. To put it more concretely, what was it about Jean Gaudet's procession that transfixed those who were on hand, as opposed to the reactions to the single most expensive event from this commemorative cycle, an exhibition in Paris that was generously supported by the federal government? Visitors to this exhibit had handheld devices to guide them through a labyrinth of screens that provided information about Canada. Typical of the comments written in the book reserved for visitors' feedback was one that read: 'Too much technology kills the enjoyment!'[17] This is, of course, an extreme comparison, but it dramatizes the point that some public references to the past make a significant difference, while others exercise an ephemeral impact. From this perspective, then, the book ends with some reflection on the legacies from the Acadian commemorative trail, which were not at all what I would have expected when I started the journey.

PART ONE

Stories of Beginnings

Many people told me that they had never been as wet in their lives as they were while attending a commemorative event that marked, to the day, the 400th anniversary of the first effort to establish a permanent French settlement in North America, on Île Ste-Croix, an island that sits on the present-day border between New Brunswick and Maine. On 26 June 2004 we stood in the pouring rain at festivities that were staged on the Canadian side of the border, from a vantage point that allowed the island to be easily viewed. In the course of the day, we heard speeches and music in three languages: French, English, and Passamaquoddy, in the process recognizing that there were three peoples who claimed a connection with the legacy of the short-lived settlement established in 1604 by a small group of Frenchmen led by Pierre Dugua, Sieur de Mons. Although they constructed buildings that might allow them to survive the winter, the elements worked against the Frenchmen. In a sense the rains that resulted in cutting short the celebrations in 2004 echoed the disastrous weather during the winter of 1604–5 that led to the death of roughly half of the newcomers, this in spite of the assistance provided by the Passamaquoddy, the First Nations people who occupied the territory. Having had enough of the island, when summer 1605 arrived, Dugua and the survivors, whose numbers included Samuel de Champlain, moved their settlement across the Bay of Fundy to Port-Royal, a site that they had explored in the previous year before establishing themselves on Île Ste-Croix. The Frenchmen were befriended once again by the First Nations people, in this case the Mi'kmaq, and Port-Royal served as a major Acadian site of settlement for over a century, until its French-speaking occupants were deported by the British.

The story of these settlements provided an opportunity for three different groups to remember the past, in the vicinity of Île Ste-Croix in 2004 and at Annapolis Royal, Nova Scotia (where Port-Royal stood), in 2005. Two of these peoples, the Acadians and the pertinent First Nations, could claim a concrete tie to the events from the early seventeenth century. For the Acadians, here were the beginnings of their existence as a people; as for the Passamaquoddy and Mi'kmaq there was much to commemorate, if little to celebrate, as the arrival of the Dugua expedition marked the beginning of a new stage in their existence. The English speakers who now constitute the population in the immediate vicinity of these sites, since the Acadians do not live there anymore, also had reason to remember the past. In part, they felt a connection to the beginnings of European settlement, viewing themselves as continuing the European presence that had begun with the arrival of Dugua and his men. In addition, however, they were motivated by the commercial possibilities that existed in marketing the legacy of the Dugua settlements to a larger audience.

All three groups had reason to look back to these founding moments, but each had its own distinctive connection with that past, and within each group there were frequently differences of opinion as to why (or whether) and how that past should be remembered. Chapters 2 through 4 consider the early-twenty-first century perspectives in turn of the Acadians, the English speakers who now live near the sites of memory, and the pertinent First Nations people: exploring their connections with the events of the early seventeenth century and how their interest in telling stories about that past reflected much about their contemporary situations. Before exploring the commemorative events of 2004–5, however, chapter 1 looks at how earlier anniversaries of the Dugua settlements were marked at regular intervals throughout the twentieth century. While the voices of three different peoples could be heard on the commemorative stages of 2004–5, such was not always the case at earlier celebrations.

1

Birthplaces in the Twentieth Century

While most chapters in this book begin with a story from my travels, this is obviously more difficult for a chapter that ends long before I became acquainted with the sagas of Île Ste-Croix and Port-Royal. However, if I had been on hand for the beginning of efforts to communicate these stories to a larger public, I would have found myself in the office of J.W. Longley, the attorney general of Nova Scotia, who was the chief organizer of what came to be known as 'DeMonts' Tercentenary,' an intricately choreographed celebration that took place in 1904 on both sides of the Bay of Fundy. Longley's efforts to stage such an event placed him in the mainstream of leaders in both North America and Europe who were investing considerable time, energy, and resources in creating commemorative events of various types.[1]

If there were anything out of the ordinary in this case, it was that Longley, whose Nova Scotia roots had led him to the Port-Royal story, chose to stage the tercentenary on the 300th anniversary of the settlement on Île Ste-Croix, but only the 299th of the Port-Royal adventure. However, Longley did not want such a detail to get in the way of building an event in which Annapolis Royal would play the leading role. Writing from his Halifax office to the prime minister, Sir Wilfrid Laurier, he played fast and loose with the facts by observing that 1904 would mark 'the tercentenary of the founding of Port Royal in 1604.' From Longley's perspective, this event was significant because 'it was the first landing and settlement of Europeans in the Dominion of Canada and, with the exception of St Augustine, the oldest European settlement in North America.'[2] Longley twice used the term 'European' because it allowed him to get beyond the fact that he had no personal connection with the French beginnings of the settlement. While Acadians might have viewed the establishment of Port-Royal as the start of their existence as a people, they had little opportunity to offer their perspective on this past, as they were no more than bit players on Longley's program; as for the Mi'kmaq, who might also have spoken more directly to the events of the early seventeenth century, no one seriously considered including them in the festivities.

After the celebrations at Annapolis Royal, the tercentenary tour moved on to Saint John, New Brunswick, to mark the naming of the St John River by Champlain three hundred years earlier, and finally to the shores of both New Brunswick and Maine to commemorate the settlement on Île Ste-Croix. At each of these stops, local English speakers, accompanied by various dignitaries, explained the significance of the commemorative celebrations, largely in the absence of individuals who might have claimed a more direct connection with the events from the early seventeenth century. There was, however, nothing inevitable about this outcome. With Longley's leadership, the settlement at Port-Royal, and not the one at Île Ste-Croix, was given centre stage; and then there were the peoples who were either excluded from (in the case of First Nations people) or marginalized on (in the case of the Acadians) the various stages. However, over the course of the twentieth century, in celebrations that took place to mark significant anniversaries, the situation that had allowed English-speaking leaders to dominate the tercentenary evolved, and with that change different stories were told, different sites of memory gained prominence, and different peoples were given the opportunity to speak, in the process setting the stage for the quadricentenary celebrations to come.

An Island on the Border, A Region on the Margin

It has been centuries since French speakers occupied the sites where Pierre Dugua, Sieur de Mons, tried to establish settlements in the early seventeenth century. The story of those efforts began in the fall of 1603 when the king of France, Henri IV, made Dugua the lieutenant general '"of the coasts, lands and confines of Acadia, Canada, and other places in New France.'"[3] In the following spring, seventy-nine men set out, both Protestants such as Dugua and Catholics such as Samuel Champlain (he subsequently added the 'de' to give himself the appearance of nobility), who would go on to greater glory a few years later with the founding of Quebec City. The expedition crossed the Atlantic and then searched for a propitious site to establish a permanent settlement. After sailing along

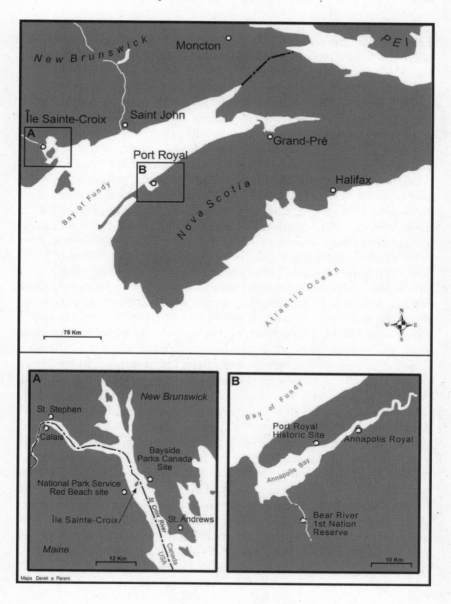

Map 1: Sites of Acadian beginnings

the south shore of what would become Nova Scotia, the expedition entered the 'Baie française' (later Bay of Fundy), soon exploring the site where the settlement of Port-Royal would be established in the following year. On this occasion, however, the Frenchmen kept sailing, ultimately entering, on 24 June, the mouth of a river that flowed into the bay and which was named by Champlain the 'Rivière St-Jean' in honour of St John the Baptist on his feast day. Dugua and his crew continued west until, two days later, they sailed up another river, where they found an island located near a point where two streams entered to form a cross, thus leading them to name both the river and the island 'Ste-Croix.' ▢

Dugua chose to settle on an island, and not on the mainland, in order to observe any unwanted visitors trying to approach the settlement. With the benefit of hindsight, Marc Lescarbot, one of the early settlers at Port-Royal, criticized this decision, noting: 'I shall always be of the opinion that any man who goes into a country to possess it should not settle down in islands to make himself a prisoner therein.' Taking a different point of view, Champlain noted in his journal, 'Vessels could pass up the river only at the mercy of the cannon on this island.'[4] Such concerns about defence proved to be misplaced, however, when winter came exceptionally early, making it difficult, if not impossible, for the Frenchmen to leave the island due to the danger created by the ice in the surrounding water. In the end, there were insufficient supplies to keep all the men alive, with the result that half died of scurvy. The results might have been even worse had it not been for the help provided, as spring approached, by the Passamaquoddy First Nation. The crisis only really passed completely when a supply ship from France brought much needed provisions in June.[5]

After the winter of 1604–5, Dugua had no intention of continuing the settlement on the island. He ordered his men to take down the buildings that had been constructed during the summer of 1604, so they might be transported across the Bay of Fundy, to Port-Royal, where the French adventure in the New World would now continue. Île Ste-Croix played no role in the last 150 years of French settlement in the Americas, and only became an object of any real interest once again, for a brief moment in the 1790s, when a boundary dispute between the British and the Americans hinged on the identification of the island as the site of Dugua's settlement.[6] In the end, the island was declared to lie in American waters, ultimately becoming the property of the U.S. National Park Service, which restricts access to the general public given its ecological fragility. The island had been one-third larger in 1604, and so needed to be protected to prevent its literal disappearance due to erosion. However, even if people could easily visit the island, they would find no visible trace of the Dugua expedition. While Dugua's fallen comrades are buried on the island, there are no markers to indicate the graves; nor are there any remaining traces of the buildings from that one winter.[7] In fact, the only physical evidence indicating that the French had ever been on the island is a commemorative plaque that was installed on the tercentenary of the establishment of the settlement.

While Île Ste-Croix would never be home to permanent residents, such was not the case for the surrounding region that started to attract settlers in significant numbers in the late eighteenth century. With the end of the imperial struggle between the French and the British in 1763, traders and fishermen started to enter the St Croix valley from New England without fear of attack. However, settlement of any significance only began following the American Revolution, which prompted a considerable movement of Loyalists to the part of the region that remained British, and which in 1784 was separated from Nova Scotia to form the colony of New Brunswick. The region possessed seemingly endless resources in its forests and streams, and the British badly wanted to secure provisions for itself and its remaining colonies, now that the American sources had been lost. In short order there were nearly two thousand residents on the British side of the area, with St Andrews, which had previously been the centre of Passamaquoddy life in the vicinity, quickly emerging as the centre for both trade and settlement.[8]

The American side was settled somewhat more slowly as land was granted to speculators who did not immediately make their holdings available to potential residents. Nevertheless, by the start of the nineteenth century, there was already a regular movement of people and goods across the international boundary, which remains a characteristic of life in the St Croix valley. Although there were interruptions caused by wars and trade policies, by and large the region's development had more to do with the market for its resources than with the impact of the border. Accordingly, throughout the 1800s, the growth of the population in both New Brunswick and Maine (which was split off from Massachusetts to become a state in 1820) was closely linked to the region's forests.

Towns such as St Stephen, New Brunswick, and Calais, Maine – which were like twin cities separated by the St Croix River – grew in lock step with the demand for the lumber sawn and the ships built, in the process attracting a fair share of the immigrants from the British Isles who came to North America in search of a better life. Writing in 1875, the Reverend

I.C. Knowlton could chronicle the steady growth of the two towns. He believed that 'a locality of this size and importance deserved to have its history rescued from oblivion.'[9] However, by the end of the century, the forests had been badly over-cut, with the result that 'the cutting of a large tree had become something of an event.' Shipbuilding faced a similar pattern of decline, occasioned by the shift from wind power to steam. By the mid-twentieth century, 'except for some fishing boats, lighters carrying freight to the islands, a few pleasure craft, and an occasional tanker or collier, there [was] no navigation on the St Croix.'[10]

Other sources of employment emerged with the decline of lumbering and shipbuilding. Bolstered by its link to the Canadian Pacific Railway, St Andrews became a resort town, a refuge for the wealthy from metropolises such as Montreal and Boston. These visitors were housed at the Algonquin Hotel, constructed in the 1880s by American interests who sought to provide healthful saltwater baths to their elite clientele, with water drawn from Passamaquoddy Bay. Recognizing a good investment when it saw one, the CPR acquired the hotel in 1903, holding on to it until the 1970s. By then, however, the exclusive nature of St Andrews had been lost as the automobile made the town accessible to a middle-class clientele. Today, with many of its homes having been retained in their original state, St Andrews continues to be a tourist destination, and in 1998 was declared a National Historic District.

Although its economic base was seasonal, St Andrews fared better than other towns in the region that tried to diversify their economies. For instance, in St Stephen, the largest town in the vicinity of Île Ste-Croix, once the lumber and shipbuilding industries declined, the only industry to consistently provide employment was the Ganong Brothers chocolate factory, created in 1873. By the start of the First World War, the factory employed roughly four hundred workers, a level of employment that continued to exist on the eve of the 400th anniversary of the settlement at Île Ste-Croix. In recognition of Ganong's role in the town, St Stephen is 'Canada's Chocolate Town' and hosts an annual Chocolate Fest. Throughout most of the twentieth century, Ganong used the image of Evangeline, Longfellow's heroine of the Acadian deportation, to market its product, which exhibited the same 'purity, excellence, constancy, romance, and sweetness' that she had shown. In fact, on the quadricentenary of the Île Ste-Croix settlement, Ganong produced a 100-kilogram sculpture of this Acadian icon.[11] However, this was as much Acadian content as was ever evident in places such as St Stephen, where less than 3 per cent of the population has French as its mother tongue.

Much less successful than Ganong Brothers in the long term was the most significant effort at industrial development in the region. The St Croix Cotton Mill was established in 1882 in Milltown, now part of St Stephen, but in the late nineteenth century an independent municipality. At the outset there were six hundred workers, and the firm was viewed as 'the cornerstone, the anchor, of a vastly changed economic future for the St Croix area.'[12] Over the years, the workforce varied between four hundred and one thousand workers, through good times and bad, and through difficult working conditions that led to a number of strikes that had a significant impact upon the local economy. Following several changes in ownership, by the 1950s the mill found itself in an industry with excess capacity, which led to its closure in 1957. Bill Eagan, the son of two workers put out of work with the end of the mill, has written, 'I left Milltown in 1960 but returned often for visits. It was not long before a visitor could see the face of Milltown changing in ways big and small. You could see it markedly in the way homes were maintained, in the decline of municipal services, in the struggling businesses. After all, a small town cannot lose a major industry that employs hundreds of workers and injects tens of thousands of dollars into the local economy every week without devastating impacts, both personal and economic.'[13]

After the collapse of the lumber economy, times were even more difficult on the American side of the border. For a while, Eastport, 45 kilometres down the coast from Calais, was home to a thriving sardine-packing industry that drew on herring stocks harvested by New Brunswick fishermen and employed both American and Canadian workers on a seasonal basis.[14] However, the industry was in decline throughout most of the twentieth century, with the last cannery closing in the 1980s. As for Calais, it limped along with nothing as significant as 'the sardine canneries, the cotton mill, or Ganong Brothers candy factory' to provide an alternative, however fleeting, to replace the sources of prosperity from the golden years of the nineteenth century.[15]

By and large, the economic situation in the region as a whole was fragile throughout the twentieth century. Writing in 1950, even before the closure of the St Croix Cotton Mill, Harold Davis, a keen observer of the local economy, remarked that with the passing of lumbering and sailing vessels, 'decline was inevitable. Agriculture, the remaining industries, and the increasingly important tourist trade will probably be sufficient to maintain the present level of existence. For anything more than this a major economic miracle ... will be necessary. Until then enterprising younger people will continue to seek their fortunes elsewhere, and the others, along with their elders, will go on spinning out their uneventful but not altogether unhappy lives along the St Croix.'[16]

The economic difficulties of the St Croix Valley led some local leaders to look to the island as a tool to draw tourists to the region. In 1942 Barrett Parker, whose family owned part of Île Ste-Croix at the time, described the area just across from the island on the Maine side, as having 'passed from days of keen activity to days of decadence and slackness, and some despair.' He hoped that the government would acquire the island to allow 'the re-erection of the settlement of Sieur de Monts as it was in the summer of 1604 ... [to] exert a stimulating and extensive influence upon the entire surrounding country-side.'[17] Parker's words were echoed by leaders from the Annapolis valley of Nova Scotia who similarly viewed Port-Royal, their site of memory, as a tool to attract tourists. Accordingly, after the tercentenary in 1904, the mayor of Annapolis Royal was delighted that ten thousand visitors had been drawn to a town of barely more than a thousand permanent residents. As he observed, the town 'never had a better advertisement.'[18] In spite of these similarities, however, there were also some fundamental differences between the paths that brought leaders of the St Croix and Annapolis valleys to their encounters with the commemoration of the Dugua expedition.

Packaging the Past at Port-Royal / Annapolis Royal

When Dugua and his comrades left Île Ste-Croix in 1605, they literally packed up the buildings and transported them across the Bay of Fundy to Port-Royal, a site that they had visited a year earlier and which Champlain had called 'the most suitable and pleasant [place] for a settlement that we had seen.'[19] Dugua returned to France soon after setting up the new settlement, leaving only a few of the veterans from Île Ste-Croix, including Champlain, along with forty others who had arrived earlier in the year on the ship that saved the survivors from the island. Most of this group stayed on for the following two winters; relatively few died, and the Frenchmen achieved some success in growing crops that would allow the settlement to be self-sufficient. Nevertheless, in 1607 Dugua's charter was revoked, and it was necessary for all the Frenchmen to return home, leaving in charge Membertou, the chief of the local Mi'kmaq First Nation, with whom the colonists had developed cordial relations and who would go on to be the first aboriginal convert to Christianity in the Americas. The French returned to Port-Royal in 1610, but this stay was also to be brief, ending three years later with the destruction of the settlement by the British, who wanted to eliminate potential competition for their own, newly established colony in Jamestown.

Over the next century, *Acadie* would change hands several times between the French and British crowns. Following one such transfer in the 1630s, the site of Port-Royal shifted twelve kilometres from where the habitation had been located. The second Port-Royal became the most important Acadian settlement of the time. Dugua and Champlain were Frenchmen, who never developed deep roots in the Acadian soil. However, over the course of the seventeenth century, families from France slowly claimed the land as their own, building dykes to reclaim marshland for farming, in the process working together as members of an Acadian community. And no community was more firmly implanted than the one at Port-Royal, which emerged not only as the largest in terms of population, but also as the hub from which others developed. As Naomi Griffiths put it, at the turn of the eighteenth century, 'Port Royal remained the centre of official life, of political and religious activity, and of commerce.'[20]

Given its strategic importance, when the British set out to remove the French from *Acadie* in 1710, they focused their attentions on capturing Port-Royal, which, as it turned out, changed hands for the last time.[21] Even though control over the rest of *Acadie* had yet to be established, the British immediately changed the name of the settlement to Annapolis Royal (in honour of Queen Anne) and made it the capital of what became, with the formal ceding of the territory in 1713, Nova Scotia. Skirmishes continued in the vicinity, and so the capital was moved to Halifax with its establishment in 1749. However, even in the days when Annapolis Royal served as the source of British civil and military authority in Nova Scotia, Acadians continued to constitute the bulk of the town's population. By and large, they remained neutral under British rule, even during French efforts to retake the colony, but this good behaviour did them little good when the decision was taken in 1755 to deport the Acadians, a subject that provides the focus for the second part of this book. By this time, other Acadian settlements had displaced Annapolis Royal as the centre of Acadian life, including the area surrounding Grand-Pré, whose destruction has loomed large in the Acadians' collective memory of the *Grand Dérangement*. Nevertheless, in December 1755 a convoy of seven vessels left Annapolis Royal with over 1600 Acadians (of an estimated 2000 Acadian residents in 1755) en route for the New England colonies, where the deportees who did not perish in transit might be assimilated into the larger population.[22]

With the Acadians removed from the scene, the lands in the vicinity of Annapolis Royal were taken over by Planters, New England farmers who were brought in to take the place of the earlier occupants; and their ranks were bolstered by the arrival of Loyalists, including a significant number of African-Americans later in the century. The new, English-speaking occupants created a profitable agricultural economy in the region. In the process, Annapolis Royal became a centre of trade, aided by the presence of a British garrison at Fort Anne (the site of the earlier French fort at Port-Royal) and the town's location that provided easy access to the Bay of Fundy and the ocean beyond. Both shipping and shipbuilding thrived, but with the closure of the garrison in 1854, the future of the town was thrown into doubt. Prospects improved in 1869 with the completion of the Windsor and Annapolis Railway that made the town the terminus of a line that would link it to a larger hinterland. As one writer observed in 1897, 'The products of the upper part of the county, as well as the regions to the south, which began to be peopled and developed, have been brought to its wharves for export, and the producers have frequented its stores and workshops to buy, and the volume of business has induced a prosperity and infused a life that have changed the face of the town.'[23]

By the end of the nineteenth century, however, Annapolis Royal was facing various challenges to its prosperity. In 1891 the rail line was extended to Digby, thus robbing the town of its strategic importance as a site that was both a port and the terminus of rail traffic. More generally, the town suffered the fate of numerous communities (including St Stephen and Calais) that had difficulty making the transition from the age of wind and wood to that of steam and steel. While the population of Annapolis Royal stood at roughly a thousand at the start of the twentieth century, it soon began to decline; but while the residents of the area surrounding Île Ste-Croix had little to fall back upon with the demise of the old economy, Annapolis Royal began refashioning itself through packaging the past.

Fort Anne, which had been left to decay, was given a new lease on life by local citizens who first lobbied for funds to repair its crumbling buildings, then had the fort declared Canada's first national historic site in 1917, and finally in 1935 had it renovated as an interpretive centre for the history of the Port-Royal/Annapolis Royal region. In a similar manner, in 1923 the site of Dugua's habitation from 1605 (located a short distance from Annapolis Royal) was declared a national historic site, and during 1939 and 1940 the habitation itself was reconstructed by the federal government, thanks largely to the efforts of Harriet Taber Richardson, an American who summered in the area and was attracted by the romance of the French past.⌨ These federal sites attracted tourists to the town, as did the efforts to preserve historic buildings by the Annapolis Heritage Society, an organization created by local residents in the 1960s. Several heritage buildings were converted into museums, while others were returned to their earlier grandeur. For these efforts, the town was declared a National Historic District in 1985.

Just as the two Dugua settlements experienced very different fates, so too did the efforts at economic development led by English speakers who constituted the local populations following the departure of the French, in one case voluntarily and in the other by force. In both cases, commemoration of the sites of memory loomed large in the plans of local leaders that surfaced regularly during the twentieth century. While efforts to marshal the past as a tool of economic development were more successful in Annapolis Royal than in the St Croix valley, in neither context did local leaders take into account the perspectives of those who could claim a more direct connection to the founding moments of 1604–5. However, during the second half of the twentieth century, the increased assertiveness of Acadians forced the English-speaking leaders to recognize that others might also make claims on the legacy of the early 1600s.

Mr Longley's Party[24]

The most significant twentieth-century effort to remember the Dugua expedition took place in 1904, on the tercentenary of the Île Ste-Croix settlement. Across Europe and North America at the turn of the century, monuments were being constructed and commemorative events of various kinds were being staged to tell stories from the past at a time when Western societies were experiencing significant changes. Buffeted by a wide array of forces, ranging from industrialization to immigration, and from imperialism to the extension of the franchise, members of the elite frequently looked to the past to provide lessons that might justify their continued hold over the larger population. In the Canadian context, while events such as the tercentenary in 1908 of Champlain's founding of Quebec City may have looked like a show of self-confidence by local, national, and imperial leaders, in fact they reflected the insecurities of men who seized on the opportunity to stage spectacles that might bolster their uncertain place in the world.[25]

In the case of those Quebec City celebrations, the leading figure was Earl Grey, the governor general, who was on a mission to generate support for the empire, particularly among French-speaking Quebecers, as it geared up for the impending battle for supremacy with Germany. Grey did everything he could to encourage a celebration that would trumpet the good relations between French- and English-speaking Canadians under the umbrella of the British empire. The high point of these efforts came through pageants mounted on the Plains of Abraham, which ended with Wolfe and Montcalm, the two generals who died on that battlefield in 1759 – one the conqueror and the other the conquered – now entering the amphitheatre as allies. Closely related to Grey's imperialist dreams was the creation of the Plains of Abraham as a public park. A significant nationalist movement had emerged in Quebec in the early twentieth century, and so Grey's packaging of the past said as much about a certain insecurity as about any sense of confidence.

In much the same way, J.W. Longley, the attorney general of Nova Scotia, emerged as the single individual most responsible for the 1904 tercentenary of the Dugua expedition. A member of an old Nova Scotia family, he was born not far from Port-Royal, in Annapolis County, which he had represented in the Nova Scotia Assembly since 1882.[26] He wanted to mark the anniversary of the establishment of Port-Royal in 1605, and might have logically waited until 1905 to celebrate the event. However, to have done so would have provided the opportunity for others to go off on their own in 1904 to create celebrations that might upstage the ones he imagined for Annapolis Royal, whose significance as a site of initial French settlement was unchallenged at the time. Accordingly, he took steps to piggyback on the anniversaries that could more logically be marked in 1904: namely the 'discovery' in June 1604 of the St John River and the establishment of the settlement on Île Ste-Croix a few days later. In a bit of commemorative creativity, Longley justified the inclusion of Annapolis Royal on the 1904 tour by the fact that Dugua and his comrades had *visited* the site in 1604. As he put it, this had been the 'first landing by Europeans on the soil of North America resulting in a permanent settlement.'[27]

As president of the Nova Scotia Historical Society, Longley worked closely with his counterparts in sister organizations in New Brunswick and Maine to create one intricately choreographed celebration that would parallel the Dugua expedition of 1604, beginning in Annapolis Royal and ending in the St Croix valley, with a stop in between at Saint John. Longley and most of his associates were English-speaking Protestants who had to be aware of the economic challenges that they faced in the age of steel and steam. While new industrial firms such as those established in St Stephen in the late nineteenth century provided an alternative to the decline in the economy based on wood and wind, some of these firms were faltering by the start of the new century, which would not belong to Atlantic Canada.[28] Nevertheless, the organizers of the quadricentenary constructed spectacles that looked positively to the future, barely making reference to the problems that beset them and refusing to allow people with backgrounds different from their own to play roles of any significance. Neither First Nations people nor Acadians were given much opportunity to have their voices heard, even though it was their forebears whose paths had crossed three hundred years earlier.

Longley's concrete involvement with the tercentenary began in 1902 when, following some preliminary discussions among community leaders, he was appointed to a committee of the Nova Scotia Historical Society that was given responsibility for mounting a celebration at Annapolis Royal.[29] Coming only a few years after the first steps had been taken to bring Fort Anne back to life as a tool to reinvigorate the local economy, here was an opportunity to allow outsiders to see what their town had to offer. Accordingly, Longley wanted to put on a show that might capture the imagination of visitors. He observed that 'a mere local celebration [of the landing at Port-Royal] could easily have been arranged but the circumstances seemed of such moment as to justify an international celebration which would involve a demonstration of a some what [sic] imposing character.'[30]

Longley invited every conceivable public figure in Canada, as well as the presidents of both France and the United States, and representatives of historical societies and universities from across North America. Recognizing the extent of Longley's dreams, the governor general, Lord Minto, wrote to a confidant, 'Longley asked the King and the President of the French Republic to come in person! – he may for all I know have invited the Sultan and all the crowned heads of Europe.' In the end, however, Longley could not even get the governor general to come. Viewing Annapolis Royal as 'an enormous distance for me to go for a short ceremony,' Minto feared that if he attended part of Longley's tour, 'it might make it difficult for me to get out of other things that would at once be proposed at St. John and elsewhere.'[31]

As for the elected officials in Ottawa, neither Sir Wilfrid Laurier nor any cabinet minister made the trip east, claiming that they were too busy because Parliament was in session.[32] Of course, the prime minister and his colleagues could have found the time, had they wanted to. After all, representatives from France and the United States did manage to attend.

While Laurier's cryptic response to Longley, claiming that he was too busy, is not particularly revealing, one has to wonder if the prime minister was not staying clear of a commemorative celebration that, as we shall see, was dominated by English speakers such as Longley and which might have been viewed with a jaundiced eye in Quebec, where he had to deal with a growing chorus of *nationaliste* opponents. Indeed, in 1908 he would do everything he could to discourage the organizers of the tercentenary in Quebec City, recognizing that someone would inevitably be alienated by reference to the past. In the end, he could not avoid the Quebec tercentenary, although he limited his participation as much as possible. However, Annapolis Royal was far enough away and sufficiently insignificant (from his perspective) that he could remain comfortably in Ottawa, delegating the local MP to represent his government.

Despite these difficulties, Longley did manage to line up representatives from both the United States and France, as well as a commitment from those two nations, as well as England, to send military vessels to mark the occasion. The town was packed with visitors, and after the crowds had left the mayor expressed satisfaction 'that a very favorable impression had been made upon all the visitors to the ter-centenary celebrations, particularly the Commanders of the warships, and the guests of the Historical Society who spoke in glowing terms of the hospitable treatment they had received ... The Town had reason to congratulate itself on the success of the whole celebration.'[33]

True to Longley's preference for events that were 'intellectual rather than spectacular,'[34] over the course of the two-day celebration there were numerous speeches, a visit to the site where the Port-Royal habitation had stood, and the laying of the cornerstone for a monument to Dugua, which would be completed later in the year on the grounds of Fort Anne, adding to the revival of the site. The inscription for the monument indicated (wrongly) that this had been the site of the 'first settlement of Europeans north of the Gulf of Mexico,' in the process marginalizing the earlier settlement at Île Ste-Croix. However, no one seems to have been bothered by Annapolis Royal's assertiveness. While the St Croix valley was already reeling from the collapse of the lumber-based economy, the leaders of Annapolis Royal believed that their connections to a tourist market, via both rail and water, as well as their first steps towards the construction of tourist infrastructure with the start of work on the Fort Anne site, placed them in a position of leadership.

Sensitivities might also have been bruised by the fact that Dugua was given centre stage at an event that had been unambiguously billed as his

1.1 Poster for Annapolis Royal tercentenary (Fort Anne National
Historic Site; available on microfilm through the Historic
Restoration Society of Annapolis County)

tercentenary, with Champlain given scant attention. In this regard, it
was significant that Dugua had been a Protestant, and Champlain a
Catholic who had already achieved heroic status among French-speaking
Canadians. The marginalization of Champlain was strikingly evident in
the speech at the opening of the affair by the lieutenant governor of Nova
Scotia. A.G. Jones placed Dugua in the company of 'other illustrious men'
such as Columbus, Cabot, Cortes, and Pizzaro, not giving Champlain as
much as a mention in passing. Champlain did not necessarily deserve
special mention in the context of the establishment of Port-Royal, since
he had been no more than a humble member of Dugua's crew. However,
if Jones were prepared to recognize the larger contributions to the
European occupation of North America of those such as Columbus and
Cabot, one has to wonder why he could not mention any of the leading
French-Catholic figures such as Cartier or, closer to home, Champlain.

The question of choosing individuals for heroic treatment was a matter
that was given careful consideration by those responsible for staging pub-

lic spectacles across the Western world during the golden age of commemorative activity. The men in charge of these events were not involved
in some abstract effort to amuse the population, but rather wanted to
advance a certain vision of the present and future by reference to the
past. In this context, drawing attention to figures they deemed as heroic
was a means to an end. Just as Grey focused attention on Wolfe and
Montcalm in 1908, pushing Champlain to the side, in order to advance
his campaign to secure support for the Empire, so too did Longley and
his English-speaking Protestant associates marginalize the French-Catholic
hero. They dwelled instead upon Dugua, whose religion spoke to a world
in which people such as themselves might feel some sense of control, free
from the influence of outsiders, represented in this case by Champlain.

In his own speech at Annapolis Royal, Longley avoided reference to
Champlain, or for that matter to the presence of any Catholics on the
1604 expedition, a presence that might have anticipated Canada's emergence as a country with two founding (European) peoples, one Catholic
and the other Protestant and, by extension, one French- and the other
English-speaking. A supporter of closer economic ties between Canada
and the United States, Longley once remarked that much could be
gained through 'a union of English-speaking people on this continent,'
apparently writing French speakers out of the equation.[35] At Annapolis
Royal in 1904, he characterized Dugua's expedition as one 'sent out
under the authority of a French king, ... commanded by a Frenchman
and ... composed of French colonists.' By secularizing Dugua and his
colleagues, Longley avoided reference to divisions that complicated the
story that he and his colleagues wanted to tell.[36]

There were others, however, who interpreted the events of 1604 differently. The *Halifax Herald*, for instance, observed that while 'this earliest
colonizing expedition was entirely French, there were in it both Catholics
and Huguenots, accompanied by Catholic priests and Protestant ministers – a happy augury of the religious freedom and good will that was to
prevail on this continent.' In the spirit of duality, the newspaper went on
to warn that 'so much attention is likely to be paid to the leader that all
others are in danger of being forgotten. Champlain, of course, must be
equally honoured with De Monts.'[37]

However obvious this may have appeared to the *Herald*, it remained
for the two French Canadians on Longley's program to make that point
in public. While no other province had an official delegate at Annapolis
Royal, Adélard Turgeon, the Quebec minister of colonization, was dele-
gated as its representative. Turgeon was an orator of note, and in 1908

would be asked by Laurier to speak on his behalf at one of the major public events of the Quebec tercentenary. Even on this occasion, Longley described him as both representing Quebec and 'in the absence of Sir Wilfrid Laurier ... speak[ing] in the name of the French population of Canada.'[38] Addressing the crowd mostly in French (so that Longley recorded none of his comments in the 'official' account of the festivities), Turgeon remarked that he stood with those who had 'seen in the maintenance of the French element a token of greatness, of progress and even of security for our Confederation ... National dualism is not a bar to the growth of a young nation.'[39] Laurier could have said the same words had he chosen to attend, but probably recognized the risk of presenting a message that might not have been universally embraced.

The other speaker from Quebec was Charles Langelier, the sheriff of Quebec City, who was on hand to represent the Institut Canadien, a literary organization in the *vieille capitale*. Langelier, like Turgeon, would occupy a key role in the Quebec tercentenary, playing the part of Champlain in the massive pageants staged on the Plains of Abraham. On this occasion, however, he stood out from the other speakers by giving Dugua a religion: 'Although De Monts was a Calvinist he brought with him Catholic priests and Protestant clergymen, showing thus that his colony was open to all, what[ever] may be their religious beliefs. Yes I proclaim it to be the honour of Nova Scotia, your Province has always shown a great religious tolerance. We have never seen among you those religious conflicts which have caused such crises in other Provinces, and which have caused dissension to endanger our national progress ... You have well understood ... that the diversity of worship is not a necessary cause of weakness of national sentiments ... If the celebration of today was only to remind us of those things, it would be sufficient to greet it with joy as a national festival.'[40]

Turgeon and Langelier carefully avoided giving Champlain credit that he did not deserve in terms of the settlement at Port-Royal. Nevertheless, they played upon the religious toleration within the expedition of 1605 to advance a message that had a particular meaning in the summer of 1904, in the context of the on-going debates surrounding the rules that would be established in the soon-to-be-created provinces of Alberta and Saskatchewan regarding denominational schools. This was only the latest in a series of controversies since Confederation about the role of Catholicism in public education, one of which – in New Brunswick in the 1870s – had weighed heavily on Acadians.[41] By the time of the tercentenary, Laurier had already made it clear that he felt that the Catholic minorities in the two new provinces 'were entitled to some form of separate school system.'[42] Of course, this was not the dominant view across English Canada, and to indicate his opposition to the prime minister's goals, Clifford Sifton, the minister of the interior, noisily resigned from the federal cabinet early in 1905. For their part, Langelier and Turgeon reflected the dominant perspective from French-speaking Quebec, namely that Catholics had a historic right to recognition in the educational institutions of the country. This point of view might have been advanced by Laurier had he seen fit to travel east, but was probably not shared by the others on the podium, who chose to avoid reference to religion altogether.

While Turgeon and Langelier spoke about diversity, there were other French speakers who might have addressed those issues with greater authority in the context of the Maritime provinces. In the end, however, Acadian leaders occupied a marginal part in celebrations that might have been constructed to mark the start of their existence. Although Longley invited the Société nationale l'Assomption, the leading Acadian organization of the time, to play a part in the Annapolis Royal festivities, in the end no Acadian spoke. To be fair, Senator Pascal Poirier, the president of the Société, did not participate because he was ill; and Rémi Benoit, who was there to represent Acadians living in New England, declined to speak 'owing to the lateness of the hour.'[43] Nevertheless, one can understand the frustration of the Acadian newspaper L'Évangéline, which observed after the fete was over: 'There were Acadians on hand, but our most accomplished speakers, whom we would have wanted to see on the platform, were absent from this assembling of representatives from three countries who were on hand to honour the memory of the discoverers of Canada after three long centuries. The Province of Quebec was proudly represented; we only wish that we could say the same in regard to Acadie.'[44] The only consolation that L'Évangéline could find in light of the Acadians' marginal status was the satisfaction that 'those individuals whom we honour were in our hearts and minds.'[45] The individuals in question were, of course, Champlain and Dugua, presented in that order by L'Évangéline, which seemed to share Quebec's reverence for the former.

This pairing of Champlain and Dugua, in whatever order, was rare in the 'official' descriptions of the celebration, but was presented graphically in the intensive coverage of the event by the Quebec City newspaper Le Soleil, whose ties to Laurier were well known. The newspaper stood apart from other newspapers by leading every report from Longley's celebration with an image of Champlain superimposed upon one of Dugua, the images ringed with the words Champlain–De Monts, 1604–1904. Whether Champlain 'deserved' equal billing with Dugua at Annapolis Royal is beside the point. *Le Soleil* was trying to underscore the messages of Canadian duality delivered by Turgeon and Langelier, which might have been reinforced had the Acadians spoken. Here they were in black and white, the Catholic and Protestant 'founders' of Canada.[46]

As soon as those festivities at Annapolis Royal were completed, most of the dignitaries boarded a steamer that would take them to the next stop along the tercentenary tour. Longley had worked with the organizers at Saint John and in the vicinity of Île Ste-Croix to guarantee that one series of events would seamlessly blend into the next. However, at least two of the speakers from Annapolis Royal went home after that celebration was over, this in spite of the comment by Alfred Kleczkowski, the French delegate to the tercentenary, who wrote to his superiors back in Paris that 'everyone who participated in the celebrations at Annapolis Royal was invited to take part in those being held at Saint John, and no one would be allowed to be absent.'[47] *Le Soleil*, which also disappeared from the scene, reported that Adélard Turgeon and Charles Langelier returned to Quebec after a series of meetings in Halifax.[48] While the two men had been invited to continue on to Saint John aboard the steamer that Longley had reserved for the occasion, one has to wonder how welcome they were after their speeches in Annapolis Royal. On 21 June, while Turgeon and Langelier would still have been at Longley's celebration, one of the leaders of the Saint John festivities wrote to a colleague that 'Hons Langelier and Turgeon will speak at our meeting if needed.'[49] Something happened, however, by the evening of the 22nd, when the steamer set sail. Were they no longer needed, or had they decided that they had had enough? In either case, their departure underscored the marginal status of anyone at Annapolis Royal whose view of the founding of Canada was more complex than Longley and his associates had conceived it.

Reinforcing this point, Sir Wilfrid Laurier, who had stayed safely out of the way in Ottawa, received an angry letter early in 1905 from Judge A.W. Savary, a local leader in Annapolis Royal, who had played a bit role in the festivities there during the summer of 1904. The federal government had made a contribution towards the construction of the Dugua monument, whose cornerstone had been laid at the time of the celebrations and which was completed later in the year. Savary was shocked by the fact that the inscription placed on the monument was in English only. He wrote to the prime minister: 'I am strongly of the opinion that the inscription on the monument should be in French as well as English. In

1.2 Medal: Tercentennial of Champlain's landing at Saint John, 1604–1904
(New Brunswick Museum, Saint John, NB: X6121-20)

this, I am sorry to say, the Honourable Mr Longley decidedly differed from me, and sent forward the inscription written by me, without instructing a French version of it to be placed on the monument ... [Dugua] was a Frenchman; he founded a French colony, and a large proportion of the people of Canada speak and will always speak the French language.' In the end, Savary's was a voice in the wilderness. As even he recognized, this had been Longley's party, and the English-only inscription would survive until a French one was finally added in the 1980s.[50]

Dressing Up in Saint John

While Turgeon and Langelier headed home, the other dignitaries made their way across the Bay of Fundy to Saint John, where a celebration took place with many of the same characteristics as the one just completed at Annapolis Royal.[51] This similarity is not entirely surprising given that Longley also had his hand in the organization of the Saint John events. From his perspective, Annapolis Royal was the main act in the tercentenary tour, and Saint John little more than a sideshow given that there had been no effort to establish a settlement at the site of New Brunswick's largest city in 1604. Rather, Saint John was included only because the river on which it was located had been named by Champlain 300 years earlier.

Convinced that he was the leader of this tercentenary tour, Longley did not hesitate to direct the actions of the Saint John leaders. Although members of the New Brunswick Historical, Natural History, and Loyalist societies discussed the celebrations from time to time starting in 1902, they had not really made much progress by late 1903. This foot-dragging led Longley to write to the Reverend W.O. Raymond, an Anglican minister and local historian of note, that 'if no accident happens, the celebration at Port Royal will be one of the most memorable occasions in Canadian history. My suggestion is that the St. John celebration should be timed so as to follow instantly on the Annapolis [one] ... I have already spoken to the Admiral of the Fleet about sending one or more ships of war to Annapolis and of course, if he does so, these ships would move promptly on to St. John.'[52]

Longley subsequently came to Saint John to give his pep talk to the entire tercentenary committee, which immediately signed on. Accordingly, by the start of 1904 work was being done to give the celebration some substance, so much so that Longley, watching from the attorney general's office in Halifax, could write: 'I am very much pleased to hear that your St. John committees are waking up.'[53] As this letter suggests, Longley viewed the Saint John organizers with some condescension, and he displayed the same attitude when he learned several months later that no invitation had been sent from Saint John to the governor general. As we have seen, Longley felt that Lord Minto was needed to legitimize these celebrations, and so he was shocked when he found that the work had not been done: 'When I was in Ottawa the other day, I found that no invitation had yet been sent to the Governor General and so far as I learned no steps had been taken by your Society to interest him in the matter ... I think it is time the St. John invitations were sent to all the Societies and Institutions of which [we] sent you the list.'[54]

Longley was even more pointed with his criticism, however, when he learned of the ambitious program that the Saint John organizers had in mind. While the Annapolis Royal celebrations avoided the sort of public spectacles that had become part of the turn-of-the-century commemorative repertoire, the Saint John people were determined to construct a carefully orchestrated affair. As a result, they were preoccupied with their finances, so much so that Longley admonished them: 'You entirely overestimate the necessity for money ... Expensive side shows are very nice from a spectacular point of view and please the masses but my idea of historical celebrations of this character is to have them intellectually commemorative and this can be done for much less money.'[55]

Longley's criticisms aside, the Saint John leaders were in the mainstream of commemorative organizers of the time, as they tried to build an event that might capture the public's imagination. After lobbying both the provincial and municipal governments for funds (Longley never had to do this), they constructed a program whose main event was a re-enactment of the landing of Champlain at Saint John on 24 June, precisely 300 years after he had first visited the site. The Neptune Rowing Club and the Royal Kennebeccasis Yacht Club received $500 each, the former so that its members could take to their canoes dressed as First Nations people. They would then welcome Champlain and his crew (the members of the yacht club) who were aboard a reconstruction of his ship, the *Acadie*. While the landing of Champlain during the tercentenary of Quebec City would feature 'real' Natives, in this case the French impersonators would be met by 'sham Indians in canoes.'[56] One member of the rowing club had suggested that 'genuine Indians could be got for the Champlain welcome.' However, there is no evidence, in this case or in any other part of the tercentenary events of 1904, that any serious effort was made to have Natives play themselves.[57]

Following Champlain's landing, the Frenchmen left their ships to make their way to Market Square, 'where they made gifts to the Indians and smoked with them the pipes of peace. They took possession of the land, with formal ceremony in the name of the King of France, and their new friends danced the war dance about them.' Professor William Francis Ganong of Smith College, a native of New Brunswick and a member of the family that owned the chocolate factory in St Stephen, went on to praise 'this part of the ceremony [which] was extremely effective. In fact, so well was it done that I quite forgot for a time that it was a show.'[58] With the close of this ceremony, Champlain, his entourage, and the Natives made their way, along with an imposing number of soldiers and sailors, to the site of a memorial that had been erected in the north end of the city in honour of the soldiers who had fought in the Boer War. While local leaders had been waiting for just the right moment to unveil the monument, why would they have chosen this particular day, dedicated to remembering the arrival of a French-Catholic explorer, to honour the veterans?

At least part of the explanation can be found in a certain discomfort that existed throughout the Saint John festivities with the celebration of a French-Catholic hero. While Dugua could easily be given pride of place

1.3 De Monts–Champlain tercentenary celebrations – The landing, Market Slip, Saint John, New Brunswick, 24 June 1904 (New Brunswick Museum, Saint John, N.B.: X11237)

at Annapolis Royal, it was more difficult to ignore Champlain at Saint John since he was the one who had named the river (and by extension the city). However, if Champlain could not be ignored, he could be domesticated by using him (or his re-enactor) as part of the ceremony to unveil the Boer War memorial. Here was the Catholic servant of a French state being pressed into a celebration of New Brunswick volunteers who had fought to defend the interests of the British empire.

At other moments in Saint John, it appeared difficult for local leaders to embrace Champlain too warmly on his own terms. For instance, at the very start of the process of organizing the Saint John events, the minutes of the meetings of the Loyalist Society consistently referred to 'the tercentenary of the discovery of the River St. John,' never mentioning the 'discoverer' by name.[59] In a similar manner, the appropriation of municipal funds for the tercentenary was resisted by some who felt that Champlain had been 'an ancient mariner with whose adventure we are nowise concerned.'[60] The grudging celebration of Champlain was also evident in some of the speeches that were made at a 'literary evening' staged on the night preceding the return of the discoverer. Attorney General Longley, in his only public appearance, managed to avoid mentioning Champlain's name, always referring instead to 'De Monts' land[ing] at St. John.' For his part, Dr A.A. Stockton, the vice-president of the New Brunswick Historical Society, was more pointed. He began by identifying himself as 'a descendant of the Loyalists' and went on to observe: 'We do well to honour the memory of the French discoverer, but we do only half our duty unless we also honour the Loyalists who came nearly two centuries later to these shores. Beside the tablet to Champlain should be one in memory of the Loyalists.'[61]

The tablet in question was to be unveiled on 24 June, following the return of Champlain and the unveiling of the war memorial, on the occasion of the opening of the new public library. The Historical Society had considered the construction of a memorial to Champlain, which might have paralleled the one to Dugua in Annapolis Royal, but this idea was quickly pushed aside, to be replaced by the 'erection of a tablet to Champlain and De Monts' at the new library.[62] Champlain just could not stand alone in the eyes of some, and even though he had been paired with Dugua on this occasion, there were those who were bothered that the Catholic hero might be given precedence over the Huguenot. In this context, Reverend Raymond, who stood out throughout the affair as an unapologetic advocate for giving the French-Catholic hero his due, argued, undoubtedly to the displeasure of some, that

'Champlain was the greater man ... He was the father of Canada and left his impress upon it, while De Monts left no memorial.' Raymond cut to the heart of the matter when he observed, 'At St. John, de Monts left absolutely nothing to show that he had ever visited it ... And yet today the Historical Society, in the tablet to be unveiled, would make the two central characters of our celebrations partners in the honours of the tercentenary.'[63]

If Dugua had been added to the Champlain tablet to make it more palatable to residents of Saint John, the manoeuvre did not have its intended effect. Even with both heroes slated for inclusion, it was no mean feat to raise the $160 needed to construct the tablet. Although the official tercentenary committee blessed the idea of erecting such a tablet in early May, it appropriated none of its $4000 budget to the effort. Instead, there was to be an appeal for funds from the general public, but these accumulated very slowly, so that by early June, two weeks before the unveiling ceremony, only $65 had been collected.[64]

In this context, the secretary of the tercentenary committee wrote to Senator Pascal Poirier, president of the Société nationale l'Assomption, asking that Acadians pay for half the tablet. While Poirier politely responded that this might be difficult 'as we are a community destitute of worldly goods,' within days of the request for Acadian support, the treasurer of the Société, Judge Pierre-Amand Landry, appealed to the 'descendants of the Acadian settlers of 1604 to take the initiative and make a voluntary contribution for the monument project; I ask my fellow Acadians to send modest gifts – $1 or less – which I will be honoured to send to the treasurer in Saint John.'[65] By the time of the unveiling, $50 of the $150 so far subscribed for the tablet had come from Acadians, and further contributions came in the days that followed.[66]

While tercentenary organizers needed Acadian dollars, they showed little enthusiasm otherwise for including Acadian leaders in the celebration, which was perhaps to be expected in a town in which the French presence was even less significant than had been the case in Annapolis Royal.[67] In spite of the high-minded talk of tercentenary boosters that their fete would benefit all New Brunswickers, Acadians did not really figure in their calculations. This blind spot was reflected in the *New Brunswick Magazine*, which condescendingly observed, 'While there are some descendants of the earliest French settlers and many of others of more recent date the country is British, the language English, and the sentiment of the people irrespective of nationality that of loyalty to the British crown and Constitution.'[68]

Although there had been talk of planning tercentenary celebrations in Saint John since 1902, there was not a single reference to any Acadian involvement until late May 1904, when Senator Poirier tried to interest organizers in Acadian participation.[69] However, all that Poirier's intervention seemed to achieve was the request from tercentenary leaders for Acadian contributions for the tablet for the library. Invitation lists prepared by the tercentenary organizers at the start of June did not contain the name of a single Acadian leader; nor for that matter was the Société nationale l'Assomption on a list of organizations to contact that included societies with varied interests from across North America. One week before the start of the celebration, Senator John V. Ellis, a Laurier appointee from Saint John, sent a telegram pointing out that 'St. John NB might be wise to assign Senator Poirier or some representative Acadian place on public program.'[70] Only after this intervention from Ottawa did Judge Landry and Rémi Benoit (the representative of Acadians living in New England) receive invitations to speak at the 'literary evening' that preceded the day of Champlain's return. With the representatives from Quebec, Turgeon and Langelier, preparing to take the train back to Quebec, Landry and Benoit were the only French speakers on the program.

Given an opportunity to address the crowds, Landry spoke not about the legacy of Champlain, but rather the achievements of the Acadians who had surpassed other Canadians in their ability to speak both languages. 'The Acadians were progressing educationally and asked the privilege of walking hand-in-hand with their English fellow citizens in the work of nation-building.' For his efforts, Landry received, according to the *St John Daily Telegraph*, 'earnest applause,' this in contrast with the 'hearty and long continued applause' that greeted Commander Dillingham, the American representative who had made the journey from Annapolis Royal.[71] In the end, various voices were heard at Saint John, but some were taken more seriously than others.

Two Countries (Briefly) Remember Dochet Island

While large crowds flocked to Annapolis Royal and a spectacular re-enactment marked the events at Saint John, the tercentenary tour seemed to be losing steam as it moved on to Dochet Island, as Île Ste-Croix was officially known before the summer of 1904. Perhaps that was to be expected, since nothing came of the Dugua expedition's tragic stay there over a single winter. The island had a brief moment of notoriety in the late eighteenth century as it served as the marker for drawing the border between the United States and British North America, but it then fell back into obscurity. Throughout most of the nineteenth century, even the name of the island as it had been known in 1604 had disappeared from view, replaced by the name 'Dochet' (pronounced Doeshay) apparently a corruption of the name of a local woman (Theodosia) who had had some relationship to the island, although its precise nature varied depending on who told the story.[72]

On the eve of the 1904 tercentenary, the bulk of the island was in the hands of the American government, which used it as a light station. The rest was held by private interests who did not live on the island. Rather, their land remained in 'unimproved condition ... a pasture for the lightkeeper's cow, and a picnic ground for all who care to use it.' Writing in 1902, William Francis Ganong called upon the State of Maine to take control of the privately owned section. Anticipating the ultimate fate of the island, he observed that 'it would be a misfortune if even a part of the island in whose history so many feel a deep interest ... should be closed against the free access of all who desire to visit it. It is a good thing for a people to take pride in their history, and this they do the more if they can study it freely upon the actual sites of their historic events, and surrounded by the charm which always hovers over places which have witnessed historic scenes.' Looking ahead to the tercentenary and thinking that this was an event of interest to both Americans and Canadians, he hoped that the Maine and New Brunswick historical societies might mark the event by 'dedicat[ing] ... the island to the free use of the people forever' and by erecting a 'graceful monument recording and commemorating the persons prominent in its history. May the wish prove a prophecy!'[73]

As it turned out, Ganong was far ahead of public thinking about Île Ste-Croix. While he claimed that many felt 'a deep interest' in the island, this was not evident in terms of the tercentenary events staged in its vicinity. In spite of his call in 1902 for the pertinent historical societies to start preparing for 1904, it was not until early in the tercentenary year that any action was taken, and most of that initiative came from the American side of the border. While Longley started haranguing the leaders in Saint John in late 1903, there is no evidence that he ever pushed the organizers in the St Croix valley to act; and when the day for the Île Ste-Croix tercentenary arrived, Longley did not even attend, although he had been at the Saint John events only one hundred kilometres away, this in violation of his own edict, apparently followed by the other dignitaries, that they should stay on the tour from beginning to end. Of course, Longley's apparent dismissal of the significance of the St Croix saga is not entirely surprising as that story challenged the claim that Port-Royal had been the first permanent French settlement, and so perhaps it was better to keep the island out of view.[74]

Nothing of substance had been done to stage the St Croix tercentenary events until the secretary of the Maine Historical Society and Baptist minister Rev. Henry Burrage became involved in early 1904, corresponding with Longley, on the one hand, and with the municipal governments in the vicinity of Île Ste-Croix, on the other.[75] However, Burrage seems to have had more of an impact upon the Calais, Maine, city government, which immediately moved into action, than upon that of St Stephen, New Brunswick, just across the border, which took no steps to move the tercentenary forward. When a committee with representatives from towns on both sides of the border was formed to look after the local arrangements, the Americans clearly provided most of the initiative. In the end, there were two main events that constituted the Île Ste-Croix celebration, one on the island and the other in Calais, Maine. There was an event held just across from the island on the Canadian side, but it was inexplicably staged 'while the services were in progress on the island,' so that 'the attendance was not large.'[76]

In the absence of Canadian leadership, the Maine Historical Society took charge of the St Croix events, but even its championing of the island's significance was muted, as the tercentenary celebration was only one in a series of commemorative events that it promoted. For instance, in 1901 the Historical Society sponsored what it called 'the commemoration of the millenary anniversary of the death of King Alfred the Great.' Placing the Society's interest in the past in the broadest of terms, its president, James Phinney Baxter, observed: 'It has been the practice from the earliest times for civilized people to publicly commemorate important episodes in the lives of those who have made themselves conspicuous by their achievements, not alone for the purpose of showing reverence for the mighty dead, but for the loftier one of keeping bright the memory of virtues worthy to be emulated by the living.' Alfred was particularly worthy of respect because 'of what he wrought for a great race from whose loins we sprang.'[77]

Moving closer to home, starting in 1903 and continuing to 1907, Baxter and his colleagues were involved in a series of celebrations to mark the anniversaries of various incursions by Europeans along the Atlantic coast of Maine. The celebration of 'De Monts' settlement and Champlain's voyage along the coast in 1604' was just one link in the chain. Perhaps reflecting the experience of the Maine Historical Society in organizing such events, Henry Burrage did not seem too concerned when he wrote to Longley in February 1904, 'We have not yet fixed a date, but shall endeavour to conform to the dates of your celebrations.'[78] There was still no permanent organizing committee in place until late April, but perhaps the slow pace was possible because this was designed to be a small affair. After the fact, one local newspaper observed that the Ste-Croix celebration had been 'less varied' than the one at Annapolis Royal and 'less spectacular' than that at Saint John: 'With little money to spend, it was simple, solemn and grand.'[79]

While there were no carefully orchestrated spectacles, just two events largely dominated by speeches, the words that were spoken at the Île Ste-Croix stop brought into relief some of the themes that had stood out at the two larger (and thoroughly Canadian) events. While there had been moments at both Annapolis Royal and Saint John when the mere mention of Champlain's name seemed unacceptable to some, there was no such reluctance on this occasion. Even though the celebration was formally referred to as the 'De Monts Tercentenary,' the tablet that Ganong had hoped for and which was unveiled at the brief event on the island included the names of both Dugua and Champlain, given equal credit for establishing on Île Ste-Croix what was 'then the only settlement of Europeans north of Florida.' While Dugua had received more credit than he deserved in Saint John, the same could be said of Champlain at Île Ste-Croix. The equal treatment of the two men continued in the three main speeches that were delivered over the course of the day, the first of which dealt with Dugua, and the last with Champlain. In between the two, Professor Ganong went out of his way to describe the landing at Île Ste-Croix of 'two [men who] bore the unmistakable stamp of leadership.'[80]

While there had been a few English-speaking voices at Annapolis Royal and Saint John that had presented Champlain and Dugua as presaging the existence of two founding people in Canada, there had also been those, such as Longley in the former case and the leaders of the Loyalist Society in the latter, who could barely bring themselves to utter Champlain's name. They seemed to feel that in the Canadian context the parallel treatment of the two men somehow legitimized the recognition of two cultures. In the end, the only voices from the Canadian stops of 1904 that consistently spoke about duality in this regard were the French speakers, and they were of course few in number.

At Île Ste-Croix, when Judge Landry was unable to attend, there were no French Canadians, but there were also few English Canadians. Instead, most of the speakers were Americans whose references to Champlain and Dugua had different political implications from what they had had

1.4 Commemorative marker on Île Ste-Croix, 1904 (National Park Service photograph)

at either Annapolis Royal or Saint John. When Henry Burrage referred to the presence of both Catholics and Protestants at Île Ste-Croix in 1604, he saw them not as harbingers of Canadian biculturalism, but rather as having anticipated American freedom of worship: 'In this French colony, Protestants and Catholics were found side by side, both minister and priest being included in the personnel of the expedition.' While religious liberty suffered setbacks in France, 'it was to have a rebirth on this side of the sea ... And now to us, religious liberty is so common a thing that we fail oftentimes, Protestants and Catholics alike, to estimate aright our indebtedness for a boon of such priceless value.'[81] Burrage did not focus on two founding nations, but rather on a much broader acceptance of all religious persuasions. Nevertheless, Turgeon and Langelier, by now back in Quebec City, might have wondered why they had been the only ones to have spoken such words at Annapolis Royal.

Acadians Return to Port-Royal

In 1904 it had been fairly easy to marginalize the Acadians, who were still struggling to reconstruct their society following the deportation. It was telling, for instance, that there was a significant ceremony in Caraquet, New Brunswick, that was held only weeks after the close of the tercentenary. The papal delegate, Mgr Donato Sbarretti, was on hand in July 1904, which provided an opportunity for various Acadian leaders, both lay and clerical, to make the case for the elevation of an Acadian to the rank of bishop (a feat that was achieved in 1912) so as to restrict the power that Irish prelates were exercising over them, challenging the survival of their language in the process. As the president of the Société de l'Assomption, Dr F.-X. Comeau, put it: 'The Catholic faith, obedience to the Pope, and devotion to the Virgin Mary – this was all that the survivors of 1755 were able to take along to the places of exile where their oppressors sent them.' Comeau concluded by noting that Acadians 'want to remain Catholic more than anything, [but] they also want to remain French.'[82] Sbarretti apparently understood the message, since he responded to his Acadian hosts, expressing the hope 'that their rights will always be recognized and granted freely.'[83]

On this occasion, 400 years after the arrival of the Dugua expedition, all the Acadian references to the past were to the deportation. Abbé Stanislas-J. Doucet, the curé of the nearby town of Grande-Anse, remarked that 'Acadians are a people with a deep sense of memory.'[84] However, this memory did not seem to stretch back to 1604, leading Robert Pichette to observe that Doucet's sermon 'had nothing to do with the 300th anniversary of the establishment of Sieur de Mons on Île Ste-Croix, an event which was being celebrated at the time by the English-speakers of the Maritime provinces.'[85] The focus of Acadian leaders was on rebuilding what had been destroyed in 1755, instead of waxing nostalgic about a world that no longer existed.

In the aftermath of the various forced movements of the Acadians that constituted the *Grand Dérangement*, a French-speaking population slowly re-emerged in the regions that would constitute Atlantic Canada. Even though they were free to return to British soil with the end of war with France in 1763, they could not return to their former lands, which were now occupied by English speakers, such as those whose heirs constituted the twentieth-century population of places such as Annapolis Royal. The Nova Scotia–centred *Acadie* of the early eighteenth century was gone forever. Nevertheless, in various pockets of the region, Acadians did rebuild their lives. A significant number avoided deportation by heading to the undeveloped lands of what would become New Brunswick, where they were joined by others who returned from exile. This was not the population of roughly 14,000 that had been uprooted after 150 years of life in the old *Acadie*.[86] Rather, at first the *nouvelle Acadie* was a scattered population that had considerable difficult in getting by, starting from scratch. It also had few means to make its feelings known through political representation or lobbying efforts by organizations of its own.

During the second half of the nineteenth century, this situation began to change, albeit slowly. After 'cent ans dans les bois (one hundred years in the woods),' to borrow Antonine Maillet's expression, Acadians found themselves in a position by the late nineteenth century to begin constructing a new national identity with its focus upon New Brunswick. While the first post-deportation census, carried out by Mgr Pierre Denaut in 1803, indicated roughly equal numbers of Acadians in New Brunswick and Nova Scotia, with much smaller numbers in Prince Edward Island, the situation changed quite radically during the nineteenth century, with a steady growth in both the percentage of the Acadian population living in New Brunswick and the percentage of the New Brunswick population that was Acadian.[87] In line with these population changes, the first Acadian newspaper and the first Acadian institution of higher education were established in New Brunswick during the 1860s. These developments reflected the emergence of a new elite that in 1881 staged, also in New Brunswick, the first of several *conventions nationales* to plot a new course for Acadians.[88]

While the initial public gathering of this emerging elite imitated a similar convention of French Canadians from across North America held in Quebec City in 1880, its most significant moment came with the decision that Acadians should have a national holiday of their own. Rejecting the Quebec celebration of the St Jean Baptiste holiday (24 June), the Acadians opted instead for the Feast of the Assumption (15 August). In order to complete their creation of the symbols of national identity, at a subsequent convention in 1884 the Acadian leaders opted for a flag of their own (the French tricolour with a yellow star that symbolized their attachment to the Virgin Mary) and their own national anthem ('Ave Maris Stella,' a hymn to Mary). To cap off this exercise in nation building, so typical of the late nineteenth century across the Western world, in 1890 they established a permanent organization to promote Acadian interests, the Société nationale l'Assomption.

The single individual who best represented this Acadian renaissance was Pierre-Amand Landry, the only Acadian to have mounted a commemorative stage during the 1904 tercentenary. Landry was one of the first students admitted to the Collège St-Joseph when it opened its doors as the first Acadian institution of secondary education in 1864. Following an active role in the Acadian battles against attacks by English speakers on their schools, he was made the first Acadian minister of a New Brunswick government in 1878. In the 1880s Landry chaired the three *conventions nationales*; as a result, his biographer called him 'the unchallenged leader of the Acadians.'[89] In the late nineteenth and early twentieth centuries, Landry also played a key role in the Acadian drive to secure some control over the administration of the Catholic church in the parts of New Brunswick where they were concentrated. This drive achieved a measure of success in 1912, with the naming of the first Acadian bishop to head one of the two dioceses in the province. A leading figure in the Société nationale l'Assomption, after a stint in federal politics, Landry was named the first Acadian judge, and near the end of his life, in 1916, became the one and only Acadian to be knighted.

For all these successes, however, there were also limits to how aggressively Landry felt that an Acadian could promote his people's cause. As Jean-Roch Cyr has noted, 'For a nationalist leader, he seems to have paid a disproportionate amount of attention to the anglophone majority. He wrote to other politicians (even French-speaking ones) in English. He even spoke in English to Acadian audiences.'[90] As we saw in the case of his behaviour in regard to the tercentenary, Landry never seemed troubled that he had been marginalized, which perhaps was a predictable response for a leader whose people were rebuilding their lives after a traumatic experience.

If Landry moved cautiously, so too did the umbrella organization created to look after Acadian interests. Michel Roy has argued that bodies such as the Société nationale l'Assomption helped create 'a structure within which the Acadian clerical-professional elite perpetuated the domination of its own people, serving as a link between the English-speaking majority and ordinary Acadians ... Not a word was said at the *conventions nationales* against the real oppressors, the English newspapers would observe. The Acadian leaders did not want to challenge the powers that be so that they might be able to hold on to the crumbs they were able to take from the table.'[91] Unwilling to attack the structures that were holding Acadians back, such organizations had little to offer in the early twentieth century, so much so that the *conventions nationales* which had been held with some regularity before the First World War ceased to occupy a central place in Acadian public life. A decade passed following the convention in 1927 until the next, and it was nearly twenty years after that of 1937. As Philippe Doucet has observed, 'The progression of the Acadian people was so slow that, from many points of view, the first half of the 20th century can be considered a period of darkness.'[92]

There were good reasons for the cautious behaviour of Acadian leaders who had to deal with a backlash against their efforts to assert their interests, however modestly. In the face of expectations among certain English-speaking leaders in New Brunswick that Acadians would remain passive, talk of 'French Domination' was common during elections, perhaps encouraged by the growing percentage of the provincial population that was Acadian. Léon Thériault has pointed to the fact that the Ku Klux Klan was active in the province during the 1930s, alongside the Orange Lodge, which convinced the provincial government to scrap 'regulations favouring greater use of the French language in New Brunswick's Acadian schools.'[93] For his part, Doucet has described a difficult situation during the same period provoked by calls from Acadian leaders to patronize the Moncton shops of French-speaking merchants. 'The Anglophone reaction was so hostile that it intimidated most Francophone clients! Decidedly, Acadians did not yet feel strong enough to display their uniqueness, at least not in the business world and especially not in Moncton where they were a minority.'[94]

In this context, on the eve of the bicentenary of the deportation in 1955, a series of commemorative events discussed at length in chapter 5, there was much public commentary about this apparent slide of Acadian leadership into irrelevance. In 1950, in their first discussion of the bicentenary, the leaders of the Société nationale l'Assomption expressed the hope that 'the bicentenary would give new life to the *Société*.'[95] Four years later, in a brief to Maurice Duplessis to secure Quebec government support, the organizers stressed that it was crucial that the events have 'a lasting impact ... In order to assure that there will be continued activity beyond the bicentenary, La Société Nationale l'Assomption wishes to create a permanent head office staff (*un Sécrétariat Permanent*), that would help all worthy causes. This staff would coordinate our activities, channel our energies, and help us avoid wasted effort when two or more organizations work towards the same end without a master plan ... The *Sécrétariat Permanent* would become the brain or central nervous system of Acadie beyond the bicentenary.'[96]

In the aftermath of the bicentenary, steps were taken to create a new, more vital body to represent Acadians. The Société national des Acadiens (SNA) was established in 1957, with its much vaunted *secrétariat permanent*. However, while the first president of the SNA, Louis Lebel, wanted to put into practice 'the best techniques of modern management,' he wanted to do so in order to achieve the same modest goals as had the Société nationale l'Assomption. As Lebel put it, 'The means that assured the success of the Société nationale l'Assomption are outmoded. While our objectives remain the same, it is necessary to change the means employed towards those ends.'[97]

The Acadian leadership's concern about being too assertive was also reflected in the very events organized for the bicentenary. While the summer of 1955 saw an unprecedented effort on the part of Acadians to take control of the streets of places such as Moncton, the message that was communicated in the process was designed so as not to threaten those who were quick to see 'French Domination.' There was repeated talk from commemorative stages about the providential nature of the deportation, a perspective with deep roots in Acadian society, and a reluctance to speak in an accusatory tone about the perpetrators of what was often referred to euphemistically as 'l'épreuve [the trial] de 1755.'[98]

The Société nationale l'Assomption played a central, albeit cautious, role in the various bicentenary events, and such behaviour continued when it watched over one final event that had nothing to do with the deportation. The year 1955 marked not only the bicentenary of the deportation, but also the 350th anniversary of the founding of Port-Royal. Since 1904, Port-Royal's status as a site of memory had been bolstered by the reconstruction of the habitation in the late 1930s, and its continued status as the leading site of memory with a connection to the Dugua expedition was further reflected by the staging of not one, but two commemorative events during the summer of 1955.

The first of these two celebrations had many of the same characteristics as the tercentenary events at Annapolis Royal. Between 30 July and 3 August a group of local English speakers (there was not a single individual with an even vaguely Acadian name on the organizing committee) staged a celebration of 'Annapolis Royal's 350th Anniversary,' thus even removing the French name of the original settlement from view. The timing of the event had nothing in particular to do with the founding moment from the French régime, but rather was designed to coincide with Natal Day, the summer's big civic holiday. In his introduction to the printed program for the fetes, the mayor managed to sketch out the festivities without ever using the words 'France' or 'French.'[99]

Over the course of five days, the only words of French were delivered by the governor general, Vincent Massey, who also stood alone in pointing to the fact that the history of Annapolis Royal had been marked by 'the confused interplay of races and peoples – French and Indians, British and New Englanders, and the steadily emerging native Nova Scotians.'[100] Throughout the rest of the festivities, there was little reference to the town's French roots. This was evident, for instance, in the messages conveyed in a parade of historical floats that passed through the town. While one float drew attention to Dugua's receipt of his charter and another pointed to the construction of the habitation, nothing suggested that an Acadian community had had deep roots here for more than a century.[101]

The marginalizing of the Acadian experience was even more striking in the historical pageant that was staged on the last day of the celebration. The pageant was a re-enactment of the siege of Port-Royal in 1710, which had led to the British takeover of the town and its renaming as Annapolis Royal. In Quebec City in 1908, when a pageant was constructed around the battle on the Plains of Abraham, care was taken to soften the message of French defeat, which would not have been well received by its French-speaking residents. In this case, however, since there were few French speakers still on the scene, such reconciliation was unnecessary. At the end of the pageant, the French simply marched away, both the soldiers who had been defeated in battle as well as women and children.[102]

Leaving in this manner, the estimated six thousand people on hand might have concluded that the French presence at Annapolis Royal had come to a close in 1710. Of course, the Acadians continued to live there, and elsewhere in Nova Scotia, for another forty-five years until their deportation. However, as was the case in other commemorative events staged in the Annapolis Valley during the same era, it was just easier to write the Acadians out of the story if their presence was too inconvenient.[103] Even the governor general's relatively inclusive comments never mentioned the word 'Acadian,' in the process conveying the sense that there had been a French imperial presence, but a temporary one at that. In any event, the Acadians were to be distinguished from what Massey described as 'the steadily emerging native Nova Scotians.' By this he presumably meant the Planters and Loyalists who followed the Acadians into this territory after the deportation, another word that was avoided during this upbeat event. However, the deportation would be very much on the minds of the Acadians who came on their own to Annapolis Royal several weeks later.

The official events to mark the bicentenary of the deportation were carefully choreographed to take place mostly in and around Moncton, but they closed with a symbolic pilgrimage to Grand-Pré, which had already taken on the role as the most significant Acadian site of memory in Canada. Over roughly the same period that had seen the reconstruction of the habitation of Port-Royal, Grand-Pré had emerged as a major tourist destination, to a considerable degree for English speakers who were enamoured with the Longfellow story of Evangeline. Nevertheless, there were Acadian pilgrimages as well, and on the occasion of the bicentenary, as part of the very tentative Acadian awakening of the time, there was a request that they should be able to exercise some control over the development of their most sacred of sites. It was in this context that the bicentenary tour moved on to Grand-Pré in mid-August 1955, but the celebrations did not end there, although the lavish attention paid in the media to the Grand-Pré events might have given that impression.

While most of the Acadians who had made the journey to Grand-Pré returned to their homes, many boarding special trains that took most of them back to New Brunswick, others continued their journey, travelling the slightly more than one hundred kilometres to Annapolis Royal for 'the last events of the bicentenary.'[104] This was the first major assemblage of Acadians at this site since the deportation, and so it put the closing act of the town's own 350th anniversary, with the military defeat of the French, in some relief. Newspapers reported the presence of 'dignitaries of church and state, monks, nuns, women dressed in colourful Acadian costumes and hundreds of Acadians and their friends.' As for the platform from which the dignitaries spoke, it was decked out in the *bleu, blanc, rouge* of the Acadian flag.[105] Even the master of ceremonies, Justice V.J. Pottier, who went on to become the first Acadian to serve on the Nova Scotia Supreme Court, stood out because he could trace his roots back to Charles de la Tour, an early seventeenth-century governor of *Acadie*, thus providing a living connection between the Acadian past and present.

While the Acadians had been completely written out of the 350th anniversary events at Annapolis Royal, the program several weeks later was carefully constructed to provide a balance between French and English speakers. The official part of the day saw the unveiling of commemorative plaques at the habitation, in both English and French, in the presence of both English- and French-speaking federal cabinet ministers. For its part, the Nova Scotia government was represented by two speakers, one of whom had Acadian roots, and at the end of the ceremony there was the singing of both 'Ave Maris Stella' and 'God Save the Queen.' Perhaps tipping the balance in favour of the Acadians, the program also included the French consul to the Maritime Provinces, who spoke about the legacy of Champlain, and two speakers from Quebec. Colonel Marquis, the president of Quebec City's Samuel de Champlain Historical Society, talked about the origins of Port-Royal, while Paul Massé, the president of the Montreal-based Société du Bon Parler français, provided awards to six Acadians, all but one of whom hailed from New Brunswick, thus pointing to the *nouvelle Acadie*.

While this recognition from Quebec was no doubt appreciated, it underscored the absence on the stage that day of any of the major Acadian figures of the time, most notably the leaders of the Société nationale l'Assomption, an organization whose need for revitalization had been closely connected with the bicentenary of the deportation from the start. This slightly sour note aside, the event at Port-Royal was exceptional as what appeared to be the last act in the bicentenary turned into a commemoration of the 350th anniversary of Port-Royal. Only a few weeks earlier, the English-speakers of Annapolis Royal had managed to purge the lengthy connection of Acadians with the site from the narrative; on that occasion the only 'Acadians' on the scene were the local people dressed up as Acadians for a pageant that had them departing in 1710. By contrast, at the close of the bicentenary, the French legacy at Port-Royal/Annapolis Royal was feted, in the presence of Acadians, both in the crowd and on the stage. While this might appear to be a small matter, it marked the start of the Acadians' public involvement with the story of their beginnings.

An Island Remembered

While the Acadians returned, albeit in small numbers, to Port-Royal in 1955, there is no evidence that they had even considered a similar pilgrimage to Île Ste-Croix in 1954, on what would have been the 350th anniversary of the first French settlement in North America. In this regard, the Acadians were in good company. Following the insignificant celebrations in regard to the island in 1904, it fell back into the oblivion that had been its fate for the better part of three centuries. While the New Brunswick Historical Society, which had also been responsible for the events at Saint John in 1904, staged another celebration in the province's largest city in 1954, there is no indication that anyone even vaguely considered marking the winter that Dugua and his men spent on Île Ste-Croix.

The Saint John events in 1954 were much like those held fifty years earlier, generally focusing upon Dugua and Champlain as a team and rarely allowing the Catholic hero to stand alone, even if it was his act (the naming of the St John River) that was being remembered. While the minutes of the New Brunswick Historical Society, which played a leading role in the celebrations, at first referred to 'the 350th anniversary of the arrival of Champlain,' within weeks this expression had been reformulated so that the events to be staged in June were now called the 'Champlain–de Monts Commemoration.'[106] The Champlain focus was further marginalized as the week of the naming of the St John River morphed into 'the Champlain–deMonts Commemorative Week and Lancaster Day Celebration,' the latter a reference to the natal day celebrations for the city that bordered upon Saint John.[107] By the time that the fetes were held in June, there were also ceremonies to mark the actions of the Saint John Fire Department during the fire that destroyed large parts of the city in 1877 and to remember the bravery of Captain Fogarty Fegen, an Irishman, whose armed merchant cruiser had been sunk in 1940 in defence of a convoy under German attack.[108]

Even with these additional events, Champlain and Dugua (or de Monts as he was always referred to at the time) were the major figures to be remembered. Strangely, however, in the months leading up to the 350th anniversary, there were occasional reports from local newspapers that cast Champlain's achievements in a negative light. In one case, *The Loyalist* ran a headline that screamed out, 'Gomez was here! Champlain Got the Credit,' an effort to set the record straight by pointing to the 'discovery' of the site of Saint John by a Spaniard in 1524.[109] On the very eve of the anniversary celebrations, roughly equal space was given to the two heroes of the moment by the *Evening Times-Globe*, even if they were far from equally responsible for the event being remembered. The newspaper provided unqualified praise for Dugua, who 'financed the expeditions and who had the foresight and imagination to realize the importance of the settlements which they founded. A good sailor, an efficient leader and a master of organization, Champlain is said to have lacked the spark of humour and enthusiasm supplied by de Monts.'[110]

It was necessary to look elsewhere to find enthusiastic celebration of Champlain. For instance, one of the few reports in the local papers that really dwelled upon the Catholic hero, without mention of his Protestant colleague, noted that the Quebec City–based National Samuel de Champlain Society (whose president would attend the ceremonies at Port-Royal at the end of the deportation bicentenary in 1955) would be sending delegates to Saint John in June so that it might 'lay a wreath at the foot of the Champlain monument.'[111] Similarly, at a banquet designed to mark how the two men had 'named the swirling waters the St. John, in honor of St. John the Baptist,' the only emphasis upon the role of Champlain came via the participation of Père Clément Cormier, a leading figure in the development of Acadian higher education. Although

Acadians were represented in Saint John by a delegation from the Société nationale l'Assomption, Père Cormier was the only one to have been given a chance to speak, and when he did the English press referred to him exclusively as president of the New Brunswick Museum, thus avoiding any reference to the fact that he was Acadian. As for the substance of his remarks, he stood alone in observing that 'even though de Monts was officially in charge, the outstanding figure of the expedition was undoubtedly Champlain. He is rightly called the Father of New France.'[112] As had been the case on the occasion of the tercentenary, Champlain was given a position of uncontested prominence only when the Acadians had a chance to speak.[113]

With the conclusion of the Saint John festivities, the events of 1604 once again disappeared from public view. Of course, in the case of Île Ste-Croix, this disappearance stretched back to 1904. Even on the occasion of the tercentenary, interest in the island had largely been restricted to the American side of the border, where both economic and political power was at a premium given the poverty of this part of Maine. Nevertheless, in the 1930s some local residents began a campaign to have the American government declare the island a historic site, both to protect it against tidal erosion and to promote it as a potential tourist attraction. These first efforts, which included the introduction of a bill in the U.S. Senate, ran up against reluctance from Washington, which did not want to become involved with the process of buying the land that remained in private hands.

In the midst of further lobbying efforts in the 1940s to promote the tourism possibilities connected with the island, H.E. Lamb, writing in a local newspaper, observed: 'Other places use their historical sites, many of them of much less importance to advertise the places and to MAKE MONEY out of them.' Lamb hoped that if the settlement from 1604 were reconstructed on the island, then visitors might spend some time in the area: 'Perhaps those who stayed over night might not buy fur coats, clothes, shoes, autos or such things; but they would have to be fed, and they would have to be accommodated for the night; they would have to have gasoline and oil for their cars and they would buy something in the stores, and the people of Calais would better be enabled to buy fur coats, clothes, shoes, autos and such things.'[114]

Lamb urged local citizens to lobby their political leaders, and his efforts bore fruit when Maine Senator Owen Brewster introduced federal legislation that would make the island a national historic monument, but only when the government had secured title to the land. This bill became

law in 1949, and provided the occasion for a modest event in Calais attended by representatives, as in 1904, from the United States, Canada,
and France. It took another nineteen years for the process of acquiring
the private property to be completed, resulting in yet another dedication
ceremony in 1968. On this occasion, a senior official of the National Park
Service, which now owned the island, spoke at length about the start of a
'new era.' Ernest Connolly led his audience to imagine that there would
be a reconstruction of the habitation on Île Ste-Croix, since he hoped
that 'this site would in every sense become the companion site to Canada's
Port Royal Habitation ... Perhaps in time this will become an international monument, or better yet, one segment of a combined site or a com-
bination of sites in one international historic site on both sides of the Bay
of Fundy.'[115]

No doubt encouraged by Connolly's ideas, the ceremony ended with
remarks by Frank Fenderson, a Calais resident who had organized the
event. He could barely control his enthusiasm at the thought that 'extensive plans are about to be implemented to make the island available to all
who wish to visit it.' He then ended by imagining what these plans might
mean for the local economy: 'While I do not want to indulge in the commercial vein, I do want to point out the tremendous potential this per-
petual attraction will have for the economics of our area. Thousands of
people throughout our nation make it a hobby to visit every U.S. National
Monument regardless of expense or distance. We have added a great
asset to our growing economic status here in Washington (Maine) and
Charlotte (New Brunswick) Counties.'[116] In spite of these hopes, as soon
as the ceremony ended, the representatives from both sides of the border once again dispersed, so that there was nothing until the 1980s to
indicate that the island had, in fact, become a site of historic significance
worth remembering.

The dramatic change in the public memory of Île Ste-Croix came with
the involvement of Canadians, and more particularly Acadians, in the
process. Even though the 1968 designation of the island as a national
monument led to a recommendation from the Historic Sites and
Monuments Board of Canada that the federal government should take
action, nothing concrete occurred until a series of public consultations
were held in early December 1980 under the shared authority of the
governments of the United States, Canada, and New Brunswick. These
consultations were part of a process designed to lead to a joint commitment by the two countries to promote the historical significance of the
island. Public meetings were held in the immediate vicinity of the island,

as well as at other locations, such as the Acadian regions of New Brunswick, where there were individuals with an interest in Île Ste-Croix. This input was solicited via newspaper, radio, and television stations on both sides of the border – and in Canada, in both official languages.

This last point is crucial to understanding the island's emergence from obscurity. While it had been possible in 1970 for a joint Canadian-American planning team with the task of making proposals for the future of Île Ste-Croix to include 'an Irish-Canadian and an Irish-American and a Hungarian-Canadian and a Norwegian-Canadian and an English-American and couple of mixed bags,' a decade later the Acadian perspective on the island could no longer be ignored.[117] While most of the public consultations attracted only 'a modest turnout of citizens,' the situation was considerably different at Moncton and Caraquet. In the former locale the meeting, given significant coverage by the Acadian newspaper *L'Évangéline*, was held on the campus of the Université de Moncton, itself a symbol of the *nouvelle Acadie*, so that in addition to those who made presentations, the Canadian and American government officials made 'contact with several hundred students.'[118] As for the meeting in Caraquet, it allowed for 'a good discussion with officials of Acadian Village (Village historique acadien) and other interested individuals of the vicinity. The essential concerns involved an on-going need for close co-operation on interpretation and liaison with franco-American historic groups of Acadian extraction.'[119]

The comments collected from the consultations in 1980 were published, but without identifying those responsible for the various remarks. Nevertheless, the role of the Acadians (or Acadian sympathizers) in the process was unmistakable. Some participants noted that 'the Island is considered by Acadian people to be more important historically to Canada than to the United States.' Other, presumably American observers pointed out that 'the Island is a significant part of Canadian heritage, particularly to the Acadian people, ... why is there need for international status? Canada should be initiating action on its own.' And then, to put that same issue in a different light, still other participants observed that 'St Croix Island is also very important in Maine history and for Maine people, especially the sizable Franco-American and Acadian population for whom the French language and traditions are still a part of daily life after more than 375 years.'[120]

There were also numerous comments about the nature of the facilities that should be constructed. In a reprise of comments that went back decades, some participants noted that 'the international commemoration of

St Croix Island will be very important to the local economy ... The developments would help to keep visitors in the area for a longer period of time.' As for the story that should be told in regard to the island, the Acadian content was front and centre in many of the comments collected. One respondent noted: 'Interpretation of Acadian history is generally poor in Canada and there is a need to ensure that proper interpretation is undertaken in keeping with the Island's importance to the Acadian people.' Another observer, assuming that the Acadian story would dominate any interpretive centre that might be constructed in regard to Île Ste-Croix, asked that a Loyalist one be built in Saint John, to give both 'sides' equal exposure.[121] This comment was about as negative as any of those collected, and so the two national governments followed up on the consultative process by signing a memorandum of understanding in 1982, in which they committed themselves to the development of interpretive facilities, in part to give prominence to the 'cradle of the Acadian presence on the continent.'[122]

While Acadians were instrumental in promoting the significance of Île Ste-Croix in the early 1980s, only twenty-five years earlier they had indicated little interest in the island. In the 1950s, on the 350th anniversaries of the Dugua settlements, some Acadians made the journey (at the tail end of the deportation bicentenary) to Port-Royal, which they viewed at that moment as the site of the start of their existence as a people, paying no attention whatsoever to the settlement on Île Ste-Croix. Twenty-five years later, by the time of the 375th anniversaries, Port-Royal had lost much of its status, so that the events staged there in 1980 to mark the occasion were seen by Acadian leaders much more narrowly, as 'the 375th anniversary of the establishment of *Acadie* in Nova Scotia.'[123] The Acadians made no claims, as they had in 1955, that Port-Royal was the site of the beginning of the larger Acadian experience, and there was a slim Acadian participation at Annapolis Royal, both on the stage and in the crowds.[124]

As in 1955, when Acadians made the trek to Port-Royal, the largest event in 1980 coincided with the Acadian national holiday, *le 15 août*. Although, as we shall see, Acadians had, by the 1980s, become accustomed to being appropriately represented on such occasions, no Acadian dignitary was given the opportunity to speak on a day that also included a re-enactment of the landing of Dugua and Champlain. The main speech of the day was presented by Prime Minister Trudeau, who spoke about the importance of recognizing that Canada was a country of minorities. Without ever referring specifically to the Acadians, Trudeau thought that the landing was significant because it brought together 'a white man (Champlain) with a black man (Mathieu Da Costa) to meet the red man.'[125] The crowd to which Trudeau spoke was estimated at no more than five thousand people, a far cry from the expected fifteen thousand; and while the weather may have kept down the numbers, there is no evidence that organized groups of Acadians came in 1980, as they had twenty-five years earlier.[126]

In particular, the Acadians of New Brunswick had little enthusiasm to make the journey to Nova Scotia, since by 1980 their leaders had already consecrated 1604, the year of the landing on Île Ste-Croix, as the starting point for their history. That this was a fairly recent development can be pieced together from the activities of the Moncton-based Société historique acadienne. In 1970 the Société made a pilgrimage to Île Ste-Croix that was organized by 'our members from New England.' That same group of New England–based Acadians was also busy lobbying at the time 'to secure a commitment from the American government that it would reconstruct the Champlain Habitation from 1604.'[127] A decade later, in response to the call by the joint Canadian-American team that was collecting the views of interested parties regarding the future of the island, the Société historique was no longer deferring to its American members, insisting in its own right that the governments of Canada, New Brunswick, and the United States must be involved and calling for the construction of interpretive sites on both sides of the border. Recognizing that 1604 was the start of Acadian history, it urged that 'something be done at the very least before the 400th anniversary in 2004 of this historic beginning.'[128]

The conviction by the late 1970s that Acadian history began with the events of 1604 was reflected in the staging, in 1979, of anniversary events that were widely advertised in the Acadian media not merely as the 375th anniversary of the short-lived settlement on Île Ste-Croix, but rather as 'the 375th anniversary of the founding of Acadie.' Yvon Fontaine, the secretary general of the Société nationale des Acadiens, was to the point in observing: 'It was on Île Ste-Croix in 1604 that the first Acadian settlers landed. These men were the founders of what came to be known as *Acadie*. Starting from this date, Acadie and the Acadians have occupied an important place in history.'[129]

Starting from the premise that 1604 marked *l'an I* of the Acadian calendar, the Société des Acadiens du Nouveau-Brunswick (SANB), which took responsibility for the events, put together an ambitious program under the slogan 'On est venus c'est pour rester (We Came … To Stay).' While there would be various commemorative events, they were to be interspersed with activities designed to assert the Acadian presence in the one province where they constituted a significant percentage of the population. In this context, Gilberte Jean, the president of the SANB, provided a rallying cry to members at the organization's 1979 annual meeting: 'We were here first; we have lived with respect, and the time has come for us to claim all the rights we deserve and to proclaim with pride and confidence that we are Acadians.'[130]

Jean's comments pointed to the overtly political nature of the 1979 commemorative events, by far the most explicitly political ones to be discussed in this book. While all commemorative celebrations have a political element, usually some effort is made to conceal such motivations to make the events more palatable to a cross-section of the population that might want to take part and to governments and other organizations that might provide funding. However, on this occasion there was not the slightest effort to pull punches. Speaking at a press conference designed to launch the 375th anniversary year, Yvon Fontaine again set the tone, noting that Acadians had experienced '375 years of struggles in order to assure our survival ... We have had to struggle against all the forces in society including our governments which have tried by all means possible to have the Acadians disappear.'[131] Recognizing that there were a variety of political gains that they wanted to achieve, the committee responsible for the celebrations observed: 'We are not celebrating simply for the sake of celebrating.'[132]

The assertiveness of the organizers of the 375th anniversary events reflected changes among New Brunswick's Acadians in the quarter-century since the bicentenary of the deportation, the previous occasion on which they had taken to the streets in large numbers. While the number of New Brunswickers of French ethnic origin constituted 40 per cent of the provincial population for the first time in the 1971 census, this growth concealed the fragility of the Acadian situation. The portion of the population with French as their mother tongue (as opposed to being of French ethnic origin) declined steadily between the 1951 and 1981 censuses, to a considerable degree a sign of the anglicization of significant numbers of Acadians. Indeed, in 1971, when data first became available in regard to the home language of the population, there was a significant gap between those who had French as their mother tongue and those who actually used the language at home.[133]

In spite of these difficulties, the political situation of Acadians did appear to improve as their political leaders flexed their muscles, encouraged to some degree by the changes that were taking place in Quebec with the coming of the Quiet Revolution. Accordingly, the 1960s were marked by the governments of Louis Robichaud, the province's first elected Acadian premier (1960–70), who brought in legislation making New Brunswick officially bilingual. Acadians were now better represented in the provincial civil service, a situation aided by changes in the educational system. An Acadian university, the Université de Moncton, was created in 1963, and in the following year the province's Department of Education was divided into two linguistic sections, thus providing Acadians with some control over their schools.

While these gains provided Acadians with the hope that they might soon achieve equality with their English-speaking neighbours, there were still signs that this was far from the case. Acadian incomes continued to lag behind those of English speakers, and there was no evidence that the assimilation of Acadians into the English-language community was slowing down. To make matters worse, there were some English speakers who believed that Acadians had already been treated too generously. The most visible incarnation of this backlash was Leonard Jones, the mayor of Moncton from 1964 to 1973, who categorically refused to provide city services in French.

In this context, some of the newly minted leaders of Acadian society started to question whether the strategies that had been put in place during the Robichaud years were likely to bear fruit. Since many of the reforms had centralized power in the hands of the technocrats of the New Brunswick government, in the process sapping the strength of traditional Acadian institutions, some questioned whether Acadians were heading in the right direction. Others who were sympathetic to the rise of state-run institutions but suspicious of English-speaking bureaucrats running them from Fredericton, created the Parti acadien in 1972, with the avowed aim of dividing New Brunswick into two linguistically defined provinces. This belief that new structures might be in order was similarly reflected when Acadian leaders in New Brunswick formed the SANB in 1973 to take charge over their own affairs from the more broadly based Société nationale des Acadiens.

With the coming of the 375th anniversary of the Île Ste-Croix adventure, the leaders of the SANB saw an opportunity to give their concerns some visibility, aided by Quebec's Parti québécois government, which provided a public relations consultant to get the planning process started.[134] In the end, it was impossible to separate the commemorative events that ran from June through le 15 août from an aggressive campaign to advance various Acadian causes. Along the way, the anniversary was linked to efforts, all of which ended in defeat, to make the Acadians' annual fete a legal holiday, to fly the Acadian flag in front of the legislative assembly in Fredericton, and to secure redress for the Acadians who had been evicted from their lands in the late 1960s and early 1970s to allow the creation of Kouchibouguac National Park, just north of Moncton.[135]

In addition, the 375th anniversary was directly linked to a convention scheduled for the fall of 1979. The Convention d'orientation nationale des Acadiens (CONA) was created by the SANB to allow the province's Acadians to reflect on their political future, the creation of a separate Acadian province being one of the options on the table. Seventeen hundred delegates from various walks of life were chosen to attend the convention in Edmundston, but well before they made their way there, the 375th anniversary celebrations were used to focus Acadians' attention on the convention to come. In June, the SANB issued a statement indicating that 'these 375th celebrations form part of the lead up to the convention because they will encourage Acadians to be proud about themselves and their ancestors. This year, by means of the 375th anniversary, the Acadians have shown their ability to work for a common goal and they will be able to show their political power by working together at the *convention nationale*.'[136] To reinforce this point, on *le 15 août* the SANB ran a full-page ad in the Acadian daily, *L'Évangéline*, that graphically linked the commemorative events of the day with the convention to be held in the fall.

In the end, CONA turned out to be an event of limited long-term significance. While the delegates indicated considerable support for the creation of an Acadian province, their enthusiasm did not lead to any concrete action; nor for that matter did the Parti acadien last long beyond the 375th anniversary events, ending its short life in 1982.[137] By contrast, the event that marked the end of the commemorative season both symbolized the newfound assertiveness of Acadians and became a permanent fixture of subsequent Acadian national holidays. Until 15 August, the public celebration of the 375th anniversary had been modest, frequently taking a back seat in *L'Évangéline* to reporting of the build-up to CONA. However, the anniversary events culminated with the staging of *tintamarres* through the streets of Caraquet, Moncton, and many other municipalities. With its roots in the Middle Ages, the tintamarre, much like a charivari, mardi gras, or other such public challenges to 'ordinary' life, brought people into public spaces where they dressed up in outlandish costumes and made as much noise as possible. As we will see in greater detail in chapter 5, the first *tintamarre* was staged in Moncton on the occasion of the bicentenary of the *Grand Dérangement* in

LE 15 AOÛT, NOUS

INVITONS TOUS LES ACADIENS

ET ACADIENNES À CÉLÉBRER LEUR

FETE NATIONALE

C'est le jour de l'Acadie,

fêtons-le en grand!

Soyons fiers de notre histoire

LA CONVENTION

. . . pour bâtir notre avenir.

1.5   375th anniversary of *Acadie* (*L'Évangéline*, 15 August 1979;
Centre d'études acadiennes, Université de Moncton)

1955. This was a significant event in which Acadians, not prone to making too much noise, took to the streets. As it turned out, however, the 1955 *tintamarre* was a one-time affair, until another was held in 1979, starting a 'tradition' that continues to this day.[138] In the spirit of the time, Acadians were insisting on making themselves heard.

In the midst of a period of intense questioning about their future, the Acadian leaders of the 1970s managed to convince large numbers of their counterparts to view 1604 as the start of their existence as a people. Never before had Acadians marked so forcefully an anniversary of their founding moment. Nevertheless, there was still considerable reluctance to embrace all aspects of the 1604 story. There were those, for instance, who seemed to miss the point of the exercise, celebrating instead moments from the Acadian renaissance of the late nineteenth century. On the date that Dugua and his men landed on Île Ste-Croix, the leaders of the Société nationale des Acadiens had little to say about the early seventeenth century, focused as they were upon the prospect of marking two years later the centenary of the first 'congrès national acadien.' In much the same spirit, on the Acadian national holiday, the Village historique acadien at Caraquet staged a re-enactment, not of the arrival of Dugua in 1604, but of the convention of 1884 at which the Acadian flag had been selected.[139]

Even when the 1604 date was respected, there was still considerable reluctance to embrace either the leading figure of the moment, Dugua, or the place where he and his men landed, Île Ste-Croix. While Champlain had long been the Acadian hero of the expedition because of his religion, the tides were starting to shift as Acadians felt more self-confident and less inclined to embrace a *québécois* icon. Nevertheless, old habits die hard, and so towards the close of the 1978-9 school year, in order to stimulate enthusiasm among students for the commemorative season ahead, a number of New Brunswick school boards engaged Champlain re-enactors. In response, the organizing committee for 'le 375e' remarked: 'De Monts was responsible for the expedition of 1604, a fact that should be kept in mind if we are going to trot out Samuel de Champlain.'[140]

As for Île Ste-Croix, the only commemorative event to mark the site of the landing of Dugua and his men in late June 1604 was a formal affair held in Moncton and open only to an invited few, which was followed by a small excursion to the island over the Canada Day weekend. More generally, much of the talk about 1979 having been the 375th anniversary of *Acadie* failed to make reference to where the founding moment had occurred. Such was the case, for instance, in June 1979 when, at an event to launch the 375th anniversary, there was a mural with some of the major dates from the Acadian past. While this chronology began in 1604 and ended in 1979, what made it stand out was the claim that the former date marked the landing that year of Dugua and his men at La Hève (in present-day Nova Scotia) where the expedition first touched North American soil.[141]

To be sure, much information was disseminated in 1979 that described what had taken place on Île Ste-Croix over that winter of 1604-5; and Acadians went on from the 375th celebrations to take a leading role in promoting the development of an international plan for making the island's story well known. In that regard, the SANB, in the midst of preparations for the anniversary celebrations, issued a press release urging the Canadian government to match the actions already taken on the American side to recognize the historical significance of the island. Failing that, Acadians would have to conclude that 'as far as the federal government is concerned, *Acadie* is of no importance in Canadian history.'[142] Nevertheless, there remained a certain distance, both physical and psychological, between the Acadians and what some of their leaders were claiming to be their place of birth, but this was not entirely surprising given the short stay of the Frenchmen (who after all were not Acadians) on the island.

Towards the 400th

As had happened following the various earlier commemorative occasions described in this chapter, once the 375th anniversaries were over, most people stopped thinking about the two sites of memory from the Dugua expedition. Visitors continued to come to Port-Royal to see the reconstructed habitation, but not in anything like the numbers that had come to Annapolis Royal on the three major anniversaries of the twentieth century. As for Île Ste-Croix, while it had become an object of interest to both Canadian and American governments, only in the mid-1990s would any further thought be given to how it might be developed to tell a story from the past. In the closing years of the century, when the 400th anniversary of the Dugua settlements loomed on the horizon, individuals with a wide array of interests began thinking once again about the stories that might be told, this time with an eye to 2004 and 2005. For all intents and purposes, however, twentieth-century efforts to present the story of these sites to a large public came to a close as the last sounds from the 1979 tintamarre faded away and the last spectators from the re-enactment at Port-Royal in 1980 went home.

In spite of prolonged periods of silence between the various anniversaries, these commemorative events did build on one another. It was as if there were an ongoing conversation about the past, which faded from time to time, only to reappear on regular intervals. That conversation was dominated at first by English speakers who lived in the vicinity of the two sites of memory, who were anxious about the economic prospects of their communities, and who hoped that public events to mark the start of French settlement in North America might provide a much-needed shot in the arm. By and large, these English speakers were untroubled by the fact that the past they were presenting was someone else's history. In fact, Acadians only entered the scene when they became sufficiently self-confident and influential to take to public stages, often in communities in which they constituted a very small minority. As part of the process that saw Acadians begin to take charge of their institutions, by the time of the 375th anniversaries, they made it clear that it would henceforth be impossible for someone to tell their story without their participation. Closely connected to the newfound assertiveness of the Acadians, the commemorative conversation also evolved over the course of the twentieth century in terms of the relative importance accorded to the two sites of memory. While the tercentenary events in 1904 presented Port-Royal as the birthplace of Canada, Île Ste-Croix's stock was clearly on the rise as the century came to a close.

Quite aside from questions of who had the power to present some past to the public, there were also significant shifts in the commemorative repertoire over the course of the twentieth century. While J.W. Longley claimed in 1904 that it was possible to present the past in 'intellectual terms' without recourse to large-scale and frequently expensive spectacles, by 1979 it was understood that something out of the ordinary was required to keep an audience involved. By that time, historical re-enactments had become commonplace, and the *tintamarre* (although hardly something 'new') suggested a novel departure that made the audience part of the show, instead of keeping it on the sidelines. Such changes reflected the fact that commemorative events had to compete with late-twentieth-century forms of popular entertainment. At the time of Longley's events at Annapolis Royal, silent film was still in its infancy, but by the time of the 375th anniversaries, organizers had to appeal to audiences that had become accustomed to modern motion pictures and television. The organizers of the 400th anniversaries would also have to contend with the Internet.

When the conversation started once again in the 1990s, the same interest groups continued where they had left off at the close of the

375th anniversaries. It would not take long, however, for new voices to be heard, most notably First Nations people who had their own perspectives on the arrival of the first French settlers. The discussion would also be changed as the sky-rocketing costs of such affairs brought government agencies into the conversation because of the financial support they might provide. In the end, there is nothing inevitable about how commemorative events are organized, who runs them, or the nature of the messages they communicate. J.W. Longley could not possibly have imagined how the public memory of the Dugua settlements would evolve over the subsequent seventy-five years; nor could the people who began to meet in the mid-1990s have predicted how the 400th anniversary events would unfold.

2

Building a New Founding Myth

Fontainebleau

The Château de Fontainebleau, just outside Paris, was the venue for a lavish celebration on 8 November 2003 that brought together Acadians and their French sympathizers, members of the group Amitiés acadiennes. We were there to mark the 400th anniversary of Henri IV affixing his name to the charter that made Pierre Dugua, Sieur de Mons, the lieutenant governor of a territory called La Cadie, in the process making possible the voyage to Île Ste-Croix in the following spring. On the face of it, this was just another commemorative event. There were speeches from dignitaries from both sides of the Atlantic, as well as re-enactors playing the roles of the two principals, Henri IV and Dugua. However, put in the context of previous celebrations of the beginning of the Acadian adventure in the New World this was a special event, and not simply because it took place at such an imposing location.

On the 375th anniversary, neither the island in question nor the leader of the expedition was paid much attention, but much had changed since the fetes of 1979. Shortly after those celebrations and in response to the emergence of support for the idea of an Acadian province carved out of New Brunswick, Fredericton passed legislation in 1981 affirming the equality of the province's two linguistic communities, recognition that became part of the Canadian constitution in 1993. Acadians were provided with the means to succeed more readily in the legal profession when, in 1978, the Université de Moncton created a law faculty that provided training in common law in French; and in the world of business there was considerable evidence of Acadian success stories. For instance, there was the case of Léopold Belliveau, the first Acadian mayor of

Moncton, from 1989 to 1998, and a businessman in his own right. Further symbolic evidence of the rise of a new entrepreneurial *Acadie* could be found in the construction of the Assomption Vie tower in Moncton. This mutual insurance company, the largest Acadian-owned firm, has since the 1970s occupied the tallest building in the city, assuming this distinction from the clock tower of the Cathédrale de l'Assomption, the symbol of an older *Acadie*.[1]

On the basis of these successes, Acadian leaders were prepared to provide their people with the last outstanding signs of national identity. Some of those attributes, such as a flag, a national anthem, and a national holiday, had been the legacy of the leaders of the late-nineteenth-century Acadian Renaissance. As the leaders of the early twenty-first century looked ahead to the 400th anniversary of the arrival of the Dugua expedition, they recognized an opportunity to provide Acadians with a story about their beginnings that was unambiguously their own. These leaders were seeking to provide their people with a new founding myth, but by 'myth' I am not suggesting that they were advancing a perspective that was inherently false (or inherently true). Rather, a founding myth is designed to provide a nation with a sense of its identity. There is nothing inevitable about the contours of a nation, which have to be imagined for a collectivity to be more than an unconnected collection of individuals. As Benedict Anderson has put it, 'Communities are to be distinguished, not by their falsity [or] genuineness, but by the style in which they are imagined.'[2]

Part of the process of creating a new Acadian founding myth entailed imagining Dugua as the undisputed father of *Acadie*, in the process pushing Champlain, the *québécois* hero, to the side so as to emphasize the distinctiveness of the *Acadiens*. It was in this context that the Acadians and their friends were at Fontainebleau in 2003. Previous stories of the Île Ste-Croix adventure indiscriminately interchanged the leadership roles of Champlain and Dugua, since both had been on the scene and since Champlain contributed much of what we know of the expedition through his own writings. By now starting the saga with Henri IV signing the charter, only Dugua could be at the centre of the story, since Champlain had not been there.[3]

In addition to focusing attention upon Dugua as the founding father, the 400th anniversary also provided an opportunity to create a calendar that was unambiguously Acadian. Again, the events at Fontainebleau were pertinent, since for the first time in the history of Acadian commemorative events, 8 November was given a certain visibility as a date that marked, if not the birth of *Acadie*, then perhaps the moment of its conception. On 8 November 2001, exactly two years before the festivities at Fontainebleau, the Société nationale de l'Acadie (with a Dugua re-enactor on hand) unveiled the logo for the 400th anniversary events; and on the same day (and at the same time) as the Fontainebleau cele-brations, Acadians in Moncton marked the occasion with festivities of their own (with yet another Dugua re-enactor on stage). As for the Acadians' date and place of birth, the 2004 celebrations would see con-siderable emphasis upon 26 June and Île Ste-Croix, so that the vague talk about beginnings that had been evident in 1979 would not reappear. For his part, Maurice Basque, the director of the Centre d'études acadiennes at the Université de Moncton, viewed the winter on the island as 'the dif-ficult beginning of the Acadian adventure.' He recognized that for many Acadians this story was 'relatively new,' and he could only hope that 'in 2004, Île Ste-Croix will make its second appearance on the map.'[4] In es-sence, the 400th anniversary was an occasion to provide Acadians with a completed birth certificate.

In self-confidently moving the story of the Acadian experience away from the deportation, the leaders of such organizations as the Société nationale de l'Acadie,[5] whose president played a prominent role in the events at Fontainebleau, sought to create a definition of the Acadian 'nation' that emphasized its modernity and marginalized its legacy of trauma and victimization. However, this conception of Acadian identity had relatively little meaning to the diasporic population scattered across the globe, and concentrated in such parts of the United States as Louisiana and New England. The version of the past that was showcased on 8 November 2003 was particularly designed for the population of Atlantic Canada, and even more pointedly for the population of New Brunswick, where 85 per cent of the French speakers of that region lived and where many of the successes of the previous decades had taken place. It was significant that representatives of the diaspora were not in-vited to the Fontainebleau event, because this was not their story.

The diaspora had various opportunities in the years leading up to the 400th anniversary events to present a version of the Acadian past that spoke more directly to the experience of deportation, and less to the founding moments of 1603–4. The Congrès mondial acadien (CMA), a meeting of the dispersed Acadian clan, was first staged in south-eastern New Brunswick, in the vicinity of Moncton, in 1994; a second edition was staged in Louisiana in 1999, while a third was held in Nova Scotia, the land from which the Acadians had been expelled, during the summer of 2004. These were opportunities for members of dispersed families to rediscover one another, and so the CMA offered a different Acadian perspective on the past from that taken by the 400th anniversary celebrations.

Even before the staging of the first CMA, there were conflicts among its organizers as to whether the diasporic or Atlantic Canada definitions of *Acadie* should prevail, so much so that some referred to it as the 'Conflit mondial acadien (the Acadian World Conflict, instead of the Acadian World Congress).'[6] In that context, it is little wonder that during the summer of 2004 the very presence of the Congrès mondial acadien appeared to be an affront to some of those who wanted to build a strong, modern *Acadie* in Atlantic Canada, and who feared that playing to the diaspora would result in 'turning Acadians into an ethnic group and their culture into folklore.'[7] At a session held within the confines of the program of the CMA, Maurice Basque questioned whether those in the audience, most of whom were from the diaspora, were really Acadians. Many listened through headphones that were providing simultaneous translation from French to English as Basque lectured them: 'We are 300,000 Acadians who live in French on a daily basis in the Atlantic provinces, and who advance our interests in terms of the Acadian people. I know that many people talk about an Acadian diaspora, but history has shown that *Acadie* is based here and it is still like that today.'[8]

Not surprisingly, some in the audience were offended by Basque's remarks. Clive Doucet, a writer from Ottawa, returned to the subject of Basque's edict in a talk of his own at the CMA. He cut to the chase by observing: 'It's not the place of an academic elite to tell me how I should live my life as an Acadian.' Doucet's outrage was mirrored in that of the historian Caroline-Isabelle Caron, who asked: 'Am I to understand that I do not really form part of Acadian society because I live on the Îles-de-la-Madeleine?'[9] For his part, Basque found support for his perspective from the sociologist Joseph Yvon Thériault who, in the midst of the 2004 Congrès mondial, expressed satisfaction that 'we are finally retreating from the very large and all encompassing definition of *Acadie*.'[10]

Basque and Thériault envisioned an *Acadie* that was firmly rooted in Atlantic Canada, a perspective that stood to benefit from the 400th anniversary of a founding moment that had taken place in this part of the world. They hoped that such a view of the past would move the defining moment of Acadian identity away from the deportation, in the process working against a diasporic definition of what it meant to be Acadian. In this regard, they echoed the views of the leaders of the Société nationale de l'Acadie, who saw that 2004 provided an opportunity for Acadians to see themselves in an entirely different light. These leaders hoped that

'this redefinition of our self-image will have some long term consequences for our understanding of Acadian history.'[11]

Such re-constructions of the past are rarely received without contesta-
tion, particularly in a case such as this one that involved such a fundamental redefinition of Acadian identity. The 400th anniversary celebrations sought to provide a narrative of the Acadian past that was not
grounded in the deportation, and by upsetting long-accepted notions of
the past was met with a certain amount of resistance from various quarters. The federal government had difficulty accepting this new Acadian
vision, given its adherence to the view, strongly held in Quebec, that
French-Canadian history began with the founding of Quebec City in
1608 and was embodied in the person of Champlain; English speakers
from the vicinity of Île Ste-Croix could not accept notions that the site of
memory in their backyard somehow belonged to Acadians; and perhaps
most significantly, ordinary Acadians did not rally to the idea that an island where their forebears had spent only a single winter should be
viewed as the site of their beginning as a people.

Acadie at the Start of the Twenty-First Century

During the various events marking the birth of *Acadie*, leaders would
typically present a stump speech focusing upon the successes of Acadians.
At the Château de Fontainebleau on 8 November 2003 and at Bayside,
New Brunswick (with Île Ste-Croix in the background), on 26 June 2004,
the presidents of the Société nationale de l'Acadie used exactly the
same words to describe Acadians at the start of the new century, viewing
them as 'a people who continue to shine through their dynamism, their
cultural richness, and their unstoppable desire to affirm their existence.'[12] Of course, the reality was much more complicated than such
self-congratulatory messages could convey. As Euclide Chiasson, the
president of the Société nationale de l'Acadie, explained to me outside
the Château de Fontainebleau where he had just provided a predictably
upbeat speech, the message of the 400th anniversary celebrations was,
'After 400 years, we are still here, speaking French. It is possible not only
to survive, but to thrive. Still, it is necessary to struggle on a daily basis to
obtain our schools and our services. We must be prepared to struggle
daily. *Acadie* is a constant struggle.'[13] 🔲

This struggle was more daunting in some parts of Atlantic Canada
than it was elsewhere. While French speakers constituted roughly one-
third of the population of New Brunswick, according to the 2001 census

nowhere else did the French-mother-tongue population exceed 4 per cent of the provincial population. However, the situation was even worse if judged by the language spoken most often at home. On this basis, outside New Brunswick, there was no Atlantic province where more than 2 per cent of the population used French exclusively at home. With a limited critical mass of French speakers outside the one province where French had an official status, roughly half of the population with French as its mother tongue spoke another language (usually English) at home. With such high rates of assimilation, the French-speaking populations of these provinces were in decline in 2001 from what had been reported in previous census reports, both in absolute terms and as a percentage of the provincial populations.

The situation was much better in New Brunswick, where roughly 85 per cent of the French-speaking population of Atlantic Canada resided. As a result, most of the leaders of organizations such as the SNA were from New Brunswick, and sometimes gave a gloss (at least in public) to the overview of Acadian fortunes that reflected the situation in only one province. Even in New Brunswick, however, there were causes for concern that were expressed at the Convention de la société acadienne du Nouveau-Brunswick held in the fall of 2004. Much like the Convention d'orientation nationale des Acadiens that was staged on the 375th anniversary of Dugua's expedition, the 2004 convention provided 'an opportunity to bring the celebrations of the 400th anniversary of *Acadie* to a close.'[14] On the issue of the rate of assimilation in New Brunswick, the best that could be said was that the figure had remained relatively stable since the 1990s, so that roughly 10 per cent of the French-mother-tongue population spoke English at home. This situation led Pierre Foucher to remark at the Convention: 'Even if the rate of assimilation for French speakers in New Brunswick is the lowest [for the linguistic minorities] outside Quebec, it is still too high; at this rate, taking into account such factors as the declining birth rate and the mobility of the population [to English-speaking regions], *Acadie* will no longer be French on its 500th anniversary.'[15]

Foucher's predictions were probably a bit overblown, but they did touch on a reality that was not proclaimed from the 2004 commemorative stages. By and large, the percentage of the New Brunswick population that was Acadian, measured either by mother tongue or the language used at home, had been in steady decline since the Second World War. This relative decline even continued when the New Brunswick population shrank between 1991 and the 400th anniversary celebrations.

While speakers at commemorative events trumpeted the successes of Acadian artists, business leaders, and public figures, there was another reality that was not much discussed from commemorative stages and which makes the population figures more understandable. The available data on the incomes of Acadians in New Brunswick show no improvement in their economic status over the twenty years leading up to the 400th anniversary, a period during which they secured legislative gains and exhibited considerable public confidence in the future. A study of the 1981 and 1991 censuses reported that 'francophones in New Brunswick [have] incomes far behind those of their anglophone counterparts,' a fact confirmed by the two most recent census reports, which showed Acadians consistently earning average incomes that were roughly 90 per cent of those earned by English speakers in the province.[16] This wage gap has largely been attributed to the continuing concentration of a large part of the Acadian population in small communities, in the south-east, north-east, and north-west corners of the province, where the economy was dependent upon the availability of natural resources, often from the ocean or the forests, to survive. While the point has been made that English speakers who resided in these regions of New Brunswick were also poor, the fact is that Acadians were disproportionately concentrated there and so suffered more from the consequences of their location, such as intermittent employment and the need to migrate, often to English-speaking regions where their language would be vulnerable.[17]

The situation was not so grim elsewhere in New Brunswick, and in fact it was this side of the coin that was trumpeted in 2004. In particular, *Acadie* seemed alive and well in the vicinity of Moncton, an ironic twist of fate since the town had been named after General Robert Monckton, who played a central role in the brutal campaign against the Acadians in 1755. The general might well have wondered where he had gone wrong had he returned to Moncton in 1999, where he would have seen a summit meeting of the leaders of the *francophonie,* an event that in its own right pointed to the vitality of *Acadie* in this one corner of New Brunswick.[18]

While the Acadian population was in decline everywhere else in the province as the 400th anniversary approached, the trend was moving in the opposite direction in the city of Moncton, but even more so in the neighbouring town of Dieppe, where such Acadian institutions as the Société nationale de l'Acadie have their head offices. While the population of New Brunswick declined between 1996 and 2001, Dieppe's increased by nearly 20 per cent; the French-speaking population, which made up roughly 75 per cent of the population of Dieppe, increased even more rapidly, growing by nearly a quarter in only five years. Moreover, while Acadian incomes lagged well behind those of English speakers everywhere else in the province, here the Acadians actually had higher incomes. In a reversal of the pattern for the province as a whole, in Dieppe the average incomes of Acadians were more than 10 per cent higher than those of their English-speaking counterparts.

As a sign of this growth, the town fathers of Dieppe paid respect to the 400th anniversary of *Acadie* by launching, shortly after the commemorative year closed, plans for a major downtown development that would be called 'Place 1604: Centre urbain de l'Acadie.' The developers were Acadian businessmen whose project would reflect 'the spirit of the Acadian urban community,' while paying homage to the 'first Acadian settlement in North America.' For the mayor of Dieppe, Yvon Lapierre, sounding as if he were on a 400th anniversary stage, the project reflected 'the modernity of Acadians and the determination of its citizens to assert themselves and to extend their horizons. In the image of modern Acadie, our new city centre is vibrant and reflects the dynamism, perseverance and aspirations of its citizens.'[19] As for the name of the new complex, the mayor observed, 'This title is designed to pay tribute to the journey of the Acadian people, to mark the incredible changes they have experienced, and to highlight their modernity that dates back to the first official settlement.'[20]

This was a classic formulation of Acadian history on the occasion of the anniversary of its birth, which managed to efface the existence of the deportation by giving Acadians the mark of modernity from the start of their experience. This effort paralleled those of leaders in Quebec in the aftermath of the Quiet Revolution who sought to purge from the historical record aspects of its past that might have cast it in anything but a 'modern' light.[21] Such formulations, of course, did not draw attention to the difficulties of Acadian populations outside New Brunswick and, within the province, for those outside the metropolitan area of Moncton. Groups such as the Société nationale de l'Acadie were, of course, aware of such problems. In 1986, at a conference looking ahead to the new millennium, delegates recognized that 'the walls surrounding *Acadie* are closing in.'[22] Nevertheless, such reflections were not part of the positive face put upon Acadie's 400th anniversary in the years leading up to 2004.

Myth Making

Although 2004 would mark their 400th anniversary as a people, Acadians were relatively slow off the mark in organizing events to mark the occasion. English-speaking residents from the vicinity of Île Ste-Croix set to work in 1995 to mark the arrival of Dugua and his men. As for the federal government, building on the momentum that came from the declaration of 1999 as the *Année de la francophonie*, in conjunction with the summit meeting of the leaders of the *francophonie* in Moncton, it had already prepared a draft program before that year was out. This draft did not view the events from 1604 as significant in their own right, but rather as part of a process of French exploration and settlement that would culminate with the founding of Quebec City in 1608. As for the Société nationale de l'Acadie, it did not even have a committee dedicated to 2004 up and running until 2000, and did not hire its co-coordinator for such activities, Chantal Abord-Hugon, until 2001.

If it took a while for the SNA to move forward on this dossier, it was not for lack of conversation among its leaders. In early 1995 the board of directors recognized that 'in light of the upcoming celebrations of the 400th anniversary in 2004, the SNA has the responsibility to start thinking about this important event which will be marked across *Acadie*.'[23] In this and in numerous subsequent meetings, there was no reference to the place where the Acadian adventure had begun. By 1997 the plans for marking the anniversary had scarcely budged forward, as members of the *conseil d'administration* reflected on how they might choose 'the site for a major event in *Acadie*' in 2004, still never having mentioned the name of that small island.[24] Writing to the board to encourage it to think hard about whether Île Ste-Croix was even worth remembering, an Acadian leader from Nova Scotia was to the point, asking, 'What significance does this island really have for Acadians at the end of the 20th century? The place is uninhabited, belongs to the United States, has never been home to an Acadian population, and as a site of French settlement only lasted for a few months, never to be colonized again.'[25]

The same correspondent also expressed doubts about focusing upon 2004, noting the other options that existed. If Acadians wanted to mark 'the *founding* of *Acadie* ... maybe we should celebrate 2003 and not 2004,' the earlier date marking the granting of the charter for the Dugua expedition. While the Nova Scotian conceded that 2004 might mark 'the *coming* of the French,' he observed that they had landed 'at several locations in the Maritimes,' including Port-Royal. Once the Port-Royal option was out of the bag, the correspondent then reflected on the possibility of focusing on 2005, the quadricentenary of Port-Royal's founding and the 250th anniversary of the deportation. As he put it, here was an opportunity to 'kill two birds with one stone ... Wouldn't it make sense to focus on 2005 to draw attention to the two anniversaries?'[26] Reflecting their own confusion as to what to do, the exasperated members of the SNA board asked: 'So what year should we celebrate?'[27]

While planning began in earnest in 1999 for the anniversary of the deportation, the 400th anniversary file remained in limbo. Committees came and went, with no discernable impact, until a *comité central pour les fêtes 2004–5* was created in 2000, which advanced the idea that there should be celebrations lasting 400 days, beginning with the anniversary of the landing at Île Ste-Croix in late June 2004 and ending 400 days later (in late July 2005) with an event to mark the continuation of the Acadian adventure at Port-Royal. In creating this calendar, which would also include the 250th anniversary of the signing of the deportation order on 28 July 2005, the leaders of the SNA seemed content to include the two fundamentally different anniversaries within a single commemorative project.[28] Moreover, to make it perfectly clear that Île Ste-Croix was not to be the primary focus of the celebration, the *comité central* insisted that the goal in 2004 should be to '*celebrate the beginnings of Acadie, the start of Acadian history, and not the first permanent French settlement in North America.*'[29]

Within months, criticism of this plan began to emerge, most notably in a report from a group of historians that the SNA assembled and which included Maurice Basque. The historians were very conscious that the SNA was already playing catch-up, and looked upon the actions of the English speakers in the vicinity of Île Ste-Croix with some suspicion, viewing them as reluctant to give Acadians their rightful place in the events. Accordingly, the historians insisted that the 2004 celebrations be organized 'by and for Acadians.' They were equally suspicious of the federal government, given its desire to build a long-term commemorative program that would culminate with a celebration of the founding of Quebec. In this regard, the historians concluded, 'It is essential that Acadians decide how they want to celebrate their 400th anniversary; and only subsequently should they insert their own program into the one being constructed at the national level.'[30]

The historians seemed to share Basque's insistence on projecting a view of Acadian history that was pertinent to the Acadians of Atlantic Canada (and not to the Acadians of the diaspora), and so they left no doubt that the anniversary of Dugua's landing needed to be divorced from that of the deportation. As they put it, 'the 400th anniversary of Acadie and the 250th anniversary of the start of the Grand Dérangement are two distinct anniversaries, and it is important to mark them very differently.' They recommended that if it were important to use the 400-day concept, then the SNA could begin its fetes on 8 November 2003, the date on which Dugua received his charter, finishing towards the close of 2004, in the process leaving 2005 unambiguously as the year to mark the deportation.[31]

Within weeks, in November 2000, this proposal had been accepted as the official calendar for the events to mark the anniversary of the arrival of the Dugua expedition, and the text released by the SNA to announce its plan reflected the language of the historians, insisting that Acadians should be 'actors in and not just observers of their history.' This forceful-ness was required so that Acadians would be able to advance their perspec-tive 'in the context of the initiative of the Minister of Canadian Heritage to celebrate the 400th anniversary of New France.'[32] By this time the fed-eral government had already been working for more than a year on its own plans for what it invariably referred to as the anniversary of 'the ar-rival of *Champlain* on Île Ste-Croix.'[33] In announcing its determination to start its 400-day celebration on 8 November 2003 (marking an event that did not involve Champlain), the SNA was firing the first of many shots in its war to make Dugua, the Acadian hero, the man of the hour. As these Acadian leaders put it quite pointedly in announcing the outlines of their plans for 2004: 'It is important to point out that [Champlain] was not in command at either Île Ste-Croix or Port-Royal.'[34]

This emphasis on Dugua was relatively new and reflected the assertive-ness of an Acadian leadership that consisted of intellectuals such as Maurice Basque and community activists such as Euclide Chiasson, one of the founders of the Parti acadien, who would head the SNA from 2000 through to the eve of the quadricentenary events in 2004. They hoped that Acadians might distance themselves from a Catholic hero whom they had adopted with relatively little reflection on earlier occasions, per-haps in part because the English-speaking Protestants in New Brunswick and Nova Scotia had just as easily gravitated towards Dugua, their own co-religionist. Of course, by the late twentieth and early twenty-first cen-turies, these religious factors had become much less pertinent than they may have been on earlier commemorative occasions, and so the Acadian leaders slowly embraced Dugua, in particular as he stood to provide a tool for distinguishing their identity from that of the Québécois, who continued to hold Champlain in high esteem.

As for the bureaucrats in Ottawa who were in charge of the commem-orative dossier within the Department of Canadian Heritage, they just as-sumed that Champlain must have been the central figure in the 1604 ex-pedition, never really listening to the Acadian insistence to the contrary.

However, there were apparently those within that department who were concerned about the Champlain focus. One such bureaucrat observed during the summer of 2000, before the SNA plan had even been launched: "Before we go too far down the road of presenting New France through the person of Champlain, do we know that there is a consensus among historians concerning this question or are we running the risk of finding ourselves in the midst of a controversy?"[35] There is no evidence that historians were consulted; if they were, then Maurice Basque and his colleagues must have been avoided, since they would have made the case for Dugua.

In the years that followed, the Acadians' insistence that Dugua should be front and centre in 2004 was only part of their campaign to secure recognition that their history had a beginning that was worthy of celebration in its own right, and not simply as an appendage of a fete for Champlain that would culminate in Quebec City in 2008. Along the way, they exhibited the sort of determination that they often claimed had allowed their survival, struggling against forces more powerful than they. At the front line of the struggles with the federal government was Chantal Abord-Hugon, the SNA's point person for coordinating the 2004 celebrations. Having taken up her post early in 2001, within a matter of months she became aware that 'the 400th anniversary of *Acadie* is a politically sensitive issue.' In particular, she felt that her efforts were being undermined by the support of the SNA for a private member's motion (M-241) that was before the House of Commons in the fall of 2001. The motion, championed by Stéphane Bergeron, a Bloc québécois MP, and strongly opposed by the Liberal government, asked the Crown to apologize for the deportation of the Acadians. As Abord-Hugon put it, 'The debates on M-241 did not make things any easier. We can complain that such partisan battles should not be involved, but that is the reality and we have to deal with it.'[36]

Abord-Hugon felt the wrath of the federal authorities personally when she was refused the right to make a presentation (although she could take part in discussions) at a meeting of representatives from Canada and France who met at the end of October 2001 to compare notes about joint plans for 2004. In the end, a federal bureaucrat had to speak for the SNA. In an email message sent at the time, Abord-Hugon observed: 'This was very embarrassing and quite surprising for the French representatives and even for some Canadians.' She was equally surprised when, at the same meeting, Norman Moyer, the assistant deputy minister of Canadian Heritage, explained that the dossier was now referred to as

'Champlain 2004' and was conceived as an opportunity to celebrate 'across Canada,' and not only in *Acadie*. Abord-Hugon observed with considerable bitterness: 'I had the impression that *Acadie* was only mentioned half-heartedly and that it wouldn't have been mentioned at all if I hadn't been there.'[37] Concerned that the SNA was being locked out of its own celebration, following Abord-Hugon's experience, Euclide Chiasson wrote to Moyer asking that his organization have a seat at the table in future discussions with the French that touched upon 2004 celebrations: 'We insist that the role of *Acadie* be recognized in celebrations marking the beginning of the history of Canada.'[38]

Abord-Hugon could also see that the minister of Canadian Heritage, Sheila Copps, had little sympathy for the SNA's plans for 2004 when the two ran into each other at an event in November 2001, shortly before the vote on motion M-241. Abord-Hugon tried to give the minister a 400th anniversary flag, but 'it was obvious that Mme Copps did not want to talk about 2004. My impression was confirmed when I heard the comments that she made about the SNA and the question of celebrating the 400th, before a group of young Liberals … Mme Copps is opposed to providing financial support for the 400th anniversary of *Acadie*.'[39]

Before the debate over motion M-241 was done, the minister had also alienated the Acadian population at large during a visit to the Monument Lefebvre in Memramcook, just outside Moncton, a site that marked the contributions of Père Camille Lefebvre, who had established there the first Acadian institution of higher education. Trying to turn Lefebvre's iconic status to her advantage, Copps claimed that he would never have waited for an apology from someone in order to advance the interests of his people, who had always managed to move forward due to their determination to survive 'in spite of the English, in spite of the Church, and in spite of History.' Along the way, she leaned upon her distant Acadian roots to refer to the Acadians as 'nous.' Here was a member of the diaspora trying to provide advice to those who faced the challenges of living in French in Atlantic Canada on a daily basis.[40]

The debate over motion M-241, which was predictably defeated in late November 2001, indicated that the SNA was taken for granted by the federal government, which figured that funding some of the group's activities (including Abord-Hugon's position) should have made it more reliable politically. On another level, the debate tarnished the image of the Chrétien government among Acadians, who strongly supported the movement for the apology from the Crown.[41] Perhaps to improve the government's standing with heretofore loyal supporters, once the debate was over the first inklings began to emerge from Ottawa that there would be financial support for the 400th anniversary events.

Funding the 400th

The federal government was prepared from early in 2002 to provide $10 million to aid the 2004 celebrations, under the rubric of a new program called the 'Atlantic Canada Cultural and Economic Partnership.' The 'partnership' in the title reflected the fact that two government agencies, the Department of Canadian Heritage (Copps's ministry) and the Atlantic Canada Opportunities Agency (ACOA), were working together. There was nothing here to indicate that there was any partnership with Acadians, or that the program had anything to do with *Acadie*. In fact, in the earliest internal government document that I could find regarding this program, the stated goal was to encourage groups in Atlantic Canada 'to celebrate the 400th anniversary of the foundation of Canada'; one looks in vain for any explicit reference to what had happened 400 years earlier or any indication that the event in question had had anything in particular to do with the Acadians.[42]

Even though this plan existed, albeit only on paper, from the start of 2002, it would not be formally announced until the Acadian national holiday, on 15 August. The fact that the internal documents had been signed was a badly kept secret, and only served to antagonize Acadian leaders, who saw the days until the start of their 400th anniversary events ticking away. The Acadians would have been even more agitated had they known that at the end of a meeting in January 2002 where plans about possible government investment in quadricentenary projects were discussed, the following cartoon was presented as part of a PowerPoint presentation. No doubt, the sketch was intended to be tongue-in-cheek, but it also suggested a cavalier attitude towards a dossier that many people in Atlantic Canada took very seriously.

In March, the SNA committee responsible for overseeing the celebrations learned that there were as yet no funds to mark *le 400ième*. This point was reinforced during a conference call from Ottawa with Gilles Déry, the executive director of the 2004–8 Secretariat that had been created within Sheila Copps's department. As the title of the Secretariat indicated, no doubt to the frustration of the Acadians, Déry's mandate was to watch over 400th anniversary events across Canada that would culminate, of course, with fetes to mark the founding of Quebec City. One can only imagine the eyes rolling in the room in Halifax where the

And Champlain said : "Let's hope that 400 years from now the civil servant at Parks Canada will invest lots of money to commemorate us"

2.1 Champlain searches for funding (Gilles Babin and Jean Desautels, 'Presentation of Champlain 2004–2008 Project,' Parks Canada, 30 January 2002; document secured via ATIP request)

SNA representatives were meeting when Déry told them: 'We share a common goal: the 400th anniversary of Champlain in North America.' When Jean-Guy Rioux, of the Société des Acadiens et Acadiennes du Nouveau-Brunswick (SAANB), asked testily whether there would be '*an acknowledgment of the role of Acadie within celebrations to mark the 400th anniversary of modern Canada,*' Déry responded, probably convincing no one: 'It was never the intention of the 2004–8 Secretariat to downplay the importance of *Acadie*.'[43]

When that same SNA committee reassembled two months later, nothing much had changed, except for the level of irritation in the room. Not knowing what else to do, the leaders created a strategy whereby they would threaten the principals in Ottawa that if they did not act quickly, there would be a press release indicating the SNA's chagrin. There was something sad about this empty threat, since there had already been numerous newspaper reports indicating that Acadian patience (which probably had no end) was running out. Further underscoring the problems faced by the SNA leaders was the fact that even this meek effort to

move the dossier forward was opposed by Vaughne Madden, the executive director of the Congrès mondial acadien, who remarked that 'the
funding requests for the CMA 2004 are making progress.'[44] Apparently,
the prospect of tens of thousands of diasporic tourists arriving in Nova
Scotia carried more weight than relatively powerless French-speaking
residents of Atlantic Canada wishing to mark their beginnings.

In the months of 2002 that followed, Acadian leaders continued to
complain, while federal bureaucrats and politicians said that the official
announcement of the funding was just around the corner. Feeling the
heat that was coming from various quarters, Claude DeGrâce of Parks
Canada quipped, 'It's not easy to reconcile such divergent points of view.
I have the impression that the seas were calmer in 1604.'[45] Finally, on *le
quinze août*, the Acadian national holiday, Sheila Copps formally committed the government to the $10 million package to mark the '400th anni-
versary of *Acadie*.'[46] There was no reference to Champlain on this occasion, and while the Acadians might have preferred some explicit reference
to Dugua, or to Île Ste-Croix, that was probably asking for too much, particularly in light of Copps's intemperate outburst on the occasion. While
delivering the good news, she managed to lecture the Acadians one more
time: 'It's not money that generates a sense of belonging. It comes from
the heart. It's not the government, it's not an apology, and it's not money
that is going to allow the survival of *Acadie*.'[47]

Even with Ottawa's formal announcement, it would still be some time
before funds for the 400th would be made available to event organizers.
Nearly a year later, Jean-Guy Rioux, president of the SAANB, vented his
frustration about the tardiness with which funding decisions were being
made, noting that some events had already been abandoned. '"There
were people who submitted applications last December. Here we are now
in July [2003], and they have still not received definitive responses. You
can't celebrate 2004 in 2005!"'[48] In September 2003, with the Fontainebleau
event only weeks away, the SAANB committee responsible for 2004 events
observed: 'Very few events have been placed in the official Calendar because we are still waiting for responses to requests for financing.'[49]

Rioux's frustration was echoed by Marc Chouinard, the director general of the Théâtre Capitol in Moncton. As he explained in July 2003, he
had already submitted applications for six different projects. 'Three of
these have been rejected, two others have yet to be adjudicated, while we
removed one from consideration.' Along with many other Acadians,
Chouinard was critical that 'the announcement of the $10 million came
so late in the day,' but he was also troubled by the distribution of the

funds. 'The funds have been badly distributed so that they have given some large sums to a few large projects, and that's the end of the story. It would have been better to give smaller amounts to a larger number of projects. This way they were able to be done with the whole dossier more easily. Congratulations to those who received funding, but there remain many more who feel aggrieved.'[50]

In the end, the available funds went to 76 projects, so that each, on average, absorbed over $130,000; or to put it another way, and to confirm Chouinard's concerns, over 75 per cent of the funding went to the 23 funded projects that received in excess of $100,000. As for projects that received support of less than $50,000, they secured less than 10 per cent of the total package. When contacted as part of a follow-up study after the 2004 events had come and gone, some applicants observed that smaller organizations worked at a disadvantage, since 'project selection tended to favour projects submitted by organizations with administrative capacity owing to the complexity of the application process.' Moreover, smaller projects, which might have had difficulty in explaining the economic benefits that would have come from receipt of funding, were disadvantaged. Accordingly, some of the respondents to a survey about the program 'complained that this criterion had eliminated good projects.'[51]

By far the largest grant, totalling $1.6 million, went to the Congrès mondial acadien, which was much more closely connected to the diasporic definition of *Acadie* than to the Atlantic Canada definition that Acadian leaders wanted to promote by means of a new founding myth in 2004. In addition, two other large grants went to organizations not even based in Atlantic Canada, whose projects had only the weakest link to the Acadian story. Historica was provided with $400,000 in order to develop a 'Champlain Learning Model,' including development of its website 'Champlain in Acadia,' which lavished considerable attention upon earlier celebrations of Champlain – in Quebec City.[52] For its part, the Association for Canadian Studies was provided with $250,000 in order to focus upon heroes such as Champlain as part of a project dealing with 'explorers and pioneers.' A poll paid for under this funding asked which of a number of explorers had been 'associated with the first permanent European settlement in what became Canada.' The association's executive director, Jack Jedwab, bemoaned the fact that, in 2003, 'as the federal government begins preparations for the 400th Anniversary of the establishment of the first permanent settlement, most Canadians are unaware that its founder was Samuel de Champlain.' While Jedwab was disappointed that Jacques Cartier outpolled Champlain, Dugua was not even one of the options.[53]

The specific Acadian focus on 2004 was more evident in the various large projects that were based in New Brunswick. In each case, an existing institution was provided funding to create something special on the occasion of the quadricentenary, in the process showcasing the *Acadie moderne* that individuals such as Maurice Basque had hoped to promote. Basque's own Centre d'études acadiennes received over $800,000 to create a new exhibit on the history of *Acadie* at the Musée acadien of the Université de Moncton, and to encourage the creation of a network among museums and historic sites in *Acadie*. For its part, Le Village historique acadien, in Caraquet, used $575,000 to mount 'Les défricheurs d'eau,' a production that played into the modern depiction of *Acadie* through its use of imaginative staging to tell the story of 400 years of Acadian history. In a similar manner, the Festival acadien de Caraquet secured over $250,000 to develop a project that became the CD 'L'Acadie en chanson,' on which well-known Acadian artists sang thirty songs from the Acadian repertoire.

While these projects built upon the understanding among Acadians that they were celebrating an anniversary, they spoke only obliquely to the particular reason why 2004 was a year worth marking. The single large-scale project that might have done this most effectively was the actual commemoration of the landing of Dugua and his men on Île Ste-Croix. While some of the other large projects had been up and running since the fall of 2002, the Ste-Croix 2004 Coordinating Committee did not receive any significant support in the first two rounds of funding decisions; it still had not received a penny of a promised $452,000 of support for its events only weeks before they were to be held, thus making it difficult for organizers to either prepare or promote the quadricentenary. Although they had been working on this project since 1995, the organizers were told by an official from Canadian Heritage on 9 June 2004 that final authorization for payment had not yet arrived, and that when it did come through, it would be another ten working days until the cheque might arrive. There is no evidence that this official understood that 26 June was, at that point, exactly twelve working days away.[54] While the situation of the Ste-Croix organizers was unique in that they were mostly English speakers trying to promote an Acadian event (an issue discussed in chapter 3), their experience reflected the stalling that had characterized federal efforts to mark this anniversary from the start.

The French Connection

In addition to unhappiness over the timing of the funding, there was also considerable concern about the amount that had been provided in the first place. This perception was fuelled as details came to light in May 2003, during a visit to Canada of the French prime minister, of federal government plans to spend over $18 million, or nearly twice the amount committed to events in Atlantic Canada, for a series of projects that would be managed out of the Canadian embassy in Paris to mark four hundred years of ties between Canada and France. Long before any money was on the table to mark the quadricentenary on Canadian soil, Prime Minister Chrétien, in a speech in Paris in 2000, announced that 'Canada and France are going to celebrate together in 2004.'[55] By the fall of that year, the team at the embassy responsible for crafting the program was able to present its broad outlines, noting that it was being designed 'to transform French perceptions of Canada; to reinforce the ties and create new partnerships between the two countries; and to achieve some tangible results.'[56] One looks in vain, however, in either this or subsequent versions of this statement for any reference to the fact that this program had anything to do with the birth of *Acadie*. At one point the SNA could not help but deplore 'the absence of the word *Acadie* in the publicity in France for the project, CANADA-FRANCE 1604–2004.'[57]

In fact, celebrating the founding of *Acadie* had never been the point of the program, which used the quadricentenary events as 'a stepping stone' to develop closer ties with France. As Terrence Lonergan, who led the team within the embassy, explained to me, he and his colleagues were engaged in an exercise in 'public diplomacy' working to change the views of the larger French public, and not just other diplomats, about the nature of Canada. In this specific case, they were trying to emphasize Canada's status as a modern, technologically advanced nation. In Lonergan's view, 'The time has come to update French perceptions of Canada … We want them to say goodbye to sugar shacks and polar bears, and hello to high tech, cultural diversity, linguistic duality.' Lonergan recognized that 'the 400th anniversary of the first French settlement in Canada' would be marked by 'some commemorative events and a good dose of history. But the point of the program [Canada-France] is of an entirely different nature.'[58]

Consistent with the program's goals, each of the major projects, which collectively absorbed the bulk of the $18.8 million, had a significant technological element.[59] Leading the way was the most expensive project, an exhibition called 'Le Canada vraiment,' a multimedia presentation staged in Paris at the Cité des sciences et de l'industrie. The exhibition, which had a nine-month run, cost roughly $8 million, half of it provided by Lonergan's program. By showing visitors aspects of Canada at the start of the twenty-first century through the use of museum technology that had not heretofore been used, the embassy hoped to dispel any lingering notions that Canada was the land of 'quelques arpents de neige.' There was not a single object in this exhibit, largely owing to the insistence of embassy officials to 'highlight technology.'[60]

The other large projects had a closer connection to the past, but even here the emphasis was, to some degree, on technology. In Brouage, the birthplace of the illustrious cartographer, Canada contributed roughly $2 million towards the construction of a Maison Champlain, which contained a series of large screens on which the story of Champlain and Brouage was told via a video presentation, enhanced by the emission of relevant scents (the sea, the forests, and maple syrup) at appropriate moments. Another $2 million allowed Library and Archives Canada and the Archives nationales de France to work together to digitize over a million items so as to create a massive database on the Internet for researchers interested in the history of New France. A further $2 million was invested in the Programme de recherche sur l'émigration des Français en Nouvelle-France (PREFEN), which had the goal of encouraging demographic research by linking a wide variety of records dealing with those who left France for Canada. This research centre was based in the French town of Alençon, in the Perche region of Basse-Normandie. Following on that theme, another $500,000 went to the construction of the Maison de l'Émigration française au Canada in the nearby Perche town of Tourouvre.[61]

Quite aside from the fact that the federal money invested in France dwarfed the sums available in Atlantic Canada for 2004 events, there was also the unavoidable impression that the history-related projects had more to do with Quebec than *Acadie*. For instance, the Maison Champlain unambiguously sang the praises of the founder of Quebec City, and was situated in a town so closely related to Quebec that its main street is the Rue de Québec. During a visit to Brouage during the summer of 2004, I was told that the local promoters of the project had something much less grandiose in mind for 2008 – to mark the quadricentenary of Quebec City, until embassy officials came along with their funding that had become available for 2004. This was a 2008 project whose time had come earlier than expected on the back of the Acadian anniversary.[62]

The Quebec connection was similarly evident in the focus of the projects dealing with emigration from Perche, which was essentially an exodus to the St Lawrence valley. Thus, in promotional material for the Maison de l'Émigration française, there was reference to the various families that 'established themselves in Canada [meaning the St Lawrence valley], and in the lands that extended beyond, all the way to Louisiana.'[63]

No reference was made to *Acadie*, but this should hardly be surprising, since Tourouvre, a bit like Brouage, has a distinctly *québécois* feel about it. As I made my way around town, I strolled through the Place du Canada, which bordered on the Rue des Frères Juchereau, so named in honour of the 'first emigrants from Perche to New France in the 17th century.' Describing her own journey, Lysiane Gagnon observed: 'At Tourouvre, there is a large restaurant that is often filled with Québécois who come on tour buses. At the local cultural centre, there is a hall named after Félix Leclerc, which is next to the one in honour of Georges Brassens. The stained-glass windows in the church tell the story of the departure of local residents towards the St Lawrence valley in 1640 ..., and of the return to the same church in 1891 of the premier of Quebec, Honoré Mercier, whose forbear, Julien, had been baptized there.'[64]

Given this Quebec connection, there was talk from the start of the projects in Perche about constructing a parallel facility in Quebec City (most likely for 2008). Writing in 2001, Terrence Lonergan noted his concern that as long as a Parti québécois government was in power, there would be opposition to 'federal involvement in a project dealing with genealogical research touching on the Québécois.' This concern about matters *québécois* stood in contrast to the evident disinterest on the part of Canadian officials about matters *acadien*, leading the Acadian MP Yvon Godin to remark that there was not 'a big role for Acadians in France. Most of the projects [in France] will concentrate on 2008 when Champlain moved to Quebec.' He speculated that 'Atlantic Canada lost out on funding because there are more Quebecers than Acadians working at the Canadian embassy.'[65]

The Quebec focus of the Canada-France program was also evident from the source of its initial funding. From the time that he became Canadian ambassador to France in September 2000, Raymond Chrétien was supportive of the Canada-France program. Shortly after his arrival in Paris, he expressed the hope that the project might continue until 2008, 'anniversary of the founding of Quebec City, an event that Canadians, Quebecers and Acadians might celebrate together.'[66] While Ambassador Chrétien imagined Acadians celebrating the 400th anniversary of the founding of Quebec City, he indicated little interest in celebrating the founding of *Acadie*. Be that as it may, the ambassador showed considerable frustration by the spring of 2001 when there was still no funding available for the projects to be administered out of the embassy. He found that French partners, who had shown initial interest in the various projects, were now 'perplexed, apprehensive and losing interest.' Accordingly, he sought 'short-term financing so that planning underway might continue and make progress.'[67]

The required funds were soon delivered by way of an appropriation of $1.3 million from the Unity Reserve Fund, which subsequently came under considerable public scrutiny in the context of the Gomery commission's investigation of the Chrétien government's sponsorship program. The fund came into existence in the early 1990s, and before it was abolished in 2004, as part of an effort to respond to the scandal swirling around the Liberals, nearly $800 million had been disbursed 'to support national events, celebrations, projects and initiatives to strengthen Canadian unity throughout the country.'[68] Of course, in practice 'Canadian unity' was code for providing support for projects that might have been of interest, at least in the minds of Chrétien loyalists in Ottawa, to Quebecers. While some of those funds disappeared into Liberal-friendly pockets, most supported projects that had some Quebec connection, such as the Canada-France program.

Following upon this initial support, the rest of the Canada-France funding was approved in September 2002, but the program was only officially launched the following spring during a visit to Canada by the French prime minister, Jean-Pierre Raffarin. Shortly thereafter, in the midst of much public condemnation of foot-dragging over the $10 million promised to Atlantic Canada for 2004 events, a deluge of criticism fell upon the Canada-France program, whose very existence, with its *québécois* orientation, was the last straw for both Acadians and their English-speaking neighbours in Atlantic Canada. Newspaper reports, television and radio broadcasts, and letters to the government from indignant citizens, all expressed outrage with the imbalance between the size of the investment in France and that envisioned for Atlantic Canada. Jean-Guy Rioux of the SAANB, perplexed by the discrepancy, remarked, '"We really have to wonder … what significance the Canadian government attributes to the 2004 celebrations."'[69] Euclide Chiasson, the president of the SNA, diplomatically expressed 'disappointment that there [wasn't] more money to celebrate the anniversary here … It seems that some ministers have more influence than others when it comes to getting project money.'[70] By contrast, those who had to deal with the 400th anniversary dossier on a daily basis were less discreet. Chantal Abord-Hugon, writing privately to one of her contacts within Canadian Heritage, remarked bluntly that 'the Embassy in Paris is celebrating the 400th anniversary without any mention of Acadie or of Atlantic Canada, and hardly any mention of [Île] Ste-Croix.'[71] However, it was Norma Stewart, the leader of the group dedicated to commemorating the quadricentenary of the Dugua landing on Île Ste-Croix, who put it most succinctly when she observed: 'You know what it's like ... you always get screwed at the place of conception.'[72]

The Bilingual Province

Not to be left out of the opportunity to pounce on the federal government over its use of funds in France was the premier of New Brunswick, whose province was the only one where Acadians had an official status through constitutional guarantees for the equality of the two linguistic communities. Bernard Lord, himself an Acadian, echoed the remarks of others in viewing the Canada-France program as the action of a government 'losing touch with the Canadian public ... And now they decide to spend twice as much money in France to celebrate something that actually happened in Canada, to me, is quite stunning.'[73] In fact, however, Lord was on thin ice in criticizing the federal government, since his own government had been slow off the mark in supporting a celebration that stood to take place largely in New Brunswick.[74]

Although there were discussions in Fredericton as early as 2001 regarding the province's involvement with the 400th anniversary events, funding was slow in coming. By early in 2002 the province had given its project a name, 'Initiative 2004,' and was contemplating a budget of over $2 million. The name that was chosen provided no indication of what, in fact, was going to be celebrated in 2004. As for the funding, there was no sign that a formal announcement committing the province to this project would be made any time soon, which made it difficult to take too seriously the various denunciations by provincial representatives that Ottawa was moving too slowly. Sheila Copps, whose own credibility on the issue was weak in May 2002, months before the federal program was announced, was able at the very least to point out there was, as yet, no money – or even the prospect of money – coming from Fredericton. As she put it, 'It's very challenging to basically say [St Croix Island] is a very important historic site – except they [the New Brunswick government] are not willing to put up any money.'[75]

Ultimately, a program to make the $2 million available was announced in March 2003. While Fredericton had been contributing operating expenses for the group working on the Île Ste-Croix celebrations, its own commitment to a larger quadricentenary program came long after the federal government's was up and running. Never missing a chance to

blame Ottawa, the province noted that 'the province tried on several occasions to create a joint program with the federal government, but these
efforts were all in vain. Ottawa preferred to go it alone in order to reap
as much publicity as possible.'[76]

In light of all this delay, Acadian leaders castigated both Ottawa and
the provinces. As Euclide Chiasson put it during the summer of 2002,
'We just can't wait any longer for the federal and provincial governments
to make a financial commitment.'[77] There were also concerns, however,
about the focus of New Brunswick's efforts to mark the 400th anniversary,
which seemed at times to lose track of the story of Dugua and Île Ste-
Croix. For instance, in early 2001 an interdepartmental committee that
was working on the 2004 dossier was far enough along that it was able to
articulate 'what [was] significant about 1604,' indicating that it marked
the 'first milestone in the establishment of French civilization in North
America (and) the beginning of the journey for Champlain and fellow
travellers.'[78] While some of New Brunswick's pronouncements over the
years that followed would make reference to both the leader of the expedition and the site where he and his comrades had landed, such references were intermingled with hollow statements such as this last one,
which made Acadian leaders wonder if their new founding myth even
held much currency in the one province where they had some clout.

Such concerns surfaced in 2002 when a presentation from the ministry
in charge of 'Initiative 2004' indicated that the celebrations would be
modelled after those that had marked the bicentenary of the province in
1984. Accordingly, there was much about the 2004 events that was phrased
using the same platitudes that had been evoked twenty years earlier, such
as the desire 'to celebrate our heritage and build for the future.'[79] Alarmed
by the direction the province was taking, Fidèle Thériault, who worked in
various capacities to advance the story of Dugua at Île Ste-Croix, wrote to
provincial authorities: 'I have just finished reading on the Internet your
website entitled "Initiative 2004." I would like to have some more information about this page. Why does it say CHAMPLAIN, 1604–2004 and not
DUGUA 1604–2004? Why do you refer to the colony established by Dugua
at Île Ste-Croix as having been temporary. You make it sound as if Dugua
would have said, when he landed in 1604: "Here we are establishing a
temporary settlement until we can find a better location." According to
your research, where was the first permanent settlement in North America
and when was it founded?'[80] Thériault's concern proved justified when, at
the time of the official announcement of the funding package in 2003,
there was no reference to Dugua, and when, in a proclamation from the

lieutenant governor noting the significance of 2004, the leader of the expedition had to endure, yet again, second billing to Champlain.[81]

As for the actual funding, while much of it was targeted for projects with a 2004 theme, broadly defined, New Brunswick also funded projects to celebrate the province's 'bilingual heritage' and its role 'as a centre to promote culture and heritage both in Canada and on the international scene.'[82] In addition, funding was provided for projects that seemed a very long way from the Dugua expedition, such as a conference on immigration (although in a sense Dugua might have been considered an immigrant) and another (also supported by the Canada-France program) dealing with the 'integration of disadvantaged youth.' As for those projects that unambiguously had a 2004 theme, numerous small grants permitted over twenty communities, particularly in the Acadian parts of the province, to create local events, while a number of larger grants supported significant theatrical or musical productions, again primarily in the Acadian regions.[83]

In terms of the support provided directly to fund the events at Île Ste-Croix, there was only a grant of $44,600, roughly what was made available for the development of the ballet 'Les portes tournantes' by a company in Moncton.[84] While Fredericton provided support (not included in its $2 million package) to defray some of the administrative costs of staging the Île Ste-Croix events, the direct funding from its flagship program was minimal, leading one newspaper to observe: 'In practical terms, this funding has little to do with the first French settlement in North America, and will consume most of the available funds that are needed for the St Croix project.'[85] In New Brunswick, as at the federal level, the new Acadian founding myth received less than overwhelming support. However, in this case, there was assistance for Acadian projects, particularly those to be carried out in the Acadian parts of the province, even if funding may have been minimal in terms of Île Ste-Croix.

The distribution of funds by the New Brunswick government reflected a certain reluctance by some of the province's Acadian leaders to encourage investment in an English-speaking region, even if this meant working against the new founding myth that the SNA was promoting. This reluctance was reflected in the conclusions drawn by Parks Canada's Claude DeGrâce at the end of a tour in 2002 during which he met with interested parties, none of whom led the major Acadian organizations of the time (and so Euclide Chiasson was not on the itinerary) or had played a role in the SNA's articulation of its plans (and so Maurice Basque was also not on the list). DeGrâce was collecting various perspectives as to what should be celebrated in 2004, and concluded that there was concern about investing 'in any region that was not Acadian ... What would be the reaction if we wanted to commemorate the Loyalists in an Acadian community?'; or to put it another way, why 'invest at Ste-Croix instead of an Acadian region?' Instead, his informants preferred that funds 'ought to be made available to allow the Acadian community to celebrate the 400th anniversary in Acadian regions.'[86] In this regard, DeGrâce heard a perspective that reflected the behaviour of ordinary Acadians, who in 2004 exhibited a strong connection with their communities and a weak one to the story of Dugua and Île Ste-Croix.

Missing the Message

In trying to redefine the popular understanding of early Canadian history, among both Acadians and Canadians more broadly, Acadian leaders were engaged in an exercise that would have been difficult even if more generous funding had been available. For instance, no amount of funding would have been sufficient to convince leaders in Quebec that Île Ste-Croix had been the site of the first permanent settlement in what would become Canada, an admission that would have displaced both Quebec City and its founder, Champlain, from the genesis of the French-Canadian experience. In 2001, for instance, Sheila Copps received a cold response from the Quebec government when she indicated interest in securing the province's support for Ottawa's yet to be articulated plans. As Joseph Facal, the minister responsible for relations with French speakers outside Quebec, put it: 'Quebec has no intention of associating itself directly to the federal government's celebrations in 2004.'[87]

When the actual funding from Ottawa was announced, however, while there was little formal response from the Quebec government, it was quite another story in the case of the mayor of Quebec City. Jean-Paul L'Allier took offence at 2004 events getting attention that should instead have been lavished on his own city, which was gearing up for the 'real' anniversary of the start of French Canada in 2008. He pointed out in early 2003 that his city's celebrations 'are not simply the anniversary of Quebec City, but are designed to mark the permanent establishment of the French fact in North America ... That is no small thing ... It is on a different scale of importance from Port-Royal.' Quite aside from the fact that L'Allier did not know where Dugua (whose name he did not mention) had landed in 1604, he was being disingenuous in adding that the two celebrations were not 'en opposition,' since he most certainly believed they were.[88]

L'Allier was prepared to be philosophical about Ottawa's $10 million contribution in Atlantic Canada if $100 million would be provided for Quebec City in 2008. As the mayor put it, 'We are pleased that much effort is being put into celebrating Port-Royal [*sic*] because we are looking at something like a menu: They (the federal government) are investing significantly in the appetizer and so it should be ready to invest proportionately when it is time to have the main course.'[89] In spite of this condescension, the mayor posed as a defender of Acadian interests, accusing Ottawa (described here as 'les fédéralistes') of seeking not only to 'lessen the significance of the celebrations in Quebec City' but also to 'push to the side the deportation of the Acadians.'[90] In this last regard, L'Allier was correct in pointing to efforts at marginalizing the place of the deportation in the narrative of Acadian history, although he was wrong in blaming the federal government for the reinterpretation of the Acadian past that Acadians themselves had undertaken.

The commemorative events of 2004 apparently had little impact upon L'Allier's view of the past, because in the fall of that year, in the context of a meeting of leaders of the francophonie in Burkina Faso, he challenged Paul Martin's view that the settlement of 1604 had marked 'the real founding moment for Canada.' As the mayor put it, 'I have much respect for Acadie, but Canada as we know it was born at Quebec City in 1608; every historian would be in agreement on that score.'[91] For her part, the Acadian journalist Carol Doucet wondered which books L'Allier had been reading: 'A small group of French settlers arrived at Île Ste-Croix in 1604 and spent a winter there, not just a week-end! From there, they went to Port-Royal … L'Allier might think about reading some history books himself.'[92]

Irritation over *québécois* efforts to diminish the significance of *Acadie*'s anniversary also surfaced in connection with a celebration held in 2003 to mark, as the Quebec minister of culture described it, 'the 400th anniversary of the arrival of Champlain in North America.'[93] More specifically, Champlain was feted for the role he had played in concluding a peace treaty with the Innu chief Anadabijou. This alliance had been forged at Baie Ste-Catherine, just across the Saguenay River from Tadoussac, where a trading post had been established in 1600; and on this occasion a commemorative sculpture was unveiled in a ceremony that dwelled on the role that Champlain had played in reaching out to the 'other.'

The Champlain focus continued as many of the dignitaries and a delegation that had come from France continued on to Quebec City. Flowers were placed at the base of the Monument Champlain, and then there was a conference at Université Laval on the occasion of the quadricentenary of Champlain's 'arrival on the banks of the St Lawrence.' The tone for the conference was set in the opening session by Michel Tétu, who had been in charge of the entire Champlain celebration, which included a tour of *Acadie* by visitors from France.[94] In this talk, Tétu praised Champlain for his 'open mind' in being able to reach out to the Innu, and in a pamphlet published for the occasion he called Champlain a 'visionary' worthy of being feted by 'Quebecers and Acadians, but also by natives.'[95]

Tétu's assumptions that all were eager to fete Champlain were soon contested. At the celebrations at Baie Ste-Catherine and again at the opening session of the conference at Laval, Ghislain Picard, the Quebec regional chief of the Assembly of First Nations, wondered how much cause there was for aboriginal people to celebrate, a perspective that would resurface in regard to the efforts to mark the 400th anniversaries of the Dugua expedition in *Acadie*. Picard thought the time had come, on these commemorative occasions, to go 'beyond moments of rejoicing. It's fine to celebrate our respective heroes, but we ought to think about some concrete actions that might lead to some needed changes.' He deplored the 'emphasis that has been placed on the start of the French presence and upon the courage shown by the settlers, without recognizing the same qualities among the aboriginal people.'[96]

Picard was not alone, however, in being reluctant to celebrate the events of 1603. Acadians also had reason to question this emphasis upon Champlain, which seemed to push their own anniversary in 2004, with its focus upon Dugua, into the shadows. Only a few weeks before the events organized by Tétu, Maurice Basque observed, at a conference of individuals involved with organizing 400th anniversary celebrations in Atlantic Canada, that there were those who were trying to draw significance away from what had happened at Île Ste-Croix. He looked warily towards the 'international conference at Tadoussac and Quebec on the 400th anniversary of the French presence in Canada because for many leading Quebec historians ... the real story does not begin in 1604, it begins in 1603. This is, of course, a very political question.'[97]

In the end, however, Basque was fighting a losing battle if he was hoping to convince Quebecers, or for that matter Canadians beyond Atlantic Canada, to embrace the new Acadian perspective on the early seventeenth century. Websites created by high-profile organizations to mark the 400th anniversary events, even if they recognized the significance of what had happened on Île Ste-Croix, focused on Champlain, in the process playing into a view of the early seventeenth century that led, inevitably, to Quebec City in 1608. As we saw earlier, Historica created a site called 'Champlain in Acadia,' which in fact paid considerable attention to Champlain in Quebec City. As for the CBC, its 'Champlain Anniversary' site focused more squarely on events in *Acadie*, but still conveyed central importance to someone who was not the centre of attention as far as the Acadian leaders were concerned.[98] In spite of efforts by groups such as the SNA to promote a narrative in which the Acadians had their own birth date (26 June 1604), place of birth (Île Ste-Croix), and father (Dugua), the Acadian leaders largely failed to unseat long-established notions about early Canadian history that had been constructed by Quebecers. While it may have been frustrating to see the power of these *québécois* constructs outside *Acadie*, it must have been even more discouraging for Acadian leaders who had to struggle to have their own people embrace the 400th anniversary in a manner that would shift the focus of Acadian identity from a long-standing emphasis upon the deportation and the Acadian renaissance that followed.

During the summer of 2004, bolstered, especially in New Brunswick, by funding that came from both the federal and provincial governments, festivities were held in most Acadian communities to mark *le 400e*. As I drove in early August along the coast from Moncton to Caraquet, nearly every town was decked out with the *bleu-blanc-rouge* of the Acadian flag and banners that read, 'Fêtons 400 ans,' and many individual houses were decorated to draw attention to the anniversary. However, a very different scenario had been discovered by a reporter for the Acadian daily newspaper, *L'Acadie Nouvelle*, at the time of the celebrations in late June to mark Dugua's landing at Île Ste-Croix. In an article entitled 'On the Eve of the 400th: Where Are the Decorations?' Steve Hachey tried to resolve a mystery:

> The tourist passing through Acadie these days would not be able to tell at first glance that we are in the midst of celebrating an historical event of great significance. Departing from their normal behaviour, Acadians have been oddly reluctant to dress up their communities. Ten years ago, at the time of the first Congrès mondial acadien, nobody would have doubted that something important was going on, as Acadian houses, businesses, and institutions were all decorated with flags, banners, and posters–all with the Acadian colours ... But not this time. There is little to show that this is a special year, that is outside of St Stephen, an English-speaking community that is close to Île Ste-Croix.

Hachey set out to study 'this apparent lack of interest in the 400th,' and was offered a variety of theories. The owner of a company that produced a considerable quantity of 400th anniversary paraphernalia said that sales had been good, but that poor weather (and there was much of that) had prevented people from showing their colours. For his part, Denis LaPlante, the director general of the SNA, was probably closer to the mark in observing that 'Acadians are simply waiting for the celebrations [on 15 August] before decorating their communities.'[99] Of course, if this were the case, then it begged the question of whether this year was different from any other, at least in terms of Acadians embracing the idea that their history had begun with the Île Ste-Croix adventure. In fact, on the very day of the Île Ste-Croix anniversary, Hachey's own newspaper incongruously ran an editorial dealing with St-Jean-Baptiste festivities in Quebec, along with announcements for such commemorative events as the twentieth anniversary of the Ville de Beresford, the centenary of the parish of St Thomas d'Aquin de Lac Baker, and the twenty-fifth anniversary of the founding of LeBlanc Brothers Boatbuilders in Wedgeport, Nova Scotia.[100]

Although some Acadian leaders may not have wanted to face this fact, the evidence suggests that ordinary Acadians did not embrace the Île Ste-Croix story since it was so distant from their day-to-day lives. Refusing to accept the limited interest of French speakers, the historian Fidèle Thériault responded with a certain impatience to a reporter who wondered if there were a problem because 'there are so few French speakers in the immediate vicinity of [Île Ste-Croix].' Thériault replied, 'This is like asking me if Jerusalem should not be remembered by Catholics simply because it is now home to Jews and Muslims ... It is important that Catholics remember this place, and that they remember it because it was a turning point in history. It is the same situation here. Île Ste-Croix is a turning point in the history of Canada and in the history of *Acadie*.'[101]

While the events staged at Île Ste-Croix are the subject of the next chapter, suffice it to say that ordinary Acadians did not make their presence felt. While their leaders stood on commemorative stages speaking about the modern *Acadie* that was claiming 26 June as its birthday, relatively few French speakers, other than those who were on hand in an official capacity, were in the crowd. While there were some enthusiastic young people who had made the trek for the performance of Wilfred Le Bouthillier, the Acadian singer who had won the Star Académie competition (the French Canadian answer to *American / Canadian Idol*) in 2003, they were the exception that proved the rule.[102] This point was underscored just hours before the big day, when Jay Reamer, co-owner of the Windsor House Inn in St Andrews, New Brunswick, only a few kilometres from the island, told me that he and the other innkeepers in town had plenty of empty rooms. This suggested that the Acadians were not coming in large numbers, or were not planning to stay very long. While the main street of this solidly English-speaking vacation town was festooned with Acadian flags, actual Acadians were much harder to find.[103] 💻

When Acadians did assemble in large numbers to witness the 400th anniversary spectacles, created by leading lights in their artistic community with the support of government programs designed to mark the significance of 2004, they were hardly encouraged to take the events of June 1604 very seriously. For instance, one of those productions, Antonine Maillet's *Odyssée 1604-2004*, staged at Le Pays de la Sagouine, a theme park an hour's drive from Moncton, told the story of four hundred years of Acadian history, with the characters created by Maillet playing various roles from the past. Those characters were ordinary folks who tended to have a cynical view of the powerful, and indeed much of the performance was disrespectful of sacred cows – even mocking the whole process that made funding for 400th anniversary events (such as this one) possible. In that context, there was nothing exceptional about the whimsical presentation of the landing of the French in 1604, except that they landed at Port-Royal! Moreover, it was striking that the light-hearted mood, which could not be maintained during the scene of the deportation, also was abandoned with the appearance of the leaders of the Acadian renaissance of the 1880s, who had fought against the ravages of the deportation by establishing such markers of a tangible Acadian identity as a distinctive flag, holiday, and anthem. These leaders were not laughed at, but rather revered; and when the story arrived at the identification of 'Ave Maris Stella' as the Acadian anthem, the crowd rose en masse to sing, before returning to the dominant mood of the evening, helped along by a blistering satire of Jacques Chirac's presence in Moncton in 1999 for the meeting of the leaders of the francophonie.

By and large, the same mood was created by Emma Haché in *Les défricheurs d'eau*, performed at the Village historique acadien near Caraquet. On this occasion, the French, led by Dugua, did manage to land at Île Ste-Croix, before moving on to Port-Royal to build a paradise that ended with the *Grand Dérangement*. With the imaginative use of trees that took on various shapes and forms, the post-deportation era was presented in abstract terms until, again, the real birth of *nouvelle Acadie* arrived with the Acadian renaissance. As in *L'Odyssée*, the mood became deadly serious with the calling of the *conventions nationales* of the 1880s and the arrival of some of its major figures, including Pascal Poirier and Pierre-Amand Landry, both of whom figured in the efforts of Acadians to play a role in the commemorative celebrations of 1904 discussed in the previous chapter. As was the case in Maillet's rendition, Haché's engaged the audience with the singing of 'Ave Maris Stella,' following which there was a summary presentation of the past century of Acadian history.

In both productions, given the fact that *Acadie moderne* had little connection with the events of the early seventeenth century, the real moment of birth, and the one that visibly connected with the audiences, was the emergence of elements of a new Acadian identity in the late 1800s. From that perspective, if the French were described as having landed at the wrong location, it hardly created a ripple, perhaps reflecting the marginal place reserved for the Île Ste-Croix experience in Acadian memory. In that context, only weeks before the St Croix quadricentenary events, a new edition of Bona Arsenault's *Histoire des Acadiens*, first published in 1966, was produced. On the back cover of this edition, advertised as having been 'revised and expanded,' it was noted that the Acadian adventure had started with 'the establishment of Port-Royal in 1604.' The recurrent reference to Port-Royal was not simply a historical 'error,' but rather reflected the blind spot among Acadians as to where their birth had occurred. So distant was the Île Ste-Croix story from collective memory that when a poll posted on the Internet site CapAcadie.com asked Acadians (one presumes), 'What ought to be the crowning act of the celebrations marking the 400th anniversary of *Acadie* in 2004?', none of the four choices made any reference to Île Ste-Croix, or for that matter Dugua; over half of the votes supported the idea that 15 August (the Acadian national holiday) should be made a legal holiday in New Brunswick.[104]

In fact, the celebrations of 15 August 2004 were among the largest that had ever been seen, their size increased by publicity that promoted the idea that this was a special year. It was *Acadie*'s 400th birthday, even though it was unlikely that many of the revellers were much concerned about the events from 1604. Among the numerous celebrations held across New Brunswick, as far as I can tell, the only one that included a re-enactment of a founding moment took place in the town of St-Basile in the Madawaska region at the northwestern corner of the province, in an event that marked the arrival in 1785 of the first Acadian settlers to the region.[105] In the end, such events of local significance or ones that harkened back to the deportation and the renaissance that followed won out during the summer of 2004 in these Acadian communities over opportunities to trace a history that went back to an island where no Acadians had been born and which was hundreds of kilometres away from where most Acadians now lived.

A month before the celebrations to mark the arrival of Dugua on Île Ste-Croix, Chantal Abord-Hugon, the SNA's point person for the 400th anniversary celebrations, was doubtful that many Acadians would make the trek because 'Ste-Croix is not a place with deep meaning for Acadians; it is not a place that they have been able to think of as their own. It is always necessary to remember that Ste-Croix was important as the site of the beginning of Acadie, but it only lasted for a year. For me, it is significant that no one was born on the island. For Acadians, there are no ancestors from that site to help make the connection. There are no emotional or familial ties.' Given this context, she viewed the selling of Île Ste-Croix to the average Acadian as 'a challenge,' particularly when there would be a large number of community events, especially in the Acadian parts of New Brunswick, as well as the Congrès mondial acadien, to be held in Nova Scotia, in recognition of its place in popular memory as 'the cradle of *Acadie*.'[106]⌨☐

The Gathering of the Clan

The commemorative summer of 2004 ended on 15 August in two very different ways. On the one hand, there were the events staged in predominantly Acadian communities, mostly in New Brunswick, which feted the *Acadie de l'Atlantique*, championed by many of the leaders of the 400th anniversary celebrations. At the same time, the Acadian national holiday marked the closing of the third Congrès mondial acadien (CMA), with events that began at Grand-Pré and finished with a musical spectacle at the Citadel in Halifax. The Congrès mondial was designed to reunite the Acadian family that had been torn asunder by the deportation, and so it spoke most clearly to the diaspora. Holding the closing ceremony at Grand-Pré made sense given that it had long been the most evocative Acadian site of memory connected with the *Grand Dérangement*. Nevertheless, it was hard to avoid feeling that the messages being communicated on this occasion drowned out the uphill efforts to provide Acadians in 2004 with a way to see their past that did not have the deportation at the centre.

The events at Grand-Pré began with an open-air mass, which only served to push Dugua, the Protestant, even further into the background.[107] As the crowds, estimated at nearly ten thousand, entered the field where the ceremony would take place, they positioned themselves near signs which identified the different families that had assembled from across the world for the CMA. Indeed, the family was the central organizing concept for the Congrès, even more so than the Acadian nation, whose Atlantic Canada–based population was the imagined audience of organizers of 400th anniversary events.[108] When the CMA had begun two weeks earlier at the Université Ste-Anne, Nova Scotia's Acadian university, each family took part in a procession during the opening ceremony, entering behind the same banners, before dispersing to various corners of the province for intimate gatherings of the clans. ▫

From beginning to end, the CMA did not pretend to be and did not function as a 400th anniversary event. Nevertheless, at those opening ceremonies, the lieutenant governor of Nova Scotia, perhaps displaying an excess of local pride, welcomed visitors to an event that was being staged, in part, in Nova Scotia to mark the 400th anniversary of the founding of Port-Royal. Not far from where she spoke, a large building had been set aside for the sale of Acadian crafts and souvenirs. In between the lobster traps and lighthouses decked out in Acadian colours, there was one item that particularly caught my eye, a large quilt with 'L'Acadie 1604' at its centre. Surrounding this focus were references to various moments from the subsequent four hundred years, including the establishment of the settlement at Port-Royal and the deportation embodied by Evangeline. Missing from this narrative was any reference to Ile Ste-Croix. In any event, this quilt held much less interest for the visitors from the diaspora than a framed copy of the royal proclamation recognizing the suffering experienced by the Acadians during the deportation, which was being sold nearby.[109] The undoing of the deportation was also palpable at the CMA's musical finale at the Halifax Citadel, a site that stands as a symbol of the imposition of British rule over the colony, where an Acadian flag was raised to show just how much had changed in 249 years.

The same distance from the 400th anniversary celebrations was evident during the time that I spent in Annapolis Royal (the site of what had been Port-Royal) for one of the many family reunions at the heart of the CMA, in this case the gathering of roughly six hundred members of the Melanson and Breau clans. With the exception of a lone pilgrim from France, these Acadians came in roughly equal numbers from Canada and the United States. Among the Canadians, the vast majority were from Nova Scotia, far outnumbering the contingent from New Brunswick, this in spite of the fact that Acadians from New Brunswick outnumber those

2.2 Family banners at opening of the CMA, 2004 (photograph by the author)

from Nova Scotia by a ratio of roughly seven to one. To be sure, the Nova Scotians had a much shorter distance to travel, but the New Brunswick Acadians also had their own mid-August celebrations to attend.[110]

As for the program at Annapolis Royal, it included the launching of a book on the history of the Melanson family, and two well-attended sessions in which genealogists helped individuals construct their family trees. At the outdoor mass, on the grounds of Fort Anne (where Port-Royal once stood), Père Albeni d'Entremont never once used the word 'Acadian.' In this regard, the lieutenant governor of New Brunswick, Herménégilde Chiasson, observed that the family-centred organization of the CMA reflected a certain 'lack of common identity.'[111] Without the negative edge of Chiasson's remarks, Caroline-Isabelle Caron has similarly pointed to the power of genealogical connections for many in the diaspora. For these individuals, 'belonging to Acadie ... is secondary, because what is important is a connection to the past of a community, to the ties that connected the family to its immediate surroundings and which were given pride of place in the narrative of the family's history.'[112]

The emotional high point for many of the Melansons was the public recognition by the federal government that the 'Melanson Settlement,' just outside Annapolis Royal and not far from the reconstructed Port-Royal habitation, constituted a site of 'national historic significance.'[113] Although the buildings on this site had been burned at the time of the deportation, archaeological remains have allowed researchers to piece together some of the history of a settlement where four generations of Melansons lived between the 1660s and the tragic events of the 1750s. In the speeches that preceded the unveiling of a plaque that gave public recognition of the site's importance, Maurice Basque provided some context. Not surprisingly, given his attachment to *Acadie de l'Atlantique* on the occasion of its quadricentenary, he spoke mostly about the Melansons of the seventeenth century, 'who were the real builders, the true pioneers; they came, stayed and had families. They are the real builders of this land.' His remarks barely made reference to the deportation.

As for the Melansons on hand, they had little interest in 400th anniversary celebrations. A man from Idaho, who had saved up for the reunion for years and who was only going back when his money ran out, told me about how he had begun with his own family tree, but had moved on to the Melanson family history more broadly. Without a nod towards Acadian roots, he said that he had been 'energized' by the reunion. In a similar manner, when I asked a group from the Halifax region about their interest in the past, one responded (with the nodding approval of the others), 'We don't practice *Acadie.*' Presumably, they did 'practice' Melanson. Another in that group, when asked about the relative importance of 1604, 1605, and 1755, responded without any need for reflection that 1755 was the date of importance because 'the deportation is *the* most important story.' Another Melanson, from British Columbia, dismissed the significance of what had happened in 1604, while one from Moncton objected to there having been too much publicity about the 400th anniversary, feeling that it had detracted from the Congrès mondial acadien.[114]

This last point of view was exceptional, and yet it stood out because it reversed a sentiment that I heard from time to time from those who had been involved with 400th anniversary events: namely, that it was the CMA, with its link to the deportation, that had detracted from efforts to recall the arrival of Dugua and his comrades. Compared to the relatively modest celebrations scattered across Atlantic Canada to mark the quadricentenary, the CMA was a very large machine, which attracted over 200,000 participants to its various activities, generated economic activity worth $180 million, and had a budget of $7.5 million, which came in equal parts from the public and private sectors. As we have seen, the most significant element of the public funding was a contribution of

$1.6 million from the $10 million fund designed to support 400th anniversary events.

While no Acadian leader involved with the quadricentenary events ever publicly observed that funds for the CMA were potentially funds coming out of their pockets, the fact remains that the Congrès mondial did compete with the 400th anniversary events for the attention of Acadians. The easy blurring of the lines between the CMA and the 400th events was reflected in a publication by the Atlantic Canada Opportunities Agency, one of the federal government agencies responsible for the $10 million fund, which asserted in 2002 that the CMA would include 'a number of key celebrations such as the 400th anniversary of the arrival of the French in North America.'[115] This competition, whether desired or not, brought the identity crisis of Acadians, described at the start of the chapter, into sharp relief by the time of the Acadian holiday in mid-August 2004. Writing in *L'Acadie Nouvelle*, Rino Morin Rossignol observed that the diaspora was viewed differently by the two currents of thought that vied for supremacy on the 400th anniversary of the arrival of Dugua. On the one hand, there were those who still saw the deportation as the central event of Acadian history and who retained 'a bitterness that the centuries have not weakened.' For these Acadians the reuniting of the diaspora was welcome, but such was not the case for 'those who, with a certain post-modernist revisionism, seek to lessen the tragic dimensions of this event and to insist (more than is appropriate) upon the successes of modern-day *Acadie*.' Rossignol concluded that 'in this context, Acadians from the diaspora run the risk of becoming like children of divorced parents who argue about custody.'[116]

Le Tour Pierre Dugua de Mons

During the summer of 2004, Robert Dugas and Jean-Marc Godin cycled from Tadoussac, where Pierre Dugua landed during a first voyage to the Americas in 1600, to Port-Royal, where he led the expedition that created a settlement in 1605. In all, Dugas and Godin stopped in over twenty, mostly French-speaking communities in Quebec, New Brunswick, and Nova Scotia 'to make Pierre Dugua de Mons better known, which he deserves since he was the main architect of the establishment of France's foothold in the Americas.' In each town, the cyclists showed the film *Sur les pas de Pierre Dugua de Mons*, produced by Marie-Claire Bouchet, from Royan, the French town where Dugua was born.[117] While the screenings were intimate gatherings, and not the large crowds of the CMA, the organizers were pleased that at each stop they were asked: 'Why has this page of history been hidden from us, and why have we not spoken about the important figure who was Pierre Dugua de Mons?' The tour might have been larger had the province provided funding, 'but the government preferred to fund activities such as bagpipe concerts rather than a bicycle tour that might have made the founding of *Acadie* better known.'[118]

This bicycle tour stands out in a summer that might have focused upon Dugua, but which – aside from the attention lavished on him by English speakers from the region of Île Ste-Croix – pushed him oddly to the side. By and large, we have seen that the ideas of those who were behind the construction of a new founding myth for *Acadie*, complete with a place and date of birth, and the identification of the father, failed to capture the attention of Acadians (in the more limited sense of the term). Even Herménégilde Chiasson, who had supported the efforts to promote the quadricentenary events, had to admit that the fetes had failed, if the goal had been to change Acadians' view of their past. At the end of the summer of 2004, by the time the celebrations had come and gone, the *Grand Dérangement* remained the central moment from the past. As the lieutenant governor put it: 'The deportation is the central moment, the founding myth, Year I of Acadian history.'[119]

While the Congrès mondial acadien may have contributed to diverting attention away from Dugua and his initial settlement, we have seen that the difficulty in selling a new founding myth to Acadians had very deep roots. The power of the image of Champlain, for centuries the pre-eminent Catholic hero of French Canada, together with the particular draw of the *Grand Dérangement*, made it difficult to convince Acadians to see their past in an entirely new way. In 1979, in the highly politicized environment that existed on the 375th anniversary of Dugua's landing, large numbers of Acadians for the first time recognized 1604 as their moment of birth, but even then they had been circumspect about embracing either Dugua or Île Ste-Croix in the process. Reflecting on those celebrations twenty-five years earlier, Chiasson remembered with a certain 'nostalgia' that they had been 'more authentic ... more political and militant' than the ones staged in 2004.[120] ⌨

The lieutenant governor found that Acadians exhibited a certain 'lack of enthusiasm' in regard to the 400th anniversary events, part of which he attributed to the form of the celebrations in which 'the use of a rigid formula' led to predictable spectacles in which the same politicians gave stump speeches and 'the same predictable artists sang the same songs in the same manner.'[121] However, quite aside from the form of the 400th anniversary events, which by Chiasson's own admission were not all that different from those that marked the Congrés mondial, there was the more fundamental problem that Acadians continued to remain unmoved by an event from some distant pre-deportation past, on an island far from their homes, led by someone who left little trace behind.

Much has been written over the past twenty years about commemorative events as tools that can shape identity, the assumption being that if a population's view of its past can be altered, so too can its view of its present and future. However, most of that literature has been framed in terms of the successes of leaders who managed to have their visions embraced by the larger population. Leaning on the expression coined by Eric Hobsbawm, those leaders have been perceived as engaging in the 'invention of tradition,' successfully imposing their new perspectives on the past upon a gullible population that uncritically accepted such inventions as if they had had long traditions.[122] From this perspective, ordinary people amounted to little more than pawns, incapable of playing any significant role as agents in the process.

As we have seen, however, the efforts by Acadian leaders to use the quadricentenary to promote a new founding myth largely failed when most Acadians saw little reason to dispense with one of the cornerstones of their identity that had long been in place and which most people believed had served them well. By their actions, Acadians showed the inadequacy of, as the Irish historian Guy Beiner has put it, 'simplistic explanations that misleadingly chart the influence of official commemoration on [popular understanding of the past] through a one-way (top-down) flow of information ... Subjected to popular reception, the ideological messages projected by official commemoration were either rejected or accepted, and even then they were frequently readapted and transformed.'[123] Providing further support for Beiner's perspective, Jocelyn Létourneau has shown that while Quebecers have been lectured by their historians over the past thirty years that the Conquest constituted a passing moment in their past, they continue to embrace it all the same as the turning point in their history.[124] Similarly, most Acadians retain the deportation as the crucial moment in their national narrative, in the process pushing stories about Dugua, Île Ste-Croix, and 1604 to the side.

Stewards of the Sites

Field of Dreams

In southwestern New Brunswick, just off a quiet stretch of Highway 127 not far from the resort town of St Andrews, a modest installation marks the site much trumpeted in 2004 as the location of the first French effort to establish a permanent settlement in North America. Even though Parks Canada has put up a signpost to alert passers-by that they are approaching Île Ste-Croix, I have frequently driven right by (and I know what I am looking for), since there is little to catch the eye. Just beyond a small parking lot stand three unimposing sculptures that were put up to mark the quadricentenary of the Dugua expedition; and just beyond the sculptures a short interpretive trail recounts the story of the winter of 1604–5. Both the sculptures and the trail are at the top of a hill, several hundred metres from the banks of the St Croix River. While the island can be easily viewed from this vantage point, visitors are not permitted to come any closer to the site of the Dugua settlement.

In fact, there had been a plan to provide visitors with a more direct connection to this site of memory. Beginning in the late 1990s, a group of local leaders, from both sides of the international border, started to consider how they might mark the 400th anniversary of the arrival of the French on what the English speakers of the region refer to as St Croix Island. While they were eager to stage commemorative events to mark the quadricentenary, their long-term goal was to use the 400th anniversary as the launching pad for the construction, at the bottom of the hill and within a stone's throw of the island, of the Dugua settlement as described in Champlain's drawings. While some Acadian leaders may have viewed 2004 as an opportunity to create a new founding story for their people, the supporters of the Bayside settlement (so called because the site was situated within the limits of the town of Bayside) were primarily concerned with a project that might give life to a flagging economy. From the perspective of Norma Stewart, who headed this effort beginning in 2003, it was important 'to establish St Croix Island as a tourism icon, as a place for visitors to come, to make it a tourist destination.'[1]

In the end, the settlement was not built on the land that fronted on the river and which was owned by the New Brunswick government, and so all that remains is a field of dreams. Although Fredericton had at one point indicated its readiness to lease the property to Norma Stewart's group for a nominal fee, that offer was rescinded at the end of 2004, which suggests that the commemorative events of the previous summer had not provided the impetus to make the project a reality. There were various reasons why the Bayside settlement was never constructed, but it is hard to ignore the fact that the English-speaking promoters were operating at a disadvantage in the midst of a celebration designed, at least to most Acadian leaders, as the start of their existence as a people.

In that context, Maurice Basque reflected the perspective of some of his peers in complaining that English speakers, such as the leaders from the St Croix valley, were only interested in making profits from someone else's past. He noted in the spring of 2004 that 'in many parts of the Acadian community, there is some frustration – surprise, but also frustration – that all of a sudden, many English speakers are claiming that this history also belongs to them.' Speaking directly to these English speakers, Basque observed: 'You are lining up to mark the 400th anniversary of Acadie because it is of interest, but also because there is much money available to organize these celebrations.'[2] In fact, as we have seen, the amount of money made available to these English speakers was relatively limited and provided only at the last minute. More likely, Basque's irritation was fuelled by the occasional expressions of resentment by the leaders from the St Croix valley, who were suspicious of 'outsiders,' Acadians included, who were trying to take over celebrations they felt were rightfully theirs. In this atmosphere of mutual suspicion, nothing was about to be built.

English speakers in Annapolis Royal also saw their own dreams turn to dust as they tried to mark, in 2005, the 400th anniversary of the arrival of the Dugua expedition at Port-Royal. In 1904 the Annapolis Royal events had taken place over several days and were attended by a wide array of dignitaries. This success was directly connected to Attorney General Longley's decision to mark the Port-Royal 300th anniversary a year early, in order to piggyback on the celebrations that were being staged on the New Brunswick side of the Bay of Fundy. By contrast, his early-twenty-first-century counterparts, believing that the Port-Royal settlement had been the site of the 'real' start of *Acadie* (since the Île Ste-Croix adventure had been so ephemeral), chose to mark their anniversary in 2005. Whether Acadians embraced all elements of the new founding myth that their leaders were promoting, there was no escaping the fact that 2004 had been widely accepted as the year that marked their birth as a people; by 2005 Acadians had moved on to focus on yet another and very different moment from the past, the 250th anniversary of the start of the *Grand Dérangement*.

In the end, commemorative events were staged in July 2005 to mark the quadricentenary of the arrival of Dugua and his comrades at Port-Royal, but they would amount to little more than a small, community celebration, without even the pretense of an Acadian connection. Few Acadians could be found in the crowd; and no Acadian official of any significance was even contacted to take part in the formal events until the eve of the celebration. As for the federal government, since it had bought in (in however miserly a fashion) to the idea that 2004 was the year of the birth of *Acadie*, it participated very discretely in a celebration being staged just down the road from where Acadians, a few weeks later, would be marking, at Grand-Pré (the pre-eminent site of memory of the de-portation), the first federally proclaimed 'Journée de commémoration du Grand Dérangement.' As in the case of the English speakers from the St Croix valley, the leaders from Annapolis Royal occasionally expressed resentment that they were not given support for efforts to mark a moment from the past with which they could identify as stewards of a site, if not in any more personal way. As we will see, both English speakers and Acadians made claims on these sites of memory, occasionally framing them in exclusive terms. Ultimately, such claims raise questions about who 'owns' the past, as if anyone can ever claim sole possession.[3]

Whose Island?

Île Ste-Croix had not been the object of much public attention until the 400th anniversary of the Dugua settlement was on the horizon. A long process that resulted in the island falling under the protective custody of the U.S. National Park Service was only concluded in 1968, and it was not until the early 1980s that the Canadian and American governments formally committed themselves to spreading the word about the significance of what had happened there in the early seventeenth century. While Acadian interest in the island had been instrumental in moving the Canadian government to act, that interest, as we have seen, was limited. Accordingly, the island emerged from the shadows largely due to the efforts of English speakers who lived on either side of the international border on which Île Ste-Croix is located.

While Acadian leaders were drawn to the island by an interest in redefining their people's past, there were much more prosaic factors at work for the residents of the St Croix valley. The golden age of an economy based upon the region's resources was already a thing of the past at the time of the 1904 tercentenary. Subsequently, alternative sources of employment emerged from time to time, and while some projects succeeded better than others, as the 400th anniversary of the Dugua expedition approached, there was no escaping the fact that this was a relatively poor region. This was particularly the case for Washington County, Maine, whose largest town, Calais, hoped to benefit from developments connected with the quadricentenary. By almost any statistical measure, Washington County is the poorest county in Maine, and Maine has long ranked among the poorer American states; and within Washington County, Calais has median household incomes even lower than those for the county as a whole.[4] Not surprisingly, in the face of this bleak economic reality, the populations of both Calais and the larger county declined during the 1990s, at the same time that the state population slightly increased. In this context, Lee Sochasky, the executive director of the St Croix International Waterway Commission, stressed the importance of developing the tourism potential of the island for 'Calais, at the heart of economically depressed Washington County.'[5]

The situation was somewhat better on the Canadian side of the border, largely thanks to the tourism industry already in place that centred upon St Andrews, only a few kilometres from Île Ste-Croix. Accordingly, the median individual income in St Andrews in 2001 exceeded that for all of Charlotte County by 20 per cent. The figure for the county as a whole was roughly the same as that for New Brunswick, which was well below that for all of Canada. However, outside St Andrews the situation in Charlotte County was far less positive. For instance, the median income in St Stephen, the largest town in the county, was well below that for Charlotte County as a whole. Paralleling the distinction between St Andrews and St Stephen in terms of incomes was the fact that the former, a tourist town, experienced some population growth between 1996 and 2001, while St Stephen, reflecting the situation in the rest of the county, saw its population decline. St Stephen and Calais were connected with one another by both an international bridge and some hard economic times in the early twenty-first century.[6] Accordingly, when Lee Sochasky stood back and assessed the importance of tourism as a stimulus for the economy of the St Croix valley, she observed, without reference to the border, that here was a 'sparsely-populated, economic-ally-depressed area on the fringe of government focus.'[7]

Within this gloomy economic context, efforts to mark the 400th anni-versary of the start of French settlement in the Americas began in July 1995 in an elementary school in St Stephen. Long before the pertinent Acadian organizations or government agencies had become involved, community leaders from both sides of the international border met to discuss how the 400th anniversary of the settlement on Île Ste-Croix might be celebrated. This was an unprecedented event, since it brought together people from the towns that surrounded this island to try to build something of their own. In 1904 the Maine Historical Society, which operated out of Portland, had taken the lead, and on subsequent anniversaries during the twentieth century, nothing had been done to mark the significance of the winter spent on the island, this in contrast with the various celebrations to draw attention to the founding of Port-Royal or the passage of Dugua and his men past the site where Saint John would later be established.

Among the group that met in 1995 were two men who would lead the local organizing committee throughout most of its existence. Keith Guttormsen, who would serve as its American co-chair, came to the pro-ject from his position as executive director of the St Croix Valley (Calais) Chamber of Commerce. He stressed the importance of using the 2004 anniversary to educate the larger population, throughout North America, about the significance of Île Ste-Croix. He looked forward to a time when 'people will say "Let's go see St Croix Island or the surround-ing area." Then you bring in tourist dollars. That helps the economy, and it helps everybody.'[8]

Echoing this emphasis upon the tourist dollar was Guttormsen's Canadian counterpart, Allan Gillmor, who was the mayor of St Stephen when the quadricentenary project was first discussed. Like others in the community, Gillmor did not see the event as an Acadian anniver-sary per se. In an interview in 2003 he expressed concern that an Acadian focus might exclude the participation of English speakers: 'Our committee is primarily an anglophone committee and we're cele-brating because of the geography.'[9] That geography, the site of the first

permanent French settlement in North America, provided an opportunity to develop the local tourist industry. On the eve of the quadricentenary, Gillmor described discussions within the organizing committee that pitted 'the history aspect vs. the tourist aspect. Some wanted
to be true to the history and that the celebration should be held with
historic lectures and that's it, but the committee as a whole embraced
the idea that it goes beyond that. There is no doubt that the history is
there, but it goes beyond that.'[10]

The views of Guttormsen and Gillmor were shared by most of the
English speakers who would serve on the organizing committee working
towards the quadricentenary. Theirs were not, however, the only perspectives on how the 400th anniversary of the settlement on Île Ste-Croix
should be marked. In particular, what became clear from that first meeting in St Stephen in 1995 was that the Acadians who had enough interest
in the island to make the journey were drawn to the project because the
island was the site of the start of the Acadian experience, and not because it was a heritage resource that might generate tourist dollars. Given
their different starting points, it was often hard for the local leaders and
their Acadian counterparts to see eye to eye.

The organizers of this brain-storming session created, as a working
title for the 400th anniversary events, the expression 'Celebration 2004.'
Such a formulation may well have been designed so that no one would
be offended, since the object of the celebration was left unstated.
However, their deliberations provided some clues, just the same, particularly in terms of the limited impact of the interventions by the Acadians
in attendance. One looks in vain, for instance, to any reference – however vague – to 2004 marking the start of the Acadian experience. Along
the same lines, while the proceedings of the workshop indicated that
2004 would provide the opportunity to make contact with France
(through exchanges of various kinds), little was said about making contact with French speakers who were much closer at hand.[11]

In spite of these differences, the local English speakers and their
French-speaking visitors resolved to press ahead by creating a coordinating committee to take charge of the 400th anniversary events. After
some false starts, that committee – which included Acadian representation from its inception – began to work in earnest in 1998, but it soon
became apparent, as it tried to craft a mission statement, that the gap
between the two groups had only widened. In April an Acadian member of the committee suggested a statement that viewed 2004 as an opportunity to highlight 'the international significance of France's first

attempt at establishing a permanent settlement in North America.'[12] As innocuous as this may have sounded, alternative versions soon surfaced that managed to avoid the use of the word 'French' altogether, leading to a debate that would only be resolved six months later. One of these 'English' versions saw the committee's job as being to 'plan and encourage events and foster the development of a permanent legacy in commemoration of the 400th anniversary of the establishment of North America's first permanent settlement on St Croix Island by explorers De Mons and Champlain.'[13] Quite aside from the exaggeration in this formulation that ignored Spain's earlier settlement at St Augustine, it made no reference to the country that those explorers were representing. Another English text even removed the names of the explorers, focusing instead upon the opportunity to 'increase both domestic and international visitors to Charlotte County, in New Brunswick and Washington County in Maine.'[14]

In the end, a convoluted solution was found that allowed the committee to move forward, but which could not entirely hide the fact that there were local leaders interested in different issues than the Acadian representatives. The mission statement that was agreed upon made reference, towards its end, to the '400th anniversary of North America's first permanent French settlement.'[15] This was a far cry from a version that had been proposed months earlier that would have focused upon 'the continuous presence of French culture in North America [that] began at St Croix Island (Île Ste-Croix) in 1604.'[16] In the end, however, such an emphasis at the start of the statement could not win support among the English speakers. The final version referred to the island only in its English form and made no reference to the long-term existence of a French civilization in North America. Moreover, the statement that was approved began with an emphasis upon the committee's determination to 'educate people of many backgrounds,' in the process playing to notions of multiculturalism without providing any particular emphasis upon the existence, 400 years later, of a vibrant French population that constituted roughly a third of the population of New Brunswick. Just to make it clear that the matter remained unresolved, the French version (drafted by the Acadian representatives) made no reference to 'people of many backgrounds' and stated from the start that the point of the exercise was to 'commemorate the 400th anniversary of the first permanent French settlement in North America.'[17] It was no overstatement when, at a meeting in early 1999, the minutes noted that there were still 'mixed agendas.'[18]

Throughout the years leading up to the 400th anniversary events, English-speaking organizers, not only in the vicinity of Île Ste-Croix but also those who were starting to think about the 400th anniversary of the founding of Port-Royal, had difficulties in connecting with Acadians who should have been natural allies in promoting their local projects. Only months after the St Croix 2004 committee began its work in earnest, several of its members crossed the Bay of Fundy to share notes with their counterparts in Annapolis Royal. Upon their return home, they reported what had been discussed, including the need to 'make Acadians feel that this is their event [since] it is!' Towards that end, there was a suggestion that Acadians, whose connection to the Île Ste-Croix region was recognized as weak, might be 'invited to plan and hold a major activity there, maybe an August 15th event' to mark the Acadian national holiday.[19] However sincere the idea to draw in the Acadians may have been, the August 15th idea disappeared from the deliberations of the St Croix organizers until after their celebrations in 2004 were over. The organizers recognized late in the day that Acadian assistance could be useful as they struggled to move forward the project to reconstruct the habitation from 1604 in order to promote long-term economic development for the region. Even with this incentive, however, the August 15th idea appeared to have been forgotten as quickly as it was raised.[20]

The difficulty on the part of the English-speaking organizers in accommodating the Acadians was also evident in other actions over the years leading up to the 2004 events. While there were recurrent efforts to improve the ability of the residents of the St Croix valley to speak French so that they might be able to communicate with visitors to the quadricentenary, in 2003 the Canadian patron of the 2004 St Croix events, Senator Viola Léger (best know for having played Antonine Maillet's La Sagouine) expressed concern 'about the Committee's connection to Acadians in New Brunswick.'[21] Only months before the big event, a communications firm hired to come up with a marketing plan warned that 'the region is viewed as having limited "Acadian" flavour and limited French service capacity ... There are sensitivities within the province and various groups regarding the anglophone nature of the St. Croix region.'[22] To underscore these concerns, Chantal Abord-Hugon, the SNA's coordinator for 400th anniversary events, observed that 'the website for the 400th anniversary of Ste-Croix makes no reference to *Acadie*.'[23]

As Acadians began to organize their own celebration of the 400th anniversary of the Dugua expedition, aggravation with the English speakers surfaced with a certain regularity. In 2000, just as the Société nationale de l'Acadie was putting its plans in place, a committee of historians, including the omnipresent Maurice Basque as well as Fidèle Thériault, who would serve on the St Croix coordinating committee, expressed concern that 'the Acadians might not feel included in the different celebrations organized by some "anglophones." We have to make sure that there will be major activities organized by and for Acadians.'[24] That there was cause for such concern was made clear by the less than cordial welcome provided to a representative of the SNA who visited the St Croix committee in 2001 to describe how the organization hoped to 'create Acadian awareness and pride in their origins, as well as project *Acadie* as a thriving and dynamic culture.' There was nothing particularly surprising about such intentions given the mandate of the SNA. Nevertheless, in the discussion that followed 'it was noted by several committee members ... that there is a danger of becoming parochial, and that the SNA may have too narrow a focus because St Croix is more than just an Acadian moment.'[25]

In the fall of 2002 the organization representing Acadians in New Brunswick expressed its concern 'on the one hand that the ceremonies [in 2004] take place in an acceptable French and, on the other, that the anniversary of the founding of *Acadie* be given a prominent place in the celebrations.'[26] From what I could tell, however, such concerns had made little impact upon the members of the St Croix Coordinating Committee, with whom I chatted in St Stephen a year later. On that occasion, the Canadian co-chair, Allan Gillmor, expressed concern that an Acadian focus might 'leave me out because I'm an anglophone.' His American counterpart, Keith Guttormsen, was more pointed in observing: 'Well, I've always thought in the background that if this whole coordinating committee, if the majority of members had French last names we would have had a much easier time.' This remark was followed by laughter from the other members of the committee. I then asked what he meant by that, to which Guttormsen responded: 'Oh, I think we would have had access to money sooner, quicker and more cooperation.'[27]

It was ironic that Guttormsen might have thought that the Acadians had some inside track to funding for 2004 events. As we saw in the previous chapter, they had their own difficulties in having the various levels of government fund 400th anniversary activities. Nevertheless, this perception that the difficulties in financing had something to do with the Acadians, or French speakers more broadly, was reflected in a comment by the executive director of the St Croix Coordinating Committee not long before the big event in June 2004. As Norma Stewart put it, her group had been 'swimming against the tide in order to get the recognition from the levels of government. There is no denying that this island and this river was the site of that first settling in 1604. But because we are an anglophone community, we were constantly banging our heads up against the bureaucratic wall of the francophones.'[28] 🖳 Maria Kulcher, the Canadian secretary of Stewart's group, echoed these concerns, noting that the Acadians failed to see the larger picture: 'The French descendants in New Brunswick are Acadian. Of course they are going to take hold of this celebration and say it is about themselves. The problem, of course, is not realizing that it was the beginning of something greater and grander than just being Acadian. It's the beginning … of the entire settlement of a land that eventually became Canada. I am a very proud Canadian and my roots are not French nor are they English. They are from middle Europe, but I am a Canadian and that is my island.'[29] 🖳

In the end, there was no resolution to a conversation that was about ownership of the past. While the English speakers from Washington County (Maine) and Charlotte County (New Brunswick) felt that there was some pot of gold that Acadians were holding back from them, there was, similarly, the sense, expressed by some Acadians, that the English speakers really had no right to meddle in the telling of a story that was not theirs. It was in this context that Maurice Basque accused the English speakers of being out only for financial gain, as if the story had nothing to do with them or as if there really were millions of dollars on the table. He made this point most clearly in a presentation delivered to a conference organized in Amherst, Nova Scotia, in May 2003 by the Federation of Nova Scotia Heritage. As the program for the conference indicated, it was designed to bring together individuals involved in 'offering commemorative and interpretive products such as events, tours, exhibits and publications in 2004–5.' By and large, the individuals in attendance, including Norma Stewart, were English speakers who, in one way or another, were involved in presenting some version of the Acadian past to the public. Feeling that he had a much more personal connection to the anniversaries than the English speakers he was addressing, Basque observed that 'for Acadians, 2004 is considered *our* birthday.' He quickly tried to qualify this claim of ownership, by saying that his intent was not 'to close doors' to others who might want to join the party. Nevertheless, there could be no mistaking the fact that he resented the imposition of the agendas of 'outsiders' upon the anniversary of his people. This was made abundantly clear when he observed: 'Let's be honest. If it was not for the millions of dollars, less attention would be directed to 2004.' 🖳

In order to sugar-coat the message he was delivering, Basque spoke to his audience about the birthday of an imaginary woman named Mary Smith, who was a pillar of her community. Everyone spoke highly of Mary, an English speaker chosen by Basque to stand in for the Acadians, but when it came to the actual celebration of her big day, she found that others had intruded upon the scene, and Mary was forced 'to team up with [her] neighbours from different cultures. She didn't mind having these people here, but it made her wonder if she still existed. She asked herself, "Will I be able to speak my language since I am supposed to be the focus of the event?"' Falling out of character, Basque observed, 'On my birthday, I would be a bit offended, if everyone in my house did not shake my hand. I would look around and say, who are these people; am I paying for this; who is picking up the empty bottles; and who's bringing the cake?'[30]

When I asked Basque about this story on the eve of the 400th anniversary, he assured me that he was hoping that 2004 might provide 'some great opportunities to build bridges,' but neither his words nor those of the English speakers from the St Croix valley made that seem likely.[31] To be sure, there were efforts to smooth over differences. For instance, in the spirit of bridge-building, the president of the SNA, Euclide Chiasson, also speaking on the eve of the quadricentenary, told me that he thought that it was 'terrific that the organizers of the event … are making the effort to draw attention to the arrival of the French in 1604.' However, he went on to express the hope that the involvement of English speakers 'was going to help them better understand the existence of the Acadian people, because for some of them, we still do not really exist.'[32] Was it really likely that Norma Stewart and her colleagues were unaware of the existence of the Acadians? In any event, suspicions about the St Croix organizers were less subtly expressed in February 2004, when an English-speaking representative of Stewart's group made a presentation to the SNA committee looking after the quadricentenary. As soon as the presenter left the room, concerns immediately surfaced that 'the Ste-Croix 2004 Committee does not seem entirely convinced that 26 June 2004 is an important date for *Acadie.*'[33] As we have seen, such suspicions also marked the appearance of a representative from the SNA before the St Croix committee, and underscored the unresolved tensions over ownership of the quadricentenary.

Singing in the Rain

With the story of missed connections between English speakers and Acadians never far from the surface, the St Croix Coordinating Committee set out to construct the quadricentenary events for June 2004. For years the group had planned to have a celebration with significant events spread over a ten-day period from 26 June (the date marking the arrival of Dugua) through to the Fourth of July (including Canada Day in the process). Only weeks before the actual staging of the quadricentenary, in the face of significant financial difficulties, this schedule was pruned back so that it amounted to little more than a long weekend. The firm that had been hired to organize the commemorative events recommended this contraction because 'the reality is that we don't have as much money as we had all hoped.'[34] In part, the shortfall was caused by 'the delays and changing commitments from our federal partners [that] have limited our use of resources and money.'[35] As we have already seen, the federal government was slow in making funding for 400th anniversary events available to the parties that needed them. In this regard, both the English speakers and the Acadians might have felt equally aggrieved. Ultimately, the federal government committed itself to provide roughly $450,000, most of which was committed to staging events on the single day that marked the anniversary of the landing by the French. However, on 9 June, only two weeks before the big day, none of this funding had yet been transferred.[36]

The other problem faced by event organizers was an inability to raise money from the corporate sector. For much of the spring, Agenda Managers, which had been contracted to do this fund-raising, had been writing to Norma Stewart with tales of woe. In April it admitted that 'our experience has not been encouraging ... We have received a significant number of negative responses ... including companies like [St Stephen-based] Ganong [which produced the 250-pound Evangeline out of chocolate] ... who we felt were among our most likely prospects considering their connection to the local communities. We feel that not having this local support has been an obstacle in our securing other corporate support. If the largest "home town" corporate partners do not step up, why should they.'[37] In the end, the fund-raisers had to admit that they did not come close to raising the $500,000 that they had projected. In fact, the St Croix Coordinating Committee reported that it only raised $12,000 over the course of 2004.[38]

Nearly all the events with any hope of attracting significant crowds were packed into the single day that marked the anniversary of the landing by the French. While there were relatively small ceremonies (discussed in the next chapter) in St Andrews and on Île Ste-Croix to mark the role of the Passamaquoddy during the time spent by the Dugua expedition on the island, the main events of the day were to be staged on the land that the federal government owned in Bayside, New Brunswick, immediately across from the island being honoured. Since Ottawa provided the bulk of the funding and owned the site, it was able to chart the schedule for the day, which began with an official event, organized by the federal government, called 'Acadie: First Dialogues – The Meeting of Two Worlds,' that combined speeches by dignitaries (including Jacques Chirac by satellite feed and Paul Martin only two days before a federal election) and performances by Acadian and aboriginal artists. The local organizers who had prepared for the day for nearly a decade had little formal role to play. In fact, after the event Norma Stewart observed that the absence of anyone on stage from the local community 'was the only negative comment that we received about the commemoration – about *our* commemoration – and we did receive it from a number of people and not just local people.' In fact, she noted, the only English to be heard coming from a resident of the St Croix valley 'was my voice over the loudspeaker ... The commemoration was beautiful, that mixing of the music of the aboriginal drumming and the Acadian fiddle stuff still makes my skin tingle, it was beautiful. But regrettably, the anglophone people felt left out. They didn't feel it was for Canadians. And that was regrettable – but that was not our program, that was the Government of Canada's program.'[39]

Whatever might be said about the federal government's handling of the 400th anniversary dossier, there was considerable logic in highlighting the meeting of two worlds in 1604, an encounter that had occurred roughly 175 years before English speakers came to inhabit the St Croix valley. Perhaps Norma Stewart was unhappy that the event had not spoken to the history of the region over the previous four centuries, but that was not the perspective chosen by the federal bureaucrats working for Canadian Heritage in the Atlantic region, many of whom were Acadians who would have felt no connection to the St Croix valley outside the context of the Île Ste-Croix adventure. Of course, as we have seen, for most Acadians, even this moment from the past had little draw, a point that was underscored by the thin Acadian presence in the crowd that day.[40]

If Norma Stewart and her colleagues had been disappointed by the absence of local voices during the first major event of the day, they had little reason to expect much more from the second, an extravaganza in which Acadian stars such as Edith Butler and Wilfred Le Bouthillier would be featured.[41] However, the evening festivities were under the direct control of the leaders from the St Croix Valley, who relished the opportunity

– after all these years – to be in charge. In the end, just as the federal
government's event came to a close, the rain that had been falling most
of the day and had kept the crowds down to no more than three thousand, intensified and the St Croix committee's show was cancelled.[42]
Given the difficulties that the St Croix 2004 leaders had had in moving
their various projects forward, there was something fitting (even inevitable) about their own show being scratched. The crowd, or what was left
of it, made its way to cars that were parked in a nearby field, which had
long since turned to mud. Drivers spun their wheels trying to climb a
shallow hill, getting nowhere fast, much like the well-intentioned members of the local community.

The final indignity for the St Croix committee came with the demise of
its plan to construct a replica of the habitation from 1604 on land owned
by the New Brunswick government along the banks of the St Croix River,
only metres from the stage where the events of 26 June 2004 were
staged (or should have been staged). The quadricentenary had been
linked to the opportunity of attracting tourists by means of the habitation from the start, and so this subject occupied the coordinating committee as early as 2000, when it hired an architectural firm to prepare
plans. According to this scheme, visitors coming off the highway would
first pass through a reception centre before heading downhill, along
'an interpretive trail that meanders through a meadow. The idea behind this casual walk is to allow visitors time … to get in a positive frame
of mind for their journey back to the year 1604.' The trail would end
with the visitors' arrival at the reconstructed settlement 'built to scale,
complete with fencing and gardens as per Champlain's drawings.' Still
closer to the river, an amphitheatre was envisioned, 'designed with elements reminiscent of Versailles,' where performances of various types
might be staged. Further downhill, there would be picnic grounds and
an aboriginal area.[43]

As befitted a site inspired by Versailles, whose grandeur was evoked
several times in the master plan, the budget for this project was set at $7.5
million, very little of which was ever raised by the leaders of the St Croix
valley, who soon found that their dreams far surpassed their means. In a
memo from March 2002, Parks Canada indicated that 'resources were
not available to support the proposed development at Bayside … New
funding will be required to implement the major projects expected by
the community.'[44] By the fall of that year the provincial government had
also indicated its unwillingness to fund an infrastructure project, fearful
that it might end up with costs for upkeep that could last for years.[45] In

the absence of any meaningful connections with the Acadians, neither level of government could see much reason to support these plans, and so the leaders of the St Croix valley went back to the drawing board to come up with a project that might be within their means.

In the summer of 2003 they came up with a new feasibility study suggesting that with an investment of $1.5 million the facility could be constructed. This figure was arrived at by keeping only those parts of the original design to be constructed on the provincial land that ran from the settlement's projected site to the water's edge. However, the study did not explain how this part of the $7.5 million project might now be built for so little, when the historic settlement alone had had an estimated cost of nearly $1.4 million in the original design; nor for that matter was it particularly clear as to where the capital for construction would be found.[46] In the absence of government sources, the St Croix Coordinating Committee tried to raise corporate funds, but was no more successful in this regard than in raising private funds to finance the 2004 celebrations. While its fund-raiser was still hoping, as late as May 2004, that it might come up with $500,000 for the project, by the end of 2004 the Committee's 'Historical Settlement Savings Account' had a balance of roughly $25,000, little of which had come from corporate contributions.[47] In that context, the New Brunswick government removed from the table its offer to lease the land to the St Croix organizers, fearing that if there were to be a shortfall, a reasonable expectation at the time, it might end up having to pick up the pieces.[48]

The settlement was never constructed, and so all that remains at the Bayside site to indicate that the quadricentenary had ever taken place are three diminutive sculptures commissioned by Parks Canada, which are located at the crest of the hill on the edge of a parking lot. Before 2001, when the idea for a sculpture project first emerged, the St Croix Coordinating Committee believed that the federal government was going to be a partner in building the Bayside settlement. Allan Gillmor, the Canadian co-chair of the committee, observed that it was as if a 'lead balloon' had fallen on the dream of the settlement when Parks Canada announced that it was going to erect a monument of some sort on its land near the highway, in lieu of participating in the construction of the settlement.[49] Accordingly, Gillmor and his American counterpart, Keith Guttormsen, wrote to Sheila Copps, the minister of Canadian Heritage, to express 'disappointment that we were not part of any consultation ... The proposed sculpture ... would enhance but should not replace the habitation recreation at Bayside.'[50] Their unhappiness

3.1 Bayside triptych. The empty field beyond the sculptures
is where the reconstructed settlement might have been; and Île Ste-Croix
can be seen beyond the field (photograph by the author)

made little difference, and in 2003 Parks Canada called for the submission of proposals for sculptures from New Brunswick, Aboriginal, and French artists. One proposal from each category would be selected so as to create a 'commemorative triptych.'[51]

In a sense, from the perspective of the leaders of the St Croix Valley, the sculpture project reflected the sense of powerlessness they had felt from the start. In the end, the Acadian, French, and aboriginal artists spoke to the 'meeting of the two worlds' concept that had driven Ottawa's participation in the quadricentenary, leaving the residents of the region without a voice. As Norma Stewart put it, 'It's my understanding … that Parks Canada actually have a mandate, they're mandated to work with communities in areas where they do have parks.' Instead, she found that the federal agency had failed to work 'in concert, or in cooperation with the community that lives in the area.'[52] Never far from the surface, however, was the sense that there was something particularly 'Canadian' about this failure. Sitting in her office in St Stephen in the fall of 2003, Stewart could literally see a large facility, the Downeast Heritage Center, that was being constructed as a 400th anniversary project just across the border in Calais; and not far down the road, the National Park Service had constructed a commemorative trail at Red Beach, on the American shore across from Île Ste-Croix, which was to be opened to the public the next day. So how was it that the various levels of government on the American side of the border managed to invest roughly $6 million (U.S.), when such investments were out of the question in Canada?

The Real Owners of the Island

While Acadians and English-speaking leaders of the St Croix valley sniped at each other as to whose claim on the past was stronger, there was another party that could say without fear of contradiction that it literally owned Île Ste-Croix. The American government, and more specifically the National Park Service (NPS), had been the sole proprietor of the island since 1968. Over the years that followed it entered into various agreements with its Canadian counterpart, Parks Canada, under which the two agencies agreed to work together to make the story of Île Ste-Croix known to the larger public. In practice, however, the political realities on each side of the border governed what could actually be achieved. As we have seen, the situation in Canada approached paralysis, as Acadians were reluctant to be too strong in their support for the construction of projects far from where they lived and disconnected from their sense of identity. As for the English speakers of southwestern New Brunswick, their claims on a French past were never taken seriously by the powers that be. Accordingly, the field remains empty at Bayside.

By contrast, these political constraints did not exist on the American side of the border, although the actual appropriation of funds still did not come quickly. Indeed, in 1999 Lee Sochasky of the St Croix International Waterway Commission wrote to convince federal authorities to restore funding that had previously been committed for interpretive facilities across from Île Ste-Croix in Maine. She found that it was 'acutely embarrassing to have the United States draw back on simple and long-overdue site improvements on the eve of a historic commemoration.'[53] Nevertheless, the Maine congressional delegation put its weight behind the effort, and Washington ended up providing roughly $600,000 for the interpretive trail at Red Beach and another $2 million as its share of the cost of the facility in Calais. In this last regard, the drive to secure funding was led by Maine's senators, who pushed through legislation that authorized funding for the Calais heritage centre, which also benefited from significant state, municipal, and private support.[54]

This funding was secured without evidence of rancour regarding who actually had the right to speak about the past, a pattern that continued as the various commemorative elements were implemented on the ground. This was particularly the case in terms of the imaginative trail constructed at Red Beach, which focused upon various moments from the expedition of 1604–5. Deb Wade, who was in charge of the dossier for the NPS, was extremely attentive to the concerns of the various interests that might make a claim on the history of the Dugua settlement. However, she had the luxury, unlike her Canadian counterparts, of being sheltered, for instance, from the lobbying of Acadians, who might have preferred infrastructure investment closer to where they lived. She was similarly sheltered from concerns about representing the role of the Passamaquoddy during that fateful winter, since that tribe had legal recognition in the United States, but not in Canada.

In this environment, Wade was able to work with professionals and interested American parties to build a project with which everyone might feel comfortable, in the process fulfilling the NPS's role as the steward of the island. The agency's responsibility in this regard was apparent, for instance, in its determination to return to the island, as part of the quadricentenary attention to the site, bones from the Dugua expedition that had been exhumed by the archaeologist Jacob Gruber in 1969. Gruber took the bones back to Temple University, where he was a professor and where they were housed until 1995, when they were returned to the possession of the NPS. Then, with the quadricentenary on the horizon, a team of scientists established exactly where the bones should be reinterred on the island, so that they would rejoin the remains already there. In advance of the reburial in June 2003, Wade and her colleagues organized a religious ceremony on the island that included clergy from both the Catholic and Huguenot churches. The inclusion of the latter was an effort to recognize the bi-denominational nature of the Dugua expedition, an aspect of the early-seventeenth-century adventure that was rarely (if ever) discussed in the highly charged atmosphere of Canadian identity politics in the early twenty-first century.[55]

Sensitivity to the various interested parties was similarly evident in the construction of the trail at Red Beach, which was organized around a number of drawings that represented key moments from the Dugua expedition, starting with one that depicted the Passamaquoddy viewing the arrival of the French and ending with a sketch of the Europeans' departure a year later. To complete the trail's design, each drawing was accompanied by a life-size bronze sculpture of one of the depicted characters. In this regard, Wade worked closely with individuals with a stake in this

3.2 and 3.3 (facing page) Bronzes from the Red Beach Trail
(photographs by Robert Thayer)

story. In particular, she was in regular contact with Donald Soctomah, the Passamaquoddy Tribal Historic Preservation Officer, regarding the two aboriginal bronzes that would be installed on the trail.[56]

One of the bronzes was supposed to depict a female Passamaquoddy figure standing on the shore, watching the arrival of the French. Wade had two proposals to consider in this regard. In one maquette, she explained, 'the stance of the woman … was with eyes downcast. The other [see figure 3.2] was of her looking outward toward the river. I chose looking outward, as our message … is that the [Passamaquoddy] People were living here for thousands of years before the Europeans and were watching as the ships came up the river.' In the case of the second bronze, Wade began from a drawing that depicted two aboriginal figures who were accompanying the French as they explored the area to the south of Île Ste-Croix. At first, there was a proposal for a bronze of one of the Passamaquoddy characters, an interpreter, who was shown with his arm up in the air. While the interpreter was presumably providing greetings, Wade feared that he 'looked horribly like a cigar store figurine or awful cowboy western stereotype saying "how."' Accordingly, she opted for the other figure (the one holding a kettle in figure 3.3) from the drawing, which would cause no offence.[57]

It was not that Parks Canada lacked staff with the sensitivity evident in the NPS's handling of the Red Beach trail. Indeed, Nathalie Gagnon, Deb Wade's Canadian counterpart, worked closely with Donald Soctomah to create an award-winning trilingual (English, French, and Passamaquoddy) children's book about the winter of 1604.[58] However, Gagnon never had the opportunity to put her skills to work on a public project as substantial as the ones funded on the American side of the border. While the Americans acted, the Canadians dithered. By 2002, with the American projects already well under way, Parks Canada's Claude DeGrâce was able to justify further inaction, noting that 'a major exhibit [regarding Île Ste-Croix] is already being planned at the heritage centre in Calais, and a reconstructed village in Bayside might be a costly duplication.'[59]

In a sense, this was a repeat of the situation in 1904, when the major events to mark the tercentenary of the arrival of the Dugua expedition at Île Ste-Croix took place on American soil, where the bi-denominational nature of the expedition might be embraced. In Canada, where the political sensitivities of the English speakers largely precluded the involvement of the Acadians, such inclusiveness proved much more difficult, a situation that was, to some degree, recreated on the occasion of the quadricentenary. In Canada there were no Passamaquoddy with whom to speak (Soctomah was an American), since they did not (officially at least) exist; the Acadians had an ambivalent relationship to the story of 1604; and local English speakers feared ceding control to their fellow New Brunswickers from the other end of the province. In that atmosphere, governments could not or would not act, and Gagnon was left supervising the construction of those sculptures that garnished a parking lot.

Multiculturalism at Annapolis Royal's 400th

At roughly the same time that those interested in marking the 400th anniversary of the settlement on Île Ste-Croix first met, a group interested in doing the same in terms of Port-Royal in 2005 was beginning its deliberations. In 1994 some informal discussions took place among community leaders that resulted a year later in the incorporation of the Port Royal 400th Anniversary Society. On the face of it, the English speakers from Annapolis Royal and neighbouring towns were engaged in the same type of project as were their counterparts across the Bay of Fundy. In 1999, following consultations towards the creation of a strategic plan, the Society listed as its top priorities the creation of 'greater awareness of the Western

[Annapolis] Valley as an important tourism destination' and the development of 'opportunities for community economic development.'[60]

Since the English speakers could not celebrate their own beginnings at these sites, the past was used for practical ends, detached from issues of identity. In the case of Île Ste-Croix, local organizers recognized from the start that they needed to legitimize their activities by drawing in others who had a much closer connection to the story of the early seventeenth century – both the Acadians and the Passamaquoddy. As we have seen, the efforts to accommodate the Acadians were not always smooth and sometimes seemed half-hearted. Nevertheless, once 1604 had been identified by Acadians as the start of their existence as a people, the leaders from the St Croix valley had little choice but to try to play the Acadian card, inviting them to their deliberations from the very start.

By contrast, the local leaders behind the Port-Royal celebrations showed remarkably little interest in drawing in the Acadians. While there were seats on the St Croix Coordinating Committee's board set aside at various points in the process for Acadian and Passamaquoddy representatives, the Port Royal 400th Society made no such efforts to diversify its leadership. In part, this reflected the context within which the Annapolis Royal leaders needed to think about the Acadians. Since 2005 was identified by Acadian leaders as an opportunity to focus on the 250th anniversary of the *Grand Dérangement*, what had happened at Port-Royal in the early seventeenth century had very little hold on the Acadian imagination. As in 1979, when the 275th anniversary of *Acadie* was linked more closely to Île Ste-Croix than to Port-Royal, in 2005 Port-Royal was not really on the Acadians' radar.

Quite aside from questions of how the Acadians might have viewed Port-Royal on the occasion of the quadricentenary, there were also issues about how the residents of Annapolis Royal regarded the involvement of outsiders in the affairs of their community. Unlike the St Croix committee, which never claimed to be a grassroots organization and was made up of leaders from the community, membership in the Port Royal 400th Anniversary Society was much more widespread, thanks to an energetic drive to sign up local residents as members, who paid a small fee that provided them with some concrete link to the project. These links were reinforced by the provision of awards for volunteer service to the Society. As the chair of the Volunteer Committee noted in 2001, 'We are always looking out for new ways to recognize and express our appreciation to the many great volunteers who are actively involved in running the organization and participating in its varied activities.'[61] Towards that end, certificates of appreciation were provided to a select group of members and stories on individual volunteers were run in the local newspaper.

At one point there were over 300 members of the Port Royal 400th Society, drawn almost exclusively from the immediate region.[62] This was no small achievement in a town of only 550 residents, but the inhabitants of Annapolis Royal lived in a very rarified environment from that which existed in the St Croix Valley, with its considerable economic difficulties. While the incomes in Annapolis Royal in 2001, however calculated, were slightly below the provincial norm, the town dramatically stood out in terms of the composition of those incomes. While over 70 per cent of the incomes of Nova Scotians came from employment earnings in 2001, the figure fell below 50 per cent for Annapolis Royal. The other half of the town's incomes came from government transfers and sources such as pensions. This last factor is significant, since the population of Annapolis Royal, with a median age of fifty-one, was considerably older than the province as a whole, whose median age was thirty-nine; or, to put it another way, the percentage of the Annapolis Royal population over sixty-five was twice that for the province. The town also stood out at the other end of the age spectrum with relatively few young people, meaning that the incomes in Annapolis Royal (even if slightly below the provincial norm) could go far, in the absence of the various costs related to starting up and raising a family.[63]

The residents of Annapolis Royal approached their quadricentenary already possessing significant tourist attractions that (as we saw in chapter 1) had been assembled over the course of the twentieth century, providing a certain level of employment, some of it seasonal and, accordingly, well suited to a population that was not necessarily in need of permanent, full-time work. Only 20 per cent of those with earnings in 2001 worked full-time, a figure that reached 50 per cent for the province. Moreover, the leisure time enjoyed by the somewhat older local population fuelled the culture of volunteering that drove the activities of the Port Royal 400th Society and helped earn Annapolis Royal the distinction of being named the most livable small town in the world in 2004.

The LivCom Awards, endorsed by the United Nations, are designed to recognize communities in which care is taken to manage the local environment, and take into account both the policies put in place and the involvement of the local community in devising them. With its high concentration of heritage buildings and its strong community spirit, Annapolis Royal was a natural candidate. As the town's deputy mayor indicated in her presentation to the LivCom judges: 'The big advantage of the small town is that you have a manageable number of people who are all willing to do their part ... There is no shortage of volunteer opportunities. There are many service groups, four churches, a Health Centre, two schools and various community project committees. Most of the attractions are operated by independent non-profit organizations. As well the community is invited at every opportunity to help shape the Town's development.'[64]

This community spirit provided a solid base from which the Port Royal 400th Society could build its projects. However, this commitment to the community also provided an obstacle to sharing responsibility for the quadricentenary with others who had a stake in the story, but lived elsewhere. Accordingly, 'outsiders' were not incorporated into the day-to-day affairs of the Society, which committed itself to 'establish alliances with outreach groups,' including the Mi'kmaq, Acadians, and African Canadians. As we will see, all these parties could claim a connection to the story of what happened in 1605, but none of them would be involved in the actual decisions regarding the story to be told.[65] Accordingly, the precise shape of the quadricentenary was determined by the local English-speaking population, which incorporated elements of other peoples' stories as it saw fit.

In the process, the local leaders placed emphasis upon a story that was self-consciously multicultural, albeit in a manner with which they could feel comfortable. At the first annual meeting of the Society's members in 1996, the point was made that 2005 represented '400 years of natives, Europeans and Africans living and working together ... Tact, care and the commitment of people representing the native, African, and Acadian communities will be required.'[66] In practice, however, the Society seemed more at ease with the Mi'kmaq and African-Canadian involvement (however limited) than it did with that of the Acadians. The greater comfort with some stories than with others was evident as the Society struggled to find the right wording for its 'Vision Statement.'

The Society went through numerous versions of the statement, along the way holding a community think tank, Forum 400, in 1998 and hiring a consulting firm to provide a strategic plan in the following year. The first version of the statement, which was supposed to provide a sense of what was being remembered, pointed to the fact that a French flag had been planted at Port-Royal in 1604, followed by the erection of the habitation a year later. However, neither in this formulation nor in those that would follow was the word 'Acadian' ever used. Only at the very end of the process, following consultations with the Confederacy of Mainland

Mi'kmaq, which represents six communities (including the nearby Bear River First Nation) in Nova Scotia, was reference made to the fact that the events of 1605 'introduced an enduring French presence.' The role of the Mi'kmaq in bringing about the inclusion of the 'French' simply underscored the long-standing ties between those two people, and drew attention to the distance between the local English speakers of Annapolis Royal and the Acadian community.

The very fact that the Mi'kmaq were directly consulted distinguished them from the Acadians in the formulation of the Society's 'vision.' While the generic term 'French' was used throughout this process, never specifying the Acadian branch of the French family, the Mi'kmaq were recognized almost from the start, although how they were perceived in the history of the region evolved quite dramatically over time. In a 1998 version of the Society's statement, the Mi'kmaq were depicted as having been on the scene in 1605, although their earlier presence was left unstated. A year later, there was recognition that the Mi'kmaq had been present in the region for 'thousands of years' before the arrival of the French. In the final version of the statement, following the consultations with the Mi'kmaq, the aboriginal presence was further emphasized with the recognition that 'the Annapolis Basin is part of the traditional territory of the Mi'kmaq people.' Accordingly, 1605 marked the entry of the French into 'the Mi'kmaq district of Kespuwitk.'[67]

In addition to focusing on the Mi'kmaq, the leaders in Annapolis Royal saw that 'the presence of an African at Port Royal adds yet another dimension to the interaction of people at this early European settlement.'[68] The African in question was Mathieu Da Costa, who was allegedly on hand at Port-Royal at its beginnings, even though the evidence regarding the travels of this late-sixteenth- and early-seventeenth-century interpreter is thin. A man of African descent who spoke a wide range of European languages, Da Costa is believed to have spoken a version of 'pidgin Basque' that made it possible for him to communicate with the Mi'kmaq. He first surfaced in a formal document in 1608 when Dugua signed him to a contract, following some competition with the Dutch, to work for the French as an interpreter in the New World. One might speculate that he was in demand because of previous voyages to the Americas, but there is no concrete evidence that he ever actually set foot on what would be Canadian soil, and thus claims that he was the first 'named' African to have been here are problematic, to say the least. As one historian has put it, 'There is no indication of where or when Da Costa was born, who his parents were, whether or not he was married or had children, what he looked like, or where or when he died. Similarly, there are no details to indicate where or when he might have travelled in North America, how long he stayed, for whom he worked, and with whom he might have interpreted.'[69]

Such doubts did not overly concern those who wanted to use the occasion of the quadricentenary to celebrate Da Costa's arrival at Port-Royal as the start of the African-Canadian experience. Leading the way in this regard was Ken Pinto, the director of the Atlantic Fringe Festival in Halifax, who as early as 2001 was promoting the idea of a 'Da Costa 400' celebration for 2005. Indicating no doubt whatsoever, Pinto observed, 'With the French settlers was a Portuguese Moor – an interpreter who spoke micmac and the trade languages – Matthew de Costa, and he was the first known black person in Canada and the US. Ever … At the Port Royal stockade in 1605, de Monts and Champlain welcomed the grand chief of the Micmacs, Membertou – in the middle between them translating was de Costa.' In case such a perfect multicultural moment was not sufficient to sell his idea, Pinto also played to the role of the tourist dollar in such commemorative events, pointing out that 'Black Americans have never been richer … The black American tourism market is basically untapped. They find Canada safe. de Costa would be a perfect brand for Nova Scotia / Canada's black history to be sold to the huge / even wealthier black American middle class.'[70]

Whether Da Costa, or another African, actually arrived in the Port-Royal settlement during its early years is beside the point. After all, by their very nature commemorative events are creatures of the imagination. Nevertheless, it is telling that the English speakers who showed so little interest in Acadian stories (but were more forthcoming regarding those of the Mi'kmaq) wanted to incorporate the African story into the quadricentenary. This point was not lost upon Fidèle Thériault, whom we saw earlier in regard to the celebrations at Île Ste-Croix. Writing to Claude DeGrâce of Parks Canada, also involved with the events of 2004, Thériault was stunned that at public consultations held in 1998 regarding the Port-Royal quadricentenary, no one questioned the role played by Da Costa, even though 'there was no evidence that Mathieu DeCostes had actually come to *Acadie*.' There were representatives of Parks Canada at the consultations, but 'nobody said a word to get the facts right. They let falsehoods be accepted as if they were fact, and so became accomplices. I find it unacceptable that the anglophones are once again telling us how to interpret our history in a way that works to our disadvantage.'[71]

Thériault correctly picked up on the repeated reference at the 1998 consultations about the need to pay respect to the non-French actors from the Port-Royal adventure. As one participant in that process noted: 'We must specifically develop projects to focus on aboriginal and black cultures and recognize their contribution';[72] and in the years that followed, Acadian stories continued to take a back seat to ones focusing upon either the Mi'kmaq or the African Canadians, although even in those cases it took some time for connections to materialize. For instance, in terms of aboriginal participation in the quadricentenary, it was not until 2003 that the Society's minutes referred to its partnership with the Bear River First Nation to develop a dramatic portrayal of the past, starting before the arrival of the French and continuing up to the deportation of the Acadians. Until 'The People's Story' became a part of the planning for 2005, the Mi'kmaq whose reserve was only twenty-five kilometres from Annapolis Royal did not figure in Society deliberations. In 1999 the organization representing the Mi'kmaq at the provincial level had been consulted in the preparation of the vision statement, but until 2003 Bear River was not part of the picture.[73]

The Bear River Reserve was established in the early nineteenth century on land that was once part of the Mi'kmaq district of Kespuwitk,[74] which was led in 1605 by its grand chief, Membertou, remembered on previous commemorative occasions as having been the first aboriginal convert to Christianity in the Americas. On none of those occasions, however, was any effort made to bring the people of L'sitkuk, as Bear River is known in Mi'kmaq, into the process. While the exclusion of First Nations people from such commemorative events was widespread until fairly recently, there were aspects of the Mi'kmaq story that may have been particularly difficult for English speakers to tell, since it invariably spoke to the close ties that developed between the aboriginal people and the French newcomers. Intermarriage between the two was common, and they fought together against the English on various occasions. Ultimately, by the mid-eighteenth century, both the Acadians and the Mi'kmaq were identified as enemies by the English, and at the time of the deportation the latter provided assistance to those who managed to escape the net of Lawrence and his men.

As the quadricentenary approached, however, a new relationship developed between the residents of Annapolis Royal and the members of the Bear River First Nation. In the spring of 2003 the Port Royal 400th Society was turned down by the special program of the federal government created to fund 400th anniversary events. Established in 2002, this fund of $10 million (described at length in the previous chapter) was accessible only to those planning events that would be held in 2004, so as to coincide with the year of the Île Ste-Croix quadricentenary; as for 2005, it was to be the year to remember the *Grand Dérangement*. Given the terms of the program, the Society saw its first effort to secure support rejected, leading its president at the time, David Kern Jr, to look for other partners who would not be tied to an Acadian chronology. One idea was to stage a re-enactment of the Battle of 1710, at which Port-Royal fell to the British. As Kern readily recognized, this was a story that would not curry much favour among Acadians, but might attract support from other organizations interested in military re-enactments.[75]

A second project was 'The People's Story,' which was slated for completion in 2004 so that it could receive federal funding, have its debut within the federal guidelines, and then continue as part of other events in 2005. In the end, Ottawa rejected the military re-enactment idea, but 'The People's Story' secured a $47,5000 grant. Ironically, the play did not have its premiere until 2005, which would have made it ineligible for federal support had that point been made in the application promoted by the Society. Be that as it may, it remained an important part of the 400th anniversary events. In 2005 several performances of 'The People's Story' were staged at a newly constructed cultural centre on the Bear River Reserve, but in addition the performers were brought in to provide an important element for the official ceremonies staged in July 2005 to coincide with the date of the arrival of Dugua and his men four hundred years earlier.▣

On a spectacularly sunny day (in contrast to the torrential rains in 2004 at Bayside for the Île Ste-Croix celebration), spectators were treated to an edited version of 'The People's Story' that focused upon the initial contact between the Mi'kmaq and the French, without the sections dealing with the conflicts of the eighteenth century that culminated in the *Grand Dérangement*, a subject that would have been out of place at Annapolis Royal, even though 2005 did mark the 250th anniversary of the deportation. While the pre-contact world was described in idyllic terms, there was nothing catastrophic about the arrival of the French, with whom the Mi'kmaq forged 'lasting friendships' based upon 'mutual respect.' There was considerable intermarriage, and so, a Mi'kmaq performer remarked, 'We were one people.' The fall only came with the arrival of the English, burning and pillaging as they seized Port-Royal in 1613. The French returned in the 1630s, which resulted in much rejoicing on the part of the Mi'kmaq. This version of 'The People's Story'

3.4 Performance of 'The People's Story' at 400th Anniversary of Port Royal
(photograph by the author)

concluded with a celebration of the ties that still existed in 2005 between
the Acadians and the Mi'kmaq, which constituted the legacy of 1605.[76]

There was one significant addition to the cast on this occasion. As Hal
Theriault, the manager of the Bear River First Nation Heritage and
Cultural Centre and writer-director of 'The People's Story' observed in
regard to this specific performance: 'Of special importance was the inclusion of an African Nova Scotian, representing the fact that several western
European countries carried African translators and negotiators, including Matthew deCosta, on their voyages to the "New World."'[77] By incor-
porating this African character, Theriault was being true to the spirit of
the Society's efforts to emphasize this aspect of the story. David Kern was
in contact with parties interested in commemorating the contribution of
Da Costa as early as 2003, and a significant moment in the formal commemorative ceremony, following the performance of 'The People's Story,'
was the unveiling of a plaque by Parks Canada on the grounds of the reconstructed habitation in recognition of the role of 'Mathieu Da Costa:
Explorer, Translator, Free Man.' Even though the inscription provided no
evidence that Da Costa ever set foot on this soil and that 'research on Da
Costa continues,' he served as a symbol for 'an early African presence in
the Americas.'[78] Members of the Valley African Nova Scotian Development

Association were on hand for the unveiling of this plaque, which was designed to become part of a Mathieu Da Costa African Heritage Trail that would eventually stretch across western Nova Scotia.

As for the dignitaries invited to speak that day, they were, in many ways, the usual suspects. John Hamm, the premier of Nova Scotia, was on hand as had been New Brunswick's Bernard Lord for the Île Ste-Croix event in 2004; and Chief Frank Meuse, from the Bear River First Nation, occupied the place that had been filled by Hugh Akagi, the Passamaquoddy chief in New Brunswick. As for the other members of the official party, this was not quite the 'A' list that had graced the stage in New Brunswick a year earlier. While a French minister had introduced Jacques Chirac via satellite hook-up at Bayside, on this occasion there was the French consul for Atlantic Canada, who apparently missed the point of Chief Meuse's comments about the role of the Mi'kmaq in the story of 1605 by focusing upon how Canada had been built by 'two founding people'; and instead of Paul Martin, who was in the vicinity on the day preceding the ceremonies but was apparently unavailable for the big event, there was the minister of Canadian Heritage. In place of the president of the Société nationale de l'Acadie was its vice-president, Gérard Boudreau. Perhaps more significant than the identity of the SNA representative was the fact that he was only invited at the very last-minute for an event that had been in the planning stages for over a decade, in a sense recreating the last-minute invitation of Acadians in 1904. Only days before the staging of the quadricentenary, I was assured by the directeur-général of the SNA that no contact had yet taken place.

Weren't There Acadians at Port-Royal?

By and large, the Acadians were marginalized from a ceremony that marked the beginning of a French presence at a site that would become an important centre of pre-deportation settlement. In a sense, it was the misfortune of the Annapolis Royal organizers that their site had been founded in 1605, a year whose quadricentenary coincided with the 250th anniversary of the deportation. Accordingly, they were put in the position of having to decide whether to go ahead with a celebration of the start of *Acadie* in a year dedicated to marking its most tragic moment. Since 2004 had been proclaimed the year of *Acadie*'s birth, it would have been easier to stage the Port-Royal event then, and indeed there was precedent for such a change since, in 1904, Attorney General Longley had managed to mark the tercentenary of Port-Royal on its 299th birthday. However, the leaders of the 400th Anniversary Society did not seem inclined to accommodate Acadian sensitivities.

Having been forced to choose between abandoning the 'real' year for their anniversary or going against the grain in 2005, Society members seemed at times resentful about an Acadian emphasis that was working against them. For instance, they showed a certain reluctance to support the activities of Acadie 2003–5, an umbrella organization designed to promote '2003–2005 celebrations commemorating the arrival of the French in Acadie.'[79] The Society was one of a number of groups in Nova Scotia, some of which were predominately Acadian, that joined together to promote commemorative events, most of which were linked to sites of memory from the early seventeenth century. The English speakers within Acadie 2003–5, including the president of the 400th Anniversary Society, were at times uncomfortable with what they saw as the imposition of undue influence by the Société nationale de l'Acadie. In a meeting during the summer of 2000, the Society's president, Céleste Thibodeau-Stacey, complained about the SNA, which had to understand that it 'needs to fit the goals of the group.'[80]

At times the Society itself appeared uncomfortable with its place within Acadie 2003–5. In November 2001 the Society's executive committee expressed 'concerns regarding what this organization is positioning itself as.' A few months later the Society's board refused to support the Acadie 2003-5 advertising and sponsorship policy, a matter that was discussed at some length at a meeting in May 2002.[81] David Kern expressed the view, also shared by others, that the umbrella organization was promoting the idea that 2004 was *the* year for celebrations. As he put it, 'Why are so many organizations marking 2004 as their commemorative year?' Another board member, speaking in much the same terms, remarked that 'there is a misconception out there because of the way things came together that 2004 is it. There is so much publicity regarding 2004 to date that it appears to most that this (2004) is the commemorative year in Nova Scotia – and this is confusing.'[82]

The mood of the board did not improve when the official announcement was made a few months later in 2002, on *le quinze août* (the Acadian national holiday), to provide funding exclusively for 2004 events. Only a few weeks after the bombshell there was a meeting to decide how to proceed. Members expressed the sentiment that there was 'no clear direction other than to celebrate history and culture particularly in the official language minority.' Nevertheless, they decided unanimously to submit an application that was doomed to failure; and to make a point as

they were on their way to defeat, they chose (again unanimously) to provide the government with only 'a bilingual introduction with a note that
the full bilingual application [could] be forwarded upon request.'[83] As
expected, the Society was turned down early in 2003, but undeterred it
applied once again – and was turned down once again, leading David
Kern to go public with his frustrations in a series of newspaper articles,
in one of which he minced no words: '"I seriously question the federal
government's decision to identity 2004 and not 2005 as the 400th anniversary year of l'Acadie ... The attempt to settle St-Croix wasn't the first
effort to settle the region and like all other prior attempts was a failure.
Had it really been significant, the government should also come up with
a funding structure to commemorate LaRoche's try on Sable Island in
1598. At least this attempt [which is often discounted because of its use
of convict settlers] lasted more than a year [ending in 1603]."'[84]

Shortly after this outburst, Kern's term as president of the Society
came to an end, and a new board set out to construct the celebration
that was possible within the limits that had been established. Instead of
beating their collective heads against the 2004 Acadian wall, the Town of
Annapolis Royal sought and received $250,000 from the federal govern-
ment when it was granted the Cultural Capital of Canada Award for 2005,
winning in the competition among towns with fewer than 50,000 people.[85]
With this relatively limited funding in place, the event that might have
proclaimed Port-Royal's significance to the world could not be constructed, particularly at this late date. Nevertheless, true to its community roots, the Society now had the means to present a story with which it
could feel comfortable. It was in this context that the formal ceremony
was staged in July to mark the date of the arrival of Dugua and his comrades. There was little evidence on the morning of the big day that anything out of the ordinary was taking place. Little effort had been made
to attract visitors from far away, and the Acadians had other things on
their minds only weeks from major events to mark the 250th anniversary
of the *Grand Dérangement*. This was just another event for the town, so as
shoppers went about their business at the Saturday morning market
there was little sense that the day was in any way exceptional.

The three thousand people who assembled that afternoon at the habitation were warmed up by various musical acts, including a group from
Bear River (which would also take part in the re-enactment described
above) and the local duet of Wayne Currie and Jeanne Doucet-Currie,
who provided the Acadian content. Doucet-Currie performed holding
an Acadian flag, one of the few in view that day. (There was no Mi'kmaq

flag on hand.) She waved it particularly enthusiastically during a song dealing with the flag that had the refrain: 'Rouge, blanc, bleu, étoile dorée, Notre drapeau flotte avec fierté' (Red, white, blue and star of gold, The flag waves proud and bold).[86] While she tried with all her might to get the crowd to sing along in French, she had no success and earned more than a little grumbling from my part of the audience. Undeterred, she tried once more in a song about Frenchy's (an Atlantic Canadian institution akin to the dollar store) with the refrain, 'Deux pièces et demi' ($2.50), but which elicited no more response than the first effort.

As the weekend wore on, the community-focused nature of the celebration became clearer as the African Canadians disappeared, the Acadian content remained minimal, and even the Mi'kmaq component receded, 'The People's Story' now to be performed at the Bear River Reserve. There was a recreation of the Order of Good Cheer on the evening of the official ceremony, a re-enactment of the club for eating and drinking founded at Port-Royal four centuries earlier. On those occasions, Membertou had been a regular guest, but on this one none of the Mi'kmaq were on hand, nor was there even an aboriginal re-enactor to balance out the Champlain impersonator. The only Mi'kmaq moment came with the singing of a song with the ironic refrain 'Membertou, Membertou, We Remember You.'

On the following day the absence of the Mi'kmaq continued with the performance of the 'Annapolis Royal Suite,' composed by Ron MacKay. The first movement, according to the notes distributed at the premiere, was designed to 'capture the excitement as the travelers left France … It culminates in the celebration of their arrival in the "New Land."' Of course, Dugua and Champlain did not come directly from France, but from their experience at Île Ste-Croix. That said, nothing in either the notes or the actual performance suggested that another people had already occupied this land, which of course was not so new to them. Next came 'The Order of Good Cheer,' which was based on French airs and so Membertou's participation was again excised. The last historical movement focused on 'The Siege of Fort Anne' in 1744, as French forces tried – unsuccessfully – to displace the British. The Acadians did not support the French imperial forces on this occasion, and so the actual Acadian presence at the site of Annapolis Royal did not have to be confronted.

In the end, however, the most striking example of local memory on the occasion of the quadricentenary came with the performance, only a few weeks after the formal 400th anniversary events were over, of 'Connections,' a series of historical vignettes by the local playwright Peggy Armstrong. 'Connections' was made up of five moments from the past that had been performed over the previous years, in the lead-up to the 400th anniversary. They constituted a collaboration between Armstrong, who had staged other historical plays at Annapolis Royal, and the local Costume Animation Committee that had been working since 1999 to develop an inventory of historical garb. Local people met weekly for years to design and produce costumes that might be worn on various occasions connected with Annapolis Royal's efforts to attract visitors to its collection of historic sites and heritage buildings. However, from the start the committee worked closely with Armstrong, who would produce one vignette per year, starting in 2000, so that a full sweep of the early history of the town might be presented on the occasion of the quadricentenary.

Armstrong's story began, much like the 'Annapolis Royal Suite,' with the departure of a number of Frenchmen, off to settle at Port-Royal, in the process excising the existence of Île Ste-Croix, from which the original settlers arrived. In the commemorative politics of the 400th anniversary, there were frequently references to the fact that the Île Ste-Croix settlement had been 'temporary' while the one at Port-Royal was 'permanent.' Of course, no one could have known that the first settlement would last only a winter, and in fact the Dugua adventure at Port-Royal was short-lived in its own right. Nevertheless, there was obviously a local conceit at work that there were colonists who had set out in 1605 directly for Port-Royal to create the first permanent French settlement.[87] At the moment of departure from France, one girl asked her brother to bring her back a present, while one of the men gleefully proclaimed, 'We're off to *Acadie*,' as if embarking on a holiday.

The play then turned to the early years of the settlers at Port-Royal, who seemed to live in a land theretofore uninhabited (as in the 'Annapolis Royal Suite'). Everything seemed to be going well until Dugua learned that he had lost his monopoly and so they would have to return, a reinforcement of the point that the 1605 settlement had been, in its own right, temporary. Having provided no evidence of a permanent French settlement at the site, the third vignette then focused upon the creation of a family in 1630 during the period when the territory was under British control and was being settled to create a New Scotland. The story was built around a Scotsman, Taig, already in the colony, who befriended a woman and her child who were found as stowaways on a ship about to return to England. Unable to see her cast aside, he took them in to form a real family, the first one that Armstrong presented to her audience.

In order to balance out the Scottish settlement at Port-Royal, she might then have looked to the establishment of ordinary Acadian families following the return of the territory to France in 1632. In fact, one looks in vain for any such Acadian family in this story. Instead, Armstrong provided a vignette built around the intrigue between Charles de Saint-Étienne de La Tour and Charles de Menou d'Aulnay. During the 1630s and 1640s the two were constantly at odds over control of *Acadie*, with a number of their encounters taking place at Port-Royal, thus making them fair game for Armstrong. La Tour was discredited in the 1640s when he solicited English support for his cause, but was ultimately rehabilitated following d'Aulnay's death in 1650. In Armstrong's telling of the tale, the story concluded with La Tour's marriage, at Port-Royal, to d'Aulnay's widow.

While there can be no denying that the La Tour–d'Aulnay struggle took place, it ended up being the only story pertinent to the French presence at Port-Royal beyond 1632, when a French *Acadie* blossomed, with its centre at Port-Royal. La Tour and d'Aulnay were Frenchmen, not Acadians who developed roots in this part of the world, and so no truly Acadian story was ever told in Armstrong's production, which then went on, in the final vignette, to examine the period following the deportation. In a sense, skipping the *Grand Dérangement* was facilitated by the fact that the Acadians never really existed in this version of the past. Instead, the last part of the story, 'Starting Over,' focused upon the arrival of the Loyalists, who had been dispossessed as a result of the American Revolution.[88]

The Loyalists, not the Acadians, were the individuals driven from their homes in Armstrong's telling of history, which I viewed in late July 2005, only two days after attending the first 'Journée de commémoration du Grand Dérangement,' an event largely staged just down the road at Grand-Pré and proclaimed by the federal government to mark the 250th anniversary of the deportation. However, if the fate of the Acadians received cursory treatment in 'Connections,' they did little better in another Armstrong creation that I attended in 2004, while the Congrès mondial acadien was in Annapolis Royal. 'Forever Marie' focused upon the life of Marie-Madeleine Maisonnat, who married an English officer shortly after Port-Royal's fall in 1710. She and William Winniett, who left the military for a successful career as a merchant before his death in 1741, had thirteen children, a number of whom – like their mother – married British officers. Needless to say, Marie was not deported in the 1750s, and the play shows her reflecting on her pre-deportation friends, a comical Mi'kmaq character and two Acadian children, whose own deportation is treated very discreetly, much as the deportation slipped by almost unnoticed in 'Connections.'[89]

Acadians were allowed passing appearances in Armstrong's plays, not unlike the treatment that was reserved for them during festivities to mark the quadricentenary of Port-Royal. Moreover, just as the Annapolis Royal commemorative events included characters of African ancestry to provide the desired multicultural content, Armstrong was careful to create for 'Connections' a character of African ancestry among the late-eighteenth-century (post-deportation) newcomers to Annapolis Royal. The vignette focused upon the opportunities that existed in this new land for everyone, regardless of their background. However, one looks in vain for an Acadian in the mix, or for that matter a Mi'kmaq character.[90]

The Acadians, in a sense, did make one further appearance before the quadricentenary celebrations were over via the re-enactment of the Battle of 1710 that saw the fall of Port-Royal and led, as it turned out, to the permanent transfer of *Acadie* to the British. This was not the first time this battle had been re-enacted. Fifty years earlier, on the occasion of Port-Royal's 350th anniversary, there had been a similar re-enactment that ended with the defeated French marching away. It was difficult for this story to end any other way, and yet here it was once again, being celebrated only weeks after the deportation had been remembered in lavish ceremonies at Grand-Pré. On this occasion, re-enactors came from both Nova Scotia and the United States. However, there is no evidence that Acadians were involved, other than in their depiction as the vanquished.

The re-enactment of 'A Common Valour' was funded in part by the American-based Society of Colonial Wars, which provided $25,000; other support for the quadricentenary came from both the federal and provincial governments in similarly piddling amounts. Even when added together, however, such funding was a drop in the bucket compared to what the organizers of the Île Ste-Croix events had sought to fund celebrations that were supposed to have an impact far beyond the St Croix valley. Of course, the price for thinking big was that the St Croix organizers were always courting disaster when their aspirations proved greater than their funding. By contrast, the celebrations at Annapolis Royal, in part out of necessity (large-scale federal funding not being available), but also out of conviction, were designed to speak to the local community, with relatively little evidence of concern about Acadian sensibilities. Such behaviour only fuelled the suspicion of Maurice Basque about English speakers who were interested in marking (and profiting from) the 400th anniversary of *Acadie*, but who seemed less inclined to engage in 'an act of reconciliation in 2005 in regard to the Grand Dérangement.'[91]

The Port-Royal celebrations were designed to be modest, so much so that they actually turned a profit, although this clearly had not been the organizers' intent. At a wrap-up meeting in early 2006, the Society's treasurer reported that he expected to end up with a surplus of roughly $25,000, which would be disbursed among various community groups.[92] In a sense, this was an appropriate way for the quadricentenary to close. Not having been overly concerned about how the inhabitants of the site for over a century were depicted, the organizers at Annapolis Royal built an event that was unambiguously for their own consumption and, as it turned out, financial benefit. Here was a town that had had some very real successes, which had a high quality of life, and which was prepared to provide glimpses of an openness to those who were at the margins of daily existence, as long as they did not appear in any sense threatening. In terms of the Acadians, there were many stories that simply were not told, but that was not a problem, since the Acadians had little to do with this anniversary of the founding of a French settlement.

Other Stewards

While the contexts faced by the English-speaking stewards of Île Ste-Croix and Port-Royal were different, a similar challenge had to be confronted in each case, namely: How do people celebrate a past that is not really theirs? In both instances, we saw that this could only be done with great difficulty. In the first case, the residents of the St Croix valley could not escape the suspicions of Acadians that they were somehow trying to profit from someone else's past; in the second, since by 2005 Acadians had moved on to mark the anniversary of the deportation, the residents of Annapolis Royal found the means of dealing with more comfortable stories of multiculturalism, trying to avoid much talk about the Acadians and how they ceased to be residents of the region.

Île Ste-Croix and Port-Royal have a certain iconic status in the early development of *Acadie*, each in its own way the site where the colony began. Nevertheless, there were also other locations that were able to make claims on the Dugua expedition on the quadricentenary of its voyage. For instance, in May 2004, a month before the celebrations in the St Croix valley, a group of English speakers organized celebrations to mark the site, on the south shore of Nova Scotia, where Champlain first set foot on the mainland of North America during this voyage.[93] Staged at a provincial park along the coastline near the location where the expedition weighed anchor before coming ashore, the Champlain Festival was a celebration of the moment of contact between the Frenchmen and the Mi'kmaq. Indeed, many of the formal events involved moments of official thanksgiving on the part of the French government, represented by its consul general for Atlantic Canada, or the Acadians, represented by the president of the SNA, who provided his society's highest honour to the Mi'kmaq Grand Chief.

For their part, the Mi'kmaq representatives made frequent reference to their Acadian brothers, noting bonds of friendship that stretched back to 1604. In his public remarks, John Joe Sark, a prominent leader of the Mi'kmaq nation, brought his people and the Acadians together by reference to their shared experience of oppression at the hands of the British. In a filmed discussion that I had with Keptin Sark just after those remarks, he noted that 'the dominant society is afraid if the two [i.e., Mi'kmaq and Acadian] peoples got together.' When I asked what he meant by the 'dominant society,' he carefully removed the Acadians from categorization as the 'white man,' leaving English speakers as the unmistakable common foe.[94]

As was the case at the Île Ste-Croix celebrations, local English speakers had little formal role to play in a celebration that was not about them. Accordingly, when one of their leaders, Karen Dempsey, a representative of the municipal government, spoke, she described this event as celebrating 'cultural diversity,' never quite making direct reference to the two peoples whose paths had crossed four hundred years earlier. She observed that 'we celebrate explorers and settlers who established l'Acadie; we celebrate the diverse cultures,' but much like her fellow Nova Scotians from Annapolis Royal, she did not speak directly to the experience of Acadians, who inhabited this territory long beyond the early seventeenth century, until the deportation, a word that was not uttered on this occasion.

After leaving this point of contact, Dugua and Champlain followed the shoreline, eventually entering the Baie française and briefly visiting the site where the Port-Royal settlement would be established a year later. In 1604 they continued on and arrived, on 24 June, at the mouth of the river Champlain would name after St John the Baptist, on his feast day, roughly forty-eight hours before they would reach Île Ste-Croix. As we have seen, Saint John went out of its way to mark the arrival of the Dugua expedition in both 1904 and 1954, although on each occasion the Acadian presence was minimal. Given the spirit of the quadricentenary, however, there was a conspicuous French role at Saint John, which was encouraged by the increased vibrancy of the local French-speaking population. Although the size of this population remained steady in the early twenty-first century at around 5000 (out of a population for greater Saint John of over 120,000), Greg Allain and Maurice Basque observed in 2001 that 'the French-speaking population has become more visible and is now an important partner in the development of the Saint John region. Not only do French speakers have their own role to play, but increasingly English speakers recognize this role and its importance to the life of the greater Saint John region.'[95] Leading the way in giving the French-speaking population greater visibility was the Association régionale de la Communauté francophone de Saint-Jean (ARCF), which provided much of the leadership for the 400th anniversary celebrations in Saint John when it was not always forthcoming from civic leaders, most of whom were English speaking.

Early in June a monument to Dugua was unveiled that went far beyond all previous tributes to the leader of the expedition, who had always been at a disadvantage at Saint John, where Champlain had a strong claim on memory, having named the river. On previous occasions, Champlain had been championed by Acadians (and their cousins from Quebec), while the English-speaking leaders largely insisted upon inclusion of the Huguenot Dugua to provide some religious balance. However, by 2004 the commemorative context had been completely transformed as Acadians had become champions of Dugua, Champlain having been jettisoned so that the Québécois could have him to themselves. There was nothing to prevent praise being lavished upon Dugua, since everyone now seemed to be on his side. The monument, a small structure that bore a commemorative text, was built on a site overlooking the Bay of Fundy. It drew attention to Dugua's role (not so much as mentioned on previous anniversaries) in naming the Baie française and gave him equal responsibility with Champlain in naming the river (perhaps giving Dugua more credit than he deserved). George MacBeath, who had also been involved with the celebration fifty years earlier, noted that he had made a mistake in 1954 when he edited the commemorative booklet produced for the occasion and entitled it 'Champlain and the St. John.' As MacBeath now put it, 'De Mons himself was there on that historic occasion, and it was de Mons who commanded the expedition.'[96]

While English-speaking volunteers played a significant role in the erection of the monument, this public enthusiasm for the quadricentenary paled in comparison with that shown by members of the much smaller francophone population, which recognized a moment to make its presence known. Accordingly, on the date marking the 400th anniversary of the arrival of the Dugua expedition, there was a re-enactment staged along the Saint John waterfront, co-sponsored by the ARCF and performed by actors from the Saint John–based Théâtre du Trémolo.

As at the Champlain Festival in Nova Scotia, the limited role of local English speakers then continued the next day, which coincided with the start of festivities in the St Croix valley. The highlight on this occasion was the appearance in Saint John of the Comédie-Française in a performance of Molière's *Le Malade imaginaire*. It was no small feat to have the oldest permanent theatre company in the Western world (which rarely performed outside France) come to an overwhelmingly English-speaking city. So as to underscore the tribute being paid to local French speakers, the French government also arranged to have the head of the ARCF, James Thériault, decorated as a 'Chevalier des Arts et des Lettres' at the same time as the appearance of the Comédie-Française. Perhaps overly impressed with its own publicity, the local French newspaper crowed triumphantly that 'the Celebrations in Saint John stole the show from those for Sainte-Croix which had been planned for years.'[97] It is hard to avoid sensing a certain satisfaction that the small French-speaking population of Saint John had somehow bested the English speakers of the St Croix valley.

A century earlier, and once again in 1954, English speakers had dominated anniversaries of the arrival of the French at Saint John, but this was no longer the state of affairs even though they still constituted well over 90 per cent of the population. As was the case just down the road near Île Ste-Croix, aside from community leaders, enthusiasm for someone else's celebration did not run deep. The situation was different in Saint John, however, because it was the only site of memory from the Dugua expedition that had a French-speaking population of any significance, let alone one which felt that the wind was in its sails, having 'entered a new era of growth and importance.'[98] There was no evidence of ill will on this occasion, certainly nothing comparable to the testy remark by one Nova Scotian active in organizing 400th anniversary activities, who complained about the assertiveness of Acadians, by observing: 'The SNA cannot come in and claim ownership.'[99] Nevertheless, there was a certain uneasiness at all of the sites touched by the Dugua expedition regarding the role of English speakers – now the stewards of the sites – who found it awkward, at best, to take part in someone else's birthday.

4

Celebration versus Commemoration

The Visitors Always Require Help

On the eve of the celebrations marking the 400th anniversary of the French landing on Île Ste-Croix, I was filming an interview with Hugh Akagi, the chief of the Passamaquoddy First Nation in New Brunswick. Near the end of a glorious early summer evening in St Andrews, he patiently answered questions on a beach not far from his home that stands on land that he considers the property of his tribe. This claim has been contested both by municipal officials of St Andrews, eager to use the property for new residential developments, and by the federal government, which does not recognize the existence of the Passamaquoddy, a trans-border tribe, in Canada. In the middle of filming, a cell phone went off with the news that camera equipment that I feared we had lost en route had in fact been left behind in Montreal. Given that a single grant was financing both a documentary film and this book, the loss of the equipment would have been catastrophic. So, when the interview was over, the members of our film crew were on a high, not only because Hugh Akagi had eloquently advanced his point of view, but also because financial disaster had been avoided.

In the midst of this euphoria, I decided that I would try to race our equipment van the short distance from point A to point B, not taking into account the curb just ahead of me. I fell face first into the pavement, and was badly bruised. There was concern among the crew that perhaps some medical advice was required. Not knowing who else to contact, they called Hugh Akagi. He came running with a friend, a paramedic, who checked me over and pronounced that I would live. Before leaving us, Chief Akagi turned to me and said, 'Why is it that whenever your people visit our territory, you need our help?'

Akagi's quip reflected a certain truth, namely, that the members of the Dugua expedition (and those French settlers who would follow them) could not have survived without the support of the First Nations people. In spite of that help, the Europeans who came to settle what was to become Canada have not always been forthcoming in providing recognition, either symbolic or substantive, to acknowledge that debt. In the case of the Mi'kmaq who belong to the Bear River First Nation near Annapolis Royal, Nova Scotia (where Port-Royal had once stood), scant resources have been made available to deal with a wide array of social and economic challenges. In the case of the Passamaquoddy, the Canadian government has to date made no concrete effort to recognize their existence as a nation in this country, preferring instead to view the tribe as exclusively American, a claim that seemed to be contradicted by the presence of Hugh Akagi and Rita Fraser, one of his band councillors, at the interview on that beach in St Andrews. The absence of recognition means that governments, at all levels, have no obligation to negotiate with the Passamaquoddy, thus precluding any discussion about rights that might have to be respected.

Given this context, there was good reason why the pertinent First Nations people might have refused to participate in any 'celebration' of the arrival of the French in 1604–5. The very fact that they were now given the opportunity to take part was one indication of how much had changed since the 1904 tercentenary, when the good burghers of Saint John dressed up as 'sham Indians in canoes' during a re-enactment of Champlain's passage three hundred years earlier. Only a few years later, at the Quebec tercentenary, aboriginal people were allowed to perform, but within a script that was carefully prepared by the 'European' organizers.[1] By the late twentieth and early twenty-first centuries, however, such open contempt for the aboriginal inhabitants was no longer possible, if only because the governments that financed such commemorative events would not agree to be involved if they stood to be embarrassed by protests from First Nations people who felt that they were being either ignored or tokenized.

A telling example of commemorative events about European beginnings in the New World that went badly wrong in terms of aboriginal participation were the celebrations in 1992 to mark the 500th anniversary of the arrival of Columbus in the Americas. A commission was established in the United States in 1985 to watch over the quincentenary, on which aboriginal concerns were given short shrift. No Native American served as a full-fledged member, and the sole Native American to be made an honorary commissioner 'resigned this appointment in 1990 and was never replaced.'[2] Not surprisingly, those – both natives and non-natives alike – who could not accept the traditional view of Columbus as the 'discoverer' were troubled by the development of commemorative programs that ignored the not-always-positive legacy of 1492, and so protests started to emerge. These protests, in turn, had the effect of scaring away funding agencies from 'supporting projects that appeared too Quincentenary-oriented and therefore controversial.'[3]

Ultimately, when many of the official projects collapsed, the events that received the bulk of media attention in 1992 were dominated by those who sought to advance aboriginal perspectives. In Philadelphia red paint was thrown on a new monument honouring Columbus only hours before it was to be dedicated. In Columbus, Ohio (the largest city in the world named after the explorer), counter-demonstrations were held to draw public attention away from the official ceremonies staged on a full-scale replica of one of Columbus's ships. As Ken Irwin, executive director of the Ohio Indian Movement, put it: 'We want to get the word out about some of the atrocities committed by Columbus – genocide, slavery ... and the taking of women.'[4] As one activist observed, 'The Quincentenary is the only opportunity we have had to call people's attention to our situation, so we have to take advantage of it before it is gone and we return to the silence in which we have always lived.'[5]

In the lead-up to the quadricentenary of the arrival of the Dugua expedition, there were certainly voices that echoed some of the sentiments heard a decade earlier in the United States. For instance, Pat Paul, a Maliseet Elder, wondered why 'the First Nations [should] join the Acadians in celebrating the 400th year of our own exploitation, destruction and demise.'[6] Similarly, Gilbert Sewell, a Mi'kmaq guide and storyteller who had been asked to participate in the ceremonies at Île Ste-Croix, wondered, 'How could anyone have the nerve to ask me to join in, when this arrival constituted the beginning of the end for us?' However, to temper this unhappiness, in the next breath Sewell recognized, 'It is true that the French have been our allies against the English. Even today, we can understand their efforts to defend their language.'[7]

Sewell's second thoughts reflected one of the fundamental differences between aboriginal memory of the arrival of Columbus and that in Canada (and neighbouring parts of Maine) regarding the coming of the French. Without overstating the point, the French were not perceived centuries later in the same light as other European colonizers of the New World. Certainly in comparison with the number of British emigrants to

North America in the seventeenth and eighteenth centuries, the number of French emigrants who made the journey was relatively small. As a result, both French imperial policymakers and French settlers were forced to establish close ties with First Nations people, so much so that the memory of the French regime remains positive, a fact reflected in some of the Acadian ceremonies described in previous chapters.

In the case of the Mi'kmaq, the period of French control over *Acadie* is still looked upon as an era of harmony that stood in contrast with the destruction that followed the takeover by the British in the early eighteenth century. Following the Acadian deportation, the Mi'kmaq often befriended those trying to escape the British net, so that there developed a sense that the French settlers and the Mi'kmaq had been the common enemy of the regime in London. In this regard, John Joe Sark wrote on the eve of the quadricentenary events that his Mi'kmaq people still remember 'the tears cried for the Acadians who suffered at the hands of the British before and after the Great Deportation of the 1700s.'[8] More specifically, for the Mi'kmaq of the Bear River First Nation who traced their roots back to Membertou, the first convert by the French to Catholicism and an associate of the early settlers of Port-Royal, there was no visceral hatred of the colonizers that might have precluded participation in quadricentenary events. While expressing some reluctance to become involved, Chief Frank Meuse recognized that it made sense for his people to take part, if only to 'revisit the role the Mi'kmaq played for that settlement.'[9]

As for the Île Ste-Croix adventure, again the memory of the French presence, although a brief moment in terms of settlement, remained positive four hundred years later. After the winter of 1604-5, the area surrounding the island became a theatre for warfare between British and French forces, with the various aboriginal people siding with the French, at least up to the transfer of *Acadie* in 1713. Owing to the French connection that survived long beyond the ephemeral Dugua settlement, Catholicism came to the Passamaquoddy via French missionaries and was maintained by French-speaking priests. Accordingly, nearly four hundred years after the first appearance of the French in the area, Donald Soctomah, the Passamaquoddy Historic Preservation Officer in Maine, could talk with considerable affection about his own memory of tribal elders still speaking French well into the twentieth century. This memory, of course, stood in contrast with the less positive one connected with the intrusion of English settlers along the New England coast to the south. As Soctomah explained to me, 'When the French landed here, the French became our friends ... If you look where the [English] landed, you don't see very many tribes left. Well, you look behind the French and all the tribes are still in existence.'[10]

This positive recollection of the French presence made it possible for these two aboriginal peoples to consider participation in the quadricentenary events, although not without considerable hesitation. In part, this reluctance stemmed from the fact that there was no reservoir of positive memories among either the Bear River Mi'kmaq or the Passamaquoddy in terms of cordial relations with the English speakers who took up residence in these regions and whose successors now, as the 400th anniversary of the arrival of the French approached, had the responsibility for making 'contact.' As I discovered when I first visited these areas, it was not so much that there were bad relations between the local English speakers and the First Nations people; it was rather that such ties simply did not exist. As Norma Stewart observed in regard to the St Croix valley, 'the native groups in our community or region don't normally get that involved in non-native activities.'[11]

On earlier anniversaries of the Île Ste-Croix and Port-Royal settlements, the original inhabitants of the two regions were largely ignored; and even in the early stages of organizing the quadricentenary events, those ties were similarly weak. In the early twenty-first century, however, it was no longer an option to ignore the role that native people had played in the events being remembered. The various governments from which funding was being sought insisted on such involvement, and so a process began, initiated by the stewards of the sites, to draw in aboriginal partners, who needed to be convinced that there were good reasons to take part, concerned that they might be used to legitimize someone else's party. Along the way, the First Nations people found opportunities to advance their interests and to tell their stories, all in the spirit of commemoration, if not celebration; and the English speakers learned about neighbours who had heretofore been an unknown quantity. While events marking contested moments from the past frequently encourage bitterness, as had been the case on Columbus Day in 1992, the quadricentenary resulted in no violence, little anger, and even some encouraging signs about the positive power of the past both for the First Nations people and the English speakers with whom they cooperated.

Do the Passamaquoddy Live Here Anymore?

The roots of Passamaquoddy involvement with the 400th anniversary stretch back to the 1980s, long before anyone was seriously thinking about the quadricentenary. At that point in time, Hugh Akagi had not yet been made the chief of the Canadian Passamaquoddy, a people who had neither a formal leader nor an organization to advance their interests. By and large, the Canadian Passamaquoddy were seen as forming part of the Passamaquoddy tribe on the American side of the border. The American Passamaquoddy had a population of roughly two thousand (ten times the number in Canada) and two reservations, one of which could be seen across Passamaquoddy Bay from Akagi's front window in St Andrews. The land surrounding Akagi's home became the focus of a public dispute that ultimately resulted in the emergence of both the Canadian Passamaquoddy as a force to be reckoned with and, by extension, Chief Akagi as a major figure in the commemoration of the arrival of the French on Île Ste-Croix.

The transformation of Passamaquoddy fortunes in Canada began in 1989 when Hugh Akagi and his siblings found themselves involved in a legal struggle with the Town of St Andrews over the land where their family had long lived. The Akagis and their forebears had occupied land near that part of town known as Indian Point, where the Passamaquoddy village of Qonasqamkuk once stood. Indian Point, an area of roughly one hundred acres, had not been developed to any great degree, in spite of its proximity to the tourist town, in part because it was traversed by the Canadian Pacific Railway. For roughly a century, from the mid-1880s until 1983, the CPR had tracks, and a right of way alongside them, on land leased from the town. Then, in the 1980s the lease lapsed, the tracks were removed, and the town found itself with real estate that it might develop. However, before going forward, St Andrews wanted to be certain that there were no other claims on the property and filed papers in order to quiet the title, that is to say, to secure judicial confirmation that there were no competing claims.[12]

The Akagi family responded to this effort by filing a petition of its own, based on the principle of adverse possession, by which title can be secured by proving the 'open and notorious possession of lands for a certain period of time.'[13] While the Akagi property only covered an area of roughly three acres, the family claimed that for generations it had openly used a much larger, 9.5-acre area that should be ceded to it, in the process stymying the development plans of the town. In the end, the 1993 ruling by Judge J. Jones provided the Akagis with slightly more than their original three acres (which even the Town acknowledged was rightfully theirs), but much less than what they had claimed.

For present purposes, however, just as important as the results of the case were the arguments used (on not used) by the Akagis.

They argued that the land in question had been occupied, going back to the 1880s, by successive generations in an unbroken line that began with Hugh's great-grandfather, who is identified in court documents only as 'Chief John Nicholas.' If Nicholas had been a Passamaquoddy chief, this was never made explicit. In fact, the 'P' word was never used during the proceedings. In the hearing of the case in 1992, the family claimed that it had a right to the land owing to both 'adverse possession and aboriginal title.' This was the only occasion on which the Akagis made explicit reference to an aboriginal basis for their claim, and yet on questioning from the Town they quickly abandoned this justification, returning to an exclusive reliance on the 'Doctrine of Adverse Possession.' The Akagis chose not to muddy the waters of their case by claiming any aboriginal right to this land, in the process tacitly accepting the assumption that had existed for much of the previous two centuries, namely, that the Passamaquoddy existed as a tribe exclusively in the United States.

Of course, for thousands of years before the close of the American Revolution, there had been no boundary dividing the Passamaquoddy into American and Canadian components. In fact, the lines that divided the Passamaquoddy from other tribes, in particular the Maliseet, who were concentrated along the St John River valley, just to the east of the Passamaquoddy territory, were far from clearly demarcated when the Dugua expedition arrived. Champlain simply referred to the aboriginal people he found here as 'Etchemins,' and so it cannot be said with complete certainty that he and his colleagues met up with a self-conscious Passamaquoddy grouping that distinguished itself from its neighbours. Nevertheless, with the emergence of written evidence that came with the arrival of Europeans, the name Passamaquoddy came to be commonly employed in treaties and other documents and was associated with a territory that roughly coincides with today's southwestern New Brunswick and adjoining regions of Maine, and which included the settlement at Qonasqamkuk.

With the end of French control over *Acadie*, the Passamaquoddy and their aboriginal neighbours, members of the Wabanaki Confederacy, entered into a series of treaties with the British. In each of these documents, Passamaquoddy representatives signed as leaders of a sovereign nation, whose limits transcended the international border that would only subsequently be established. These signatures proved significant when the Supreme Court of Canada ruled in 1999, in its landmark

Marshall decision, that the treaties into which the Passamaquoddy had freely entered still provided security for aboriginal fisherman to provide for their 'necessaries' (to use the eighteenth-century expression). Moreover, the Marshall decision provided some justification for the claim that Hugh Akagi had been reluctant to make only a few years earlier: namely, that his people had a legal claim on resources within that part of Canada that had formerly been Passamaquoddy territory.[14]

Following the Marshall decision, claims by Passamaquoddy leaders such as Hugh Akagi that the Supreme Court had validated their treaty rights in Canada were countered, as they had been for nearly two centuries, by the argument that the Passamaquoddy nation existed exclusively within the United States, and so there was no one in Canada to exercise such rights. To be sure, the bulk of the Passamaquoddy population had gravitated to the American side of the new border. In part, this was due to the fact that the Passamaquoddy, already experiencing encroachments upon their lands by the British, had supported the Americans during the Revolution, and were 'rewarded' for services rendered by entering into a treaty with Massachusetts (Maine was not created as a state until 1820) that provided them with slightly more than twenty thousand acres of land, in return for the abandonment of all claims. Even these land rights were eroded over the years and efforts were only made to correct the situation by means of an agreement entered into by the federal government and several tribes of Maine, including the Passamaquoddy, in 1980. By then the Passamaquoddy in the United States still possessed two reservations, but were compensated for past losses by being given access, along with the Penobscots and a Maine-based band of Maliseets, to a $27 million trust fund and $81.5 million to acquire a further 300,000 acres of land. At the time, this was the largest such settlement in American history.[15]

The road had not been an easy one for the Passamaquoddy in the United States. Indeed, according to the 2000 census, the tribe's Pleasant Point reservation was among the poorest communities in Washington County, Maine; and as we saw in the previous chapter, this was the poorest county in a very poor state. Nevertheless, no one would have argued that the American Passamaquoddy did not exist. By contrast, the prevailing narrative regarding the same tribe in Canada is that it was uprooted following the American Revolution, brutally displaced by the Loyalists and subsequent immigrants to New Brunswick. This process is particularly well documented in terms of the settlement of St Andrews, which started to receive newcomers from the recently created 'American' side of the St Croix River in 1783. Recognizing that the Passamaquoddy were still living at Qonasqamkuk, colonial officials made some efforts to have the Loyalists settle elsewhere, but to no avail. In fact, 'some Loyalists thought it necessary to patrol the Bay in the frigate Adriane ... "to protect their settlement at St Andrews [i.e., Indian] point from attack by Passamaquoddies."'[16]

Matters only deteriorated in the years that followed. In 1784 Lewis Neptune, a Passamaquoddy chief, reported that a cross on a Passamaquoddy burial ground at Indian Point had been 'cut down by some of the refugees and their place of worship destroyed ... [The Passamaquoddy] thence forward discontinued their worship and burials and fixed the same at Pleasant Point,' which a decade later would be the site of one of the reservations in Maine.[17] The final nail in the coffin, if one were needed, for a viable settlement at St Andrews came in the following year. As a Passamaquoddy petition from 1854 put it, in 1785 a group of Loyalists needing a place to pass the winter 'came to the Indians then living on Indian point and requested leave to be allowed to land saying that they would pay £25 for license to remain until the Spring when ... they would leave.'[18] Speaking to me 218 years later, Donald Soctomah remarked, 'You know, we never got the £25 and slowly, the village of Loyalists got bigger and bigger and kept putting more pressure on the tribe so finally, the majority of the tribe moved,' most ending up in what became Maine.[19] 🖥

The pressures on the Passamaquoddy continued into the first half of the nineteenth century due to the rapid growth of the New Brunswick population. Recognizing their difficulties, in 1842 the lieutenant governor indicated that he would 'make a provisional arrangement for the acquisition of land for them in the St Croix.'[20] These good intentions were translated into action in 1851, when New Brunswick created a reserve in Charlotte County at the intersection of the Canoose and St Croix rivers for the benefit of the Passamaquoddy.[21] The 100-acre Canoose reserve was established in response to a petition from John Lacoute, about whom little is known other than he was aboriginal and lived in an area that had been traditionally occupied by the Passamaquoddy. However, for whatever reasons, there is little evidence that these lands were subsequently occupied (at least not on a permanent basis) by aboriginal people, let alone members of the Passamaquoddy tribe, and by the early twentieth century government officials were exploring how the property might be transferred to non-natives interested in harvesting its timber resources.[22] In 1909 a representative of the New Brunswick Crown Lands Department wrote: 'For about 40 years or more the land has not been occupied by any Indian and never will be again there being no Indians in this part of the country ... The Lacoutes for whom this land was obtained have long since left the Province and now live in Maine on a Reserve there and so there seems to be no excuse for this lot being held by the Dominion Government for an Indian Reserve.'[23]

In order to repossess the land, the Crown set off in search of a Passamaquoddy inhabitant of Canada who might legally sign it away. There certainly were reports in the early twentieth century that such individuals existed. One Indian agent noted in 1904 that 'the only Indians I can learn of in Charlotte County are some six families divided between Scotch Lake, St Andrews and St George.'[24] Nevertheless, by the 1920s a signature had still not been secured, so that the discovery of an aged man named John Nicholas, seemed to offer some hope. F.H. Grimmer, a St Andrews–based lawyer, had the assignment of getting the signature from Nicholas, whom he described as the 'only representative of the Passamaquoddy tribe living here, or so far as I know, in New Brunswick.' In 1922 Grimmer indicated that 'the old Indian ... is here for a couple of days only at present, and is going back for two or three weeks to stay with his sons, one living at Pleasant Point Maine, and another near Princeton Maine,' site of the other Passamaquoddy reservation in the United States. 'He seems to be quite willing to sign release of the Canous reservation.'[25]

Grimmer did not manage to secure Nicholas's signature either on this or subsequent occasions. In 1925, admitting defeat, he wrote: 'John Nicholas has at last given a flat refusal, and says he will not sign anything, and I know it is quite useless for me to press the matter further with him. He says Indians have no rights any longer. They can't fish, can't shoot, can't take birch bark for canoe or stick of ash for basket, or camp on river or lake shores, etc. ... I find it quite useless to press him further.'[26] Nicholas appears to have died in 1925, shortly after Grimmer's last dealing with him, thus making it possible for the Department of Indian Affairs to invoke a clause in the Indian Act that allowed for the repossession of Indian land in the absence of anyone to surrender it.

In 1936 Ottawa sold the land to James Hasty, a local farmer, but this did not bring the matter to a close. Rather, the dossier took on a new life in the 1970s when the Union of New Brunswick Indians (UNBI), claiming to speak 'on behalf of the Indian people of New Brunswick,' asserted that the Canoose reserve had been 'set aside for the use and benefit of the Malecite Indians.'[27] Choosing to ignore the Passamaquoddy connection with Canoose, the UNBI preferred to believe that the Maliseet should have been consulted for the surrender of the reserve and now deserved compensation. Not surprisingly, the federal government took the view that 'the Indians' – never using the word Passamaquoddy – 'for whose use and benefit the lands were originally set apart ceased to exist as identifiable groups or bands,' and rejected the claim.[28]

For the next twenty years, there was sporadic sparring between the Maliseet (or organizations representing them) and Ottawa, neither side ever mentioning the existence of the Passamaquoddy; and why should that have been too surprising, since even the Akagis did not seem to press their specific aboriginal identity when they took on St Andrews regarding the land at Indian Point in 1989? However, the situation changed quite dramatically during the following decade. In 1999 Indian and Northern Affairs received a number of documents from an organization that called itself 'The St Croix Schoodic Band of the Passamaquoddy Nation at Quanasquamcook,' whose chief was Hugh Akagi, and which wanted to press land claims on, among other properties, the Canoose Reserve.[29]

So what had happened in the intervening years to make Akagi and the other members of the band council assert their Passamaquoddy identity, not only in their dealings with the federal government but also in the face of disregard of their existence by other First Nations? Or to put it another way, how can we explain Hugh Akagi's own apparent transformation? In 1989 this great-grandson of John Nicholas, the elderly Passamaquoddy who had refused to sign away Canoose, did not even recognize Nicholas's Passamaquoddy heritage, but a decade later was prepared to follow in his footsteps, a path that ultimately led Akagi to commemorative stages in 2004.

Akagi's assertion of his aboriginal rights was closely linked to developments in St Andrews following the quieting of the titles at Indian Point. The Akagis had tried originally to advance their case on the basis of their long-standing occupation of part of this territory, but to no avail. Immediately following the court ruling in 1993, they did not appeal 'because they could not afford additional legal costs and were afraid that an appeal could cost them their home and the small acreage they had been awarded.' However, any notions of going away quietly ended in 1995 when the town council met to consider amending its bylaws to permit a development project at Indian Point. In response, Akagi now appealed to aboriginal rights that had not heretofore been invoked. Referring to the judge from the earlier legal struggle with the town, he asserted in no uncertain terms, '"The land must be returned. Your loyalist judge may have settled with my family, but not with my tribe."' To add substance to that claim, Akagi was joined at the council meeting by Passamaquoddy from the two reservations in Maine, including Fred Moore III, the tribe's representative to the state legislature, who would play an important role in the assertion of Passamaquoddy (as opposed to Akagi family) claims in St Andrews.[30]

Moore made his presence known once again in 1997 when the town sold off a lot, not far from the Akagi property, thus triggering fears that more significant infringements on Passamaquoddy land were in the offing. Mincing no words, Moore told a journalist that 'St Andrews is to the Passamaquoddy what Jerusalem is to the Israelis.' Perhaps going farther than Akagi was prepared to go, Moore showed no interest in settling for some agreement regarding Indian Point, but rather wanted to deal with the claim that 'southwestern New Brunswick was unsurrendered Indian land,' a point that was reinforced by the unprecedented participation of the Maine Passamaquoddy in the Canada Day parade in St Andrews.[31]

For Hugh Akagi and the other Passamaquoddy in New Brunswick, the support from the American side of the border helped transform a family's campaign into one for the recognition of an aboriginal presence in the St Andrews area. As he put it some years later, the support from the Maine Passamaquoddy had made Akagi feel that he 'wasn't alone. I had been a lone voice for some time and I thought that this was my battle.'[32] Nor was this the only encouragement for his cause, since the Atlantic Policy Congress, which included chiefs from across Atlantic Canada, also expressed its recognition of 'St Andrews as the longtime capital of the Passamaquoddy people.'[33]

Buoyed by this support, forty Passamaquoddy from New Brunswick, claiming to represent a population of roughly two hundred (as opposed to the two thousand living in Maine), met in 1998 to create formally a band for their people on the Canadian side of the border. Not surprisingly, Hugh Akagi was chosen chief. While this might have been seen as a new departure for his people in Canada, he insisted that they 'were not creating a new band, but re-establishing an existing band.' As he put it, 'the "Passamaquoddy ... never left [Canada]."'[34] Of course, it was easier to create a band that might be recognized by those that already existed at Pleasant Point and Indian Township on the American side of the border, than it was to achieve some legal status in Canada, where federal officials held to the line that the Passamaquoddy were exclusively an American tribe.

In the years that followed, Akagi and his fellow band councillors secured some degree of legitimacy, in certain quarters at least, that came from this self-proclaimed band status. For instance, in 1999 when the Marshall decision regarding aboriginal fishing rights was delivered, Akagi was sought out for comment and referred to in the press as the 'Canadian Passamaquoddy band Chief'; and several years later, he was profiled in the *New Brunswick Telegraph-Journal* as the 'Chief of the St Croix–Schoodic Band.'[35] More substantively, he was front and centre when in 2001 town council considered a rezoning ordinance to allow construction of a subdivision at Indian Point. The proposition was defeated as numerous residents of the town as well as members of the two reservations in Maine came out to support the Passamaquoddy in Canada. On one occasion, the outpouring of support forced town council to hold a meeting in the local arena; on another, a petition with seven hundred names, along with strong opposition from the Atlantic Policy Congress of First Nation Chiefs, forced the motion to be tabled.[36]

The Indian Point issue returned to the council floor one more time in early 2002. With many of the town's residents who winter elsewhere unavailable to protest, a vote was finally taken and the rezoning approved, but only after the mayor cast the tie-breaking vote. Feelings ran high, with some of the development proponents playing on the fact, as one councillor put it, that "there is no officially recognized Passamaquoddy Indian band in New Brunswick or Canada.'[37] This 'victory' by those who wanted to develop the land could not conceal the fact, however, that by then the Passamaquoddy in St Andrews had achieved a certain popular acceptance, if not formal recognition. Accordingly, even when the council passed the rezoning by-law, it chose to delay any work on the land pending further study.[38] As I write these lines, the land in question remains undeveloped; however, the Indian Point controversy did have consequences, namely, the emergence of the Canadian Passamaquoddy as a force that could not be ignored. The newfound influence of the tribe would have a significant impact upon the quadricentenary of the arrival of Dugua and his men at Île Ste-Croix.

Chief Akagi Takes Centre Stage

When interested parties first met in 1995 to discuss the Île Ste-Croix quadricentenary, there was not so much as a vague reference to the involvement of the Passamaquoddy. It would only be three years later that the minutes of the St Croix 2004 Organizing Committee would first mention the tribe, and then only in the context of needing 'to consult with Pleasant Point about Passamaquoddy representation.'[39] By then, of course, the

Passamaquoddy band in St Andrews had been established, with support from the Maine bands, and so for the American Passamaquoddy to be involved without any recognition of their tribe's existence in Canada would have been complicated to say the least. Perhaps this was the context for the cryptic comment recorded in minutes from early 1999 that the committee should 'not attempt to hide any aboriginal conflicts.'[40] During the following year, Pleasant Point named various representatives to serve, but there is no evidence that they ever attended a meeting. Accordingly, it could not have come as much of a surprise in early 2000 when a letter was received 'indicating the tribe was withdrawing their participation from the Ste-Croix 2004 Coordinating Committee.'[41]

Over the following three years that saw the emergence of Hugh Akagi and his band as a significant political force in the region, the Passamaquoddy remained outside the discussions pertinent to the quadricentenary, and the organizing committee began to look for other aboriginal people who might fill the void. In late 2000 the committee's master plan for the settlement at Bayside, discussed in the previous chapter, included a 'Mi'kmaq Area,' an idea that Hugh Akagi 'found kind of interesting,' since there was no basis for imagining a Mi'kmaq presence in this part of the world.[42] More substantively, in early 2003 the committee met with Martin Paul, Aboriginal Development Officer for New Brunswick, who explained that 'provincial interest lie [sic] with, in this case, the Maliseet First Nations People.' Obviously taken by Paul's presentation, the Coordinating Committee resolved to 'recognize the Maliseet Nation in Canada and the Passamaquoddy Nation in the United States as the aboriginal peoples essential in the partnership of commemorating the 400 year anniversary of the French presence in North America.'[43] As if this were not sufficient to marginalize the Canadian Passamaquoddy, only weeks later the committee met with a representative of the New Brunswick Aboriginal Peoples Council, an organization that looked after the interests of off-reserve and non-status Indians. The Council was offered a seat on the Coordinating Committee, which led Nathalie Gagnon, who was responsible for the dossier for Parks Canada, to wonder why 'other First Nations organizations,' including the Passamaquoddy had, 'not been invited also.'[44]

Even though the town of St Andrews had by early 2003 effectively abandoned any efforts to undertake development projects opposed by Hugh Akagi and his supporters, the organizing committee seemed prepared to avoid them if at all possible. Perhaps the organizers from the St Croix valley feared that the federal government, already reluctant to support their various projects, would be even less enthusiastic were the Canadian Passamaquoddy to be involved; or perhaps the neglect of Hugh Akagi and his band simply reflected the perception, communicated to me by one of the organizers only a few months later, that 'there wouldn't be five Passamaquoddy people in Canada.'[45] In any event, the spurning of the Canadian Passamaquoddy was certainly encouraged by the various First Nations groups that seemed willing to participate in the quadricentenary, regardless of the treatment of Akagi's band. Later in 2003 the Mi'kmaq leader John Joe Sark, writing to Chantal Abord-Hugon of the Sociéte nationale de l'Acadie, remarked in regard to the involvement of the Canadian Passamaquoddy in the 400th anniversary events: 'I am sure that the Passmaquady [sic] may have some concerns, but I have no idea what they are. The Passmaquady live in the State of Maine, they may share some of the treaty rights with the Mi'kmaq and the Maliseet, however they are not Canadian or Mi'kmaq.'[46]

In the end, the formula that envisaged the involvement of the Maliseet in New Brunswick and that of the Passamaquoddy from Maine proved untenable because the latter had come too far in support of Chief Akagi to abandon him now. Accordingly, the organizers from the St Croix valley quickly realized that there had to be some acceptance of the Passamaquoddy fact in Canada, or there would be no involvement by the tribe that was most closely linked to the Île Ste-Croix adventure. As Allan Gillmor, the Canadian co-chair of the committee, put it, his group finally rejected the position that 'there would be the [Maliseet] in New Brunswick and the Passamaquoddy in Maine and all that sort of thing and then we just really said, "the heck with it, we are here to involve the Aboriginals, we're not going to get into the politics of the issue, we'll do what we feel is appropriate to the celebrations or the commemorations" … I forget what we did with the resolution [regarding the Maliseet] but we basically said, you know, "Forget it. Forget that."'[47]

Having come to this acceptance of the necessity of working exclusively with the Passamaquoddy, the first step in bringing it about came in May 2003, when Norma Stewart effectively crashed a dinner attended by the leaders of the Passamaquoddy in Maine. As Stewart puts it, until then her efforts to 'find any person that would talk to me just failed,' which is hardly surprising since her committee had been reluctant to recognize the existence of the Passamaquoddy in Canada. As she explained to me:

I just walked into the room with my gift and introduced myself and said who I was and why I was there and basically it was again, to invite them to participate because there was opportunity, economic opportunity for them and also that chance to showcase *their* culture, and who *they* are to the world ... It was difficult to gatecrash this dinner party, but about two months after that this gentleman from the tribe, Donald Soctomah, he came by to visit us and said that he would be the link between us and the tribe and that they were very interested in inclusion at this point.[48] ⌨

During the summer of 2003, Donald Soctomah, who was already working closely with the National Park Service in the development of its trail at Red Beach, began to meet with Norma Stewart. Speaking to me several months later, he recognized that his tribe had 'stayed out of the process for probably two years before we decided this is part of our history and just to sit in the back and let this event pass us by ... we're not doing anybody justice. So we decided to become part of the event, making sure everybody realizes that this isn't a celebration for us, it's a chance for us to educate, it's a chance for us to remember.'[49] ⌨ Indeed, Stewart quickly agreed that 'next year's commemoration [would have the themes of] Education and Remembrance,' thus removing the concept of 'celebration' from the lexicon.[50] In fairly short order, a Passamaquoddy patron for the quadricentenary was named, Passamaquoddy symbols were painted on the windows of the Coordinating Committee's offices on the main street of St Stephen, various projects that would spread understanding of Passamaquoddy history were agreed upon, and there was a proposal to start the events on 26 June 2004, exactly four hundred years after the arrival of Dugua and his men, with a Sunrise Ceremony that would be held at Indian Point in St Andrews.[51]

The symbolism of this last point reflected the willingness of the local leaders to accept, at least implicitly, that the Canadian Passamaquoddy, who had fought for the preservation of this land in an unspoiled state, did in fact exist. Indeed, achieving such recognition had been one of Soctomah's goals in involving his tribe. According to Hugh Akagi, Soctomah told him: 'I am going to let them get their hooks into me, then I am going to tell them that I am working with you.'[52] For his part, on the eve of the 400th anniversary, Soctomah explained to me: 'The underlying cut of this whole thing is to bring our story to light, the story that we are a border tribe, an international tribe, and for four hundred years, our people have been stiffed by the Canadian government and we're hoping that there's going to be people that are going to hear that and try to do the right thing. We're hoping people, either the public watching this or government officials will want to do the right thing in honour of their ancestors and in honour of our ancestors. So that's the underlying motive behind the whole thing.'[53]

With Donald Soctomah playing intermediary, Hugh Akagi had no formal role in negotiations regarding the shape of the quadricentenary. In that regard, he told me in the fall of 2003, when he was already a public figure in the area, that he had had 'little or no contact with them [Norma Stewart's group]. Probably the one experience I've had was dropping something off for Donald [Soctomah] and I'm sure they didn't have any idea who I was.'[54] Nevertheless, Akagi emerged as the star of the 400th anniversary events. His leading role began with the Sunrise Ceremony that he hosted at Indian Point, only five hundred metres from the property that the Passamaquoddy had long occupied. While a hundred people stood in the rain waiting for the sun to rise, Akagi, wearing aboriginal head dress in his capacity as chief, welcomed the assembled 'to his territory' and explained the rituals to follow. First, everyone took part in a smudging ceremony, in which they were 'cleansed' with smoke from a pot carried by one of the Passamaquoddy elders; then everyone was invited to place tobacco on the fire around which the ceremony was held, in order to offer thanks to one's ancestors.🖳

In the midst of the ceremony, Akagi made reference to the presence of John Craig, the mayor of St Andrews, with whom he had differed over the development of Indian Point. However, there was not the least sign of bitterness, since the point of the exercise was to spread the message that the Passamaquoddy existed in Canada, and not to rekindle hard feelings. As Akagi put it after the quadricentenary was over, 'The [sunrise] ceremony was simply a way of welcoming the day, a way of purifying ourselves, and making sure that when the new day dawns we were ready to accept it, that we were new people. That's what was happening, we had some old grudges set aside. We were comfortable we were on our own land, on our own territory.'🖳 For her part, Norma Stewart later remarked that 'to see those dignitaries and average Joes like me all sharing an experience that was unknown to all of us with the Passamaquoddy was very special.'[55]

Following this ceremony, a select group then made its way to the only event that would be held on Île Ste-Croix, so that the French government might formally thank the Passamaquoddy for the help that had been provided four hundred years earlier. While Hugh Akagi was on stage along with representatives of the reservations in Maine, he was the only Passamaquoddy leader who had an opportunity to speak from his heart, and not simply recite formal resolutions passed by the tribe. Of course, when he talked, he had to be careful not to be overtly political, since he was on American soil. Since the Passamaquoddy had never really accepted

4.1 Canadian Passamaquoddy Chief Hugh Akagi (photograph by the author)

the international border placed through their territory, Akagi was careful to avoid drawing distinctions between the status of the tribe in the two countries. Nevertheless, there could be little mistaking his Canadian perspective when he talked about his 'fears for our future.' Since the Maine Passamaquoddy had received a large settlement in 1980, the fears were entirely those of Akagi's band, and so he was still likely thinking about St Andrews when he referred to his hope that those in attendance 'would respect our heritage to this land.'▣

The day then ended (when the show for the evening was rained out) with the formal event organized at Bayside by the Canadian government and dedicated to a celebration of the 'first dialogue' between the French and aboriginal people, the latter represented exclusively by the Passamaquoddy. High above the stage were the flags of the principal parties with a connection to the quadricentenary, including that of the Passamaquoddy; and the emcees for the event introduced the various speakers and musical performers in the three official languages of the day: Passamaquoddy and the two more obvious ones. Among the speakers there was only one First Nations person, the Canadian chief of the Passamaquoddy.

Hugh Akagi recognized that this might be the largest crowd to which he would ever have an opportunity to speak, and thought carefully about what he might say. Forty-eight hours before his opportunity, he observed: 'I understand that the way I have to do it is that you have to be nice. It doesn't help to be nasty. At this point in time, it's not going to serve my people any good to go out there and scream and yell that an injustice has been done.' Only seconds before explaining his strategy, he described the behaviour of the federal government towards his people as 'a nice way of committing genocide … They are not going to put a nail through your heart, but they might as well. Because what they're cutting out is that native content. Nobody has the right to do that to another person.' ⌨ On a public stage, however, Akagi intended to take a different tack: 'I would like to tell the story of a [French] people who were starving … They were about to perish, certainly were not likely to survive. When I think about that story, I am also thinking about my people. Because my people are having the same problems today. Back then, the people on St Croix Island found a friend in the room when they met the Passamaquoddy, who helped them survive. I would like to think that the stories being similar, that we can find a friend in the room today, so that maybe we can survive too. That's the story that I'd like to get across'[56] ⌨

As befit his status as the only aboriginal speaker, Akagi was the first to take the stage. Playing on the distinction between a celebration and a commemoration, he began by surprising his audience, indicating that 'we too have things to celebrate … If you [Acadians] have need to celebrate the one winter you spent in our territory, then we need to celebrate our existence here for the past thousands of years.' He then turned to the central point of his message, as he spoke to the issue of recognition, which was being withheld by the same government that was sponsoring the event.

> Our survival is also deserving of recognition … While the culture of our Acadian brothers and sisters is flourishing strong, ours is fragile and endangered … The threat to our survival is no longer hunger and disease, but the use of a legal system under which we are forced to live … We search for justice, but are too often told that after checking their documentation that has been created for us, we no longer need to exist in our territory. Even when the Supreme Court of Canada recognized our treaty rights, we were told that we were not welcome here as a people … The lack of recognition by the government of Canada … brings a death knell for the Passamaquoddy in this land now called Canada … I have to hope that there are people who want to hear our story … I hope that you would value us not as an object to be discarded for some piece of legislation, but protected forever and a day with the recognition that we so truly deserve. ⌨

Over the course of the afternoon, as the rain became more persistent, there was little to indicate that Hugh Akagi's message had had much effect. While there were aboriginal performers on stage and speeches that referred to the role of the First Nations people in 1604, the word 'Passamaquoddy' was never uttered. Ironically, the closest that any speaker came to 'recognizing' the tribe was when Paul Martin took to the podium. At the moment in the midst of a campaign for an election that would be held two days later, the prime minister made a surprise visit that pleased event organizers, otherwise depressed over the disastrous weather that hung over their events. In regard to the Passamaquoddy, Martin's visit was delicate to say the least, since the government he led had refused to recognize the tribe's existence in Canada.

In paying his respects to the dignitaries on hand, Hugh Akagi was 'recognized' to the extent that Martin made reference to him among a number of chiefs who were in attendance, none of whom were identified in terms of their tribal affiliation. As for the body of his speech, Martin made only passing reference to the presence of First Nations people four hundred years earlier, and made no specific mention of the Passamaquoddy. Although the event had been billed as one to mark the 'first dialogue' between European and aboriginal peoples, Martin's speech was almost entirely about the beginning of *Acadie*, praising the first French settlers for having provided the basis for a society that was 'just, strong, inclusive, and tolerant.' Of course, the presence of a chief who apparently represented a people that did not exist gave these remarks a certain ironic twist.

Paul Martin immediately left the scene, on his way to the next campaign stop. He may have had the benefit of a helicopter in a neighbouring field while ordinary people tried to pull their cars out of the mud, but like many of those in the crowd, he was not going to return the next day for what turned out to be several local events, performed on the same stage at Bayside. With the sun now shining, these events focused on the Passamaquoddy. First, there was an ecumenical service, conducted in the three languages of the quadricentenary, which turned out to be a ceremony of reconciliation, with apologies offered both to the Acadians for their deportation and to the First Nations people for their treatment by Europeans. For its part, the United Church issued a statement with a veiled reference to the recognition issue in calling upon Ottawa to act in the 'spirit of welcome and inclusion ... in its rapport with the Passamaquoddy ... and other First Peoples.'[57]

The final formal act in the quadricentenary was the premiere of an orchestral work, the *St Croix Island Suite*, by the New Brunswick composer

Alasdair MacLean. The piece was performed by the New Brunswick Youth Orchestra before a local crowd, which included a number of Passamaquoddy, including Hugh Akagi, who was publicly thanked (along with Donald Soctomah) by the composer. In particular, one of the movements was based upon a Passamaquoddy canoe song, and so the tribe's presence was front and centre.[58] The political context for this composition was only reinforced in an interview with the composer following the performance. MacLean admitted that when he started the project he 'didn't know much about the Passamaquoddy other than the name.' However, he observed that by being involved in the commemorative process, 'I learned about their culture … I learned about a certain political sensibility of the Passamaquoddy as it related to this commemorative event … They have strong grievances that they cannot avoid talking about. Hugh Akagi yesterday spoke very beautifully, but he also spoke very truthfully about the sense of history that they have here and how much of what happened since the settlers have arrived from Europe has been very negative in terms of their own culture.'[59]

Alasdair MacLean literally had the last word. While we were speaking, workers were starting to dismantle the stage where the quadricentenary events had taken place. Within hours, there would be nothing left in the field at Bayside, other than some tire tracks, to indicate that a commemorative event had been held; and since the reconstructed habitation was never built, once those tire tracks were gone, no evidence would remain in the field to suggest that the quadricentenary had ever occurred. Nevertheless, the composer's words indicated that some things had changed. By being involved in the process, he had come to learn about the Passamaquoddy and had been, to use his words, 'sensitized to a particular political sensibility.' Much the same point was made by Norma Stewart, who expressed satisfaction that the Passamaquoddy had had a chance to make their point of view known. 'We learned lots about them locally … who they were, how many there are – and there are hundreds of them.' In regard to the issue of Passamaquoddy recognition, she viewed the quadricentenary as having been 'an opportunity for the Passamaquoddy to get a little impact, if you will, to make their story known, and immediately following the commemorative experience in July there was a petition that went around on the Canadian side, that said they want the Passamaquoddy recognized … From my position that's very exciting.'[60]

There was a similarly upbeat feeling among the Passamaquoddy. Rita Fraser, a member of the Passamaquoddy band council in St Andrews, was busy during the months following the 400th anniversary events in securing signatures for the petition mentioned by Norma Stewart. 'We started on that morning with the sunrise ceremony, getting names on the petitions and it's … kind of snowballed because everywhere I go, I carry this with me and if I get into a group of people I automatically just bring it out and [ask] please sign my petition; and all the time I've been doing it I think I had one gentleman who just turned and walked away and wouldn't do it. Everybody else has been more than willing to sign.'[61]

As for Hugh Akagi, he echoed Fraser's optimism: 'With the way the event has gone and the assistance of a lot of good people that have come through the door and are very serious about helping us, including the Acadian community, I think that it's going to be very difficult for the government to keep ignoring us … I'm hoping the writing's on the wall.' In fact, in the aftermath of the quadricentenary, Chief Akagi's band was given a small budget by the Department of Indian Affairs so that documentation might be assembled to see if some official status might be in the cards. While nothing has been settled as I write these lines, Hugh Akagi believed that his people were on a 'a path to our recognition.'[62]

Using the Past at Bear River

Some of the funds that the New Brunswick Passamaquoddy have received since the 400th anniversary events have gone to carry out a census, so as to establish exactly how many people belong to Hugh Akagi's band. By contrast, in the case of the First Nations people involved with the quadricentenary of Port-Royal, there is no doubt about the number of Mi'kmaq in the vicinity since the individuals in question were all 'status' Indians, carefully counted by the federal authorities. As we saw in chapter 3, the Bear River First Nation, whose reserve is only a short distance from Annapolis Royal, was associated with the anniversary events in 2005. From the perspective of the English speakers organizing the quadricentenary, the involvement of the Mi'kmaq provided both a connection with the family of Membertou, the chief who had befriended the French in 1605, and the means of attracting much needed and otherwise inaccessible funds from the federal government for activities to be held at the Bear River First Nation Heritage and Cultural Centre. Quite aside from the motives of the leaders in Annapolis Royal, the roughly one hundred Mi'kmaq at Bear River had reasons of their own for becoming involved.

Established in the early nineteenth century, there was nothing particularly exceptional about the history of the Bear River reserve over the next 150 years. Created to provide a structure within which the Mi'kmaq of southwestern Nova Scotia might look after themselves, and not be wards of the state, the reserve could never bring about the settled agricultural population that political leaders might have sought. Located in an area known as 'the Switzerland of Nova Scotia,' the reserve provided the Mi'kmaq with access to the resources of the forests and the Bay of Fundy. However, as Darleen Ricker has noted in her history of this community, the 'many attempts at farming the thin, rocky soil failed.'[63] The resources that were available frequently were harvested by individuals from outside the reserve; other times the land of the reserve was appropriated, without due process, as was the case with inroads made by the Nova Scotia Power Commission on several occasions during the twentieth century.[64]

Under these circumstances, the population living on the reserve was often lured away by better prospects elsewhere, so that a population of roughly ninety in the 1920s and 1930s bottomed out at fewer than forty throughout most of the 1960s, 1970s, and 1980s. While this situation might have led to hopelessness and despair, the band's experience over the past twenty years has been quite the opposite, characterized instead by a determination to become more self-reliant. Towards this end, in 1987 the band left the long-standing association of Nova Scotia Mi'kmaq people, the Union of Nova Scotia Indians, to join the newly created Confederacy of Mainland Mi'kmaq, which was dedicated to developing expertise in terms of such matters as resource management. In the case of Bear River, this effort to build a more self-reliant community was reflected in the introduction of a forestry management plan in 1988 and efforts to enhance salmon stocks four years later. Rather than wait for governments to provide relief, Bear River created educational programs in both regards so that its people could develop expertise that might both help the community and be marketed beyond the limits of the reserve.

The changing fortunes of the Bear River First Nation, whose population nearly tripled between the early 1980s and the quadricentenary of Port-Royal, coincided with the emergence of Frank Meuse, Jr, as its chief. First elected in 1987, Meuse reflected a determination on the part of this Mi'kmaq band to face the larger world, but on its own terms. Already in 1995, his achievements were recognized by the Mi'kmaq author and activist Daniel Paul, who wrote about Meuse's efforts to use the 'traditional Micmac way to solve community problems ... After the passage of only eight years since he was first elected, the Band is financially sound and has, while solving its money problems, accomplished many things: Alcohol and drug abuse have been reduced to a negligible problem; a new school and dozens of new homes have been built; the main road has been upgraded and paved, and secondary streets upgraded; recreation facilities, such as a tennis court and swimming pool, have been installed; and the Band is involved in many other Reserve and surrounding area activities, i.e., forest management, fish restoration projects on various streams, and so on.'[65]

Meuse's band was faced with a new set of challenges following the 1999 Marshall decision, which as we have seen also had its own impact on the fortunes of the Passamaquoddy, who found their claim for recognition bolstered by the Supreme Court of Canada. In the case of the Bear River Mi'kmaq, as for many other aboriginal communities, the Marshall decision provided the opportunity to extend their fishery operations within the limits acknowledged by the court. Fearful that expansion of the native fishery might have a disastrous impact upon their own livelihoods, non-natives sometimes reacted with anger, occasionally striking out against people who had long been their neighbours. This hostility was particularly evident on the east coast of New Brunswick, where vandals attacked the property of members of the Burnt Church First Nation.[66]

It appeared that a similar scenario was about to unfold in the fall of 1999, when non-native fishers were ready to enter St Mary's Bay, not far from Bear River, to seize native lobster traps in waters described as 'the richest lobster fishing grounds in the world.'[67] In the end, however, violence was averted due, in no small part, to the intervention of Frank Meuse, who established a positive tone by bringing an eagle feather to a meeting. As he put it, 'The feather is a symbol of the bird that can fly the highest and take our messages to the Creator the quickest ... When you receive the feather it's a sign of respect. It means you've attained a level of humility that allows you to learn.'[68] Meuse and the non-native fishers sat around talking to one another, and soon came to an agreement for sharing the lobster fishery based upon 'a shared appreciation of the principles supporting community-based management.'[69]

By 2003, all but three bands in Nova Scotia, New Brunswick, and Prince Edward Island had 'entered into direct agreements with the federal Department of Fisheries and Oceans (DFO) that allowed their members to get into the commercial fishery.'[70] One of the three bands to chart its own course was Bear River, whose chief at the time, Sherry Pictou, refused to 'enforce a concept of commercial fishing that doesn't respect Mi'kmaq culture and threatens non-native livelihoods as well.'[71] Pictou feared that negotiating with DFO might have compromised treaty rights, but she also saw good reasons to negotiate with her people's neighbours. As she put it, 'Those [non-native] fishermen are a part of nature, in a way that DFO certainly isn't.'[72]

Ultimately, the federal government blessed this agreement, but it had been the product of neighbours, natives and non-natives, finding the means of managing a resource collectively. Even within their own community, the Bear River Mi'kmaq tried to find a solution that might work for the common good. Accordingly, they chose to send out smaller than normal boats so that more members of the community might be involved. Pictou said that her band was looking towards both 'community benefit and sustainable livelihoods. The money we made from the lobster harvest went straight to the Band Council. We paid the harvesters' expenses, and they certainly didn't get rich from their work. We fish communally, not individually. Government services are being cut here, so we used the money raised by lobster fishing to provide some of those services.'[73]

The Bear River approach in the aftermath of the Marshall decision was based upon the use of traditional practices to find a place in the world of the twenty-first century, and this same strategy was employed in both developing the Bear River First Nation Heritage and Cultural Centre and negotiating a place in the Port-Royal quadricentenary. The centre began as a gym in the late 1990s, but soon expanded as part of an effort, as Sherry Pictou put it, to 'build community learning initiatives ... that involved re-claiming [our] history and traditional practices.'[74] However, when it opened in 2004 in a structure with a stylized wigwam entrance, it was not only a tool towards self-education, but also a means of providing much needed economic opportunities by drawing tourists to the reserve. Soon after opening, the centre was recognized by the Tourism Industry of Nova Scotia with its 2004 award of excellence for tourism innovation. In the following year, as the band sought to develop the programing that might draw further attention to their enterprise, over $100,000 of funding was received, mostly from the federal government, to construct a heritage gallery inside the centre. In addition, 2005 saw the first performances at the centre of 'The People's Story,' a play that provided the Mi'kmaq perspective on the previous 400 years, and was supported with $47,500 from the budget allocated by Ottawa for 400th anniversary celebrations. As we saw in chapter 3, this funding was secured with the involvement of the leaders of the quadricentenary events in Annapolis Royal, who were eager to have something new and different to attract tourists.

It would be easy enough to view the efforts at Bear River in regard to the Cultural Centre as little more than a money-making enterprise. Indeed, the local MP, Robert Thibault, described federal support for the heritage gallery as a means of assisting 'the band in capturing its share of the growing interest in aboriginal tourism in North America and help generate additional tourism revenue for band residents.'[75] As the largest structure on the reserve and with employment for sixteen staff members (out of a total reserve population of roughly one hundred), the centre's economic benefits for the band can hardly be ignored. However, such a focus on the spin-offs ignores both the hesitation of Frank Meuse, who was chief again in the run-up to the quadricentenary, to become overly committed to a commercial enterprise and the determination of the band to keep its primary focus on the interests of its people.

When we first met in 2003, while the Cultural Centre was still under construction, Frank Meuse was far from convinced that participating in the quadricentenary was a good idea for his band. In part, his reticence was based upon a certain discomfort with the aboriginal element only being taken seriously towards the end of a process that had begun nearly a decade earlier and which was now being driven by the difficulties of the organizers in Annapolis Royal to secure funding. In fact, the very notion that the band's involvement was being driven by financial considerations was deeply troubling for someone who had championed traditional ways of life as a tool for the band's revival, as witnessed in his approach to the crisis that followed the Marshall decision.

Over the next two years leading up to the quadricentenary, I had other opportunities to speak with Chief Meuse, as he became more (if never entirely) comfortable with his band's participation in the quadricentenary. Even on the day before he was to speak from the stage with the other dignitaries at the formal events at the Port-Royal Habitation, Meuse said that he was doing so 'reluctantly.' He wondered if 'we were being tokenized one more time; were we being used as a pawn for somebody else?' He was 'wishing for the best, but expecting the worse.' Nevertheless, he did come around, following some of the same path towards acceptance of an aboriginal involvement that had been trod by Donald Soctomah in the Passamaquoddy context. Like Soctomah, Meuse needed to take the time to discuss the issue with his band members, ultimately accepting some participation as long as everyone understood that the quadricentenary events were to be commemorative, and not celebratory. To the very end, Meuse was troubled when he heard the word 'celebration.' Ultimately, however, much like Soctomah, Meuse recognized that if his people did not tell their story, someone else would. Accordingly, he came to see his own participation as 'an opportunity to be in my rightful place as a chief with the other representatives of government, even if only for a commemoration.'[76]💻

The more substantive contribution of the Bear River band to the quadricentenary was the production of 'The People's Story,' which – for Meuse – raised further questions about the potential dangers of only looking at the bottom line. Accordingly, when we spoke in 2004 he expressed discomfort about 'commercializing too much' by developing 'The People's Story' for a non-native audience, fearful that appealing to the tourist gaze might determine how the past would be presented. More generally, Meuse saw the Cultural Centre as a workshop where traditional skills could be learned, but he wondered how much of the emphasis should be on selling to an outside market with tastes of its own that might skew what the band hoped to achieve. In the end, he wanted to encourage 'development as long as it was not at odds with our values,' and he felt reasonably comfortable that this might be achieved thanks to the positive experience for band members who through 'The People's Story' might experience first hand 'the pride of someone who gets on stage.'[77]

In this regard, Meuse was in sync with the approach of Hal Theriault, the founding manager of the Cultural Centre and the writer-director of 'The People's Story.' With a background in community theatre, Theriault, who is a non-native, strongly believed that such productions had the power to transform the people who were associated with them. In the aftermath of the Marshall decision, when tensions ran high between natives and non-natives, particularly Acadians, he wrote a play about Mi'kmaq history that he took to both communities as a means of healing wounds. That production brought him to the attention of Frank Meuse and eventually to his position at the Cultural Centre, where 'The People's Story' provided a logical use of his skills.

Given this background, Theriault wrote a play to be performed at Bear River that emphasized the strong ties that had united Acadians and the Mi'kmaq for four hundred years. When a version of 'The People's Story' was performed as part of Annapolis Royal's celebrations, described in chapter 3, it focused only on the early years of the Acadian–Mi'kmaq relationship, ending long before the deportation and avoiding any depiction of British wrongdoing, a chapter from the past that might not have gone over well in the town. By contrast, the version told at the Cultural Centre starting in 2005, largely to audiences from outside the reserve, took the dynamics of the relationship between the French and the 'People' (as the Mi'kmaq were described) up to the *Grand Dérangement* and beyond.

Without sugar-coating the impact of the French, who brought diseases to the very people who had helped them survive the first winters, special abuse was heaped upon the English, always contrasted with the French, who wanted 'a relationship based upon equals.' Of course, the true colours of the British came out in regard to the deportation, which saw – in this telling of the tale – the harbouring of Acadian children by the Mi'kmaq who had long been their friends; in other cases, entire Acadian families 'lived clandestinely with their Mi'kmaq allies and friends, some forever, some until the time eventually came when it was safe for the Acadians to begin to return to these shores.' Not to end on a negative note, Theriault's narrator saw that beyond 1755 the Mi'kmaq and the Acadians were not only united by 'a shared history of oppression ... but so much more importantly, by the will, the strength, the determination to emerge victorious, to keep their cultures alive and vital.'[78]

There was no mistaking the fact that this was a version of the history of the previous four centuries that was rarely heard in Annapolis Royal, where theatrical performances tended to conceal the very existence (or minimize the impact) of the deportation. Indeed, Frank Meuse wondered if 'the people in the town would understand the story; do they want to understand it?'[79] However, the nature of the story was probably not the most important part of the exercise. Reflecting the same sentiments that had been expressed by Frank Meuse, Theriault explained to me: 'What is happening with the play is beyond the obvious.' Speaking only days before the premiere of 'The People's Story' in 2005, he observed that it had taken a year and a half to get to this stage in order to encourage 'team building' among the participants, and to allow them to 'develop confidence.' It's not easy to 'get up on the stage and do it ... The problems are deep and complex.' In this context, Theriault prepared a story that required thirty-five cast members, limiting the size of any one part so as to maximize the number who might participate and to ensure that those who did would succeed.[80] 💻

In the end, the creation of the Bear River First Nation Heritage and Cultural Centre and the performance there of 'The People's Story' were examples of the tribe's ability to recognize an opportunity and turn it to its own advantage. As in other contexts, the Bear River Mi'kmaq employed traditional techniques to make gains in the modern world. With this success, the band's population has slowly increased, and it ranks well above the norm for First Nations communities in Nova Scotia on a 'community

wellbeing index' created by the federal government. Based upon an analysis of a community's performance in terms of income, education,
labour force activity and housing conditions, a score is calculated between
a low of zero and a maximum of 100. In 2001 the average score for communities (both native and non-native) across Canada was 79, with native
communities (not surprisingly) scoring much lower on average, at 66.
Bear River finished well above this level, with an index score of 77, roughly the same as was recorded by non-native communities in the province.[81]
In response to this effort at quantifying the success of the Bear River First
Nation, I can almost imagine Frank Meuse rolling his eyes, his determination to put traditional practices to work seemingly at odds with this quest
to reduce the nature of a people's existence to a number. Be that as it
may, in this case, the number was one of several reflections of a First
Nation that had found the means to make modest gains, seizing opportunities such as the one provided by the quadricentenary of Port-Royal.

Surprises from the Quadricentenary

One of the joys of following a story such as the construction of these commemorative events was the opportunity to be surprised. As was perhaps
inevitable, I developed close ties with some of the people I met along the
way, and on various occasions commiserated with them when their plans
did not work out as they might have wished. Leading the way in this regard was my disappointment that the people of the St Croix valley were
unable to move their plans for the reconstruction of the 1604 habitation
forward. It is hard for me to drive on the road that passes that site without
feeling some regret for what might have been. Nevertheless, I would not
say that I was exactly surprised by the way that that story ended, given the
political realities that stood in the way. The Acadians never really warmed
to the Île Ste-Croix story and the English speakers could not muster support for an event that did not exactly belong to them. In the end, there
was little concrete that either the Acadians or the 'stewards of the sites,'
the subjects of the previous two chapters, could point to as lasting legacies
of the 400th anniversary of the Dugua settlements. The exception that
proves this rule was the commemorative trail at Red Beach, across from
Île Ste-Croix in Maine, whose construction underscored the paralysis induced by the particular mix of players in the Canadian context, one of
which did not even exist as far as the federal government was concerned.

Most of the surprises from my quadricentenary travels came in regard
to unexpected successes achieved by First Nations people. In 2002, when

I made a preliminary tour of the St Croix and Annapolis valleys to see if there was a project worth pursuing, I did not hear a word mentioned about either the Passamaquoddy or Bear River First Nations. Of course, in the Canadian context, the former did not need to be reckoned with since they did not exist; as for the latter, they were far away up a hill, out of sight and out of mind. From such beginnings, however, something changed in the years that followed, so that the real legacies of the quadricentenary are the gains that the aboriginal people achieved. In the case of the Passamaquoddy, there is now a process under way that could lead to the recognition of the tribe in Canada; even this possibility, however abstract, is a consequence of the 400th anniversary. As for the Bear River First Nation, visitors daily approach their Cultural Centre, which stands as the only visible trace that the Port-Royal quadricentenary ever took place.

It is perhaps not so surprising that the aboriginal people who recognized an opportunity in 2004–5 seized upon it. But what is more surprising, and encouraging to an often cynical historian, is that people in the larger community, who had at first had little interest in the First Nations people pertinent to this story, ultimately came to champion their cause. To give only two examples: In the case of Île Ste-Croix, I was witness to the fascinating transformation of one of the individuals (better left unnamed to avoid embarrassment) connected with organizing the local quadricentenary events, who had no interest in the Passamaquoddy when we first met, but who was their strongest champion three years later. This individual was not hostile to the Passamaquoddy at the start, but had had little reason to deal with them. The 400th anniversary allowed 'contact' once again, and won people (or at least this one person) over to a cause. Similarly, in the case of the Port-Royal events, I can recall hearing much concern during my first trips to Annapolis Royal about Frank Meuse, who was seen as unwilling to aid in the development of quadricentenary plans. Of course, as we have seen, he was suspicious, not hostile, and over time a working relationship developed that permitted the construction of the Cultural Centre at Bear River. During one of my last visits to Annapolis Royal, Sharon McAulay, marketing manager for the town, told me that she saw the centre as *the* legacy from the 400th anniversary. Who would have thought?

Ultimately, these surprises spoke to the power of the past to bring people together in order to build things of value. Of course, most of the stories in the news about the use of the past make it seem as if divisiveness is the inevitable consequence when people mark events from an earlier time. To take only one of the many available examples of the power of memory to fuel animosities, there is the case of Northern Ireland, where every July the remembrance of the seventeenth-century Battle of the Boyne has long encouraged conflict between Catholics and Protestants. To be sure, the drama, and even the stakes, involved with the commemorative events discussed in the last three chapters can hardly compete with those at play in contexts such as the Irish one. Nevertheless, the surprises from the quadricentenary do speak to the fact that nothing is inevitable when the past is recalled. It is not inevitable that some instances of remembering must end in conflict; nor was it inevitable that the 400th anniversary events of 2004–5 had to end in unexpected successes for the Passamaquoddy and Mi'kmaq; and for that matter, it was not inevitable that those celebrations of the 500th anniversary of Columbus's arrival, described at the start of this chapter, had to end the way that they did. So the greatest, and most pleasant surprise to me was to be able to watch people of goodwill who would never have had the opportunity to meet come together in the context of an anniversary and join forces to make a positive difference.

PART TWO

Stories of Trauma

In late July 2005 I spent five days on the road with Acadians on the occasion of the 250th anniversary of the beginning of the most traumatic episode from their past, their deportation, often referred to as *le Grand Dérangement*. Between 1755 and the close of the Seven Years War in 1763, the vast majority of the roughly fourteen thousand Acadians, inhabitants of both what had been known as Nova Scotia since 1713 as well as the colonies of Île Royale (Cape Breton) and Île Saint-Jean (Prince Edward Island), which remained French until 1758, were sent into exile, most of the rest fleeing to avoid capture. Since 1713 the British had tolerated the Acadians' refusal to swear allegiance to the crown, preferring instead to remain neutral. However, as what would prove to be the final showdown with the French approached, patience with the concept of neutrality evaporated and the decision was taken to deport. By the time the dust settled, hundreds, if not thousands, had died as most Acadians were uprooted, sometimes more than once, under difficult conditions. With the close of the war, the Acadians were allowed to return to British North America, but could not reclaim their former lands. In fact, relatively few did return; the bulk of the population of the new *Acadie* was made up of those who had avoided deportation. The great majority of the exiles remained just that, mostly scattered across North America.

For three of those days in 2005, I rode on a bus with a group from Nova Scotia well versed in the details of the deportation, which we marked on the highways in song. We attended commemorative events of various types, crowned by a night-time spectacle on 28 July, exactly 250 years after the Nova Scotia government had ordered the Acadians' ouster, on the grounds of Grand-Pré, now a national historic site, but long the pre-eminent Acadian site of deportation memory. This last event, and really the whole pilgrimage, was designed to coincide with the first *Journée de commémoration du Grand Dérangement*, established by the federal government by means of a royal proclamation that recognized that the deportation had in fact occurred. As I travelled with the Nova Scotian Acadians, and in the days that immediately followed, which ended with a three-kilometre procession by foot to the Grand-Pré site, I heard various perspectives on the memory of the deportation 250 years after the fact. Some were pleased that official recognition of the deportation had finally occurred, however belatedly; others could not stomach a declaration that lacked any indication as to who had been responsible; still others wanted to *tourner la page* on the whole tragic episode; and there were those who objected to the official celebrations so much that they staged 'alternative' events of their own, the procession fitting into that category.

In short, there was no absence of remembering on this anniversary, which provides the focus for chapter 6, so much so that it might have appeared only natural that a people that had been traumatized should mark the anniversary at hand. In fact, however, for most of the two centuries following the deportation there was very little public commemoration, a situation that changed in 1955 with the staging of large-scale bicentenary events. Accordingly, the following chapter explores how the deportation was remembered (or forgotten) on anniversaries prior to the 250th. Much like the Irish after the Potato Famine and the Jews after the Holocaust, the Acadians struggled to come to grips with a traumatic moment from their past; and the events of summer 2005 indicated that there was still much controversy about how to speak about the unspeakable.

5

Silences

Searching for a Voice

Since most of the chapters have started with a description of some moment from the road to introduce the topic at hand, I have decided to continue in this vein, but not with a story pertinent to the Acadian deportation. Most of this chapter deals with the events that marked the bicentenary of the *Grand Dérangement* in 1955, but I was very young at that point and it would still be years until I would know what an Acadian was, growing up as I did in a Jewish-American family. This last point is important to my particular perspective on the silence within which memory of the deportation was shrouded for the better part of two hundred years. Growing up in a community that was almost entirely Jewish, only years after the end of the Second World War, I had no idea that the Holocaust had occurred until I was a teenager. I suspect that it was the trial and execution of Adolf Eichmann in the early 1960s that first made the Holocaust real to me, but it begs the question of how I had managed to go through the first decade of my life without ever having heard from family, friends, or teachers about the murder of six million of 'our' people.

Given this context, I read with more than passing interest Peter Novick's fascinating book, *The Holocaust in American Life*, which deals precisely with the question of how American Jews managed to 'forget' the memory of the Holocaust for the two decades that followed the end of the Second World War. As he put it, in terms that rang true, 'Between the end of the war and the 1960s, as anyone who has lived through those years can testify, the Holocaust made scarcely any appearance in American public discourse, and hardly more in Jewish public discourse.'[1] Most Jews felt that 'the Holocaust was over and done with, and there was no practical advantage to compensate for the pain of staring into that awful abyss.'[2] As for why this might have been the case, Novick rejects notions that it had to do with a Freudian repression of something that was too traumatic to be contemplated. After all, he argues, American Jews were very far away from the carnage in the camps, and with few survivors having been admitted to the United States after the war, there was little direct contact with the Holocaust in the late 1950s and into the 1960s.

Instead, Novick argues that my parents, and many like them, were motivated to avoid talk about the Holocaust out of a desire to integrate into the mainstream of American life. As he put it, 'An integrationist rather than a particularist consciousness was the norm in the postwar decades: difference and specificity were at a discount.'[3] In order to further substantiate his claim that the failure to talk about the Holocaust was more contextual than psychological, Novick points to the fact that the Holocaust only became a matter of discussion among American Jews when they wanted to be different, in contrast with an earlier desire to blend in. As he put it, writing in 1999, 'These days American Jews can't define their Jewishness on the basis of distinctively Jewish religious beliefs, since most don't have much in the way of distinctively Jewish religious beliefs. They can't define it by distinctively Jewish cultural traits, since most don't have much in the way of these either ... The Holocaust, as virtually the only common denominator of American Jewish identity in the late twentieth century, has filled a need for a consensual symbol.' Such a symbol proved particularly potent in the context of a time when in American culture there was 'a change in the attitude toward victimhood from a status all but universally shunned and despised to one often eagerly embraced.'[4]

There can be no doubt that contextual issues, as we saw in the first part of this book, play a significant role in determining what is remembered and what is forgotten, whether for a shorter or longer period of time. However, in the case of an event as devastating as the Holocaust (as opposed to the landing of Dugua et al. on Île Ste-Croix), there was also the fact, as even Novick had to admit, that here 'was a horrifying spectacle, painful and nauseating to contemplate, the sort of thing to which most of us respond by averting our eyes.' In other words, the recollection of such traumatic moments is determined by both the nature of the event and the circumstances allowing its memory, particularly in public venues.[5]

I hadn't thought much about my missed encounter with the Holocaust until I began reflecting upon the nature of public remembrance of the

Grand Dérangement, which was also characterized by silence for well over 150 years. Peter Novick observed that 'between the end of the war and the 1960s ... only a handful of books dealt with [the Holocaust], and those that did, with rare exceptions like *The Diary of Anne Frank*, had few readers.' As for literature regarding the deportation, Robert Viau has indicated that 'the first Acadian novel dealing with the deportation, published in *nouvelle Acadie*, only appeared in 1940.'[6] Even on the occasion of the 250th anniversary of the deportation in 2005, Ronnie-Gilles LeBlanc could observe that while there were various works that touched upon the deportation, 'few of these works dealt exclusively with this moment from the past.'[7]

To be sure, comparisons between the memory of trauma as experienced by American Jews and Acadians can be taken too far.[8] Since most Acadians can trace their family lines back to the events of the late eighteenth century, they can claim an immediate connection with the deportation that most American Jews cannot claim regarding the Holocaust. Moreover, the two events were very different in terms of the nature of what was being attempted. On the one hand, there was the carefully orchestrated murder of a people, while on the other there was an attempt at what we would call today 'ethnic cleansing.' The British were not particularly committed to the physical extermination of the Acadians, although many would perish as they were shipped from place to place. Rather, as most Acadians were scattered across the American colonies to the south, the goal was to see them assimilated and their culture destroyed, in what might be called 'ethnocide.' As John Mack Faragher has recently put it, the definition of ethnic cleansing as carried out in the Balkans in the 1990s 'could have been drawn from a study of the expulsion of the Acadians. The operations carried out by Anglo-American forces in 1755 included the forced deportation of civilian populations, the cruel and inhumane treatment of prisoners, and the plunder and wanton destruction of communities, practices now defined as "crimes against humanity."'[9]

As in the case of the Holocaust, it took time for Acadians to publicly remember the deportation. Such commemorative moments were rare, particularly until the infrastructure was created for *la nouvelle Acadie* in the late nineteenth century. Accordingly, there were no public ceremonies to mark the deportation on its centenary in 1855. In fact, the only evidence of public remembrance came via a pastoral letter issued by William Walsh, the archbishop of Halifax, to the Acadians of Nova Scotia 'on the subject of the suffering and virtues of their ancestors.'

Since relatively few had managed to return to Nova Scotia, particularly in comparison with those who ended up in New Brunswick, Walsh was speaking to only a small percentage of the Acadian population. Nevertheless, his words anticipated the few, more public moments of deportation commemoration that would follow in the twentieth century. In his telling of the tale, the Acadians had not been deported for any geo-political motives of concern to the British. In fact, Archbishop Walsh was so careful to avoid blaming the British that he observed that the Acadians had suffered 'at the cruel hand of persecution,' never identifying whose hand it was. What was clear, however, is that the Acadians had to go because of 'their attachment to their faith,' and not out of any concern that they might fight for France. Ultimately, the moral of the story was that the Acadians had remained true to Catholicism; they had passed a test and so constituted 'a chosen people.' The archbishop implored the Acadians in 1855: 'Reflect on what [your ancestors] endured, and learn to submit yourself with resignation, in all of the trials that you may face, to the beneficent will of our Holy Father.'[10]

Fifty years later, on the 150th anniversary, it had already been a quarter-century since the markers of national identity had been constructed in the *conventions nationales* of the 1880s. These *conventions* continued to be held into the twentieth century, and one was scheduled in 1905 for Caraquet, in northeastern New Brunswick, where some who had escaped from the deportation began construction of the new *Acadie*. Given this context, one might have thought that this gathering of the leaders of Acadian society 150 years after the deportation would give rise to references to this event in the speeches that were inevitably presented. There was all the more reason to expect that the Caraquet gathering might have commemorated this pivotal Acadian moment given the considerable enthusiasm that existed at the time (witness the DeMonts Tercentenary in 1904) for such public representations of the past. However, what is striking about the Caraquet *convention nationale* is just how little reference was made to the *Grand Dérangement*.

Reporting on the opening of the *convention* on 15 August, the Acadian national holiday, *Le Moniteur Acadien* described the presence of roughly five thousand delegates who had come 'from all corners of Acadie to discuss important questions for our people.'[11] Over the course of two days there was considerable discussion of a range of issues, from the need to develop policies that would allow Acadians to stay on the land to the importance of programs encouraging French-language education in both New Brunswick and Nova Scotia.[12] Hardly any reference was made either in the formal proceedings of the convention or in the speeches that were published in *Le Moniteur Acadien* to the fact that this event co-incided with the 150th anniversary of the deportation. One of the few such references came from Rev. Philippe-Louis Belliveau, who observed, almost in passing, 'We are just starting to rear our heads again after 150 years of persecution and of being forgotten.'[13] The word 'déportation' did not appear here, nor was it used in a speech by Onésiphore Turgeon, who noted almost as an aside that Acadians had resisted 'the sacrilegious hand of Charles Lawrence,' the governor of Nova Scotia who signed the deportation order in 1755.[14]

The exception that proved the rule in terms of marginalizing the deportation on this occasion came via a presentation made, not to one of the plenary sessions of the convention, but to a much smaller one dealing with 'Our Acadian Brothers across Canada.' At this particular meeting, Placide Gaudet spoke pointedly about 'the expulsion of the Acadians,' noting that 'at roughly this time, 150 years ago, desolation, distress and terror were starting to take hold in *Acadie*.' Gaudet, who would go on to write an important booklet regarding British responsibility for the *Grand Dérangement*, was painfully aware that 'the current generation has a weak understanding of the suffering and misery endured by our forebears.' Accordingly, on the occasion of this anniversary he tried to provide an account of the removal of the Acadians, although he was conscious of the fact that he had been given far too little time to do a proper job, only having been asked to speak at the eleventh hour.[15] In any event, Gaudet's efforts received relatively little attention. Already hidden from the large numbers of people at the plenary sessions, his talk was also ignored by *Le Moniteur Acadien*, which provided considerable coverage of many of the speeches made at Caraquet.

Mincing Words

In the years that followed the 150th anniversary, memory of the deportation slowly began to emerge from the shadows, mostly in relation to the site of Grand-Pré. Of course, in a sense, the focus on Grand-Pré only magnified the difficulties that Acadians had in publicly remembering the deportation since it was impossible to separate the development of this site from Longfellow's poem, written in the mid-nineteenth century. Many Acadian communities suffered the same fate as that of Grand-Pré, which saw the deportation of roughly two thousand of its inhabitants during the fall of 1755. However, Grand-Pré only became *the* principal site of deportation memory because the American poet popularized a story that he set there, but which might have been situated at any number of other locations. Although written in the mid-nineteenth century, *Evangeline* has remained popular, both among Acadians as well as English speakers across North America, in part owing to its romantic emphasis upon the forced separation of lovers, who only reunited when Gabriel died in the arms of Evangeline, who by then had become a nun. Evangeline was the pure heroine, who stoically accepted her fate. As Grand-Pré emerged as the principal site of memory connected with the deportation, the idea that the Acadians had willingly accepted their fate (and that no one was really responsible for it) became a central element in the story that was told.[16]

In line with the popularity of *Evangeline* in the English-speaking world, the first efforts to develop Grand-Pré as a site of historical significance came in response to the interest of tourists, mostly Americans, to visit it. When Grand-Pré was first reached by rail in 1869, roughly twenty years after the publication of the poem, banners at the station proclaimed, in English only: 'Welcome to the Land of Gabriel and Evangeline.' This rail line eventually became the property of the Dominion Atlantic Railway, which, recognizing the touristic possibilities connected with the Evangeline story, in 1917 acquired the property around the site of the church where the men had been locked up before their expulsion in 1755. The railway was picking up where John Frederick Herbin, a jeweller in nearby Wolfville, had begun. In 1907, on the centenary of Longfellow's birth, Herbin created the Grand Pré Preservation-Restoration and Acadian-Longfellow Memorial Movement. With little evident support from Acadians, Herbin soldiered on for a decade, before finally ceding the land to the railway, albeit with the condition that 'the Acadians would be able to contribute to its preservation and to construct there a church or some other commemorative monument.'[17]

Herbin had tried to interest Acadians in acquiring the land, but without success. Barbara Le Blanc has observed that 'it is not clear why the Acadians with whom Herbin had contact were so hesitant.' She wondered if it had to do with the 'fact that he was Protestant and more at home in English.'[18] For his part, Robert Viau has speculated that the Acadians did not want to be too closely connected with efforts that were more oriented to 'erect a monument in honour of Longfellow that to remember the Deportation.'[19] However, the Acadian reluctance to promote this site of memory can also be seen in the context of other missed opportunities to remember the deportation publicly, one of which had occurred in 1905, only two years before Herbin purchased the land. In any event, Herbin resisted efforts by Americans interested in acquiring the site, in the process providing the opportunity for Acadian involvement under the terms of sale to the Dominion Atlantic. As a result, in 1919, the Société nationale l'Assomption, the forerunner of today's Société nationale de l'Acadie and the same organization that had watched over the *convention nationale* in 1905, acquired – for $1 – a parcel of land from the railway on which a commemorative church would be built.

Fund-raising ensued, encouraged by frustration that arose from the unveiling in 1920 of an Evangeline statue to which no Acadian leader was invited. This ceremony was built around the presence of newspaper editors and journalists from across the Empire, so that an editorial in *L'Évangéline* referred to 'Une Évangéline impérialisée (An Evangeline for the Empire).[20] With the impetus of this snub on turf that was viewed as holy ground, funds poured in and the memorial church was opened in 1922, soon to be followed by other projects that helped Acadians claim the Grand-Pré site as their own. A statue of the Acadians' patron saint, Our Lady of Assumption (the Virgin Mary), was unveiled inside the church in 1923, and in the following year there was the blessing of an iron cross, *la croix de l'embarquement* (the Embarkation Cross), at a site two kilometres from the church where it was believed the Acadians from Grand-Pré had been loaded onto ships.[21] A further project, a museum inside the church, was completed in 1930 so that it could be officially opened on the occasion of the 175th anniversary of the deportation.

Much had changed since the 150th anniversary had passed almost unnoticed, most notably the emergence of Grand-Pré as a site of Acadian memory. Placide Gaudet, who had distinguished himself in 1905 by speaking directly to the deportation, described the developments at Grand-Pré as the 'grand arrangement.'[22] During the 1920s, there were several pilgrimages to Grand-Pré, some organized by *Le Devoir*, which sought to expose the Québécois to a different part of French-Canadian history, and others by Acadians on the occasion of events that were held nearby, although never on the Grand-Pré grounds. A *convention nationale* was scheduled to be held at Grand-Pré in 1920, but the venue was changed when it was put off until the following year, in part out of fear 'of an angry backlash from the English-speaking population.'[23] This concern that remembering their own deportation might make others feel uncomfortable would be a major element of the anniversary events that were staged at Grand-Pré in 1930.

The organization of this fete was the responsibility of a committee of the Société nationale l'Assomption that was in charge of the 'Église-Souvenir.' When it first met a year before the anniversary, the plan on the table was to hold an event on 5 September. This particular date marked the moment when Acadian men were rounded up for deportation at Grand-Pré, and – as we shall see in the next chapter – it would still hold a special meaning to some Acadians in 2005. However, that date was often seen as inflammatory, pointing as it did to the actual, physical round-up of the Acadians, and so when the Canadian government chose to set aside a date on which the 250th anniversary of the deportation might be marked, it selected the more anodyne 28 July, which spoke to the signing of the deportation order, but which sidestepped the actual deed.

Even in 1930 the commemoration of 5 September was avoided, on this occasion because it would conflict, according to Abbé J.-Auguste Allard, the head of the Comité de l'Église-Souvenir, with 'the beginning of school. Parents and students would not be able to come.'[24] As plausible as this might appear, there was also a larger context, most notably the need to reassure English speakers that the Acadians had no thoughts of somehow 'getting even' by marking this event, which might have been more inflammatory were it held in early September; and so, as the plans took shape for an anniversary in late August, considerable attention was paid to drawing in those English speakers.

François G.J. Comeau, the secretary of the organizing committee, wrote to Abbé Allard that one of their goals had to be attracting 'the English-speaking population of the Maritime provinces to join our ranks in supporting our program of *Entente cordiale.*'[25] Towards that end, Comeau penned numerous letters to Acadians who might speak at the ceremonies, all of which were in the same spirit as one he sent to R.W.E. Landry, a member of the Nova Scotia legislative assembly, who was asked to 'deliver a ten minute address of good-will.' Landry wrote to Comeau for clarification, wondering why it was necessary to make such a request, to which he received the following answer: 'What you are desired to refer to particularly in your address is the amicable relations existing between the Acadians and the English-speaking population surrounding them wherever they happen to be located, whether in the Maritime Provinces, in the New England States, or in Louisiana.'[26] To underscore this point, in writing to a journalist who was doing a story on the commemoration for an English-speaking market, Comeau advised against even using the word 'expulsion … It sounds too hard to the present day people.'[27]

Comeau and his colleagues apparently did their job well. A visitor from New York City expressed disappointment that there had not been more buildings 'in the manner of the olden, golden.' In particular, he complained that the Église-Souvenir 'was beautiful, but it seemed so ornate that I got quite a shock when I walked into it. I wanted it to look like that old Covenanter's church up on the hill outside the village.'[28] All of the talk about *bonne entente* must have encouraged the New Yorker to think that the Acadians had left voluntarily, with their buildings intact.

Quite aside from the tone that might be adopted by speakers, the very location of the event helped present the Acadians in a manner that would have been reassuring to those uneasy about stirring up tensions. While the Grand-Pré site had been seen only a decade earlier as potentially provocative, it now could be viewed in a very different light, its new structures such as the commemorative church turning the grounds into a museum of sorts, much like other outdoor museums established at the time, such as Greenfield Village near Detroit, where Henry Ford could depict a time of goodwill among all the classes, in a sense trying to cultivate the spirit of *bonne entente*.[29] In the case of Grand-Pré by 1930, the grounds spoke to an *Acadie* that was not about to return, in the process leaving *nouvelle Acadie* (where Acadians did live) in the shadows. And as pilgrims from Louisiana stole the show, the story of the 175th anniversary ended up having more to do with the rediscovery of a 'lost' part of the clan than about celebrating the new lives that had been built for hundreds of thousand of Acadians in places such as New Brunswick; or to put it another way, the people who were actively marking the past – who were claiming public space – were not so much the Acadians of Atlantic Canada, but their long-lost cousins from the diaspora.[30]

Only weeks before the big day, on 20 August, formal planning for the program had barely begun, although not much organizing was necessary for an event that amounted to little more than a mass and a series of speeches by dignitaries. Much more planning was required to coordinate the arrival of 'Acadians from all corners of the continent.' Although the delegation from Louisiana would get the bulk of attention, there would also be groups from New England and Quebec; and to add to the sense that everyone was involved in a pilgrimage, arrangements were also put in place to transport 'Acadians from New Brunswick who want to make their way to Grand-Pré.'[31] This was an unprecedented gathering of the clan, in a sense a forerunner of the *Congrès mondial acadien* movement that would start up at the end of the century. Accordingly, in spite of the fact that the deportation was the reason for the reunion, Acadian leaders could in good conscience refer to 'the celebration of the 175th anniversary of the Deportation.'[32]

Obviously, no one wanted to celebrate what had happened in 1755. Nevertheless, relatively little note was made of a sense of loss that might have dominated such an event, but which would have been in conflict with the spirit of *bonne entente*. Instead, Judge Arthur LeBlanc, president of the Société nationale l'Assomption, saw reason to celebrate the unbreakable bonds of kinship, which were much stronger than the ephemeral bonds of empire. Speaking at a time when the British Empire was in decline and the Acadian 'nation' appeared intact, he went so far as to claim (in English so that the visitors from the south would understand) that 'the defeat of the Acadians at the hands of the English in 1755 has done more for the Acadian people that it has for the English who claimed victory.'[33] Others celebrated the fact that the Acadians had proved themselves a 'chosen' people for having survived so many trials; and adding to the biblical illusions, Pascal Poirier, one of the fathers of the Acadian renaissance of the late nineteenth century, whose presence at an advanced age created quite a stir, declared that, with the reassembling of the clan, 'here we have a veritable resurrection.'[34]

Without doubt, however, the stars of the show were the *Louisianais*, who provided the emotional punch that fuelled this anniversary, what one participant called 'the crowning point for the whole affair.'[35] While there was relatively little talk in the Acadian press about planning for the formal event at Grand-Pré, there was substantial coverage of the movement of this rediscovered branch of the family. As *L'Évangéline* put it in late July, the energy put into the arrival of these long-lost cousins increased in 'proportion to the distance that separates them from the site for the reunion.' The same newspaper also heaped praise on the leader of the mission, Dudley J. LeBlanc, the public utility commissioner in Baton Rouge, whose efforts to assemble a delegation and 'to cover a distance of several thousand miles were so [laudable], so patriotic.'[36] LeBlanc clearly knew how to grab the media's attention, and so arranged to have the bulk of his delegation of forty consist of young women dressed in Evangeline costumes. These 'Evangeline Girls' were selected and subsidized by their home parishes. Each community would send 'a young Acadian girl who could speak French. Each would be dressed in a traditional outfit and each would wear a sash on which would be written the name of the town that she was representing.'[37]

With the girls in tow to provide eye candy, the Louisiana delegation set off on a journey that took it through Washington (where it was received

5.1 Evangeline Girls greeted at the White House, August 1930
(State Library of Louisiana)

by President Hoover), New York, and Boston (where it was received by
Longfellow's daughter). The *Louisianais* then boarded a ferry that took
them to Nova Scotia. En route to Grand-Pré there was a brief visit at the
sites of memory from the French régime at Annapolis Royal. However,
even after the *Louisianais* left Grand-Pré, their travels continued to be
reported, as they made their way through Halifax and Moncton, before
heading west for Quebec City, Montreal, Toronto, and Niagara Falls.
They then headed south, returning home roughly two weeks after they
had left.

In the end, the return of the diaspora became the message of the
175th anniversary celebration as they embodied 'le miracle acadien.'[38] In
his editorial, after the visitors had departed, Alfred Roy, the editor of
L'Évangéline, wrote at length about 'the return of Évangéline ... What an
incredible return! This survival is wonderful to behold!' However, the
part of their journey that most grabbed his attention was not the time
spent at Grand-Pré, but rather their visit to Moncton: 'It was at the
Moncton train station, at the moment of their departure, that the intense emotion that had overtaken the crowd was most evident. Thousands

of people were jostling for position so that they might get close to one of their "cousins" from down south. When the train pulled out, the joyous screaming and fond farewells disappeared. Instead, many were pulling out their handkerchiefs to wipe away tears … A women nearby cried out: "My God, they are leaving!" And another confided in us a bit later: "They are as Acadian as we are. So why are they leaving?"'[39]

The scene at the Moncton train station helped put the nature of public commemoration of the deportation as of 1930 in some perspective. News reports indicated that there were roughly three thousand people there to see off the *Louisianais*, this in a town where the entire French-speaking population was less than seven thousand, and at a time of day (a Friday afternoon) when 'most people were tied up working in factories, offices, and shops.'[40] Accordingly, in some relative sense, this was the most significant event of the 175th anniversary, even though it was entirely spontaneous. Acadians came to the edge of the train platforms to lavish attention upon individuals who were really only passing through. Indeed, Acadians never took to the street to mark this anniversary, staying within the territory that belonged to them at Grand-Pré. In spite of this reluctance to go where they did not feel they belonged, there were still those English speakers in the vicinity of Grand-Pré who resented even that presence, leading to what Barbara Le Blanc has called a 'backlash …, a movement to erect a monument to the English Colonel Noble and his men, who lost their lives in the 1747 Grand-Pré Battle (sometimes referred to as the Grand-Pré Massacre).'[41]

The 'massacre' in question was an attack upon British quarters, leading to the death of Noble and roughly seventy of his men. Clearly, the intent of those who wanted to erect such a monument was to establish the moral equivalency between the victims of the deportation, whose 175th anniversary had just been so delicately marked, and these military casualties. Several months before the anniversary events, François G.J. Comeau received a message from L.M. Fortier, the superintendent of the historic site at Fort Anne in Annapolis Royal, who thought such a memorial 'will completely clear the air … You might even arrange to place the tablet on the chapel [the église-souvenir at Grand-Pré] … Every side of our history can thus be brought out impartially and without disturbing the sensibilities of anyone.'[42] Sadly, we do not know how Comeau responded, although one imagines he was polite, since the Acadians bent over backwards to avoid offence.

There was so much enthusiasm for the presence of the delegation from Louisiana that it would have been difficult for any bitterness to emerge. In this regard, the speech at Grand-Pré by the leader of the 'Acadiens du sud,' Dudley LeBlanc, was interesting as it offered another perspective on what might have been remembered. LeBlanc spoke shortly after the lieutenant governor, J.C. Tory, who observed that while 'the dispersal of the Acadians was a cruel act,' it had been 'a necessity of warfare in the midst of the efforts of two empires to seize the upper hand in North America.' Others who followed Tory, including Pascal Poirier, let these comments pass unanswered; they were following the edict of Judge LeBlanc, who echoed Comeau's advice to speakers by calling on Acadians 'to bury the hatchet in the shadows of the cross, the symbol of forgiveness.' Dudley LeBlanc obviously did not feel that he had to follow the party line, and observed that it was 'his duty to offer a perspective that differed from what had been said by those who preceded him. "We do not believe that the deportation was necessary ... From the point of view of the victors, it was perhaps a military necessity, but they did not need to carry out such an act. It was not necessary."'[43]

Dudley LeBlanc, being far from home, did not have to live with the consequences of his actions, and so said what he wanted to say. However, for the Acadians of Nova Scotia and New Brunswick who were assembled at Grand-Pré, it was not prudent to be so provocative, and much easier to accentuate the positive, particularly given the presence of the *Louisianais*. In the end, the 175th anniversary was as significant for what was not done (going into the streets) or not said (speaking bluntly about past wrongs) as for what was. It was not that Acadians were silent on this occasion, but there were certainly silences.

Building the Bicentenary

In the quarter-century after the Evangeline Girls returned home, Grand-Pré continued to provide the focus for Acadian memory of the deportation. Robert Viau has called the period between the wars the site's 'Golden Age.'[44] With the construction of the Église-Souvenir, attention turned to manicuring the site, to provide it with the lush landscape that attracts visitors to this day, in the process making it hard to imagine that this had been a site of suffering. But then that had been the idea of Acadian public memory of the deportation – to turn it from an all too easy emphasis upon pain and loss to one based upon purity and rebirth.

Given this focus upon Grand-Pré, when Acadian leaders turned their sights to marking the bicentenary of the deportation in 1955, they chose this as the site for events that coincided with the Acadian national holiday.

The symbol of the bicentenary, a gigantic 'A' topped by the Acadian star, dominated the stage on which a pontifical mass was celebrated by the papal delegate to Canada. The event drew three archbishops, eleven bishops, two hundred priests, and fifty nuns; it was so large that the historian Sacha Richard has called it the 'crowning point of the fetes.'[45] If the mass were not enough, civil leaders were also on hand, and one of them, Jean Lesage, at the time the federal minister of Northern Affairs and Natural Resources, announced that Ottawa was willing to integrate this site of memory into its network of historic sites if both the Dominion Atlantic Railway (which still owned most of the property) and the Société nationale l'Assomption (which controlled the church and the area surrounding it) were in agreement. While Acadian leaders did not jump at Lesage's offer, which would continue to keep the site out of direct Acadian control, it still was a measure of official recognition of the Acadians as a people with a distinctive past.

Most accounts of the bicentenary have focused on what happened on stage that day, but relatively little has been said about the crowds. While there seems to be an unfounded consensus among historians that upwards of ten thousand people were on hand, a closer reading of the record tells a different story.[46] On the day after the event, a Canadian Press report set the number at only five thousand, leaving Adélard Savoie, the chief organizer of the bicentenary to wonder where he and his colleagues had gone wrong, since they had anticipated three times the number that actually showed up.[47] In order to accommodate such crowds, Savoie had made arrangements with the Halifax Tourist Bureau so that rooms would be set aside, most of which went unoccupied. He wrote to Leo Charlton, manager of the Tourist Bureau, that 'if the situation that developed proved embarrassing to you, I beg to assure you that it was and still is to a higher degree embarrassing to me.' Savoie explained that there had been a similar situation in Moncton, where festivities had taken place over two days earlier in the week that closed with the Grand-Pré finale. Eighteen hundred rooms had been secured in private homes, and while 'some of these were rented, [it was] a rather small percentage.' The Moncton organizers had also secured some two thousand army beds that were set up in various halls across the city; once again, Savoie confessed that 'very few of those beds were used.'[48]

When forced to reflect '*Why* there were not enough people to use the accommodations,' Savoie had various theories.[49] First, there was the rainy weather that, he thought, had kept away 'thousands of people' during the fetes in Moncton. However, this does not really explain the slim crowds at Grand-Pré, which were no larger than had been the case twenty-five years earlier, when there was less formal organization and before the expanded use of the automobile had made travel considerably easier.[50] And so Savoie wondered whether 'another reason for the failure of the people to show up was the number and the scope of the regional celebrations that had been held previously. We had figured that those regional celebrations would serve to pave the way for the final one and thus act as an inducement for the people to come. However, it would seem that they had a contrary effect, and that many people who had seen at home pageants, floats, parades, rallies, etc. felt that they had already seen enough of the Bicentennial Celebrations and that there was no need to spend time and money to see what they considered the same thing in larger scale.'[51]

These regional celebrations formed part of the ambitious program that was devised in order to celebrate the bicentenary over the course of an entire year, a schedule that would only end with the events at Grand-Pré. However, by focusing upon the fetes at this particular Acadian site of memory, it is easy to lose track of the much grander plans that leaders had put into place; and even if those plans were not always as successful as organizers might have liked, the results still spoke volumes about the relationship between Acadians and their past in the middle of the twentieth century.

By any standard, the bicentenary was the largest public event staged by Acadians until the first Congrès mondial acadien in the 1990s.[52] While the formal 'national' events, culminating with the pilgrimage to Grand-Pré, lasted for only a week, the leaders of the Société nationale l'Assomption did everything they could to keep the bicentenary in the public's eye as long as possible. With much fanfare, there was an official start for 'the great campaign to prepare for the bicentenary' in April 1954;[53] this was then followed by further celebrations on le 15 août to start the countdown to the events that would conclude exactly one year later. Over the course of that year, each Acadian community in New Brunswick, Nova Scotia, Prince Edward Island, and the Îles-de-la-Madeleine (Quebec) was encouraged to have its own bicentenary fete; and by June 1955 the local events had largely given way to more regional ones. As the newspaper L'Évangéline, which functioned as the official organ of the leaders of the bicentenaire, put it (wrongly as it turned out): 'The central committee [for the bicentenary] thought that if the local fetes were successful and if the regional ones drew large crowds, then this would assure the success of the largest [national] fetes during the month of August.'[54]

By the time that the dust settled at Grand-Pré, there had been roughly sixty parish-based events, eight regional ones, and, of course, the 'official' celebrations for mid-August 1955 that traced the history of the Acadians, going in reverse chronological order.[55] The festivities began at Moncton with a celebration of 'Acadie in 1955 ... with its organizations that take care of its religious, national, educational, social and professional needs.'[56] Then, the fetes turned to Memramcook, only thirty kilometres from Moncton, to mark 'the beginning of the [Acadian] Renaissance' on the centenary (actually the 101st anniversary) of the opening of the Séminaire Saint-Thomas, which in 1864 became the Université Saint-Joseph, the first Acadian institution of higher education. The man behind this project, Père Camille Lefebvre, was also a leading figure in staging the first *convention nationale* at Memramcook in 1881. Going back yet another hundred years, the focus then turned to Grand-Pré to remember 'l'épreuve [the trials] de 1755.' This expression was omnipresent on the occasion of the bicentenary, indicating that words were still being minced as had been the case twenty-five years earlier.[57]

For all intents and purposes, the Grand-Pré events closed the *bicentenaire*. On the following day, in an effort to push the Acadian chronology back to the seventeenth century, there were some modest events at Port-Royal to mark the 350th anniversary of the arrival of Dugua and Champlain. However, relatively few of those in attendance for the previous stops continued on to Port-Royal, which was not quite part of the Acadians' collective memory of the time, focused as it was upon the deportation and its aftermath. Following the day at Grand-Pré, *L'Évangéline* observed: 'The din from the bicentenary of the Deportation of the Acadians has died down. The special trains, the chartered buses, and the thousands of automobiles that transported Acadians from Canada and the United States to New Brunswick and Nova Scotia ... have left. The echo from the last speech has passed; the floats from parades are ready to be used elsewhere; the noise from the last fireworks show is over, leaving old *Acadie* quiet.'[58]

Putting together such a complicated program would have been a challenge for the Société nationale l'Assomption in the best of times. In fact, however, one of the principal goals of the *bicentenaire* from the start of planning had been to kick start the moribund SNA. At an early meeting of organizers, the point was made that 'the more we make the work of the Société visible, the more will people come to understand the importance of sustaining it and assisting it.'[59] There had not been a *convention nationale*, a staple of Acadian political life going back to the days of Père

Lefebvre, since 1937, and so it was from a position of weakness that the SNA set off to construct such a major event. While there were some initial meetings to chart a course in 1950, the bicentenary was not seriously discussed again until the fall of 1953, when a central committee was created to provide leadership. Then, early in 1954, Adélard Savoie, a young lawyer, was hired as the chief organizer and the project started to take shape.

Stepping into a void in terms of Acadian leadership, Savoie separated himself from an earlier generation that had been concerned largely with issues of *survivance* and had been more comfortable in building parish-based institutions than in creating a cohesive national movement. Mirroring changes in the world view of his contemporaries in post-war Quebec, Savoie took a different perspective, arguing, 'For the Acadians of New Brunswick, it is no longer a question of surviving, but of expanding our horizons.'[60] Savoie's choice of New Brunswick in this remark was not coincidental, as he was reflecting an emerging territorial view of Acadie that was focused upon New Brunswick, and which imagined central direction from Moncton over the activities of individual Acadian communities. Much like leaders of Quebec's caisse populaire movement at the same time, who were trying to break down a parish-based system so as to mobilize funds for large-scale projects, Savoie was engaged in an exercise in building a modern bureaucratic structure from the top down.[61]

Savoie's efforts in this regard were evident in the fund-raising drive that he led during the fall of 1954. While the primary goal of the campaign was to finance the bicentenary, whose costs were being estimated at $250,000 (far beyond any previous commemorative budget), there was also the hope (overly optimistic as it turned out) that a successful drive would provide support 'to place the head office of the SNA on a firm financial footing. This organization has played an important role in Acadie, and could do even more to advance the Acadian cause, if only it had the means.' To achieve these twin goals, Savoie put together an organization to extract $45,000 from the pockets of ordinary Acadians. *Comités régionals* were set up in every diocese with significant Acadian populations. In turn, those regional committees leaned on parish-based organizations that put one thousand fund-raisers out into the field across New Brunswick and Prince Edward Island for one day of canvassing on 31 October, with the goal of raising $1 from each Acadian family in what was called a 'patriotic campaign.'[62]

Savoie and his colleagues in Moncton required the goodwill of far-flung Acadians to make the drive a success, but were hampered by the not entirely unfounded suspicion that they were simply using the local leaders to achieve their own goal of building a national movement. One such leader, A.J. Saulnier, the president of the *comité régional* in Cape Breton, wrote to Savoie that 'Acadians outside Moncton are not simply pawns to be manipulated by the Head Office. Maybe this is not the case, but some of the actions taken to date suggest that it is.'[63] Faced with such suspicions, no doubt encouraged by the long years during which the SNA had been lifeless and incapable of intruding upon local autonomy, Savoie came up with a formula that would allow the *comités* to keep a percentage of the funds that they raised to help pay for their own bicentenary activities, depending on how well they did in meeting targets, which were based upon the number of Acadian families available to make the $1 contribution. A region that failed to meet its goal could keep 20 per cent of what it raised, while – at the other extreme – one that surpassed its target could keep 50 per cent.[64]

In the end, in spite of Savoie's efforts to find a formula that would maximize the funds raised, none of the regions came even close to meeting the targets that had been set for them. For instance, the diocese of Moncton had a target of $12,500, but brought in only $7000. Overall, the drive collected only $25,000, and this total would have been considerably smaller had it not been for a gift of $5000 by the Montreal financier Jean-Louis Lévesque, and another $1000 from the Quebec City–based Conseil de la vie française. When the contributions from such interested parties outside *Acadie* are subtracted, the campaign raised roughly $18,000, or about 40 per cent of its target. Perhaps the goal was unrealistic in the first place, but the resistance that Savoie received from local leaders that he wanted to employ as his own foot soldiers suggests that this story had to do with more than just the celebration of the bicentenary of the deportation.[65]

Indeed, the tensions between local and Acadian national concerns persisted as the winter of 1954–5 passed and the season for festivities began. Much as had been the case in terms of the fund-raising, Savoie and his colleagues hoped that the numerous community and regional fetes would serve the national interest, acting as the warm-up acts for the main events for mid-August. They tried to watch over the form of these local celebrations and to exercise some control over their timing, but in the end local leaders made decisions that made sense for them, regardless of the dictates from Moncton.[66] For instance, the Acadians of Haute-Aboujagane, a community forty kilometres east of Moncton, had agreed to stage their fete to coincide with Corpus Christi celebrations, known in

French as the 'Fête-Dieu,' a Catholic holiday with roots in the Middle Ages. Only a few days after the announcement of this scheduling, local leaders changed their minds so as to have a celebration that coincided instead with that 'of the Sacred Heart ... the fete for the patron saint of the parish.'[67] This simple act, which only altered the timing by a week, spoke volumes about the local nature of such events that had much more to do with the celebration of individual Acadian communities than with the larger, more grandiose plans of the SNA.[68]

Similarly, the regional fetes had as much, if not more, to do with local circumstances as with the construction of an overarching Acadian identity. This was particularly the case in terms of the one staged in Edmundston, in the Madawaska region of northwestern New Brunswick, to mark both 'the golden anniversary of the city of Edmundston and the celebrations of the Acadian bicentenary.' The town was decked out with signs with the numbers '50' and '200,' which in the process reflected the split personality of the French-speaking population of this region between a larger Acadian identity and a narrower 'Brayon' one for citizens of the 'République de Madawaska.'[69] References to both anniversaries were on display at a banquet for dignitaries in early July 1955. Similarly, there was a parade that featured floats drawing attention to such matters as 'the deportation, the forest industry, the Brayon identity, and the arrival of the Acadians in the Madawaska region.'[70] However, the high point for the fetes came with the presentation of Le Pageant d'Edmundston, by Père Laurent Tremblay, the prolific author of French Canadian historical pageants. The play was staged five times to thousands of spectators in a hall in Saint-Basile, the site – just outside Edmundston – of the first Acadian settlement in the region. As for the story told, with more than two hundred local actors, the pageant focused almost exclusively on this 'small corner of the world.' Only one of the scenes dealt with larger Acadian themes, but did not even touch upon the deportation.[71]

To one degree or another, local stories helped draw the crowds to the various regional fetes, so much so that the one at Caraquet attracted twenty thousand, which as one of its organizers bragged was 'larger than the number on hand at Grand-Pré on 15 August 1955!'[72] Adélard Savoie and his colleagues in Moncton were not particularly troubled by the large turnouts across Acadie, figuring that the local and regional celebrations were simply warming Acadians up for the grande finale in mid-August. However, when those celebrations finally arrived, the crowds were not what the organizers had hoped for and, in a case of the periphery winning out over the centre, it became easy to look to the more local events as part of the problem.

Recriminations were obviously flying after the fetes had ended, leading a correspondent to write to *L'Évangéline* who was identified only as 'Un Madawaskaïen,' his real identity kept confidential, perhaps because the issue was so sensitive. Responding to criticisms that Acadians from outside Moncton had been responsible for the small crowds, this author observed that 'if our participation was not greater at the big celebrations in Moncton and at Grand-Pré, this was not due to regionalism or indifference ... The proof that the bicentenary did not leave anyone here indifferent was that there were large fetes at both Edmundston and Grand-Sault, which were organized with considerable effort ... If we did not want to become involved in the bicentenary, then we wouldn't have acted in this manner.'[73] In a way, however, 'Un Madawaskaïen' spoke past the point that local enthusiasm had sapped support for the national events. That this may have been the case was underscored by an editorial in an Edmundston newspaper just after the festivities ended. Without any reference to local people making the trek to Moncton, Memramcook, and Grand-Pré, an editorialist in *Le Madawaska* commented on the passage *through* Edmundston of 'groups of pilgrims from French-speaking centres of population from across North America' on their way to 'the ancestral homeland, the cradle of *Acadie.*'[74]

In the end, Savoie may not have been too far off the mark when he observed, again to his correspondent in Halifax who had been left with the unused accommodations, that 'it is quite possible that we were too optimistic about the whole affair.'[75] After all, there had never been a national event on this scale before, while local celebrations had a long tradition. In fact, in recognition of such local loyalties, Savoie and his colleagues built into the Moncton celebrations a ceremony in which flag bearers from the various parishes of *Acadie,* each holding a staff with both the Acadian flag and a banner emblazoned with the name of the parish, would march together for a 'blessing of the flags' by the archbishop of Moncton, Mgr Norbert Robichaud, who was omnipresent during the fetes. In the end, the blessing that was supposed to be part of an outdoors ceremony probably lost some of its punch when rain forced it to be moved inside. Nevertheless, the press gave the event relatively little attention, perhaps because the inhabitants of those parishes did not come to Moncton in large numbers.[76]

From the earliest discussions regarding the bicentenary in 1950, organizers recognized that the local needed to be made part of the national. Far ahead of his time, Père Clément Cormier proposed that the family unit, and not the parish, should be used to 'generate interest wherever Acadians can be found. Each group would name a committee for its family. This committee would publish a pamphlet for the members of the family that would be as complete as possible. Then, each family would work at leading to the fetes as many members of its group as possible.'[77] Of course, the family has been the cornerstone for the Congrès mondial acadien movement, so much so that in 2004 – as we saw in chapter 2 – such more limited identities still frequently overpowered the emergence of a larger Acadian one. If the development of an overarching Acadian identity had still not been achieved by the early twenty-first century, it is probably no great surprise that Savoie and his colleagues did not entirely succeed fifty years earlier. Nevertheless, the show that they put on broke new ground in some significant ways, and is worth consideration for what was being said as much as for how many people were on hand to hear it.

Mincing Words (Again)

There was much about the events staged in Moncton, Memramcook, and Grand-Pré, the sites for the centrally organized fetes, that echoed the message communicated twenty-five years earlier, when *bonne entente* had been the order of the day. Even though (or perhaps because) the event being remembered had been inflicted upon Acadians by English speakers, the organizers of the *bicentenaire* went to great lengths to create events 'which would not hurt the feelings of Canadians who speak the other language.'[78] Acadian leaders were aware that some English speakers were fearful that 1955 might provide an occasion for the descendants of the deportees to somehow 'get even.' In that context, both CN and CP were reluctant at first to make arrangements to facilitate the transport of pilgrims to Grand-Pré. Colonel T.L. Bullock, who advised Savoie and his colleagues, observed that 'the railways were uneasy about the reaction of Nova Scotia's English-speaking people … Folks were frankly frightened of a revival of the Expulsion issue.' With that in mind, Savoie told everyone he could that the Acadians were determined to avoid any 'ill feelings towards anybody.'[79] 💻

So how did the leaders in Moncton manage to stage an event about the deportation without making those who may have identified with the perpetrators feel uncomfortable? Savoie and his colleagues began by making it clear that they were, in fact, not really marking the bicentenary of the deportation at all. As Col. Bullock explained to Governor General

Massey, who did not appear eager to attend, 'The celebrations were planned originally to mark the bicentennial of the Expulsion, but the organizers have decided that they might be misunderstood by their fellow-Canadians and it has been decided instead to hold just an "Acadian festival" in the course of which the Expulsion will be only one of several landmarks to be recalled.'[80] This would explain the decision to stage the bicentenary events at various sites, only one of which spoke to the deportation per se. However, effacing the deportation went even further, as even that word was rarely uttered.

The expression of choice was to refer instead to 'l'ÉPREUVE du peuple acadien (the TRIALS of the Acadian people),' in the process drawing attention to the religious mission of a chosen people, being tested – much as had been the case for the Jews – so that they might have the opportunity to prove themselves worthy to God.[81] The campaign to allay fears that Acadians might be interested in revenge also saw the leaders of the SNA craft a message to the Queen on the occasion of the bicentenary, in which they professed their loyalty – not that they had ever shown any evidence of disloyalty. Never once in the message, an illuminated document carefully prepared on parchment, was the word 'deportation' as much as mentioned. Instead, 1955 provided the occasion to mark 'a series of centenaries,' one of which just happened to be 'the bicentenary of an event that put the virtues of our ancestors to the test (à l'épreuve).'[82]

The efforts to make English speakers feel comfortable with the bicentenary went beyond the words that were avoided and continued on to the construction of the events that were staged, one of which was a folklore festival performed on four consecutive nights in Moncton. The initial idea was to bring together French speakers from Acadie, Louisiana, and Quebec, and English speakers of Scots, Irish, and English ancestry. Père Cormier, who was responsible for the festival, explained to a French-speaking correspondent, who was preparing the performance for one of the groups, that 'by including an evening of folklore in our program, our primary goal was to assure the participation of groups other than the Acadians in our festivities. The theme for the fetes is a delicate matter, and we are fearful of hurting the feelings of the English-speaking population; in order to make them feel better about participating, we thought that the folklore festival would do the trick.' Ever mindful of not offending English speakers, he advised this same correspondent that she should avoid using French as much as possible: 'We are going to try to keep the spoken word to a minimum. Each invited group should simply sing and dance.'[83]

Viewing the folklore festival from another perspective, Cormier touted its potential for encouraging diversity: 'Were we to believe that Canadian unity can be achieved solely through assimilation, the Acadian celebrations of 1955 could be labelled a dangerous initiative. But on this side of the Iron Curtain, where freedom is so treasured, unity is not mistaken for uniformity.'[84] In spite of this apparent support for diversity, First Nations people were not part of the original design. Cormier only warmed to the idea after lobbying by Col. Bullock, who reacted with some surprise when the former was prepared to leave them out because 'they might be a headache.' Bullock thought that Acadians, of all people, should have been sensitive to including the aboriginal inhabitants of *Acadie*, given their own past: 'It is not when it is strong that a race needs help, it is when it is weak and despised ... Would it not be a great thing for the Acadians, still not quite dominant themselves, to offer the first *big* gesture in modern times destined to raise the status of the Indians and give them back their pride and self-respect? ... Should not Indian chiefs be honoured guests, ... not just "actors in costume" at your main banquets?'[85] Having been convinced by Bullock, Cormier then set out to find participants, but when he visited a residential school in Shubenacadie, he found that none of the children knew about their culture. 'To my great surprise, no one there was concerned with perpetuating their traditions or teaching them the history of their ancestors.'[86]

Cormier did eventually find his Indians, who were part of a show in which each group performed on its own, and then returned at the end when all the participants came out to dance '*l'escaouette.*' The word derives from a long stick around which people danced in Acadian communities as a means of bringing families together. As the program for the folklore festival put it, 'The "Escaouette" is a truly Acadian dance ... Its symbolism represents the various ethnic groups gathered at the Bicentennial Celebrations as neighbouring families sharing in our festivities, and dancing around the wand of unity and good fellowship.'[87]

The desire to sidestep the story of the deportation was also in evidence in staging *Le Pageant de l'Acadie*, which, along with the folklore festival, was performed in Moncton on numerous occasions during the bicentenary. As at Edmundston earlier in the summer, the pageant was written by Père Laurent Tremblay, who assembled a cast of three hundred, although not without difficulty, to play the eight hundred roles in this version of the Acadian past. Perhaps picking up on the same distance between the Acadians and the central events that had been evident in other contexts, Tremblay complained to Savoie only two months before the pageant's opening that little had been done to date to draw Acadians to join the cast. In fact, some leaders had become so discouraged that they were considering the use of actors from outside *Acadie*. Tremblay, who had a long history of involvement with community theatre, reacted with horror to such an idea, which was 'anti-educational ... Staging a bicentenary has everything to do with inventing opportunities for everyone to become involved, to work, to sacrifice, and to give of themselves. The Acadian who has not been inconvenienced or has not sacrificed for the bicentenary will not have celebrated this event. A bicentenary is above and beyond everything else an opportunity to instil among the people a sense of commitment to the larger community.'[88]

As for the story that Tremblay constructed, the early scenes painted the idyllic picture that preceded 1755, while the final ones dealt with the rebuilding of Acadian life so that they became 'a happy people,' as scene 16 was entitled, once again. Of course, the complicated part was in presenting the deportation. In a draft of the scenario produced four months before the bicentenary, Tremblay was merciless in his depiction of the British, describing newcomers to Nova Scotia during the 1750s as 'a people who were greedy, lazy, fanatical, and self-centred; all they wanted was to get rid of the Acadians and take over their lands.' By contrast, in the final version presented to audiences in Moncton, the tone had been changed so that now the newcomers had 'an odd perspective in regard to the Acadians.'[89]

Tremblay's toning down of provocative rhetoric was even more apparent when depicting the events that began in 1755. In the final version, the relevant scene was entitled 'La tragédie d'un peuple,' or even more benignly in English, 'The Trials of 1755.' By contrast, his earlier draft of the same scene had been entitled 'Les Bourreaux de l'Acadie' (The Executioners of *Acadie*). It focused upon the evil of Lieutenant Colonel Charles Lawrence, who was placed in contrast with Governor Peregrine Thomas Hopson, in a classic good cop/bad cop scenario. Père Tremblay described Hopson, in this early version of the scene, as 'the most understanding and humane man you could find. For him, the matter was not very complicated: the Acadians were loyal subjects of the highest quality, who deserved to be treated as such.' In contrast, there was Lawrence, 'a monster, a blood-thirsty Nero, a hypocrite, a dishonest diplomat, a sadistic and inhumane murderer, one of the most disgusting figures in history, a stain forever on British history.'[90]

In order to make Lawrence's sins as vivid as possible, Tremblay wanted this to be 'a scene with the spoken word,' so that audiences could both see and hear the oppressor. The action took place in Hopson's residence in Halifax, just before illness took him back to England in 1753, thus allowing Lawrence to take charge. During a very brief appearance, Hopson said only a few words in which he expressed his desire to deal with the Acadians in a humane fashion. No sooner was Hopson out the door, but 'Lawrence took charge and the sad drama began.' He was soon joined by his 'accomplices,' including Lieutenant Colonel Winslow and Governor Shirley of Massachusetts, who helped him set the trap for the Acadians who came to plead their case in Halifax, not knowing what awaited their people. The scene ended with Lawrence and his sidekicks ordering the deportation and proclaiming triumphantly: 'Their goods are now ours!'

This original version, prepared by a Québécois who had apparently not yet assimilated the Acadian desire to downplay the evil of the 'other,' could never have been presented on the occasion of the bicentenary; and so when the pageant opened in August, this scene no longer was designed to depict the machinations of the British, but rather focused upon the difficulties experienced by the Acadians, the perpetrators having largely been removed from the picture. There was even a kindly British soldier who showed compassion: 'He was sensitive to the misfortunes of the victims, and had no real enthusiasm for his job.'

Père Tremblay's initial scenario in regard to the aftermath of the deportation had to be similarly edited to soften the anti-British edge. He originally called the scenes after the expulsion 'The Deportation and the Manhunt' and 'Suffering in Exile.' In both cases, there was an unremitting focus upon the 'criminal intent' of the British and the misery of the Acadians. He showed, for instance, that the British sent into exile 'the entire Acadian people.' Those who were not captured in the first sweep were then hunted down in what amounted to 'a veritable massacre. Acadians were hunted down like game. Bounty hunters were paid for each Acadian killed. They were scalped, then their bodies were stretched out and chopped into small pieces.' While the version that was actually performed hardly skimped on the misery that followed the *Grand Dérangement*, the scenes had titles that were less controversial: 'The Wandering Acadians' and 'The Difficulties of a People.' And while there was no absence of pathos in these scenes, they also focused upon the Acadians, trying to survive, instead of provocatively pointing fingers at the British.

Père Tremblay had unwittingly challenged the prevailing code regarding public presentation of the deportation, but met with resistance from Adélard Savoie and the bicentenary organizers in Moncton. Privately, Savoie had no qualms in accepting a much more inflammatory

5.2 Deportation scene, *Pageant de l'Acadie*, 1955 (Photo P133-B8:
Centre d'études acadiennes, Université de Moncton)

view of British actions in the eighteenth century, one that had been presented once again by a Quebecer. In that regard, he wrote to a correspondent shortly before the bicentenary who had been upset by a speech
by the historian Guy Frégault, one of a group of young historians making
names for themselves in Quebec at the time. Frégault referred to the
deportation as 'a terrible atrocity, a genuine war crime' that – had the
French been victorious in the Seven Years' War – might have resulted in
a situation comparable to that when 'the judges at Nuremburg' passed
sentence on more recent architects of 'crimes against humanity.'[91] Savoie
felt that Frégault's point of view, while lacking the 'sentimentality' often
found in the works of Acadian historians, had still been presented 'scien-
tifically and with objectivity.'

In a sense, it should come as no surprise that Savoie, who had indicated his modern credentials in trying to construct a new, national organization on the occasion of the bicentenary, might have expressed some support for Frégault's novel approach to the past. However, to announce his

leanings publicly was another matter, and Savoie made it clear in the same letter in which he seemed to defend Frégault that he had been advised 'by the Archbishop and his colleagues that we had to avoid at all costs any controversy in the newspapers or on radio in regard to the Deportation ... Until the fetes are over, we have to annoy the smallest number of people possible.'[92] Faithful to these instructions, Savoie even made it clear to a costume supplier from Montreal that the uniforms for English soldiers had to be as historically accurate as possible: 'We are on thin ice. Moncton is largely a town of English speakers. The pageant, which evokes the history of *Acadie*, will not be easy for them to swallow ... We don't want to give them the opportunity to criticize us in regard to the costumes. That would simply provide an opening for dismissing the whole Pageant. I am sure that you understand.'[93]

Coming Out

Preoccupied with the bicentenary events at Grand-Pré and the organizers' careful management of the message, historians have tended to dismiss the centrally organized events in August 1955 as part of an older Acadian tradition of public remembrance. Robert Viau found that 'when the bicentenary was over, there was nothing to indicate that Acadians were about to renounce the ways of their forebears.' In a similar manner, Sacha Richard has argued, 'The predominance of a traditional ideology in the language used during the [bicentenary] fetes showed how those celebrations were in line with what had come before ... The celebrations of 1955 provided no sneak preview of a new era for *Acadie*.' This point has been reinforced by Caroline-Isabelle Caron, who found that while the centrally controlled national events were stuck in the past, local celebrations were capable of breaking out of a traditional preoccupation with the deportation, even on the occasion of the bicentenary, in the process showing that Acadians were 'a courageous, industrious, well-educated and resolutely modern people.'[94]

To be sure, the leaders of the Catholic Church kept a close eye on Adélard Savoie and his colleagues, but it would be a mistake to assume, without closer analysis, that this influence would inevitably lead to an encounter with the past that could be reduced to the term 'traditionnel,' which conceals as much as it explains. Indeed, as Michael Gauvreau has shown in terms of the political ferment bubbling just beneath the surface in Quebec at roughly the same time, much of the impetus for change took place within the Catholic Church. From Gauvreau's perspective, the Quiet Revolution – normally viewed as a moment when Catholicism was rejected – was 'shaped to a considerable degree by religious identities and institutions.'[95]

From the very start of the planning for the bicentenary, many of the old Acadian themes about the deportation were trotted out one more time. Much like the Jews, the Acadians had been a chosen people who were martyred as they remained true to themselves. In exile, they never lost their resolve to retain their faith, and were rewarded by being watched over by their patron, the Virgin Mary, who aided in their rebirth, rising from the dead much like Christ himself.

The Marian references, with their long-standing tradition in *Acadie*, were omnipresent in clerical pronouncements during the bicentenary, and might have given the impression that little had changed. Upon the kickoff of preparations in April 1954, Mgr Robichaud saw an opportunity to offer thanks to 'the holy and glorious Virgin Mary for her constant attention to the Acadian people.' With that in mind, the archbishop looked forward to a celebration of 'an Acadie, both Catholic and devoted to Mary!'[96] He made similar statements on both the start of the bicentennial year and during the fetes in Moncton in 1955, and while Marian devotion officially went back to the late nineteenth century when Acadians chose to abandon St-Jean-Baptiste for a patron saint of their own, there was a context on the occasion of the bicentenary that was very different from that even twenty-five years earlier, when the deportation had last been marked publicly.

Mgr Robichaud paid particular reference to two developments from the late 1930s in his 'Sermon du Bicentenaire.' While 1912 saw the first appointment of an Acadian to the rank of bishop, it was only in 1936 that the Acadians effectively had a diocese of their own with the creation of the Archdiocese of Moncton, in a sense the first Acadian administrative unit since the fall of *Acadie française* in 1713. This led in short order to the construction of a cathedral for the diocese, which came to be known as *le Monument de la Reconnaissance acadienne envers sa Patronne* (Monument of Acadian Gratitude towards its Patron [the Virgin Mary]), and was for years after its opening in 1940 the tallest building in largely English-speaking Moncton.[97]

The visibility of Acadians had also been advanced by 1955 through the decree from Rome in 1938 declaring, again to quote Mgr Robichaud, 'the Holy Virgin ... as the heavenly Patron for Acadians "wherever they may be found."' The archbishop called upon all Acadians to learn this decree by heart 'because it amounts to the only, but authentic, charter of our official existence as a distinct entity within the Church of God.'[98] Going much further than the declaration of a diocese, here was a political document (albeit an ecclesiastical one) indicating that Acadians constituted a 'distinct society,' to use an anachronism. If Adélard Savoie was trying to provide the basis for a strong, centrally controlled Acadian organization outside the church, Mgr Robichaud was trying to do the same from within.

The archbishop's most radical act during the bicentenary had nothing to do with ecclesiastical politics. Rather, Mgr Robichaud placed himself at the centre of a significant moment in Acadian history by calling all Acadians to come out into the streets to celebrate 'un joyeux Tintamarre.' We saw in chapter 1 that the celebrations in 1979 to mark the 375th anniversary of the founding of *Acadie* on Île Ste-Croix provided the moment for the beginning of the annual Acadian street festival marked by dressing up in outlandish costumes and making as much noise as possible, a tradition that continues to this day. However, the first modern *tintamarre* took place during the *bicentenaire*, even if it did not become a part of the Acadian calendar for nearly another quarter-century.

There was nothing in Acadian history that provided a basis for the *tintamarre*, nor was there any indication in the early planning of the bicentenary that such an event was in the works.[99] Père Cormier's draft for the fetes, prepared in 1950 and largely adhered to, made no reference to such an innovation. In 1954, when plans for the year ahead were announced, the *tintamarre* was still not mentioned, and by the spring of 1955, even if the *tintamarre* was now scheduled for the evening of 10 August, it was only on the next day that fetes would officially begin.[100] It is impossible to know what had changed by August, but by then the *tintamarre* had become the high point of the opening night of the bicentenary.

For weeks leading up to the big moment, an appeal from Mgr Robichaud was widely disseminated, which called upon the involvement of all Acadians and not just those on hand for the opening of the bicentenary in Moncton. First, they were asked to drop to their knees and recite the official 'bicentenary prayer,' in its own right a fairly traditional statement of thanks by Acadians for both their 'trials' and their 'survival.'[101] This action, so typical of an older way of remembering the deportation, was all the president of the committee that oversaw the events took away from the evening. Calixte-F. Savoie was struck by the parallel between the Acadians begging for mercy from Lawrence in 1755 and now expressing their thanks in that same position two hundred years later. As he put it, 'Because Acadians always approached God respectfully on bended knee, the Acadian people had the strength to stand tall among men.'[102]

In dwelling on this act of supplication, Calixte-F. Savoie did not tell the whole story, as Mgr Robichaud asked Acadians to then rise from their knees and 'scream, ring bells, and make noise: whistles, automobile horns, bicycle bells, yelling, noisy toys, etc.' Perhaps Savoie, coming from a generation of Acadians that had tried to keep quiet and out of the way, was not sure what to make of such an event, which he did not even mention in his memoirs.[103] As for the organizers, however, that is to say the much younger Adélard Savoie and his colleagues, no stone was left unturned to make the Moncton event something special. L'Évangéline instructed people planning to take part to arrive early 'so that everything will be ready for radio and television at 7 pm.'[104]

For months before the event, the CBC – and more particularly its French-language service, Radio-Canada – was working on how to make the event accessible to as many Acadians as possible. While this may not have been a problem in the Moncton area (which had a French transmitter), a CBC official in Halifax observed that 'our real problem is to get coverage for the French-speaking people in the following locations: Wedgeport, Yarmouth, Church Point, Digby, Annapolis Royal, and Grand-Pré.' In order to deal with this exceptional opportunity, the CBC decided to turn over English-language transmitters in both Sackville and Saint John, New Brunswick, to the French service. The public broadcaster understood that 'there may be some criticism from English-speaking people in using CBA and CHSJ ... Conversely, there would be very definite criticism from French-speaking people if we did not do our best to give proper coverage to these Celebrations.'[105]

Thanks to the CBC's foresight, encouraged by Adélard Savoie and the organizers in Moncton, we have an exceptional description of the opening ceremonies, presented by Radio-Canada's star reporter, René Lévesque. With the bells of the Cathédrale chiming in the background, Lévesque introduced the various speakers who made the obligatory speeches of welcome before a relatively quiet audience. With the formalities out of the way, Savoie declared that 'the time for the tintamarre' had arrived, unleashing such a din that Lévesque could barely be heard over the crowd, estimated at five thousand (and so equal to the number that showed up at Grand-Pré), that blocked the intersection before the cathedral.[106]

While this celebration may not seem very striking decades after much larger, louder, and wilder tintamarres have become a staple of Acadian life, it was in certain ways a radical action – and one blessed by the church

– in the 1950s. There was something not very 'Acadian' about such a blatant takeover of public space. It certainly stood in stark contrast with all the painfully self-deferential talk that went into organizing the pageant and the folklore festival. Here the Acadians were in the midst of Moncton, an overwhelmingly English-speaking town, claiming turf as their own. At the same time, the good-natured fun that was at the core of the *tintamarre* took away any possible sense that the Acadians were harbouring grudges about past wrongs; and the potentially provocative nature of the event was further reduced when it was held on 10 August, and not five days later, when it would have coincided, as is now the custom, with the Acadian national holiday.[107]

The sense that this *tintamarre* was in any way threatening was further reduced by the essentially stationary nature of the crowd. Unlike modern-day *tintamarres*, or Catholic festivals that would have been well known in 1955 such as *Carnaval* (marking the beginning of Lent), or the *Fête-Dieu* (a late spring holiday to celebrate the Eucharist as constituting the body of Christ), or even the more secular St-Jean-Baptiste parade in Quebec, the bicentenary *tintamarre* did not attempt to claim territory by moving through the streets of Moncton.[108] Rather, the assembled Acadians waited patiently to be given the signal to make noise from leaders on the stage. Moreover, unlike *Carnaval* or more recent *tintamarres*, in which the identity of the revellers is obscured by the costumes worn (thus freeing the participants to act without fear of consequences), the only change to normal garb in 1955 was the widespread donning of the traditional Evangeline costume. While participants were encouraged to act up a bit because 'the police are permitting all this noise,' there really was little threat to public order.[109]

While the 1955 *tintamarre* could not live up to the power of fetes with hundreds of years of tradition, it did make an unprecedented claim on public space, an aspect of the *bicentenaire* in Moncton that was reinforced by the construction of special arches at the major entry points to the city. On this score, the Acadian leaders were leaning heavily on a tradition of the Fête-Dieu that frequently saw the construction of triumphal arches which helped mark the territory being claimed as holy. These *arcs de triomphe* were modelled after similar structures in Europe 'in order to celebrate the entry of a ruler into a conquered city.' In the case of the Fête-Dieu, 'the ruler is God who in the form of the host is led triumphantly through the streets.'[110] Following the same logic, a claim was made on public space when 'the routes leading to Moncton were marked by the construction of a series of giant 'A's made out of metal, topped off with five-pointed stars.'[111]

5.3 Logo, Deportation Bicentenary, 1955 (Photo P133-A159:
Centre d'études acadiennes, Université de Moncton)

Superimposed on a *bleu-blanc-rouge* background, the giant 'A' (for both *Acadie* and Assomption) was the central element of the official logo for the bicentenary. More famously, the 'A' was the most conspicuous element on the stage where the ceremonies took place at Grand-Pré in mid-August 1955 before a crowd of roughly five thousand. In a city of over twenty-five thousand, with thousands more living just outside its limits, many more people, the majority most likely English speakers, passed under the Moncton arches than were on hand at Grand-Pré. Nevertheless, as with the *tintamarre*, the bicentenary organizers were careful not to make too much noise about the erection of these arches, lest they be seen as a sign of Acadian assertiveness (which of course they were) in territory that – unlike Grand-Pré – was not entirely theirs. These Acadian leaders always referred to the fact that the 'high point' for the fetes would take place at Grand-Pré. Tellingly, it was the outsider Père Tremblay, never quite in touch with Acadian codes of behaviour, who observed: 'The most important events will take place in Moncton, the major centre of modern *Acadie*.'[112]

Towards the 250th

The efforts to mark the anniversary of the deportation in a town named after one of the architects of the 'trials of 1755' (spelled Monckton) had few ripples beyond 1955. With the close of the bicentenary, public memory of the *Grand Dérangement* once again focused upon Grand-Pré, and more particularly on efforts by Acadians to secure control over the site once it had been transferred to the federal government. At the very start of the preparations for the *bicentenaire*, there had been hopes, expressed by Père Cormier, that by 1955 'all the land [at Grand-Pré] would belong to the Acadian people.'[113] Given the financial problems of the SNA, this was not a realistic hope, and while an announcement was made during the *bicentenaire* that the federal government was prepared to take charge of the site, it was a far cry from securing Acadian control.

Ultimately, after much hand wringing by Acadian leaders, an agreement was reached that transferred control of the Grand-Pré site from both the Dominion Atlantic Railway and the SNA to Ottawa. While there were various promises about retaining the distinctive Acadian character of the site, they were not always kept. For instance, as Barbara Le Blanc has explained, there had been an understanding in the transfer that the *Eglise-Souvenir* would retain its Acadian character. However, by the early 1980s 'only half of the interior was dedicated to the story of the [Acadian] people. The other half commemorated the Planters and the Loyalists, later immigrants to the Annapolis Valley.'[114] In the midst of a period that witnessed their much greater assertiveness, Acadians insisted that their voices be heard at Grand-Pré, leading first to the creation of a formal Acadian consultative committee in 1985 and, more significantly, the signing in 1998 of an agreement for the site to be co-managed by the federal government and the newly created Société Promotion Grand-Pré, itself partly a product of the re-energized SNA.

It would be a stretch, however, to see the developments at Grand-Pré as somehow having grown out of the *bicentenaire*. In fact, the only initiative from the bicentenary that continued to have meaning for Acadians was the *tintamarre*, which resurfaced in 1979 as part of celebrations marking the 375th anniversary of the Île Ste-Croix adventure. On this occasion, there was an insignificant event in Moncton, which was dwarfed by the one at Caraquet, a much less contested site for Acadians, and since 1979 home to the largest *tintamarre* each *quinze août*. Just as significant as the primary location for the 'new' *tintamarre* was the context in which it was reborn. While the 1955 event had been mandated by the church and staged to mark an anniversary of the deportation, the 1979 *tintamarre* was firmly under the control of the Société des Acadiens du Nouveau-Brunswick (SANB) in order to mark a moment of beginnings, and not one of trauma.

For Acadians, or at least for those in New Brunswick, the deportation was no longer their uncontested foundation moment. Rather, there was a newfound search for beginnings that would place them on the same trajectory as other 'normal' people such as the Québécois, who had a well-defined territory of their own and European beginnings from the seventeenth century. In this regard, the Université de Moncton purchased a full-page advertisement in *L'Évangéline* on *le quinze août* 1980, the 225th anniversary of the deportation, that made no reference to the *Grand Dérangement*, and rather celebrated the 376th anniversary of the founding of *Acadie*, paying tribute 'to those who have stayed.'[115] In the background was a modern photograph of an abandoned farm, and so the tribute was not to those who had survived the deportation, but rather those who had not left the land for greener pastures. While the Acadians who had left in 1755 were given no choice, such was not exactly the case 225 years later; or to put it another way, the agent of Acadian decline was no longer the British under Lawrence, but rather economic circumstances.

That the deportation-based identity was starting to lose currency was underscored by the total absence of events in 1980 to mark the 225th anniversary of the *Grand Dérangement*. While the 175th anniversary (the previous 'quarter-century' event) had sparked the fetes at Grand-Pré that featured the Evangeline Girls, there was a very different mood in 1980, at least in New Brunswick, where the *tintamarres* were relatively insignificant events that were not promoted by the SANB, whose sights had turned to the fortunes of the Parti acadien and the creation of an Acadian province.[116] A special edition of *L'Évangéline* on the occasion of the Acadian *fête nationale* was filled with numerous articles dealing with anniversaries, but the anniversary of the deportation was not among them. Rather, there were various references to the fact that while 1979 had seen the 375th anniversary of the beginnings of *Acadie* in New Brunswick because of the landing at Île Ste-Croix, 'this year, it's the turn of our fellow Acadians in Nova Scotia, who will be marking officially the 375th anniversary of the establishment of Port-Royal.'[117] In addition, this special edition of the Acadian daily observed that 1981 would mark the centenary of the first *convention nationale*, while 1984 would mark both the bicentenary of New Brunswick and the centenary of the

5.4 *Acadie* on its 376th birthday, or the 225th anniversary of the deportation
(*L'Évangéline*, 15 August 1980: Centre d'études acadiennes,
Université de Moncton)

Acadian flag. One looks in vain for a single reference to the anniversary of the deportation.

The diasporic definition of *Acadie*, while contested, was not dead. This was evident in the some seventy-five thousand Acadians who assembled in southeastern New Brunswick in 1994 for the first Congrès mondial acadien. While families torn apart by the deportation were now brought back together, it would be an overstatement to call the CMA a deportation commemorative event, in the way that the 1930 or 1955 events were. If anything, the location of the first Congrès in New Brunswick underscored the re-centring of Acadian memory away from Grand-Pré. As Barbara Le Blanc has put it, most of the major Acadian sites with historical themes that were created in the late twentieth century were situated in New Brunswick. 'These places are vying for the tourist dollar and the iconic status achieved by Grand-Pré after 150 years of sacrilization.' Moreover, these new sites marked the history of *Acadie* since the deportation, with relatively little attention to the *Grand Dérangement* itself.[118] Even the CMA, which returned to Canada in 2004 after the second edition had been held in Louisiana, coincided with the 400th anniversary of the founding of *Acadie* (thus its focus upon Nova Scotia), and not the 250th anniversary (a year later) of its dispersal.

As 2005 approached, there remained significant silences in terms of the deportation, most notably the continued absence of both important sites of memory outside Grand-Pré and of voices that spoke in terms other than the apologetic ones that almost made the Acadians seem responsible for their misfortune. But this would all change in the early twenty-first century.

6

Tourner la page

Le seul pèlerin de Caraquet

The Sanctuaire Ste-Anne-du-Bocage, just outside Caraquet in northeastern New Brunswick, is a site for quiet contemplation. This was particularly the case when I ended up there all alone early on the morning of
3 September 2005. Of course, I hadn't planned it that way. Several weeks
earlier, I learned from Jean Gaudet, a municipal councillor in Dieppe, the
rapidly growing Acadian community on the eastern border of Moncton,
that he was organizing what he called *un pèlerinage historique* (a historic
pilgrimage) that would take Acadians (and Acadian wannabes) to various
sites of memory en route to Grand-Pré, where they would all arrive two
days later. Gaudet was experienced at organizing such adventures, having
staged a caravan of vehicles (La Caravane Pélagie) to the Congrès mondial
acadien in Louisiana in 1999 and one by both sea and land (Les Caravanes
Mer et Terre) around Nova Scotia to mark the 2004 CMA. This particular
adventure would end on 5 September 2005, which marked the 250th
anniversary, as Jean Gaudet put it in the limited publicity advertising
the event, 'of the announcement of the deportation by Winslow to the
418 men assembled in the St-Charles de Grand-Pré church.' Much larger commemorative events had taken place earlier in the summer, on
28 July, to mark the 250th anniversary of the signing of the deportation
order, but to Gaudet and others, Winslow's efforts to carry out this act of
ethnic cleansing were more significant than signatures on a piece of
paper, which constituted merely 'an administrative act.'[1] 💻

Gaudet had planned on having three separate groups whose routes
would converge near Halifax, before then travelling together for the
final push on to Grand-Pré, but no one came out for the two journeys

that were supposed to begin in Nova Scotia, and I had a feeling that maybe no one was on this part of the journey as I waited for another *pèlerin* (pilgrim) to arrive. The time on my hands allowed me to look around the site that had been carefully chosen by Gaudet and which was pertinent to some of the themes of deportation memory on this particular anniversary.

Ste-Anne-du-Bocage, unlike Grand-Pré, spoke not to the expulsion of the Acadians, but rather to the escape of a significant number of them from the grasp of their oppressors. It was first settled by Alexis Landry, whose story differed dramatically from that of Évangeline and Gabriel. When the British attacked his village near the present-day border between Nova Scotia and New Brunswick, he and a number of his neighbours headed north to the Miramichi valley, where thousands of Acadians sought refuge, many dying from starvation during the winter of 1756–7. Moving further north along the coast, Landry led hundreds of survivors who settled at Ste-Anne-du-Bocage. In the years that followed, British attacks made the lives of Landry and his fellow Acadians unbearable, and they moved on several occasions until establishing themselves, at the location where I found myself, on a permanent basis in 1769.

Ultimately, Ste-Anne-du-Bocage took on a new vocation as a site of pilgrimage in relation to a chapel located there. In 1857, on the fete of Ste-Anne (26 July), fishermen came to offer thanks to their patron saint after a devastating storm had resulted in the death of many of their fellows. By 1880 a pilgrimage there developed into an annual event by fishermen and their neighbours on 26 July; and over time it became the location of choice for local celebrations to mark the Acadian national holiday. In recognition of its status, in 1955 (when the bicentenary events at Caraquet were larger than those at Grand-Pré), Ste-Anne-du-Bocage was proclaimed a site of national historic significance, a status reconfirmed in the following year when a monument to Landry and the other *fondateurs* was unveiled.[2]

This location had a long connection to pilgrimages, and yet here I was with no other pilgrim in sight. Undeterred, I soldiered on. Jean Gaudet had given me the itinerary for this part, now the only part, of his adventure, and had told me where he was expecting to show up further down the road. And so I continued, conscientiously following his instructions. Heading south, I stopped first at Pokemouche, the birthplace of Valentin Landry, the founder of the Acadian daily *L'Évangeline*, where I grabbed a cup of coffee in the hope that someone else might join me. By the time I reached Neguac, I had pretty much come to grips with the fact that I was on my own, but on this occasion I was met by a Madame Savoie, who had been lined up to greet the *pèlerins*. Slightly disappointed that she had come out early on a Saturday morning for *un seul pèlerin* (and not even an Acadian), she still explained to me the history of her town, which – much like Ste-Anne-du-Bocage – had been founded by those, including her namesake Jean Savoie, who had escaped the deportation.

Soon after Neguac, I finally caught up with Jean Gaudet, who had three couples in tow with whom I travelled for the next two days, visiting other sites of Acadian survival in the aftermath of the deportation and (until our arrival at Grand-Pré) hardly visiting any locations that spoke to the act of expulsion per se. For instance, just after I joined the group, we visited the site of the Camp d'Espérance, a refugee camp established to harbour Acadians, such as Alexis Landry, who had escaped the grasp of the British. This was an initiative of the government of New France, whose officials embezzled funds that should have helped the refugees. The story told by the Camp d'Espérance had nothing to do with the Acadians' acceptance of their fate at the time of the deportation, and so departed from the dominant sentiment at the time of the bicentenary fifty years earlier.[3]

Before the journey was over, we also visited two further *lieux de mémoire* – one in Dieppe and the other in Halifax – that had received no particular attention prior to the 250th anniversary. Only months earlier both had been marked by monuments that spoke to the resistance of Acadians, in the process decentring the focus of deportation memory from Grand-Pré and contributing to the message, certainly important to the group with which I was travelling, that the Acadians had not gone off meekly to their fate. These monuments were the work of the Commission de l'Odyssée acadienne, of which Jean Gaudet was a member and whose efforts to tell a very specific deportation story are discussed below. However, the commission's view of the deportation and that of my fellow travellers were not the only ones on display during the summer of 2005.

As we visited these two monuments we were very much alone, while large numbers of people went about their regular routines, only metres away. Of course, it is not so unusual for monuments to become part of the scenery and ignored by passers-by. However, in the case of these monuments, the crowds had even been relatively small at their unveiling earlier in the summer, on 28 July, the commemorative date that Jean Gaudet had not much liked and which marked the signing of the deportation order. Like it or not, 28 July 2005 had been bestowed with a certain official status thanks to a royal proclamation issued by the federal

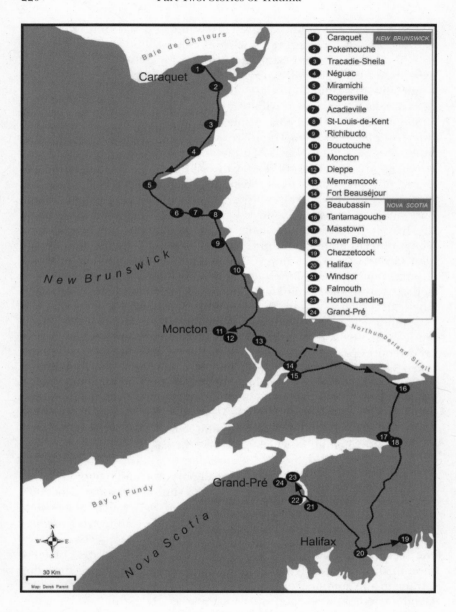

Map 2: *Pèlerinage historique,* September 2005

government as a means of responding to demands for an apology to Acadians for the wrongs they had experienced. In the end, there was no apology, only an acknowledgment of wrongs committed by some unnamed force, along with the commitment to have an annual 'Journée de commémoration du Grand Dérangement.'

If the crowds had been small for the monuments unveiled on this first day of deportation remembrance, such was not the case for a spectacular *sons-et-lumières* show that drew large crowds to Grand-Pré, during which Acadian leaders made speeches about the need for their people to *tourner la page* (literally, to turn the page). While the exact meaning of that term was much debated in the run-up to the 250th anniversary, its sense that the time had come for Acadians to put the matter of the deportation to rest once and for all was at odds with the spirit of the *pèlerinage* of which I was a part.

On a different level, the spectacle at Grand-Pré differed from the pilgrimage in the sense that the former involved spectators, while the latter was made up of participants. I already knew Jean Gaudet's biases in this regard before signing on for this early September adventure, as I had previously participated in two processions that he led over the three kilometres from Horton Landing (where Acadians had been placed on ships) to the reconstructed church at Grand-Pré: one at the close of the Caravanes Mer et Terre during the Congrès mondial acadien in 2004 and the other earlier in the summer at the close of the weekend that celebrated the first day of official remembrance of the deportation. ▣ The third such procession, described at the start of this book, took place at the end of the *pèlerinage historique*, in a sense undoing the act of deportation as the marchers, stopping at sites along the way – much as one would stop at Stations of the Cross – reversed the route from 250 years earlier. ▣

There was little sense in such an act that the time had come to *tourner la page* on the deportation; nor was there any sense that it was good enough for leaders to make speeches about the deportation or for spectators to sit in a crowd and allow the events to wash over them. Rather, as Gaudet said to the roughly forty marchers, they were to be congratulated for having carried out 'a personal commitment.' As he had told me months earlier as we talked about my involvement with his *pèlerinage*, it was important for Acadians to give evidence of 'a personal involvement' and so he even referred to the pilgrimage as one dedicated to 'learning and reflection.'[4] Perhaps this explains why there were so few of us. It was so much easier to remain passive. ▣

Crosses to Bear

For Acadian leaders, particularly those associated with the Société nationale de l'Acadie (SNA), the celebrations marking the 400th anniversary
of their people provided the opportunity to establish a new founding
myth, in the process unseating the idea that Acadian history had 'begun'
in the aftermath of 1755. Of course, if that were the case, then what was
to be done with the unfortunate occurrence of a deportation anniversary
on the heels of fetes marking the arrival of the Dugua expedition on Île
Ste-Croix? While the juxtaposition of the anniversaries of founding and
trauma was nothing new, the muted celebration of the Dugua expedition on previous occasions had spared Acadian leaders the difficulty of
harmonizing the very different memories evoked by 1604 and 1755.

While the SNA began reflecting on the 400th anniversary as early as
1994, it was only three years later that it first seemed concerned that *le
400e* might conflict with the 250th anniversary of the deportation, and so
discussions began as to 'what year we should celebrate.'[5] This question
was answered implicitly in 1998 when the SNA created a committee dedicated to celebrating the quadricentenary; it only took up the issue of the
deportation again when it was approached a year later by a group of
Acadians, led by the environmental activist Daniel LeBlanc, which had
the idea of creating the new sites of deportation memory that I visited
with Jean Gaudet's group. If there were any question as to which way the
wind was blowing, in 2000 the SNA's committee that was weighing its options for 2004–5 reported that 'our primary goal should be to celebrate
the beginnings of *Acadie*.' As for the deportation, the report suggested
that its celebration should be confided to LeBlanc's Commission de
l'Odyssée acadienne.[6]

It is little wonder that the SNA jumped at the opportunity to divest itself
of responsibility for remembering the deportation. This had all been
much easier in 1955, long before Acadians had begun to show interest in
marking the moment of their founding and while they still felt that they
had to tiptoe around the issue of the deportation, fearful that reference
to their own expulsion might raise eyebrows. However, in the fifty years
that followed the *bicentenaire*, while Acadians continued to face some significant challenges, they had also achieved some real successes: politically,
economically, and culturally. With success came greater self-confidence
and the ability to address the deportation in a number of ways. At one
end of the spectrum there were those who felt sufficiently assertive that
they would settle for nothing less than a formal apology, from the Queen

if at all possible, for wrongs that had been done; at the other end there were those who thought that the self-confidence of Acadians provided them with the option of largely letting the 250th anniversary pass without making too much fuss. This point of view probably received its clearest (and perhaps most extreme) expression in a statement by New Brunswick's lieutenant governor, Herménégilde Chiasson, who observed in the midst of the 2005 commemorative events: 'The fact is that we should never forget, yet we have to forget … I mean we should never forget because it is a historical event but we have to forget because life goes on … I think it is like someone who lost a leg. You have to say, well, there are better days ahead. For the Acadian people, I think that's how we think right now.'[7] 💻 Rather than wade into such contentious waters, the Commission de l'Odyssée acadienne provided the SNA with an opportunity to focus on the 400th anniversary events while someone else dealt with the anniversary of the *Grand Dérangement.*

Consisting of a half-dozen active members of the Acadian community, the commission began its work in 1998, a few months before offering its services to the SNA.[8] From the very start, this group sought to explore ways to avoid the earlier emphasis of deportation commemoration on its tragic dimensions, particularly through the site at Grand-Pré. Nevertheless, they soon found that it was not that easy to escape from earlier modes of memory. In particular, they struggled over how to balance their use of two terms to which they attributed very different meanings: *Grand Dérangement,* which they found conveyed a message of 'suffering and tragedy,' and *Odyssée acadienne,* which spoke to 'rebirth and continuity.'[9]

While the former term had a long pedigree going back to the eighteenth century, the latter had only received official sanction fairly recently.[10] During the 1970s, the Historic Sites and Monuments Board of Canada decided that Memramcook (the site of the first *convention nationale* of the 1880s, and one of the sites of the bicentenary in 1955) was worthy of commemorating to mark 'the survival of the Acadians.' However, by the early 1990s members of an Acadian Consultative Committee that was advising Parks Canada asked that the term *Odyssée acadienne* be adopted instead, feeling that the older term was too negative and grounded in the events of the 1750s. Instead, the expression *Odyssée acadienne* spoke to 'the evolving journey of the Acadian people through their early struggle for survival, their later period of renaissance and their current position as active participants in the issues that concern Canadians today.'[11] Parks Canada gave the new term public recognition when it became the focus for the permanent exhibition that was mounted in Memramcook at the Monument Lefebvre.

Since the spirit of the times seemed to favour distancing Acadians from the horrors of the deportation, LeBlanc and his colleagues chose at first to eschew the use of the term *Grand Dérangement* in naming their group, preferring instead to emphasize 'the commemoration of the *Odyssée acadienne*.' As they put it at the time, 'the idea is not to move away from remembering the *Déportation* but to focus on the *Odyssée acadienne*.' Within weeks, however, they had backtracked to allow their committee to be more closely 'connected to the commemoration of the *grand dérangement* rather than the *Odyssée acadienne*'; and in the years that followed they continued to go back and forth, reaching the point in the early twenty-first century where they referred to themselves as being involved with both concepts.[12] If nothing else, the commission's indecisiveness about its name reflected the difficulty in rejecting older notions of the deportation, which had become part of Acadian identity, and provided further explanation of why the SNA had wanted to keep its distance from the 250th anniversary dossier.

True to its initial inclination to speak to the *Odyssée acadienne*, the commission developed a list of sites worthy of commemoration, some of which, such as Memramcook, were to be remembered, not for any connection with the deportation per se, but rather as 'the cradle of contemporary *Acadie*.'[13] In time, however, just as the commission turned, however tentatively, to focus more squarely upon events directly tied to the *Grand Dérangement*, the Memramcook site was abandoned, replaced in southeastern New Brunswick by one twenty kilometres away along the banks of the Petitcodiac River in Dieppe, just outside Moncton, where the commission's first monument was unveiled in 2005, on the 250th anniversary of the signing of the deportation order. 💻

With the decision, in 2000, to erect a monument along the Petitcodiac, the commission committed itself to focus not merely upon the uprooting of the Acadians, but also on their resistance when confronted by the British.[14] This was a radical departure in public representation of the deportation: no longer were Acadians the victims of the British, going quietly to their providential fate, but rather they were capable of being agents in their own right. The members of the commission were plugging in to a strong current of thought in the late twentieth and early twenty-first centuries that saw the resistance to mistreatment as a group's badge of honour. Of course, it had not been that much earlier that the mere evidence of victimization had been justification for a group to seek

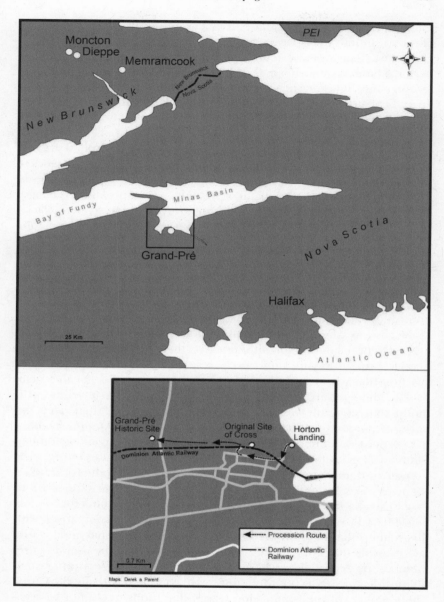

Map 3: Sites of deportation memory, 2005

some remedial action. As Peter Novick put it in terms of the inclination of American Jews to display their link to the oppression embodied by the Holocaust, 'The greatest victory is to wring an acknowledgement of superior victimization from another contender.'[15]

Over time, however, such special pleading wore thin, and so it became incumbent upon those who sought recognition to prove that they had shown some resolve in the face of adversity, in short to show some 'agency,' to use the operative expression from the last decades of the twentieth century. In terms of historical writing, there was the shift from the airing of past grievances by women, workers, and minorities of various types to their presentation as having had a certain autonomy of their own, even when faced with the most difficult of circumstances. Speaking to changes in the writing of African American history, Novick observed how 'blacks, both under slavery and thereafter, were depicted as constituting a community of resistance … In a way which had many parallels to Jewish historians' discussions of the behavior of Jews during World War II, resistance came to be equated with endurance and survival.'[16]

Similarly, in terms of more popular representations of the past, moments of resistance came to be prized alongside more conventional references to past suffering. In the case of the representation of the Holocaust, to take only one example, the development of the United States Holocaust Memorial Museum saw considerable discussion of the need to present 'significant forms of resistance … to counteract the accusation that victims went like "sheep to their graves."'[17] For the members of the Commission de l'Odyssée acadienne, the unveiling of a monument along the banks of the Petitcodiac provided the perfect opportunity to inscribe its efforts within the same language of resistance.

In order to communicate any message, however, the commission had to find a design that it could afford, no small problem for an organization that did not benefit from any official status. After some trial and error it found a formula that permitted the construction of a series of structures that had a common form and which could be built for roughly $35,000 each. While this may seem like a paltry sum in comparison with the millions that were invested in the 2004 quadricentenary events, the fact remains that governments were not falling over themselves to remember the deportation, whose message of trauma was less attractive to political leaders than the founding myth associated with Île Ste-Croix. The members of the commission feared that funds might not be available because 'the committees involved with Port-Royal and Île Ste-Croix have proposed projects requiring millions of dollars.'[18] Ultimately, the

Petitcodiac monument benefited from financing in roughly equal parts from the Canadian, New Brunswick, and Dieppe governments.[19]

Committed to going forward modestly given its financial limitations, the commission came up with a simple design, most of whose elements were agreed upon shortly after it began its work. The base of each monument was to be in the shape of a star, thus playing on the star on the Acadian flag. Rising up from the base was a pentagonal structure designed to evoke 'the hull of a ship' (an appropriate deportation reference). On the top surface, the commission chose to present a map of the *Odyssée acadienne,* an image of the international dimensions of the dispersal of which more than forty thousand copies were published in the early 1990s, when the *Odyssée* concept was in full bloom. However, by the time that the map was incorporated into the commission's design, it was referred to as depicting the *Grande Dérangement.* Along with the map, the top surface also included several classic deportation images, including one of the *église-souvenir* from Grand-Pré. At the start of the commission's work this traditional image was in the foreground, but in the final design it was pushed to the back.

Even more radical, however, was the common text pointing to the *Grand Dérangement* that was to appear on the faces of the monuments, in both official languages. Beyond presenting the context for the deportation, it also indicated that aside from those who were exiled, 'others escaped the deportations, seeking refuge in French territories and forming a resistance.'[20] Finally, each monument was to have a text that spoke to the specific circumstances that made that site one of deportation memory; and it was in this regard that the Dieppe monument spoke volumes. Entitled 'Resistance on the Petitcoudiac,' the inscription told the story of British efforts to remove the Acadians from this region in August 1755 (and so well before the expulsions from Grand-Pré) because of their 'independent character.' When the deportation began in earnest, residents of this area became 'armed resistance fighters [who] inflicted a major setback on the British soldiers ... For three years, entrenched in the upper reaches of the river and under the leadership of the Broussard (Beausoleil) brothers, the Acadians waged incessant guerilla warfare against the British.' Ultimately, the resistance collapsed, but even then the unbreakable determination of the Acadians continued: 'Even though many of these Acadians were pursued, decimated by illness and imprisoned, they still managed to avoid the Deportation, thus allowing *Acadie* to survive. While some families chose to leave voluntarily, others remained in their native land to build the new *Acadie.*'[21]

6.1 Monument of Commission de l'Odyssée acadienne (Commission de
l'Odyssée acadienne, Société nationale de l'Acadie)

The reference to Beausoleil Broussard placed the work of the commission within a larger effort to focus attention on the occasion of this anniversary on the resistance of Acadians. In that regard, for instance, the
historian Paul Surette used the opportunity to point to the actions of
those living near the present-day border between Nova Scotia and New
Brunswick, who did not fit the stereotype of the Acadians living at Grand-
Pré, who were 'innocent beings. When they were attacked by the evil,
aggressive English, they were just like lambs who offered little resistance.'
By contrast, the Acadians of Chignectou were 'more autonomous, hardy
and determined. They were capable of being resourceful, and should
the need arise, of fighting back.' So, when the deportation came, only
about one-quarter of the Acadians of the region were deported: 'The
victory here belonged to these Acadians.'[22] The single individual who
embodied this spirit of resistance was Broussard, the Acadian freedom
fighter, who had long been relegated to the shadows. While the fictional
Evangeline may have been the gentle female whose life was consumed
searching for Gabriel, the real-life Broussard (to the extent that we
understand the details of his life) was the tough male who took matters

6.2 Beausoleil Broussard as Che Guevara (drawing by Lucius A. Fontenot)

into his own hands, defying British efforts to deport the Acadians between 1755 and 1762. Following the end of the Seven Years' War, Broussard
took other Acadians with him first to Saint-Domingue and later Louisiana.
He was not a deportee, but an Acadian who had resisted.[23]

In the run-up to the 250th anniversary, Broussard was presented as a
Che Guevara–like figure on the cover of a book by Warren Perrin, a longtime advocate from Louisiana for an apology from the Queen in regard
to the deportation. Writing in 2003 that Broussard had led an 'insur-
gency,' Perrin seemed to place him in the same mould as those who were
opposing the American presence in Iraq.[24] Beausoleil also was displayed
on T-shirts (marketed by Perrin) and was celebrated in song. *Petitcodiac*,
by the Acadian band Zéro° Celsius (1995), placed him in the company of
other resistance fighters such as Louis Riel and Crazy Horse, the Lakota
leader who had led his people against intrusions into their lands by the
American government, most notably in the Battle of Little Big Horn.
Daniel Léger also provided a tribute in his *Beausoleil* (2004), which sang
the praises of a man who had managed to 'déranger [upset] le Grand
Dérangement.'

The story of resistance as expressed by the Commission de l'Odyssée
acadienne's Dieppe monument concluded with the cross that rose up
from the base. On the face of it, this was a traditional expression of
Acadian acceptance that they constituted a martyred people. Indeed,
the cross incorporated into all the commission's monuments was modelled after the four-metre-tall *Croix de la Déportation* (also known as the
Croix de l'Embarquement) that had been erected by the Société nationale
l'Assomption in 1924 on a spot roughly two kilometres from the *église-
souvenir* at Grand-Pré to mark the spot (wrongly as it turned out) where
the deportees had been herded on to ships. While the location of the
cross, adjacent to the rail line of the Dominion Atlantic Railway, allowed
passengers to sample this taste of the Land of Evangeline as they passed
by, it also took on a holy status among Acadians and those sympathetic to
their fate, who turned it into a site of pilgrimage where respects could be
paid to the victims of the deportation. In fact, the unveiling of the cross
took place in the midst of a pilgrimage to *Acadie* organized by Henri
Bourassa and *Le Devoir*.

Put in these terms, the Croix de la Déportation seemed to speak to
an older view of the past that the commission was now seeking to marginalize. Nevertheless, the members remained determined from the
start that the cross form part of the concept for the monument, even
though 'a cross might be viewed negatively in certain countries, states

6.3 Unveiling of the Deportation Cross, 1924 (Société Promotion Grand-Pré)

and provinces.' In light of such concerns, the matter was still being discussed in 2002, but the commission once again committed itself to the cross, which 'has long been a symbol of Acadian resistance; it is their faith which has allowed resistance for so long against the consequences of the deportation.'[25] The commission was appropriating an older symbol of the Catholic mission of a chosen people and expressing it in terms of the agency of a community of resisters.

In addition to the monument at Dieppe, one other monument was unveiled on the 250th anniversary of the deportation, this one on the waterfront in Halifax to mark the imprisonment of Acadians on Georges Island, which can easily be seen from the shore.[26] True to the commission's formula, this monument was identical to the one along the Petitcodiac, except for the inscription that spoke to the local circumstances that made the tiny island a site of deportation memory. Once more, that inscription spoke to the resistance of the Acadians: 'Lieutenant Governor Lawrence described the island as "the place of most security" so Acadian partisans who took part in the resistance often ended up there.' Beausoleil Broussard had been a prisoner here, along with others described as 'partisans,' a term that evokes

memories of those who resisted Nazi rule in Europe during the
Second World War.

The commission might have unveiled one further monument in 2005
had it had its way, as it supported efforts to move the Croix de la
Déportation to its rightful spot, where Acadians actually had been herded
onto ships, at Horton Landing (what had been known as La Pointe Noire
or Vieux Logis), two kilometres further from Grand-Pré than its original
location along the railway tracks. On the eve of the 250th anniversary,
the only commemorative marker on that site was a cairn that drew attention to the arrival of the Planters. In the plaque placed here by the
Historic Sites and Monuments Board, there was only a passing reference
to the Acadians, whose 'fallow lands' had been assumed by people described, enigmatically, as 'pre-loyalists,' an expression that oddly focused
more upon the people whom the Planters preceded than on those whom
they followed.

In order to right that wrong, the Société Promotion Grand-Pré, the
Acadian group that now shared responsibility for the Grand-Pré site with
the federal government, advanced the idea of moving the Croix de la
Déportation to Horton Landing. For its part, the Commission de
l'Odyssée acadienne then approached the federal government, which
owned the land, with the proposal that the massive cross might be made
part of one of its monuments 'in a larger format,' complete with its map
and explanatory texts.[27] Since its various monuments would all bear
scaled-down copies of the Cross, there was some logic in trying to incorporate the real thing into one of its projects. In the end, however, the
federal government did not want to 'increase the number of monuments
at this historic site,' and while the Cross was moved – to be unveiled as
part of Ottawa's festivities on 28 July 2005 – it was transported as it was,
leaving the explanation of its own history to one of several panels installed by Parks Canada.[28] These panels provided the Planters and
Acadians with equal attention, in the process also recognizing the connection to this site of both the Mi'kmaq and African Nova Scotians. If the
Acadians had hoped to make this site their own through the relocation
of the Cross, they did not entirely succeed.

There was one more story connected with a cross, or rather the absence of a cross, on the occasion of this anniversary. As we saw at the start
of this section, the Société nationale de l'Acadie jumped at the opportunity to give the Commission de l'Odyssée acadienne the opportunity to
take a lead role in public commemoration for 2005. Nevertheless, as the
anniversary approached it was impossible for the major organization

6.4 Logo: 250th Anniversary of the Deportation (Société nationale de l'Acadie)

representing Acadians to remain outside the activities that were being organized. While the SNA had launched its activities to mark the 400th anniversary of the founding of *Acadie* in 2003, it waited until only weeks before the 28 July events to explain its involvement in the anniversary of the deportation and to launch its logo.

While many commemorative logos lack any real interest, this one spoke to an important current of thought in official Acadian circles. In the first issue of a newsletter that appeared belatedly to communicate information about the anniversary, the SNA provided a detailed explanation of the logo's various elements. The word *commémoration* was included 'to underline the message that the Société Nationale de l'Acadie wants to communicate on this anniversary: namely that Acadians are ready to remember the past and, at the same time, to reconcile themselves with their History. There is a positive idea here of a people looking towards the future.'[29] As we shall see, the idea of coming to some final resolution in terms of the deportation so as to turn the page on the past was constantly repeated by Acadian officials during the summer of 2005. As for other elements: the colours (although not evident in the black and white version shown here) were drawn from the Acadian flag, and the four sectors of the circle represented the four Atlantic provinces. The inclusion of the dates was self-explanatory, as one would have thought were the waves, which had taken the Acadians to distant shores. However, on this occasion, they were much more benign so as to 'emphasize the importance of the sea in the lives of Acadians.' By far, however, the most striking feature of the logo, if only by its absence, was 'the Croix de la Déportation which is only hinted at, showing that this page of History has once and for all been turned.' With the horizontal section of the 'cross' in the form of the dates and its vertical section left to the imagination between the star at the top and the 'Commémoration' at the bottom, this marker of Acadian memory of the deportation for over eighty years had almost disappeared. When placed in contrast with the efforts of the Commission de l'Odyssée acadienne to make an old symbol relevant in the early twenty-first century, the logo underscored the fact that there were numerous voices in *Acadie* on the occasion of this anniversary.

Who's Sorry Now?

In 1955, on the occasion of the previous large-scale commemoration of the deportation, the idea that the British Crown might be asked to apologize for the wrongs done to the Acadian people would have been unthinkable, given that the Acadians were still using such occasions to express their loyalty to the monarch. To underscore this point, during the lead-up to the bicentenary, the chief organizer, Adélard Savoie, observed that Acadians wanted to take advantage of the occasion to extend a 'generous offer of Christian forgiveness' to those who had been responsible for the deportation.[30] For some Acadians, at least, matters had changed considerably in the years leading up to the 250th anniversary of the deportation, which came in the midst of what has been called 'the age of apology.'[31]

Beginning in 1988 with the apologies, along with reparations, to Japanese victims of internment in both Canada and the United States, there has been a steady stream of statements of remorse from governments and other institutions such as the Catholic Church. Trying to quantify the growth of the phenomenon, Aaron Lazare found that the number of articles dealing with apologies of one sort or another in the pages of the *New York Times* and *Washington Post* between 1990 and 1994 doubled during the period between 1998 and 2002.[32] The actual list of apologies from states could go on for pages, but among the ones that received much attention in the media, there was France's apology in

1995 for the acts of the Vichy government during the Second World War, Russia's in 1998 for the eighty years of 'sins of communism,' and in the same year the apology by the British Crown for its treatment of the Maoris in New Zealand. Canada was hardly immune from the trend, having apologized in 1990 for the internment of Italian Canadians during the Second World War and in 1998 for the abuse of First Nations people in residential schools, to name only two such acts.[33]

Statements from governments in regard to their previous actions have come in all shapes and sizes. While some apologies, as in the case of the Japanese internees, have come along with financial compensation, others – such as the apology to Italian internees – have not. There were also real apologies, which indicated some sense of accountability, that need to be distinguished from statements of regret that fell short of accepting responsibility. In this regard, there was the statement by Tony Blair in 1997 concerning the Irish famine of the 1840s. Blair indicated that 'those who governed in London at the time failed their people through standing by while a crop failure turned into a massive tragedy. We must not forget such a dreadful event.' While some read between the lines to see the British government's acceptance of its responsibility, others looked only at the words which never said 'I'm sorry.'[34]

Just as the complete list of 'apologies' over the past twenty years would be long, so too would be the list of reasons proposed by scholars to explain why this outpouring of regret occurred when it did. Some have pointed to the end of the Cold War, which allowed admissions of wrong-doing without 'strategic preoccupations' so that 'the global community … [could] commit itself to a higher standard of justice.'[35] Others have pointed to the rise of ethnic and national sensibilities (many of which emerged with the fall of the Soviet Union), which, in turn, encouraged the airing of grievances. According to Charles Maier, 'Ethnic grievances have become the currency of politics. For some these grievances involve past catastrophes. In any case, getting others to pay their respect is a form of national recognition. Respect must be paid, ambassadors must be exchanged, compensatory deals must be arranged, victims must be remembered.'[36]

In spite of the numerous contextual reasons for the rise of apologies, there were also considerations that led some governments either to oppose the practice in general or specific acts of contrition in particular. Leading the list were the arguments – some of which surfaced during the debate over granting an official apology in regard to the deportation – that sought to distance current governments from actions taken long ago. Robert Weyeneth has provided a guide to some of the reasons not to apologize, including: 'People alive today did not commit the past acts'; 'Why dredge up the past? It's too divisive'; and 'It was a tough decision, and people today cannot understand the historical circumstances of the time.' Weyeneth also pointed to objections to the symbolic (or lip service) aspects of apologizing that did nothing to address the current circumstances of the aggrieved party: 'It's time to look forward and not backward.' Finally, there was also resistance to any one apology based on the fact that 'There are so many past deeds for which to apologize. Why single out this one?'[37]

In the Canadian context, the most famous statement of opposition to the apology movement came from Prime Minister Pierre Elliott Trudeau, who in 1984 – on his last day in office – expressed his unwillingness to compensate Japanese Canadians for their internment. As he explained in the House of Commons, he did not close the door to 'other forms of redress' and he did express his 'regret,' but did not go any further, fearing that it would be the thin edge of the wedge. 'I know that we would have to go back a great length of time in history and look at all the injustices that have occurred, perhaps beginning with the deportation of the Acadians and going on to the treatment of the Chinese Canadians in the late 19th century. I do not believe in attempting to rewrite history in this way ... I do not see that there is much to gain by trying to apologize for acts of our great-grandfathers and their great-grandfathers.'[38]

Trudeau was prescient in the sense that no sooner had an apology been extended to the Japanese Canadians than the first suggestion emerged that Acadians should be next in line. Writing in *l'Acadie Nouvelle*, Nelson Landry argued that the time had come for Canada to have Great Britain recognize 'officially the wrongs that were done to the Acadians in 1755 ... Our ancestors lived through a trauma that was equal to, if not worse than the one experienced by the Japanese Canadians.'[39] In the end, however, Landry's was a lone voice, because it would be more than a decade until Acadians from Atlantic Canada would jump on the apology bandwagon. Instead, the movement was largely advanced by two men with Acadian roots, one of whom lived in Louisiana and the other in Quebec. This reluctance in Atlantic Canada to take a confrontational stance is hardly surprising, given the long-standing Acadian reluctance to ascribe blame in regard to the deportation. Even the members of the Commission de l'Odyssée acadienne, who were willing to talk in somewhat more assertive terms about the deportation, focused upon issues of resistance, and not the need to confront the aggressor. The commission rejected the idea that Acadians had been victims, and while the sense of martyrdom had a long pedigree in Acadian culture, until the early years of the twenty-first century the Acadian tradition was one of quiet suffering, not public agitation.

In that context, throughout most of the 1990s, as the apology boom took off, the idea for securing one for the Acadians was largely the work of the Louisiana lawyer Warren Perrin, whom we saw earlier as a promoter of the cult of his forebear Beausoleil Broussard. The fact that Perrin was both advancing a story of resistance, on the one hand, and a tale of victimization, on the other, only underscored the distance between his efforts and mainstream Acadian thinking about the issue throughout the decade. In 1990 Perrin became an object of considerable curiosity, if not unconditional support, in *Acadie* when he produced a petition to the British government that sought to 'obtain an apology for the Acadian deportation.' In fact, Perrin's petition was less than clear that an apology per se was what he was seeking, in a sense underscoring the ambiguity inherent in some of these carefully worded documents. In a summary of the six issues at play, he requested an 'official' cancellation of the deportation order (which he claimed had never been annulled), the appointment of a panel to inquire into the deportation, the erection of a monument to 'memorialize the "end of the exile,"' and – perhaps most importantly – 'an acknowledgement that tragedies occurred.' Only at the very end of the document, in an appendix, was there a proposed apology that might contribute to 'the process of healing ... between the Crown and the Acadian people.'

There was much in Perrin's petition that would have found a receptive audience in *Acadie*: He claimed that Acadians had acquired rights as British citizens to remain neutral, and that their deportation under those circumstances lacked justification since war had yet to begin with France. As he put it, 'The exile of the Acadians during a time of peace is unprecedented in history.' Moreover, he chronicled the sins of Lieutenant Governor Lawrence who, 'acting without direct authorization of superiors and contrary to existing British law, ordered unmerciful punishment for all the Acadians, treating them as rebels and criminals. However, he lacked authority to so act.' On the other hand, Perrin was on less sure ground in terms of Acadian popular opinion when he declared unambiguously that 'the British [had] engaged in genocide.'[40]

Given the mixed signals that Perrin's petition would have sent to Acadians in Atlantic Canada, it is probably not surprising that it found most of its support in the United States. Louisiana and Maine, two states with significant Acadian populations, saw their legislatures pass resolutions in 1993 and 1994 respectively in support of the petition; and further support was expressed during the second Congrès mondial acadien, staged in Louisiana, where a mock trial was held regarding the virtues of the Perrin petition. Perhaps not surprisingly, 'the 15 judge panel unanimously ruled that the Petition should proceed to conclusion.' By contrast, however, by Perrin's own admission, 'the reaction was mixed in Canada, particularly among Acadians.'[41]

Among those in attendance at the Congrès mondial in Louisiana was the Bloc québécois MP Stéphane Bergeron, who like roughly a million residents of Quebec had Acadian roots. During his journey south, he had the opportunity to meet Warren Perrin, and returned to Canada with the thought that if two American states could offer a sign of recognition for the actions taken against the Acadians, why could Canada not do the same? Accordingly, without any consultation with Acadian leaders, he offered a private member's motion in 1999 that would have asked the Canadian government to seek an apology from the British Crown for the wrongs that had been done to Acadians.[42] Only a handful of such motions ever make it to the floor of the House for debate, and this was not one of those selected by a random draw, so that Bergeron's efforts barely made a ripple in *Acadie*.

By contrast, two years later Bergeron's luck was much better when motion M-241 was selected for debate, so that the issue of a formal apology to the Acadians could get a full airing. While the Bloc MP might have thought, naively, that his efforts to champion the Acadian cause would be welcomed by Acadian leaders, he was about to have a rude awakening, when he received a call from Euclide Chiasson, the president of the SNA, who was, in Bergeron's words, '*furieux.*'[43] This anger was evident when Chiasson wrote to the Bloc MP: 'Although, obviously I agree with the principle of the motion, I must tell you that we are indignant about the fact that it was brought forward without anyone having the courtesy to consult the Société nationale de l'Acadie beforehand.'[44] Nevertheless, Bergeron pressed on, and in his speech in March 2001, upon the introduction of his motion, described questions of responsibility for the deportation as 'still taboo and ubiquitous ... as they permeate the collective psyche of the Acadian people.'[45] Apparently, Bergeron was out to repair that psyche, even if the patient had not sought his help. This failure led one Liberal MP, Jeannot Castonguay, an Acadian from New Brunswick, to remark, 'One would think that such an initiative would be made in consultation with those concerned, namely the Acadians. That is the least the Bloc Québécois could do. But its logic does not work like that.'[46]

Between 2001 and 2004 Bergeron would present various resolutions regarding the deportation that were voted upon in the House of Commons, and the Acadian MPs who were Liberals opposed each and every one of them. Their opposition stood in contrast with the support that Bergeron received from Yvon Godin, the NDP deputy from the Acadian region of northeastern New Brunswick. At one point, in regard to the mildest of Bergeron's proposals, which made no reference to an apology and only sought 'to recognize officially the wrongs done to the Acadian people,' the opposition from the Acadian Liberals stood in stark contrast with the support from the leaders of all the opposition parties in the House of Commons: Alexa McDonough (NDP), Joe Clark (Progressive Conservative), Stockwell Day (Canadian Alliance), and – of course – Gilles Duceppe (Bloc québécois).

The leaders from English Canada had little difficulty in supporting Bergeron's motion once the references to an apology had been purged. While none of the party leaders participated in a debate about a private member's motion, Peter MacKay, who would take Clark's place as leader in 2003, observed that 'some people may be surprised to see an anglophone from Nova Scotia speak in favour of this motion. After all, some people may have been tempted to see it as an insult to the British crown, the federal government or even English Canada. However … it is clear that it is simply not the case. This motion does not target the federal government and is not an insult to the crown. After all, the crown did apologize to certain people for similar acts committed in its name. I support this motion … It is simply an act that recognizes what was a horrific attempt at ethnic cleansing.'[47]

In the end, however, it was impossible for the Acadian Liberals to be so philosophical. In part, to be sure, this was a reflection of the long-standing Acadian reluctance to revisit the deportation in a manner that might stir up old passions. From that perspective, it was easier for someone like MacKay (or even Bergeron) to support a recognition that wrongs had been done than for those who would have to live with the consequences. In addition, however, the Acadian Liberals could not accept a motion that was proposed by a Bloc québécois MP, seeing the act as one designed to advance that party's political agenda in Quebec more than one made out of any sincere effort to advance the interests of Acadians. Nevertheless, the Acadian Liberals feared that other members of their party might be attracted to an apparently innocuous motion, now that it had been shorn of the apology, and so just before the vote on the amended version of M-241, 'they were making their way through the Liberal backbenches, distributing a note [written in English] which asked their colleagues to vote against the motion. "The Acadian Caucus is asking you to support them in voting against the motion," They translated this note into English to be sure that everyone understood!'[48]

The Acadian Liberals managed to hold the fort and the amended motion was defeated in November 2001 by a margin of roughly thirty votes (in a House where the Liberal government had a roughly fifty-seat majority); the original motion that included reference to the apology was, not surprisingly, defeated by a much larger margin. The Acadian MPs may have thought that they had carried the day, but the fallout from the affair suggests that their efforts to adopt an older, more submissive (or less assertive) approach towards the deportation was not universally popular among their constituents. In the spring of 2001, before the Bergeron motion had received much public attention and before it had been amended, roughly six hundred Acadians responded to an online poll at the site capacadie.com, two-thirds of whom supported the idea that an apology was appropriate. In the aftermath of the defeat of M-241, the same question was asked once again, and while the percentage in favour of any apology remained constant, the number who responded increased three-fold. The Bergeron motion had increased interest in the question without weakening support for an apology, at least among those who were prepared to weigh in. This interest was also reflected by the steady stream of letters received by *L'Acadie Nouvelle* following the defeat of the Bergeron motion. The newspaper's editor-in-chief, Bruno Godin, remarked: "'I can't recall any subject generating so much interest.'"[49] Acknowledging that some damage control was in order, Sheila Copps, the minister of Canadian Heritage who, like Bergeron, had also gone public with her Acadian roots, suggested in the midst of the final stages of the debate over M-241 that the time had come to recognize 15 August as the Acadian national holiday.

In light of the Liberals' opposition to Bergeron's initiative, the historian Stéphane Savard has characterized them as having 'helped maintain conventional references to Acadian identity ... The elected Acadian politicians see themselves as the protectors of this [traditional] definition of identity, which dovetails with their efforts to make Acadians appear folkloric.' In contrast with these elected officials, Savard found that 'the elites connected with Acadian associations in New Brunswick tend to contest such conventional references to Acadian identity.'[50] In this binary conception, Savard viewed the leaders of the SNA as solidly behind Bergeron from the start, but this oversimplifies their role in the lead-up to the 250th anniversary of the deportation.

In fact, the SNA was far from supportive when it first caught wind of Bergeron's initiative. Meeting only two weeks after Bergeron introduced M-241 in the early spring of 2001, the organization's *conseil exécutif* was not sure how it should proceed, recognizing that 'some people support the request for an apology and others vehemently refuse to be associated with such an initiative. Still others would like to see the SNA forgive the Queen for having deported us, and there are also some who would like the SNA to concentrate its efforts in regard to the 250th anniversary of the deportation to show our pride in being Acadian.'[51] The SNA was torn as to how to deal with the memory of the deportation, and in this regard shared some of the uncertainty exhibited by the Commission de l'Odyssée acadienne. While the commission distanced itself from the Liberals by unambiguously supporting the idea that 'the governments responsible for the dispersal should recognize the wrongs done to the Acadians,' its members could not agree on 'the question of an apology and that of compensation.'[52]

By the time that the SNA assembled for its annual meeting in early June, support for Bergeron's apology motion had increased, aided by the Bloc MP's own efforts to explain his initiative to Acadians during a visit to *Acadie*. The annual meeting chose to endorse M-241 and the demand for the apology that was still part of the formula, but at the same time established a committee of experts that would consult with Acadians before making recommendations that could form the basis for future action. In other words, even if Bergeron received a measure of support from the SNA for his initiative, it was conditional, recognizing that 'the dossier is very delicate and divisive.'[53] The mandated committee was headed by Maurice Basque, whom we have seen in other contexts in regard to the celebration of the 400th anniversary of *Acadie*.

The Commission Basque received petitions that contained the perspectives of 140 Acadian individuals or organizations, only three of which were opposed to M-241. As to whether the authors of the submissions really wanted to receive an apology from the Crown, this cannot be established since I could not locate the original texts.[54] Instead, we have snippets from a few of the submissions that were included in the Basque commission's report, but these indicated support, not so much for an apology, but rather for 'a recognition of the wrongs experienced by the Acadians as a result of the *Grand Dérangement*.' In this regard, one submission indicated that 'such a recognition of a wrong from the past would have some positive consequences in terms of our self-image and, more importantly, in terms of our development. This would result in our people being accepted as equals by our English-speaking neighbours.'[55]

Building on these submissions, Basque and his colleagues concluded that 'the SNA should continue its efforts to secure an official recognition by the British crown that some wrongs were committed at the time of the deportation.' Conspicuous by its absence in this formulation was any insistence upon an apology, which thus underscores once more the distance between Bergeron and the Acadians. In place of such a reference to the past, the Basque group used the opportunity to ask that the pertinent governments look to the future by increasing 'their efforts to encourage developments that would permit the Acadian communities to catch up economically, socially and culturally.'[56]

Following upon the recommendations of the Basque commission, the SNA acted with some sense of urgency in November 2001, as the final debates over M-241 were set to take place. On the day before, the SNA's *conseil d'administration* expressed its 'support for motion M-241.' However, in the next breath, it observed in no uncertain terms: 'We have made our point of view as clear as possible, namely that the term "apology" is not absolutely necessary and that if it would cause no inconvenience, we would accept instead a recognition of the wrongs done to the Acadians.'[57] Bergeron obviously got the message. The SNA could not afford the public ridicule that would have resulted from its opposition to M-241, but it also could not support the demand for an apology, which was completely out of character for an organization that would obscure the deportation cross on its 250th anniversary logo. Accordingly, on the day after the SNA's board of directors expressed itself, Bergeron amended M-241, effectively removing the question of an apology from the political arena.

Following the defeat of this motion, Bergeron would return to pursue the matter in two further resolutions introduced in the House of Commons in 2003, both of which spoke of the wrongs that had been done to the Acadians, but without any mention of an apology. In a sense, by 2003 Bergeron had already served his purpose in having helped set the parameters for debate among Acadians regarding the expression of official recognition for the misdeeds of the eighteenth century. It had already been made clear during the debates in 2001 that with the opposition of the Acadian Liberals the Bergeron resolutions had no chance of succeeding. Accordingly, the significant discussions about how to proceed were initiated within *Acadie*, and not within the House of Commons.

In the immediate aftermath of the defeat of M-241, the SNA decided that it would take the initiative to write directly to the Queen, 'asking that she recognize the wrongs done to the Acadian people as a consequence of the deportations from 1755 to 1763.'[58] In several versions of letters that were being considered for transmission to Buckingham Palace, Euclide Chiasson adopted the tone that would dominate official Acadian discourse regarding the deportation up to the 250th anniversary. In a telling expression, he characterized 'the deportation as an unhealed wound which has not yet received the balm of reconciliation.' The goal was no longer to have the British government be revealed for the oppressor it had been; rather, the point of the exercise was for Acadians to receive some recognition of past wrongs so that they might 'turn the page (*tourner la page*) definitively on this tragic episode from our past.'[59]

For nearly a year, this effort at gentle persuasion appeared to be going nowhere, but during the summer of 2003 a breakthrough of sorts occurred when the SNA received a response from Buckingham Palace that the Queen 'as Sovereign of a constitutional monarchy' could only act upon the advice of 'her Canadian ministers.' Encouraged by this opening, Euclide Chiasson wrote to Stéphane Dion, in his capacity as president of the Privy Council in what turned out to be the last months of the Chrétien government: 'We ask your government, by the means that it finds appropriate, to recognize the wrongs that were done to the Acadians during the *Grand Dérangement* and to communicate this point of view to the Queen who would then be free to deal with the matter as Her Majesty sees fit.'[60]

Negotiations between the SNA and Ottawa followed, encouraged both by Chiasson's conciliatory tone (as opposed to that of the 'bad cop' Bergeron) and by the federal government's interest in getting issues connected with the deportation out of the way before the start of the festivities to mark the 400th anniversary of *Acadie*. As we saw in chapter 2, the Chrétien government was already taking a beating in the press over its foot-dragging on the 400th anniversary dossier and did not need any further fuel to be thrown on the fire. Accordingly, by the fall of 2003, drafts of a possible royal proclamation that would be approved by the federal government and signed by the governor general were shuffling back and forth between Ottawa and Dieppe.

Starting from the idea that, at the very least, there should be a recognition that wrongs had been committed, the SNA proposed a draft in early October that described in detail the trials and tribulations of the Acadians and provided an acknowledgment by the British Crown that there had been 'wrongs committed in its name against the Acadian people at the time of the Grand Dérangement.'[61] Ottawa was not prepared to go nearly that far, even though some recognition of wrongdoing against the

Acadians seemed necessary to allow them to *tourner la page*. When the final text was released two months later, on the next to last day of the Chrétien government, the word *torts* (wrongs) was conspicuous by its absence. Instead, the royal proclamation included a terse statement acknowledging 'the historical facts and the trials and suffering experienced by the Acadian people.' No one was about to be held responsible for these 'facts,' and so the proclamation included a statement that it did not 'constitute a recognition of legal or financial responsibility by the Crown.'[62]

Having suffered from a bad press in *Acadie* over the 400th anniversary celebrations, Sheila Copps, who as minister of Canadian Heritage was also responsible for this dossier, now had the opportunity to make the announcement of the proclamation her last official act as a cabinet minister, having already been informed that she would not be part of the Martin government that was about forty-eight hours away from taking office. It is unlikely, however, that her performance on this occasion won her many new Acadian friends. As she had done previously, she expressed her satisfaction with the proclamation in terms of her 'Acadian roots,' which only seemed to be trotted out on politically useful occasions. More substantively, many Acadians must have puzzled over what was meant by her formulaic reference to how 'the proclamation will allow Acadians to *tourner la page* and make it possible for them to reconcile themselves, once and for all, after 250 years.'[63] They would have justifiably wondered exactly with whom, or with what, this reconciliation was supposed to take place.

In the end, if the Liberals wanted to get the issue out of the way before the celebratory events for 2004 began, it also appeared that the SNA was ready to move on, or to employ the much-used expression that found its way into the royal proclamation, it wanted to 'turn the page on this dark chapter of [Acadian] history.'[64] The idea that the Crown might apologize having been dispensed with, there was now not even an acknowledgment that any wrongs had been committed by anyone in particular. Trying to sell the proclamation to a population that had become sensitized to the issue during the years since Stéphane Bergeron had first raised it, Euclide Chiasson explained to *L'Acadie Nouvelle*, 'In making reference to the historical facts, there is a description of the wrongs that were committed against the Acadian people at the time of the Deportation; these are now recognized as historical facts. Maybe this is not the vocabulary that everyone would have liked, but it all comes to the same thing.'[65] At the carefully orchestrated event in Ottawa at which the proclamation was officially made public, Chiasson continued to speak in similar terms, noting, 'What we are celebrating today is not a re-writing of history, nor is it an effort to correct history. Rather, we are celebrating a recognition of a chapter from our history.'[66]

At that same event Chiasson indicated that he was pleased to be in the company of individuals who had been hostile to the various versions of the Bergeron resolution. 'Individuals who were long opposed to this effort are now supporting it.' Conspicuous in this regard was the Liberal MP Dominic LeBlanc, who had minced no words in regard to motion M-241. Now, however, he was supportive because a resolution had been found that did not require that we go 'on bended knee to a distant Queen.'[67] Of course, if LeBlanc's opposition to M-241 had only been based upon the question of an apology, he could have supported the amended version that had only referred to 'the wrongs done to the Acadian people.' In fact, LeBlanc must have felt victorious given that the wording in the royal proclamation referred only to 'historical facts' and never to 'wrongs.'

In the end, the royal proclamation did not come even close to achieving what apologies for past wrongs can produce, namely, a sense of 'moral restitution, offering recipients something of non-material value as a way to make good for an injury, loss, or damage.'[68] In the absence of the slightest recognition that any wrongs had occurred, the proponents of the proclamation referred vaguely to the therapeutic value of a reconciliation with a past in which no one was responsible for the deportation of the Acadians. Michel Cyr, Chiasson's successor as president of the SNA, spoke precisely in those terms when he explained to me that the proclamation was a means of achieving 'a concrete reconciliation with our past.'[69]

Similar expressions about the need for Acadians to close the door on the deportation came from those who found value in somehow forgetting about the *Grand Dérangement*, however unlikely that might have been. In this context, there was Herménégilde Chiasson's tortured explanation, cited at length at the start of this chapter, that 'we should never forget, yet we have to forget ...' In the same spirit, the Université de Moncton political scientist Chedly Belkhodja, in an interview for a series on Radio-Canada on the occasion of the 250th anniversary of the Deportation, observed, 'I believe that forgetting allows individuals to create a certain distance [from the past] ... There is a type of forgetting that can be helpful.'[70] These comments provoked the ire of Carol Doucet, a columnist for *L'Acadie Nouvelle*, who wrote: 'He thinks that talking too much about the deportation prevents us from developing as a people. For my part, I think the opposite. It seems to me that keeping in mind what happened in 1755 has provided us with a certain power, a certain determination. If we were able to survive that moment, there can't be anything to stop us now.'[71]

Faced with its hollow rhetoric about the need to move on, voices emerged to oppose the royal proclamation, some of which were easier for the leaders of *Acadie* to ignore than others. For instance, there was a current of thought that would settle for nothing less than an admission that genocide had been committed against the Acadians. In 2002, at a time when the SNA's efforts seemed stalled, five Acadian activists published the *Manifeste Beaubassin,* so called because it was issued on the anniversary of the date in 1755 on which the British loaded residents from the settlement of the same name onto ships to send them into exile. The authors demanded a public statement that 'the British authorities were responsible for a genocide ... It is necessary to recognize that the Acadian people were the victims of a crime against humanity and to recognize the guilt of those responsible for the deportation, taking into account the cultural, material, and human losses endured by our ancestors.'[72] Writing in a similar spirit after the proclamation had been announced, Achille Hubert described the deportation as 'a crime of genocide' and the royal proclamation as 'a deliberate maneouver to con the Acadian people ... It is only an empty shell. It is an effort to deceive Acadians and to make them forget the real wrongs that were committed against their ancestors, wrongs whose repercussions are still making themselves felt on the Acadian and Canadian psyches.'[73]

Euclide Chiasson found it easy to push aside such criticisms, observing that 'there are some people who would only be happy if the Queen was forced to climb the steps of the Oratoire Saint-Joseph on her knees.'[74] Nevertheless, there were also opponents of the proclamation who did not want to demonize the British as much as they sought some genuine recognition not merely of 'facts' that had occurred, but of wrongs that had been committed. In this regard, Jean-François Thibault observed that the wording of the proclamation was telling in its reference to the opportunity that would now exist for Acadians to 'turn the page on this dark moment from their past.' Thibault was troubled by the use of the third-person plural modifier: 'From *their* past! But wouldn't we expect that it would equally be part of the history of the British crown? ... This use of the possessive adjective effectively changed the sense of the rest of the Proclamation because the burden of the deportation has been placed entirely on the shoulders of Acadians.'[75]

Still other critics shared the same goals as supporters of the royal proclamation who sought collective therapy for Acadians by allowing them to *tourner la page.* Nevertheless, these critics doubted that this particular document was capable of achieving that end. For instance, writing in the letter-to-the-editor section of *L'Acadie Nouvelle* (which had much commentary about the proclamation), Charles Emmrys, a psychotherapist from Moncton and a signatory to the *Manifeste Beaubassin,* was able to speak directly to the alleged therapeutic value of the proclamation by referring to his own patients who have to deal with instances of sexual abuse. He observed that they are often tempted to repress thinking about such incidents: 'But denying the truth has its own costs. For the victim of abuse, the price is to lose a connection with their own experience and to any understanding of their own existence.' Emmrys tried to get his patients to recognize what had happened to them, and thought that Acadians needed to do the same: 'It is crucial to call things by their names.'[76]

The theme of the unresolved psychological trauma of the deportation also figured in other representations on the 250th anniversary. In her documentary film *Le souvenir nécessaire,* Renée Blanchar visited a New York City psychologist, Flora Hogman, to see whether Acadians suffered from their long-standing refusal to talk openly about the deportation. Hogman commented on the unwillingness of Holocaust victims (including her own mother) to reflect on their trauma, but who needed to do so to 'maintain a connection with their past.' Much like Emmrys, she suggested that Acadians needed to confront their own tragic past in some meaningful way.[77] Following along the same lines, Claude Le Bouthillier (a psychologist) populated his novel *Complices du silence?* with characters suffering from various psychological problems. Leading the way was Poséidon, who remarked at one point: 'It's Acadie that drives me crazy ... To see so much misery, so much double dealing, ordinary people being exploited, a determination to be silent [on the question of the deportation], that disgusts me.'[78] Ultimately, Poséidon's salvation came when he unearthed evidence (buried under the statue of Evangeline at Grand-Pré) that led to apologies and reparations, announced on the 250th anniversary, not only from the British, but also the Americans, the French, and even the Vatican. In a personal note at the end of the novel, Le Bouthillier described it as his 'contribution so the wounds caused ... by the deportation and its consequences might be healed.' For these reasons, he would settle for nothing short of 'apologies and compensation from the British crown.'[79]

The discussion about how Acadians might best achieve their collective liberation from the burden of the deportation seemed strained, particularly given the considerable evidence of increased Acadian self-confidence at the time of the 250th anniversary of the deportation. It would not have been obvious to a visitor to *Acadie*, just after the 400th anniversary of its birth, that this was a people in need of healing. To be sure, the rhetoric of therapy reflected larger currents of thought at the turn of the century about the need for individuals (and by extension groups) to talk openly about their traumas. In the specific case of the Acadians, as we saw in the previous chapter, there was a long history of refusal to face up to all the dimensions of the *Grand Dérangement*, and so the discussion about the possibility of an apology (or even a recognition of wrongs) encouraged Acadians to take part in an unprecedented conversation. However, there really was no closure in this case, when the royal proclamation failed to provide either any clear statement that wrongs had been committed or any identification of the responsible parties. The leaders of the SNA had hoped that the proclamation would allow Acadians to *tourner la page*. However, as Paul-Pierre Bourgeois of Grande-Digue, New Brunswick, put it in a letter to *L'Acadie Nouvelle*: If anyone had recognized responsibility for the deportation, 'I would have really felt that a page of history had been turned.' However, when no one came forward, Bourgeois remarked: 'But, my word, this page is turning out to be too heavy to turn!'[80]

Remembrance Day

In addition to its carefully crafted statement that avoided ascribing responsibility for the deportation, the royal proclamation also declared that, starting in 2005, there would an annual 'Journée de commémoration du Grand Dérangement.' As Robert Viau has observed, in the absence of any 'recognition that wrongs had been committed ... the principal goal of the Proclamation was to establish a day of commemoration,' a fact that is confirmed by the proclamation's official title, which makes no reference to the 'historical facts' that were being confirmed and which focuses exclusively on 'designating July 28 of every year' as such a day of commemoration.[81] The choice of this particular date was a red flag for some such as Jean Gaudet, the organizer of the *pèlerinage historique* described at the start of the chapter, who believed that the real deportation had begun on 5 September 1755 when the residents of Grand-Pré learned of their fate and not 28 July when the deportation document was signed. Perhaps to pay lip service to such concerns, the proclamation (perhaps a bit too cleverly) was only to come into effect on 5 September 2004, with the first 'day of commemoration' to occur the following 28 July.

Canadian Heritage recognized during the period that the royal proclamation was being negotiated that 'the date that is better known as the
start of the deportation is 5 September.'[82] Nevertheless, Ottawa decided
to choose an administrative date, instead of one that spoke to the actual
rounding up of the Acadians. Even with this toning down of the potentially inflammatory aspects of the commemorative day, Canadian
Heritage explored the possibility of further marginalizing the deportation by making no mention of it in invitations to the event at which the
proclamation was revealed to the public. While a first version invited the
recipient to attend a reception 'to mark the creation of A Day of
Commemoration of the Great Upheaval,' some of the bureaucrats in
Canadian Heritage tried, albeit unsuccessfully, to have the wording
changed so that the reception would instead be 'celebrating the vitality
of the Acadian community.'[83] If the only concrete contribution of the
proclamation was the day of remembrance and if that day was trivialized,
then what was left?

Given these beginnings, one might have expected that the first
'Journée de commémoration' would be a sanitized event, and while
there were certainly some efforts in that direction, it would be an over-
simplification to see the day in such terms. Rather, the day's activities
reflected the various voices that had emerged within *Acadie* on the occasion of the 250th anniversary of the deportation, in part, because neither
the federal government nor the SNA were able to exercise complete control over the proceedings. Accordingly, 28 July 2005 became the opportunity, as we have seen, for the unveiling of the first monuments produced by the Commission de l'Odyssée acadienne, with their references
to the resistance of Acadians, in the morning at Dieppe and in the afternoon in Halifax.

Next on the agenda was the rededication of the Croix de la déportation at its new location near where Acadians from Grand-Pré boarded
the ships that took them into exile. This event packed a punch, since it
was set to coincide with the ringing of church bells across Atlantic Canada
and Quebec at 17h55, followed by a minute of silence. Writing in *L'Acadie
Nouvelle*, Steve Hachey found that 'the emotion was intense. With heads
lowered, the people in attendance solemnly remembered their forebears
and the suffering that they endured during this difficult time.'[84] The actual ceremony marking the relocation of the cross was accompanied by
predictable speeches by officials from both Parks Canada (which owned
the site) and the SNA. However, the event transcended the obligatory

6.5 Rededication of the Deportation Cross, Horton Landing, 28 July 2005
(photograph by François Gaudet; with permission of
Société nationale de l'Acadie)

references to the need for Acadians to have some reconciliation with their
past, when a genuine act of reconciliation took place with the participation of Gordon Haliburton, whose own family had come to Nova Scotia as
Planters. Haliburton spoke from the heart, avoiding any formulaic apology for an event that his forbears did not initiate. While he acknowledged
the Acadians' pain and was pleased to take part in a ceremony that commemorated the deportation, he observed that the 'Acadians' plight was
none of the Planters' doing.' The honesty of Haliburton's comments constituted a genuine act of reconciliation.[85]

Finally, the scene shifted to the Grand-Pré site for the truly official
event under the supervision of the SNA. Weeks before this event took
place, it had become – like everything else connected with this anniversary – a matter for public debate. In early June the SNA announced its
formal plans, which did not include any opportunity for public recognition that the day of remembrance only existed because of the royal proclamation. Stéphane Bergeron, who could claim some responsibility for
this special day, remarked: 'I find that very odd.' Given the history of the

dossier that had seen an apology morph into a recognition of wrongs, and then finally a recognition of facts accompanied by a day of remembrance, Bergeron found the exclusion of any reference to the proclamation 'disturbing. This simply confirms that the Proclamation was essentially no more than an opportunity to defuse the pressure [for an apology].'[86] Coming from a different direction, the lawyer David Le Gallant, who would also have preferred an apology over the anodyne recognition of wrongs, observed: 'The Proclamation is a fraud. For my part, I am so opposed to it that I am content if it is not read.'[87]

While there could be objection to various aspects of the message communicated by the official event, no one could really argue about it being held at Grand-Pré, given the site's iconic status in regard to deportation memory for over a century. On their way to the area where the festivities would take place, spectators passed through an interpretive centre that had opened in 2003 so as to be ready to welcome the visitors who came during the following year for the Congrès mondial acadien. Visitors to the centre first viewed a film that introduced them to the site, and while the film claimed that it sought to avoid traditional depictions of early *Acadie* as a paradise destroyed by the *Grand Dérangement*, it did little to unseat those images, since all the pre-deportation Acadians appeared to be happy peasants: well fed and amicably working for the common good. In presenting the deportation, the most powerful image was that of a child begging on the streets of an American town. Departing from the *Evangeline* story that ends in exile, the film closed with the return of Acadians to the promised land to build the *nouvelle Acadie*, thus playing into the idea that this new society was built by returned deportees and not those who had escaped the grasp of the British. On the face of it, these were people ready to *tourner la page*.

After viewing the film, visitors who made their way through the permanent exhibit found a somewhat more complicated view of the past. As one interpretive panel noted: 'Although often depicted as a tranquil paradise, Acadie was often a battleground.' Starting from this premise, the exhibit tried to trace the tangled stories of the Acadians, the Mi'kmaq, and the agents of French and British imperial ambitions, so that pre-deportation *Acadie* became much more than the story of Acadians. Turning to the deportation itself, there was a particular focus on the issue of whether Evangeline was an appropriate symbol, given that she had been the creation of an American poet, and the exhibit ends, alluding to the work of Antonine Maillet, noting the search by Acadians for more 'authentic' figures of their own to celebrate. However, in making reference to those, such as Pélagie-la-Charette, Maillet's character who returned to *Acadie* (aided by Beausoleil Broussard) with her wheelbarrow, the exhibit, a bit like the film, offered a limited range of possibilities and celebrated the return of the deportees, paying little attention to those who either resisted the British or avoided deportation.[88] Many of those who built the *nouvelle Acadie* did not need to return because they had never entirely left. In any event, the story of return would be the centre-piece of a dramatic recreation of Acadian history presented on the evening of 28 July.

Before this spectacle, the SNA had arranged for speeches by representatives of the various parties connected in one way or another with the deportation. Opening the evening was Keptin John Joe Sark, of the Mi'kmaq Grand Council, who had been a frequent speaker at commemorative events marking the 400th anniversary of *Acadie*. At many of these, it was commonplace for both Sark and the Acadians with whom he shared the stage to make reference to the long history of ties between the two people that included the years of the deportation, during which the Mi'kmaq had often befriended the Acadians. On this occasion, Sark made precisely that point. Strangely, however, in 2005 the aboriginal presence on commemorative stages was minimal, and their contribution rarely mentioned, until the speech by the president of the SNA later this evening, in the various texts produced either by the SNA or by the Commission de l'Odyssée acadienne.[89] First Nations people apparently existed at the time of contact, but had largely disappeared from the scene 150 years later. To be fair, such marginalizing of aboriginal people from the narrative of Canadian history after the story of contact was told has a long history in its own right, which transcends the presentation of the past by Acadians.

Sark was followed to the podium by a representative of the British high commissioner, who expressed satisfaction that the Acadians had 'turned a page.' Of course, there were those who would have liked the British to have turned a page as well, and this false note was only reinforced by the fact, as Paul-Pierre Bourgeois put it in a letter to *L'Acadie Nouvelle*, that the high commissioner 'did not have the decency to show up himself and instead sent along a banal statement that placed responsibility on the Acadians.' Bourgeois also commented on the speech of the representative standing in for the American ambassador, whose formulaic reference to the tragedy of the deportation did not mention that 'the colonial authorities in New England had played a significant role at the time in executing the Acadian genocide.'[90]

With these introductory speeches out of the way, the main event of the evening could begin, a presentation of Acadian history conceived by Daniel Castonguay, the artistic director of Le Pays de la Sagouine, the Acadian theme park in New Brunswick where I had seen another version of Acadian history in 2004.[91] Staged on a large field with the commemorative church and the statue of Evangeline in the background, Castonguay's spectacle employed a large (and talking) willow to serve as narrator. The Grand-Pré grounds are strewn with willows, the most visible traces that remain there of life from before the deportation.

At the outset, the willow was happy to have taken root in Acadian soil; and the tree was soon joined by actors, young girls dressed in white, who represented the arrival of Acadians. The willow expressed its joy for the presence of 'men, women, and especially children who played with me.'[92] Before the arrival of the Acadians, First Nations people made only a fleeting appearance on a large video screen, almost making it seem as if the Acadians had been the aboriginal inhabitants of this land. The absence of the native population left a large void, but one that had become commonplace during 2005. In any event, the Acadians managed to live in an 'idyllic land,' an image supported by the virginal purity of the performers. However, this golden age was short-lived, as the willow was soon buffeted by 'some strong winds which were shaking everything up.' The arrival of the deportation was marked by fireworks and by the plea from the willow (repeated five times) that 'We must resist (*Nous devons résister*).' As Castonguay put it in his scenario: 'The willow, our narrator, holds on to the soil, trying to resist. He is afraid of being uprooted, of being swept away by the winds, and ultimately disappearing.' The willow, a tree with deep roots, was perfectly suited to represent the Acadians, who could not easily be displaced. In addition, the use of the term 'resist' reinforced the same expression that had been front and centre on the monuments unveiled earlier that day, although the term was used here very differently.

The devastation of the deportation was communicated by means of lighting that made it appear that the church (itself modelled after the church destroyed in 1755) was being burned down. The willow then reported that he had seen ships arriving to take away the Acadians, and one of the children hugged it before departing. The physical appearance of the willow was transformed, becoming 'rickety and decrepit; cracks were visible in its bark, lesions caused by the memory of what was happening.' Then, in a very long segment of the spectacle, the willow read out the names of the families deported, each represented by one of

6.6 Recreation of the Deportation Cross, 250th Anniversary of Grand
Dérangement: Grand-Pré, 28 July 2005 (photograph by François Gaudet;
with permission of Société nationale de l'Acadie)

the girls who left a lamp, so that when the procession was done the Croix
de la déportation had been created yet again. The purity of the performers together with the display of the cross played on older notions that the
Acadians were on a providential mission to spread Christianity.

Following a moment of silence for the deportees, the traditional nature of the tale continued when the post-deportation story was begun by
the singing of 'Évangéline,' which tells the saga of the Acadian heroine
in terms faithful to Longfellow. Emerging from behind the statue of
Evangeline, the singer Isabelle Roy was also dressed in white, reinforcing
the purity of the subject of the song. When she finished the piece, whose
last stanza begins 'There are still people who live today in your land,' the
figures who had been sent off into exile began to return and took away
the candles that had formed the cross. While the willow – now happy
once again – read the names of the families that would constitute *Acadie
moderne*, the candles were repositioned, this time to form the outlines of
Atlantic Canada. With the obliteration of the cross, the logo of the SNA

for the 250th anniversary had, in a sense, been recreated. An older version of the deportation story, grounded in Catholicism, was gone, replaced by a map that defined the territory now watched over by the SNA. As in the new interpretative centre, the Acadians had returned from their exile.

Following some remarks by a junior representative of the Canadian government, which like the Americans and the British could not manage to send a senior official, even though it was Ottawa that had declared this day of commemoration, Michel Cyr, the SNA president, then took the stage and reinforced the message that his group had been advancing since taking up the dossier several years earlier.[93] Much like the spectacle that had just been presented – and unlike the story of resistance told by others – Cyr spoke of a people that had been 'deported, dispossessed, hunted down, sent into exile, persecuted, and forced to disappear.' Nevertheless, the Acadians could not be broken, and so 'what might have been the last chapter, turned out only to be one episode – however difficult – but not the final one in a history that we continue to live.' Cyr then returned to the themes that his organization had been advancing for years, and so he called this first day of remembrance one of 'reappropriation, reconciliation, and forgiveness,' although as in other expressions of this message it was not clear who was being reconciled with what. As for the reference to 'pardon,' it begged further questions about who was being forgiven. Ultimately, inevitably, Cyr observed that 'We turned the page long ago.'[94]

The End of the Road

Isabelle Roy returned with the actors, this time forming a choir, to sing Ave Maris Stella, thus bringing the first 'Journée de commémoration du Grand Dérangement' to a close. In the days that immediately followed there would be some much smaller events, including a march led by Jean Gaudet from the new site of the Cross of the Deportation to the Grand-Pré grounds, a procession that would be repeated later that summer at the end of the *pèlerinage historique* that reached Horton Landing on 5 September, the day that Gaudet and others always thought should have been the focus for the memory of Acadians on this 250th anniversary.[95] Following Gaudet's September procession (described at the very start of this book), there were some modest events attended by small crowds at Grand-Pré, certainly nothing to compare with the carefully orchestrated spectacle in July. Among the activities at the end of that

Labour Day weekend, there was the reading of the deportation order from the steps of the reconstructed church at the same time that it would have been read exactly 250 years earlier. However, by then most Acadians had moved on to other things.

It would have been relatively easy for me to have closed this account of the commemorative events of 2004–5 here. When the activities of 5 September 2005 were done, so was my journey through Acadian memory. I retraced my steps back over the three kilometres of the Gaudet procession, put the keys in the rental car I had left at the starting point, went one last time to the Halifax airport, and returned home. However, it would not have been fair to end with a cynical dismissal of the mainstream approach to the deportation that found its way on this anniversary into the royal proclamation. Critics (and even this historian) might be able to find fault with the proclamation, and yet it obviously meant something to many Acadians on the 250th anniversary of the deportation.

An on-line poll on the website Capacadie.com, posted just before the announcement of the proclamation in late 2003, asked visitors whether they would be 'satisfied if the British crown officially recognized the wrongs committed against the Acadians during the Deportation.' Even though the question was based on the false premise that some recognition of British wrongdoing would be forthcoming, the results still reflected something of the mood of 'ordinary' Acadians. Only about a quarter of respondents indicated that they felt the need to hold out for an official apology. The remaining responses were evenly divided between those who were content to be able to officially 'tourner la page' and those who thought the whole affair had been a waste of time that had consumed energy that might have been better 'invested in regard to something more constructive.' Even the respondents in this last category showed little interest in holding out for an apology and wanted, in their own way, to turn the page.[96]

The sense that the time had come to move on may not have had the same impact as some dramatic admission of guilt from a representative of the perpetrators, but it obviously meant something to those who were present at the ceremony announcing the proclamation late in 2003. *L'Acadie Nouvelle*'s Steve Hachey, whose reporting on such matters did not tend to be overly sentimental, observed that 'strong emotions were evident during the ceremony. When the Acadian national anthem, Ave Maris Stella, was played ... a number of those on hand could not help but cry.'[97] This reaction is perhaps not surprising since the sense that the time had come for Acadians to *tourner la page* had had some currency in Acadian society well before Stéphane Bergeron began his campaign in Parliament.

Witness, for instance, the considerable popular success for the band Grand Dérangement, which released in 1998 its first album, entitled appropriately *Tournons la page*. In the prologue to the album there is reference to a new *Grand Dérangement* by which young Acadians will confidently look to the future, having 'turned the page on a distant past.' This same attitude was pursued in the album's first song, 'Y a jamais eu de Grand Dérangement (There never was a Grand Dérangement)' which, again, imagines a day when young Acadians will have 'swept away the burdens of their past.' Writing about this song, Robert Proulx has observed, 'It's as if the narrator was trying to convince himself that the depressing episode of the Deportation had never occurred or, at least, to relegate it to a past that no longer has to be considered and which no longer causes any suffering. As in the prologue [to the album], the emphasis is placed on the present and the future.'[98] Speaking on his own behalf, the composer of the song, Michel Thibault, indicated to me what he had hoped to achieve:

> I wanted to destroy with this song the idea that we are perpetually in a state of upheaval. I believe that it we Acadians refuse to accept the idea of a GRAND DÉRANGEMENT, this refusal will liberate us and allow us to accept our past without this burden of seeing all of the past in negative terms, a sentiment evoked by the term 'GRAND DÉRANGEMENT.' The word 'déportation' is hard enough to swallow without trying to make it even more funereal by attaching some melodramatic euphemisms!'[99]

Most Acadians were not interested in returning to the deportation in order to develop a sense of their resistance to British oppression, let alone to insist that Lawrence's successors should be now held accountable. They did not want to (and could not) forget the deportation, but they seemed ready to press forward. Given the long history of their own sense that the deportation had been somehow providential, this was no small change in their relationship to the past.

Epilogue:
Legacies

After having logged thousands of kilometres, spoken with hundreds of people involved with commemorative events, and partaken of more than fifty ceremonies or exhibits inspired by the Acadian anniversaries of 2004-5, I had finally come to the end of this journey. Along the way, I had the opportunity to see how even today the past still has the power to transform. On several commemorative occasions, I was on hand when an audience's presuppositions about the past, and by extension the present, were significantly altered. I also witnessed cases in which individuals involved with presenting the past were changed when they were brought into contact with other interpreters from different backgrounds whom they would never have otherwise met. For a historian who has tended to be cynical about the uses of the past, those moments were nothing short of inspirational. Taking the relationship between power and the past in another direction, I also witnessed less uplifting instances when the version of history that was presented to the public was determined by those who wield influence. There were times when it was painfully clear where Acadians (but others as well) fit into the Canadian pecking order. With these thoughts in mind, what follow, then, are some reflections on my travels on the road of Acadian memory, focusing particularly upon the legacies of the various anniversaries that had come and gone.

French Lessons

Various connections between power and the past were made abundantly clear to me when I visited the single activity (either event or exhibit) that absorbed the greatest amount of public funding over the 2004–5 commemorative cycle. As we saw in chapter 2, while the Canadian government invested $10 million in activities across Atlantic Canada to mark the 400th anniversary of the founding of *Acadie*, it placed even more funds – $18 million to be exact – in a series of projects in France managed by the Canadian embassy in Paris, the largest of which, a temporary exhibit at the Cité des sciences et de l'industrie in Paris, absorbed over $4 million for its nine-month run. While Acadian leaders (as well as English speakers promoting commemorative events near the sites of the Dugua settlements) railed against the glaring discrepancy in funding for these two envelopes, the federal government showed relatively little concern. Just as the Chrétien government seemed indifferent to the demands of Acadian leaders when they lobbied for some recognition of the wrongs committed against them at the time of the deportation, so too did the same government blithely ignore demands that the 2004 anniversary should focus upon the Acadian past instead of being used as a tool for cultivating ties between France and Canada. By insisting that 1604 had marked the beginning of four hundred years of ties between the two countries, Ottawa pushed the specific pertinence of *Acadie* on this occasion out of the picture; but perhaps this was to be expected for a population of 300,000 people, the vast majority of whom had been long-time loyal supporters of the federal Liberals and so could afford to be taken for granted.

One of the goals of the Canada-France 2004 program was to show 'Canada's emergence as a vibrant, modern nation,' and in this regard the exhibit at the Cité des sciences played a particularly crucial role.[1] Advertising plastered across Paris showed a cuddly polar bear wearing a headset. The caption read: 'In Canada, even the bears are connected!' The idea that Canada was a technologically advanced country was then reinforced when visitors arrived at the entrance to the *Canada vraiment* exhibit, where they were handed a BlackBerry-type device, a minisat, to guide them through a labyrinth of screens that could provide information about the modern Canada that existed four hundred years after the arrival of Dugua. As I made my way through the exhibit, I would beam a signal to various screens to learn more about Canada in terms of its resources, technology, and diverse population. In this last regard, the exhibit was inspired a *Globe and Mail* series 'Meet the New Canada' that ran during the summer of 2003.[2] Emphasizing the modernity of Canada, it focused on Canadians in their twenties 'as they worked, played, loved, married, struggled and participated in public and private life.' *Canada vraiment* followed the *Globe*'s lead by only featuring young people in its videos.

Each time that I beamed a signal at a screen, my selection was recorded electronically, so that I could relive my virtual experience once back

E.1 Le Canada vraiment: Postcard advertising French exhibition
(Cité des sciences et de l'industrie, Paris)

home, and readers can do the same by going to the address in this note.[3] At the very end of the exhibit, I was invited to stand in front of a Canadian backdrop of my choosing to create a postcard with my image, which readers can also produce by clicking on the appropriate link. The technology that made all of this possible was one of the points of the exhibit, which was designed to 'make the [Canadian-developed] product commercially viable.'[4] In this regard, the inspector general for the Department of Foreign Affairs and International Trade found in 2005 that while there had been some short-term benefits, 'prospects for economic spin-offs remain limited because the exhibition is over and it did not create enough interest for a travelling exhibition.'[5] Be that as it may, it is starting from a false premise to think that this exhibit had anything to do with the past, let alone with the beginnings of *Acadie*.

Fifty thousand visitors came to the exhibit, roughly half the number that had been hoped for at the outset. Some of the problems in drawing in the crowds were technological, since there were traffic jams at the entrance owing to the frequent inaccessibility of the minisats due to some 1200 cases of 'equipment breakdown.'[6] As for those who made it inside, there were complaints about the excessive reliance upon showing off new technology that probably kept still others from coming. A follow-up study indicated that 'many individuals felt that the exhibition suffered from the fact that too much importance was granted to technological development, to the detriment of content.'[7] This conclusion was confirmed by some of the remarks recorded in the exhibit's *Livre d'or*, the book made available to visitors for their comments.

While there were certainly visitors who enjoyed *Canada vraiment*, many others found the experience painful. Since I had spent a considerable part of my time at the exhibit trying to aim the infrared beam from the minisat at the target that would trigger one of the screens, I could sympathize with the visitor who observed: 'I really did not see the point of your minisat ... I think I would have been just as happy sitting on my sofa, watching a good news report on the television.' Others commented upon the emphasis on technology that could not take the place of interesting content. In this regard, one visitor asked, 'Have you overemphasized form, at the expense of substance? High tech is not the answer to everything.'[8] Given these complaints, it is perhaps not surprising that the exhibition, according to a follow-up study conducted by the Cité des sciences, had very little impact on visitors' perceptions of Canada. Even though the point of *Canada vraiment* had been to emphasize Canada's modernity, 'when ... visitors were questioned in discussion groups a few days after the visit, the traditional perceptions (nature, cold, open spaces) were restated.'[9]

These complaints would have relatively little pertinence to larger issues about the presentation of the past to the public, were it not for the fact that the French collaborators from the Cité des sciences, with whom the officials in the Canadian embassy worked, had suggested, albeit unsuccessfully, that the exhibit needed objects to engage its visitors. In the end, the Canadian officials should have listened. As Roy Rosenzweig and David Thelen have shown in their landmark work *The Presence of the Past*, museums are by far the source for understanding the past that is most trusted by Americans (with history professors far behind), precisely because they allow visitors to feel that through artefacts they can come into direct contact with an earlier time.[10] Rosenzweig and Thelen surveyed over eight hundred Americans about how they engaged with the past, one of whom 'trusted museums because by displaying objects "for everybody to see," the museum "isn't trying to present you with any points of view... You need to draw your own conclusions."' Another one of their respondents, having visited a dinosaur museum, proclaimed,

'"The bones are right there ... the bones don't lie."'[11] Needless to say, those bones did not get there on their own, and respondents who downplayed the intermediary role that curators had played in interpreting the past for them were, in a sense, not seeing the whole picture. Nevertheless, they believed – and this is no small thing – that they had come closer to the past, as opposed to the visitors to the *Canada vraiment* exhibit, who did not seem to feel that they had come closer to anything.

The preference on the part of Canadian embassy officials for technology over objects was also evident in another major project financed out of the Canada-France 1604–2004 envelope, the construction (for a Canadian investment of $2 million) of the Maison Champlain in Brouage, the birthplace of Dugua's cartographer. Brouage already was a historic site of some importance, a walled town that spoke to its splendours from early modern times. Champlain came out of that world, and Nathalie Fiquet, the site's curator, had hoped that it might be possible to take advantage of the 400th anniversary of the founding of Quebec City in 2008 to develop a museum that spoke directly to Champlain's achievements. While the French were prepared to wait, the Canadian government, oblivious to the fact that Acadians would not have been interested in promoting Champlain upon their own anniversary in 2004, provided the funding for a museum that opened during the fall of what should have been Dugua's year.[12]

Much like the *Canada vraiment* exhibit, the permanent one at the Maison Champlain lacks any objects, this in spite of the fact that there is an archaeological dig going on immediately behind the building. In fact, during my visit there, I discovered some objects on display on a separate floor, nearly hidden from view. As for the exhibit, it amounts to a video presentation that visitors can watch on one of the flat screens scattered across an austere room, which parallels the austere exterior that does not even bear the name of the Maison. Talking heads present the story of Brouage and Champlain, following an outline that regularly appears on screen, which left me feeling that I was attending a clumsy PowerPoint lecture. If the visitor were to watch the entire video, it would have taken over five hours, interrupted at times by the infusion of scents, but they hardly make this exhibit come alive. As a commentator in *Le Devoir* asked, 'What is the point of travelling so far to a superb walled town in order to be locked up in the dark for such a long period of time? This exhibition could just as easily have been presented in Canada; it could even have been watched at home with a DVD.'[13] 🖥

E.2 Maison Champlain: Brouage, France (photograph by the author)

The final major exhibition that was constructed in France with the aid of the federal government spoke much more positively, not only to the power of the object, but also to the power of place. The Maison de l'Émigration française au Canada opened in 2006 with the help of an investment of $500,000 from the Canadian embassy. The museum is located in Tourouvre, a town in Basse-Normandie, which is a magnet for Quebec tourists who seek out the *maisons de familles souches* (houses of founding Quebec families) that are scattered in the immediate vicinity. Given this *québécois* connection, reinforced by a Quebec flag at the entrance, the museum really tells the story of the settlement of the St Lawrence valley. As a result, references to *Acadie* are rare, but the marginalization of Acadians on their anniversary should by now be expected. What set this museum apart from the exhibits in Paris and Brouage, however, was the presence of objects that provided the possibility for the visitor to make some connection with the past. This was done most effectively in a room dedicated to explaining the contact between the French and the First Nations people. At each of the four corners of the room, there were screens standing at right angles to each other so that two characters from the past might speak to one another. For instance, in one of these conversations, there was a nun and a young aboriginal girl discussing her education. The images of the characters are grainy so as to make them appear as if they are out of the past, this in contrast with the sharp images of seventeenth-century re-enactors in the video at Brouage. To complete each conversation, at the foot of the screens pertinent objects were carefully displayed to reinforce the idea that there really was a past that could be touched (figuratively, of course). 💻

Lessons from Canada

The presumption in the French exhibits – lavishly supported by the federal government – that the ties between France and Canada were really those with the St Lawrence valley was, perhaps not surprisingly, reinforced by the major exhibit in Canada on the occasion of the 400th anniversary of the Île Ste-Croix adventure. *Il était une fois en Amérique française / Once in French America* was presented at the Canadian Museum of Civilization from June 2004 to March 2005. The museum was justly proud of an exhibit that incorporated 'nearly 600 objects and over 100 illustrations from 40 Canadian and foreign collections.'[14] There would be no repeat of the sterile exhibits in Paris and Brouage. However, there would be more of the generalizing that allowed the specificity of the Acadian experience, on its anniversary, to disappear from view. By and large, except for a display relating to the deportation, little mention was made of *Acadie*. In fact, special reference to its destruction – on the anniversary of its birth – was jarring, particularly given the efforts of Acadians to use 2004 to tell a story that had begun in the early seventeenth century, and not after the return of Acadians following the deportation. At the very close of the exhibit there was a reference to the fact that 2004 marked the '400th anniversary of French settlement in North America.' However, it was not obvious as to precisely where this moment of birth which would have made 2004 the birthday, had taken place.

In the end, the commemorative events of 2004–5 showed the powerlessness of Acadians to secure federal government support to tell their story – either in terms of the founding of *Acadie* or in terms of the deportation. However, the Acadians were not the only ones whose weakness was exposed. The residents of the regions surrounding the sites of memory from the Dugua expedition also found it difficult to tell their stories. This was particularly true in terms of the people from the vicinity of Île Ste-Croix who had hoped to put the past to their advantage by telling the story of the winter of 1604 on a parcel of land directly across from the island. They received little support from Acadians, who frequently felt that this story belonged exclusively to them and were powerful enough – at least in this context – to discourage the project from coming to fruition.

As David Glassberg has reminded us, reconstructed settlements, such as the one created at Port-Royal in the late 1930s, only serve to widen the gap between the past and the present. The early-twentieth-century commemorative events, starting with those marking the tercentenary of the arrival of Dugua and continuing to the bicentenary of the deportation, tried to provide lessons for the future derived from the past. There was an optimistic spirit in those celebrations that contrasted with the reconstructed settlements, emerging in the aftermath of the First World War, that showed how the 'past was receding from the present and the future, rather than leading to it.'[15] Nevertheless, the leaders from both sides of the international border that cut through the St-Croix valley would have gladly welcomed such a facility to help kick-start a flagging economy.

In the absence of the reconstructed settlement, the only legacy in Canada from the 400th anniversary of the settlement on Île Ste-Croix is the set of three sculptures that sit at the edge of a parking lot, overlooking the empty field where the settlement might have stood. The three pieces of sculpture, commissioned by Ottawa and unveiled (in the rain) on the precise date that the Dugua expedition landed, were the individual works of an Acadian, a French, and an aboriginal artist. However, based upon time that I spent near these sculptures a day later (when the sun had returned), none of them appeared to have struck a responsive chord with visitors who happened by. (Photos of the three sculpture can be found in chapter 3.) Whenever visitors seemed at least somewhat curious about the sculptures, I would ask them about their impressions. Nearly all the responses pertained to one sculpture in particular (my personal favourite), the work of the French artist Jean-Charles Pigeau, which allowed the observer to look through a disk that resembled a CD to see the island, while shadows were cast on an impressionistic map on the horizontal surface, so that the sculpture also functioned as a sundial.

Invariably, before visitors would respond to my queries, they wanted to be certain that I was not one of the artists. Once reassured they were eager to tell me what they thought, many expressing the view that the sculptures constituted 'a colossal waste of tax payers' money.' In that spirit, one man told me that he was 'a guy who doesn't like abstract art. I wouldn't have paid for it, but we did.' As for the Pigeau sculpture in particular, there

E.3 Jean-Charles Pigeau, *Le Point du jour 2004*: Saint Croix Island
International Historic Site, Bayside, New Brunswick
(photograph by the author)

were those who thought that the CD reminded them of a Frisbee; still
others suggested that the hole in the CD might have been filled with a
magnifying glass to allow a better view of the island.'[16] Since the inaccessibility of the island was one of the factors that worked against it occupying
a significant place in public memory, this last comment was particularly
appropriate. In a larger sense, however, these viewers expressed a preference for more traditional forms of sculpture, which, as James Young has
put it, can serve to 'engage viewers with likenesses of people, to evoke an
empathetic link between viewer and monument that might then be mar-
shalled into particular meaning.'[17]

There were other tangible legacies of the Île Ste-Croix quadricentenary,
but they were on the American side of the international border. The fact
that both a museum (the Downeast Heritage Museum) and the commemorative trail at Red Beach, immediately across from the island, managed to
see the light of day said something once again about the connection between power and the past. Funds could be secured for developments in
Maine, where the competing interests that bedevilled 400th anniversary

events in Canada did not exist. The National Park Service, which owned both the island and the land where the trail was constructed, did not need to be concerned about either the jostling between Acadians and the local English speakers or the involvement of the Passamaquoddy, who did exist in the United States, although not in Canada.

Without these concerns, the past was remembered in a manner that more successfully engaged the public than was the case with the sculptures in New Brunswick. The commemorative trail was constructed out of a stand of trees (and not at the edge of a parking lot) and led visitors to a lookout at the edge of the water where some contact with the island (albeit at a distance) could be made. However, what really encouraged visitors to spend some time here was the opportunity to sample the stories of individuals, some famous (such as Dugua) and others nameless (both Frenchmen and Passamaquoddy), who had a connection with the winter of 1604–5. These stories were told both through sketches on explanatory panels and, more significantly, through six life-size bronzes.

At the unveiling ceremony for the trail in the fall of 2003, I watched as local residents (admittedly ones who cared enough to come out for the ceremony) lingered to literally look into the eyes of the characters, who were not on a pedestal; and this positive reaction was reinforced by the comments of visitors with whom I spoke during several subsequent stops at the trail. I never once heard the slightest annoyance with the use of taxpayers' money that I had heard on the other side of the border, an impression that was reinforced by Meg Scheid, the National Park Service ranger who looks after the site. In late 2007 she explained to me, 'In my tenure since fall of 2004, there has never been a negative comment, and the positive comments passed along are frequent.' In particular, she noted that visitors often commented that 'the statues are fabulous; they tell the story so well; they make it seem so real.'[18]

This was not the representational art from the Canadian side, nor was it the sort of statuary that had been constructed a hundred years earlier when the Dugua monument was erected at Fort Anne in Annapolis Royal. Although the monument from 1904 lacked the various allegorical figures that were then common, a bas-relief depicting Dugua's landing at Port-Royal was designed to communicate the heroic actions of the past that might influence the present, and thus it bore the overt instructional qualities that Maurice Agulhon has described as common for such turn-of-the-twentieth-century structures.[19] By contrast, the early-twenty-first-century version of Dugua was accessible and his story could be absorbed by getting close to him. Of course, as James Young has reminded us, the downside of such realistic sculptures was that, unlike more abstract forms, they could only represent the past in a fairly straightforward manner, without the possibility for 'accommodat[ing] as many messages as could be projected on to [them].'[20]

At the unveiling, the accessibility of Dugua was reinforced by the presence of a Dugua re-enactor, a Park Service ranger dressed up for the occasion, who obligingly posed for visitors and patiently answered numerous questions about the winter of 1604. This Dugua was quite unlike the Champlain re-enactor who had performed at the tercentenary events in Saint John. Of course, the very fact that Dugua was now the star of the hour reflected a shift, however limited, in power relations, with the Acadian hero now holding some superior claim over Champlain in regard to the expeditions of the early seventeenth century. In 1904 Professor W.F. Ganong, whom we saw in chapter 1 as a participant in the celebrations at Île Ste-Croix, reacted as organizers might have hoped to the Champlain re-enactor, expressing a certain sense of awe. Ganong remarked that the re-enactment had seemed so real that 'I had some momentary impulse to approach Champlain and ask him the truth as to certain ambiguous passages in his narratives!'[21]

Ganong's sentiments were also reflected by some of those who observed the intricately staged historical pageants presented at the Quebec tercentenary of 1908. As Viv Nelles has indicated, 'The therapy of theatre, especially in the form of the mass participatory re-enactment, taught lessons in different ways, reached new audiences by making them actors, and potentially reshaped public consciousness.'[22] In both of these early-twentieth-century cases, the past was performed in a way that made its lessons seem close at hand, while the performers were kept at a distance. A hundred years later, the performer was just an ordinary person, which made him accessible to spectators, but at the same time the past seemed further away since there could be no confusion (as there had been in Ganong's mind) that this was the 'real' Dugua.

In large-scale commemorative events, from those of the summer of 1904 through to the ones staged in Moncton to mark the bicentenary of the deportation a half-century later, lessons were communicated by dramatic staging that tried to create distance between the performers and the audience. By contrast, the dramatic presentations of the past in 2004-5, particularly the Acadian ones described in previous chapters, used a variety of techniques to add to the immediacy of the experience, which was demanded by audiences in the age of the Internet. Nevertheless, because it seemed as if the performers (or the subjects of sculptures)

E.4 Two Duguas: Opening of Red Beach Trail, Maine, October 2003
(photograph by Robert Thayer)

were just like us, the past that was presented, however entertaining it
might have been, could convey few lessons for the early twenty-first
century.

Power of Place

In spite of efforts to highlight the story of the winter of 1604, Île Ste-
Croix did not emerge from the shadows during the quadricentenary of
the Dugua adventure as a significant site of memory. There were good
reasons why both Acadians and English speakers from the immediate
vicinity may have felt disconnected from the story, the former because
Dugua and his comrades moved on after the disastrous winter and the
latter because the French legacy was somehow foreign. Just as significantly, however, people could not connect with a place that they could
not visit. I had the great fortune to visit the island on three separate occasions, on one of those in the company of a team that was opening up
the graves of the casualties of that fateful winter so that bones taken away

decades earlier by an overly enthusiastic anthropologist might be returned to their rightful place. Although there are no visible remains of buildings from the early seventeenth century, I was able to see the commemorative plaque from the celebrations of 1904 that was affixed to a boulder; and I could stand at the southern edge of the island and look downstream from where the ships would have approached. In short, I was able to make a connection that few others could claim, seeing that visits to the island are now carefully monitored by the Park Service, which recognizes the fragility of the island, now much smaller due to erosion than the one that was briefly home to Dugua and his men.

If the island's inaccessibility blunted the power of the Île Ste-Croix story, some of the most moving moments from my time on the road came at places whose own significance gave power to the commemorative event at hand. Alongside objects, Rosenzweig and Thelen found that historic sites provided people with a tangible connection with the past. As they put it, 'Approaching artifacts and sites on their own terms, visitors could cut through all the intervening stories, step around the agendas that had been advanced in the meantime, and feel that they were experiencing a moment from the past almost as it had been originally experienced – and with none of the overwhelming distortions that they associated with movies and television, the other purveyors of immediacy.'[23] Of course, as in the case of objects, historic sites are only accessible to visitors after a process of selection that privileges some over others. This process clearly did not privilege Île Ste-Croix, and so if the island could not engage visitors, it was because various 'agendas' had intruded.

Nevertheless, Rosenzweig and Thelen's observation was confirmed, in regard to the Île Ste-Croix commemorative events, by a ceremony staged by the Passamaquoddy on a piece of land near St Andrews, New Brunswick, known as Indian Point. Once the centre of the Passamaquoddy culture, the land had more recently been the focus of controversy over proposals for its development that had been challenged by Hugh Akagi, the chief of a tribe that was not recognized by the federal government. However, on 26 June 2004, four hundred years after the arrival of the French, there was no sign of any ill will, as the day began with a Sunrise Ceremony under the supervision of the Passamaquoddy, who in a sense received some measure of informal recognition.

The crowd was not large and some in attendance had probably come out of solidarity with their Passamaquoddy neighbours in New Brunswick. Nevertheless, there was no ignoring the intense emotions that prevailed as the Passamaquoddy conducted a ceremony that their forebears might have led on the same site four hundred years earlier. At one point, Chief Akagi encouraged everyone to take some tobacco from a pouch he was holding and to throw it on the bonfire around which the ceremony had taken place, thinking about their ancestors in the process. Many of the participants (they were no longer simply spectators) were crying as they carried out this small act, which constituted a connection with the past. Norma Stewart, who headed up the local organizing committee for the commemorative activities, later observed: that 'There were people who told me that the [Sunrise] Ceremony was probably the most significant experience they had ever had in their life.'[24] 🖳 Recognizing that something special had taken place, Akagi observed: 'There were people that were watching us enjoying ourselves on our own turf, if you will, and they were enjoying it with us. That was the surprise that nobody was expecting. Many of them felt something very emotional as well, because when people sort of let their guard down a little bit, then there's a chance they'll discover something they never knew.'[25]

The only other moments that came even close to packing the punch of that ceremony occurred during the various processions that Jean Gaudet led from Horton Landing, the point from which Acadians were herded onto ships, to the Grand-Pré historic site. The numerous deportation-related events staged at Grand-Pré tended to be carefully choreographed official ceremonies, and while there can be no doubt that the Grand-Pré site has its impact on visitors, its carefully manicured grounds play into older Acadian constructions of the deportation that emphasized purity and rebirth, in the process marginalizing feelings of pain and loss.[26]

Horton Landing, by contrast, had no official status until the summer of 2005 when the Croix de la Déportation was moved there, but even with that change it remains largely anonymous and unlikely to be visited except on special occasions. No signs tell visitors that they are approaching a site of historic significance, and I had to ask the owners of the neighbouring farm if I had found the right place when I first went there. By starting at this bleak point, because of its landscape – dominated by a scraggly tree believed to have been there at the time of the deportation – and the events that took place at the site in 1755, Gaudet's processions became efforts to reverse the past and so, while sad, they were significant acts of self-affirmation. Unlike so many other commemorative events at which those in attendance seemed disconnected from the moment, those who took part in the processions had gone out of their way and were visibly moved by an

E.5 Willows at Grand-Pré (photograph by the author)

effort to speak to both the horrors of the deportation and the possibility of undoing its consequences. 💻

In the end, from both my own perspective and that of the people around me, the Sunrise Ceremony and the Gaudet processions captured the imagination in a way that carefully orchestrated spectacles could not. In part this was a function of the power of the site: the centre of a civilization now battling for its survival in one case and the point of the destruction of a people now on the rebound in the other. However, there was more to these two events than the significance of their sites. Both were small-scale affairs, supported by no government and led by individuals who wanted to engage those in attendance as participants, and not merely as spectators. Neither Hugh Akagi nor Jean Gaudet were telling stories that were in the mainstream, the former because his tribe did not exist as far as the Canadian government was concerned and the latter because he was unwilling to *tourner la page*. Precisely because these events were telling stories that went against the grain, had no official status, and were joined by people who had gone the extra mile to be on hand as active participants, they were special moments that truly made the past come alive.

E.6 Jean Gaudet at start of procession from Horton Landing,
5 September 2005 (photograph by the author)

Small Victories

Much like the events that stood out, the tangible consequences of the
2004–5 commemorative cycle that demonstrably changed peoples' lives
for the better were the product of actions that cost relatively little. Much
of this book has dealt with the power politics connected with efforts to
secure funding for activities of various types. Nevertheless, if anything
really changed for those connected with these two anniversaries, it did
not come out of the investment of large amounts of money by government agencies. The irrelevance of funding had its clearest expression in
terms of the Passamaquoddy population of New Brunswick. When I visited the members of the St-Croix 2004 Organizing Committee in the
fall of 2003, the efforts by Chief Akagi and his council to seek recognition were treated with some ridicule, one member wondering out loud
if there were more than a handful of Passamaquoddy in Canada. Only a
few months later, I was on hand for a meeting in Paris between officials
from Canada and France who were involved with 400th anniversary

celebrations. One of them, a high-ranking representative from Canada, told me that there could not have been more than one Passamaquoddy living in Canada.[27]

Hugh Akagi was used to being dismissed. Nevertheless, his band in New Brunswick, together with their counterparts in Maine, decided that they had an opportunity that might never come again to tell their story and chose to take advantage of it. They became involved in the process of developing the events for the anniversary of the arrival of Dugua and his men, along the way explaining their cause to neighbours who had heretofore known little about their situation, or if they did had shown little sympathy. The past brought them together, and at the end of the process, Norma Stewart, who was witness to the transformation of the image of the Passamaquoddy, observed: 'They used the opportunity and they used it wisely and they did it well, so ... it was very, very positive. The people are aware now that not only are [the Passamaquoddy] here, [but that] it is still their land and they're still on it. So there was a lot of support that came out of Charlotte County from Canadians on this side of the border.'[28] 💻

Stewart's comments that the Passamaquoddy had turned some corner in terms of public opinion were confirmed later in the year when the Irving-owned *New Brunswick Telegraph-Journal* – hardly a radical voice – insisted that

> before the curtain falls on 2004, we'd like to draw the attention of our federal and provincial leaders to some unfinished business ... We believe that the federal government officially recognized the St Andrews Passamaquoddy band the moment federal organizers asked Chief Akagi to speak at the event on [26 June]. We take it from the pride of place accorded him in the opening ceremonies that he was there not as an entertainer, but as a leader among leaders. It would be shameful for the federal government to ignore the public act of recognition and continue the pretense that New Brunswick's Passamaquoddy are interlopers on their own historic territory ... While Canadians cannot be held responsible for injustices committed centuries ago, we are accountable for the injustices our governments commit today.[29]

The Passamaquoddy victory in the court of public opinion would be hollow if there were no concrete action to report. Only months after the 400th anniversary events, Akagi commented that government officials 'haven't run away from me which is something that happened before, which is the minute Passamaquoddy appeared or the minute the name

Passamaquoddy appeared, officials seemed to disappear in a hurry and it doesn't seem to be happening anymore ... I think it's pretty hard for them to avoid the issue now.'[30] A short time after Akagi made these comments, the federal government provided a small budget so that the Passamaquoddy could carry out the research that would establish whether they are capable of holding aboriginal rights, by establishing such matters as the size of their population and their connection to the territory. To supervise this process, Akagi, who had heretofore worked (ironically) for the federal government, retired and hired some staff for a small office in St Andrews which, in its own right, stands as a legacy of the quadricentenary. As Akagi put it in an interview during the summer of 2006, 'The office itself was a step towards recognition, because now [we] are an official entity.'[31]

Another aboriginal legacy from a 400th anniversary celebration exists on the Bear River Mi'kmaq reserve, just outside Annapolis Royal in Nova Scotia. While local leaders had hoped to stage significant events to mark the founding of Port-Royal, their dreams had even less chance of success than those regarding Île Ste-Croix, given that by 2005 the Acadians along with the federal government had moved on to commemorating the 250th anniversary of the deportation; and while Acadian support for the Île Ste-Croix celebrations was sometimes lukewarm, it did exist. In this context, the celebrations in Annapolis Royal were low-keyed local events, leaving no legacy in their wake. However, twenty-five kilometres away, the Bear River First Nation Heritage and Cultural Centre stands as another unexpected consequence of marking the past. When the 400th anniversary organizers from Annapolis Royal were unable to meet the funding criteria established by the federal government, they worked out an arrangement with Frank Meuse, the tribe's chief, and Hal Theriault, the director of the Cultural Centre, to provide funding for the creation of a dramatic production, 'The People's Story.' The performance of this play was designed to bring audiences to the Cultural Centre so that it might develop into a viable enterprise, in the process helping the tribe become as self-reliant as possible.

Finally, there is also one tangible, on-going legacy from the 250th anniversary of the deportation. While most of the headlines connected with this anniversary touched upon the question of an apology to the Acadians for wrongs committed in the mid-eighteenth century and most Acadian leaders spoke about the need to *tourner la page*, the Commission de l'Odyssée acadienne quietly, and with a modest budget, went about its business, marking sites of memory related to the *Grand Dérangement*.

With a monument that played on traditional Acadian symbols, most notably the cross, the commission sought to refocus deportation geography away from its preoccupation with Grand-Pré and to reformulate deportation language so that it now included the word 'resistance.'

I had the opportunity to be on hand for the unveiling of the commission's first two monuments on 28 July 2005, the first commemorative day mandated by the royal proclamation, and since then I have passed by the sites in Dieppe, New Brunswick (on the border with Moncton), and on the Halifax waterfront on several occasions. The crowds were relatively slim on the occasion of the unveiling, and during subsequent visits I have noticed that people tend to pass by without noticing these markers that are near to the hustle and bustle of urban life. In the end, however, the power of the commission's project lay not so much in any one monument that might or might not be visited, but rather in the long-term effort to construct a series of markers of deportation memory scattered across the globe. In 2006 the commission unveiled monuments at the Camp d'Espérance in New Brunswick's Miramichi valley and at St-Basile, near Edmundston, while in 2007 Caraquet and St-Pierre-et-Miquelon were added to the list. Still other projects are on the drawing board as I come to the end of this book.

Much like the Passamaquoddy drive for recognition in Canada and the efforts of the Bear River Mi'kmaq to become more self-sufficient, the Commission de l'Odyssée acadienne used the interest in the past generated by a significant anniversary to begin a long-term project designed to generate hope among people who had long felt powerless. There was nothing flashy about these efforts that did not garner the headlines of the larger, but ephemeral, commemorative events discussed in these pages, which I thought would prove the most important ones when I began this project. However, in their quiet way, the individuals who worked outside the limelight were trying to provide their people with tools for facing the future by having them engage in some new ways with the past. These efforts were always aimed at self-improvement, never at getting even for past wrongs. After the Sunrise Ceremony was over, Hugh Akagi reflected on what the 400th anniversary events had meant. What he had to say could also have pertained to Chief Frank Meuse and the members of his tribe or to the activists – whose number included Jean Gaudet – involved with the Commission de l'Odyssée acadienne: 'I wanted to explain to [others] the Passamaquoddy story, in such a way that they would understand where we were coming from, what the problem was, and I wanted to leave them with a little hope for all of us.'[32] 🖥

Notes

Prologue

1 The figures regarding both the number of Acadians in 1755 and the number actually deported are much contested and are discussed in Part Two. A team of researchers at the Université de Moncton estimated in 2005 that there were roughly 10,000 deportees, with another 2500 avoiding capture. So, most Acadians were uprooted from their homes. (Centre d'études acadiennes, Université de Moncton, '1755: L'histoire et ses histoires,' http://www2.umoncton.ca/cfdocs/etudacad/1755/entree.cfm?&lang=fr&style=J&admin=false&linking=) As for the reference to ethnic cleansing, see John Mack Faragher, *A Great and Noble Scheme: The Tragic Story of the Expulsion of the French Acadians from Their American Homeland* (New York: W.W. Norton, 2005), 469.

2 Henry Wadsworth Longfellow, *Evangeline: A Tale of Acadie* (1847), in *Poems and Other Writings* (New York: Library of America, 2000), 57–115.

3 Gaudet also used the fourteen stations of the cross as the organizing principle for a journey around Nova Scotia in connection with the 2004 Congrès mondial acadien. Gaudet's 'Caravanes Mer et Terre,' with its fourteen stops, is discussed in chapter 6.

4 In order to emphasize the fact that this island had been settled by the French, I have used the French form throughout the book. From time to time, English speakers who live in the vicinity of the island will be cited referring to it as St Croix Island.

5 *Founding Fathers* (Toronto: University of Toronto Press, 2003).

6 Although the two terms are frequently used interchangeably, Ronnie-Gilles LeBlanc has explained that for some Acadians going back to the late eighteenth century the concepts had very different meanings. He argued

that the 'deportation' pertained to the period that started with the 1755 expulsion and ended with the close of the Seven Years' War in 1763. As for the *Grande Dérangement*, it started earlier (with expulsions that preceded 1755) and ended later (including disruptions beyond 1763) and pertained even to those Acadians who managed to escape deportation. In the same piece LeBlanc rejected the idea that the term *Grand Dérangement* began as a euphemism, claiming that Acadians of the time used it to express the horror of the deportation and not to avoid calling it what it was. Of course, LeBlanc's research does not preclude the possibility that individual Acadians may have used these terms in a variety of ways over time. (LeBlanc, 'Du "dérangement des guerres" au Grand Dérangement: La longue évolution d'un concept,' in his edited volume, *Du Grand Dérangement à la Déportation* (Moncton: Chaire d'études acadiennes, 2005), 11–20.

7 Pierre Nora, *Realms of Memory* (New York: Columbia University Press, 1998), 3: 637.

8 Eric Foner, *Who Owns History? Rethinking the Past in a Changing World* (New York: Hill and Wang, 2002), ix–x.

9 David Lowenthal, *The Heritage Crusade and the Spoils of History* (Cambridge: Cambridge University Press, 1998), 121.

10 To be sure, there are works in which the author has witnessed some part of contemporary commemorative events. In *Sinking Columbus: Contested History, Cultural Politics and Mythmaking during the Quincentenary* (Gainesville: University Press of Florida, 2000), Stephen Summerhill and John Alexander Williams had the benefit of the latter's role as someone who at one point was one of the organizers of the American events to mark the 500th anniversary of the arrival of Christopher Columbus. However, Williams was an insider, and not the fly on the wall that I was trying to be. Closer to the conception of this work is Stephen Laurence Kaplan's *Farewell Revolution, Disputed Legacies: France, 1789/1989* (Ithaca: Cornell University Press, 1995). His study, which focuses on the bicentenary of the French Revolution, includes numerous interviews with key players in the commemorative process, most of which appear to have been secured after the events were over and not during the construction of the anniversary, as is the case here. While dealing with the construction of a museum, Edward Linenthal's *Preserving Memory: The Struggle to Create America's Holocaust Museum* (New York: Columbia University Press, 2001) shares something of the spirit of the current work as the author had access to both internal documents and key players, in the latter case before the museum's opening.

11 Roy Rosenzweig and David Thelen, *The Presence of the Past: Popular Uses of History in American Life* (New York: Columbia University Press, 1993), 2.

12 Ibid., 178.

13 Of course, the map bears no reference to any place called *Acadie.* When used in this book, it is meant to refer to the French-speaking regions of Atlantic Canada.

14 Interview with Norma Stewart, 28 May 2004. (Unless otherwise noted, all interviews were conducted by the author.)

15 Interview with Donald Soctomah, 17 October 2003.

16 Interview with Maurice Basque, 26 May 2004.

17 The exhibition, 'Le Canada vraiment,' was staged at the Cité des sciences et de l'industrie from 16 December 2003 to 29 August 2004, and is discussed at some length in the epilogue. The *livre d'or* (in this case an entry from 18 February 2004) was made available to me by Pierre Duconseille and Perrine Wyplosz, who worked on the development of the project and to whom I am most grateful.

Chapter 1

1 There is a large literature dealing with such turn of the twentieth century commemorative events. In the Canadian context, to take only a few examples, see H.V. Nelles, *The Art of Nation-Building* (Toronto: University of Toronto Press, 1998); Colin Coates and Cecilia Morgan, *Heroines and History* (Toronto: University of Toronto Press, 2002); Patrice Groulx, *Pièges de mémoire: Dollard des Ormeaux, les Amériendiens et nous* (Hull: Éditions Vents d'ouest, 1998); and my *Founding Fathers.*

2 Library and Archives Canada, Laurier Papers, Longley to Laurier, 11 April 1903, 72108–9.

3 From Dugua's royal charter as cited in George MacBeath, 'Pierre Du Gua de Monts,' *Dictionary of Canadian Biography,* http://www.biographi.ca/EN/ShowBio.asp?BioId=34320&query=du%20AND%20gua. The documents from the early seventeenth century refer to Pierre Dugua (or sometimes Du Gua), Sieur de Mons. Many English writers of the turn of the twentieth century (and since) have referred to De Monts (or DeMonts) adding the 't.' There were occasions on which the English form was accepted by French speakers. Nevertheless, by the time of the quadricentenary celebrations of 2004, he was invariably referred to as Dugua, and to limit the confusion, I will do the same throughout the book, although others may be cited from time to time using the alternative expressions.

4 Marc Lescarbot, *The History of New France* (Toronto: Champlain Society, 1911), 2: 240–1; Champlain as cited in W.F. Ganong, *Champlain's Island* (Saint John: New Brunswick Museum, 2003), 60.

5 Ganong, *Champlain's Island*, 86.
6 Prior to the American Revolution, the St Croix River was the boundary
   between the colonies of Massachusetts (which then included Maine) and
   Nova Scotia. When the new international boundary was being drawn, the
   river was still to be the dividing line, but the Americans insisted that another
   river (which would have given them more land) was the real St Croix River.
   The island could prove the point, and so evidence was collected to show
   which island had been settled in 1604. When St Croix Island was identified,
   the British position was confirmed, thus establishing the boundary that
   exists to this day.
7 In 2003 the bones of some of the Frenchmen from the winter of 1604–5,
   taken earlier by an overly enthusiastic archaeologist, were returned to the
   island. However, even after the return of the bones, the graves remain
   unmarked.
8 The story of the region is told in greater detail in Harold Davis, *An International Community on the St. Croix (1604–1930)*, University of Maine Studies,
   2nd series, no. 64 (Orono: University Press, 1950).
9 I.C. Knowlton, *Annals of Calais, Maine, and St. Stephen, New Brunswick* (Calais:
   J.A. Sears, 1875), 3.
10 Davis, *International Community*, 277; 234.
11 Barbara LeBlanc, *Postcards from Acadie* (Kentville, NS: Gaspereau Press, 2003),
   87; http://chocolatemuseum.ca/archives.htm.
12 Bill Eagan, *Woven in Time: An Oral History of the Milltown (St Croix) Cotton Mill*
   (Bayside, NB: Kolby Publishing, 2004), 7–8. The early years of the mill are
   also discussed in Peter DeLottinville, 'Trouble in the Hives of Industry: The
   Cotton Industry Comes to Milltown, New Brunswick, 1879–92,' *Canadian
   Historical Association, Historical Papers* 15 (1980): 100–15.
13 Eagan, *Woven in Time*, xiii–xiv. The role of the mill in popular memory was
   reflected in the unveiling in Fall 2007 of the Milltown Cotton Mill Monument (milltowncottonmillmemorial.ca).
14 Davis, *International community*, 239; 241.
15 Ibid., 261.
16 Ibid., 307.
17 Barrett Parker, *Saint Croix Island, 1604–1942* (Cambridge, MA: Crimson
   Printing Co., 1942), 7; 18.
18 Annapolis Royal Municipal Archives, Minutes of Town Council, 5 July 1904.
   I am most grateful to Leah Butler for her research assistance in the town
   council minutes.
19 Samuel de Champlain, *The Works of Samuel de Champlain* (Toronto:
   Champlain Society, 1922), 1: 259.

20 Naomi Griffiths, *From Migrant to Acadian: A North American Border People, 1604–1755* (Montreal: McGill-Queen's University Press, 2005), 180–1.

21 The significance of the 1710 military defeat is considered from various perspectives in John G. Reid, et al., *The 'Conquest' of Acadia: Imperial, Colonial, and Aboriginal Constructions* (Toronto: University of Toronto Press, 2004).

22 Faragher, *A Great and Noble Scheme*, 363.

23 W.A. Calnek, *History of the County of Annapolis* (Toronto: William Briggs, 1897), 186.

24 Parts of the following three sections pertinent to the 1904 tercentenary originally appeared in my 'The Champlain-DeMonts Tercentenary: Voices from Nova Scotia, New Brunswick and Maine, June 1904,' *Acadiensis* 32 (2004): 3–26.

25 In his *How Societies Remember* (Cambridge: Cambridge University Press, 1989), Paul Commerton discusses the use of such events as part of a 'compensatory strategy' (64).

26 James Wilberforce Longley (1848–1922) represented Annapolis County (with only a short absence) as a Liberal member from 1882 to 1905, at which time he was named to the Supreme Court of Nova Scotia. He served as the province's attorney general from 1886 to 1905.

27 Longley, 'Demonts Tercentenary at Annapolis, 1604–1904,' *Collections of the Nova Scotia Historical Society* 14 (1910): 108.

28 T.W. Acheson, 'The National Policy and the Industrialization of the Maritimes, 1880–1910,' *Acadiensis* 1 (1972): 3–29.

29 Town of Annapolis Royal, Minutes of Town Council, 29 December 1902. A resolution was passed indicating that 'the Town Council is in sympathy with the movement to celebrate the ter-centenary of the founding of Annapolis Royal, and that the Council most respectfully request that the Nova Scotia Historical Society take the initiative and carry out the programme in connection with the celebration.'

30 Longley, 'Demonts Tercentenary at Annapolis,' 107–8.

31 Paul Stevens and J.T. Saywell, eds, *Lord Minto's Canadian Papers* (Toronto: Champlain Society, 1981–3), 2: 462. For his part, Longley later observed that 'many there are who think that [Minto] both could and should have attended on such an important occasion.' (Longley, 'De Monts' Tercentenary,' *Acadiensis* 5 [1905]: 7.)

32 Library and Archives Canada, Laurier Papers, Laurier to Longley, 23 May 1904, 85955.

33 Annapolis Royal Municipal Archives, Minutes of Town Council, 5 July 1904.

34 New Brunswick Museum (hereafter NBM), Champlain Tercentenary Fonds, Longley to D.R. Jack, 11 April 1904. In this regard, Longley stood apart

from a contemporary commemorative event promoter, Earl Grey, who played a pivotal role in shaping the Quebec tercentenary of 1908. On this and other matters related to the Quebec tercentenary, see Nelles, The *Art of Nation-Building* and my *Founding Fathers.*

35 Longley, *The Future of Canada* (n.p., n.d.), 15.

36 Longley, 'Demonts Tercentenary at Annapolis,' 118; 115.

37 *Halifax Herald*, 21 June 1904. From its founding in the 1870s, the *Herald* had been a staunch supporter of the 'Liberal-Conservative Party.' In fact, shortly after the conclusion of the tercentenary festivities, it enthusiastically supported the Conservatives, led by the native son Robert Borden, in the federal election that took place in November. In this support for Borden the *Herald* characterized Laurier's Liberals as pro-American, in the process trying to portray the Conservatives as the party of Canadian nationalists. From this perspective, the paper had little interest in supporting Longley's narrower vision of the country.

38 Nova Scotia Archives and Records Management, Nova Scotia Historical Society Records, MG 20, vol 687, S.-N. Parent to Longley, 14 January 1904; Longley, 'Demonts Tercentenary at Annapolis,' 122.

39 *Halifax Morning Chronicle*, 22 June 1904. Turgeon concluded his remarks in French, but did not repeat this sentiment.

40 *Halifax Morning Chronicle*, 22 June 1904. Like Turgeon, Langelier also appears to have spoken in both languages (*L'Évangéline*, 30 June 1904). His speech was reprinted in its entirely in *Le Trois-Centième Anniversaire de l'Arrivée de M. DeMonts à Port-Royal: Discours prononcé par l'Honorable Chs. Langelier, le 21 juin 1904* (Quebec: n.p., 1904).

41 The New Brunswick controversy resulted in a riot in Caraquet in 1875. There was a further controversy in Manitoba in the 1890s.

42 H.B. Neatby, *Laurier and a Liberal Quebec* (Toronto: McClelland & Stewart, 1973), 153.

43 *L'Évangéline*, 30 June 1904; *Halifax Morning Chronicle*, 23 June 1904.

44 *L'Évangéline*, 30 June 1904.

45 Ibid.

46 This image of the two heroes of the moment was reproduced daily in *Le Soleil*, 21–25 June 1904.

47 Library and Archives Canada, Fond du ministère des affaires étrangères (Paris), Kleczkowski to Minister, 10 May 1904 (microfilm F-2180).

48 *Le Soleil*, 25 June 1904.

49 NBM, Champlain Tercentenary Fonds, telegram from W.C. Gaynor to D.R. Jack, 21 June 1904.

50 Library and Archives Canada, Laurier Papers, A.W. Savary to Laurier, 20 January 1905, 93902. The information on the addition of the French text

was provided by Theresa Bunbury, Operations Superintendent, National Historic Sites, Southwest Nova Scotia.

51 For a very different perspective on the tercentenary events in Saint John, see Greg Marquis, 'Celebrating Champlain in the Loyalist City: Saint John, 1904–10,' *Acadiensis* 32 (2004): 27–43. Marquis points to the 'nationalist and bicultural tone of the tercentenary ... at the elite level' (38), although the record (at least as I read it) does not always support such a conclusion.

52 NBM, Champlain Tercentenary Fonds, Longley to Raymond, 11 November 1903. Raymond was active in the New Brunswick Historical Society and the author of numerous works, many of which dealt with the history of the St. John Valley.

53 Ibid., Longley to D.R. Jack, 10 February 1904.

54 Ibid., 8 April 1904.

55 Ibid., 11 April 1904. While Longley thought the Saint John organizers went too far in presenting a spectacle for the public, the *New Brunswick Magazine* found that the celebration 'was largely of a literary character and was not signified by parades and pageants that were not unnaturally looked for by the general public, though this feature was not altogether lacking' (4 [September 1904]: 9).

56 E.M. Slader, *From the Victorian Era to the Space Age*, Collections of the New Brunswick Historical Society, no. 21 (n.p., 1973), 35. Slader was on hand as a member of a militia unit that participated in the parade that followed Champlain's landing. As for the landing of Champlain in 1908, there is no evidence that the Quebec City organizers realized that they were repeating the Saint John spectacle. I describe the Quebec City landing in *Founding Fathers*, chap. 4.

57 NBM, White Scrapbook #19, Tercentenary, 1904; shelf 37a, clipping from 12 February 1904. It is tempting to speculate as to why the organizers of the three events eschewed Native participation, but they left behind no explanations in this regard.

58 W.F. Ganong, 'A Visitor's Impression of the Champlain Tercentenary,' *Acadiensis* 5 (1905): 21. Ganong was not alone in expressing wonderment at such turn-of-the-twentieth-century events. In this regard, see Nelles, *The Art of Nation-Building*.

59 NBM, Alice Fairweather Fonds, Minutes of the Loyalist Society (F16), 13 January 1903.

60 *St John Daily Telegraph*, 29 April 1904.

61 Ibid., 24 June 1904. The Loyalist Society repeated this demand for a tablet in honour of their ancestors shortly after the tercentenary (NBM, Alice Fairweather Fonds, Minutes of the Loyalist Society (F16), 15 July 1904). Although proposed, this tablet was never erected. Nor was any action taken

on the proposal to have two tablets alongside Champlain's, one in honour
of the Loyalists and the other in honour of the 'men who made St. John the
centre of trade for the Maritime Provinces before the Loyalists came here'
(*New Brunswick Magazine* 4 [September 1904]: 12).

62 NBM, New Brunswick Historical Society, Regular meeting, 3 May 1904. A
statue to Champlain would ultimately be constructed in 1910. The story of
its construction can be found in Marquis, 'Celebrating Champlain.'

63 *St John Daily Telegraph*, 24 June 1904; *New Brunswick Magazine* 4 (September
1904): 29.

64 NBM, New Brunswick Historical Society, Meeting, 7 June 1904.

65 NBM, Champlain Tercentenary Fonds, Pascal Poirier to D.R. Jack, 5 June
1904; *Le Moniteur Acadien*, 16 June 1904.

66 *St John Daily Telegraph*, 25 June 1904; *Le Moniteur Acadien*, 30 June 1904.

67 According to the 1911 census, while roughly 5% of the population of
Annapolis Royal was of French origin, this figure was only 2% for
Saint John.

68 *New Brunswick Magazine* 4 (September 1904): 14. This slight was not the only
one experienced by Acadians in early-twentieth-century commemorative
events. For instance, in 1920 a statue of Evangeline was unveiled at Grand-
Pré, Nova Scotia. Although Evangeline was supposed to represent the
Acadians who had been deported, this event featured no Acadian speakers
and little reference to their history. Perhaps this was to be expected since
the unveiling was held in the context of 'the Imperial Press Conference, of
which a hundred people have come from every corner of the British
Empire' (*Toronto Globe*, 30 July 1920).

69 NBM, Champlain Tercentenary Fonds, letters from Pascal Poirier, 22 May
and 31 May 1904.

70 Ibid., Champlain Tercentenary Fonds, John V. Ellis to D.R. Jack, 15 June
1904.

71 *St John Daily Telegraph*, 25 June 1904. A longer and more assertive text was
published in *Le Moniteur Acadien*, 7 July 1904. Since other speeches in
French were signalled as such by the *St John Daily Telegraph*, it seems likely
that Landry spoke in English and then published a fuller French text for
Acadian consumption. Although the public reaction was muted, Robert
Pichette, recognizing that Landry was in the lion's den, saw his speech as
'unprecedented, revolutionary in certain ways, and very courageous'
(Robert Pichette, *Le pays appelé l'Acadie: Réflexions sur des commémorations*
[Moncton: Centre d'études acadiennes, 2006], 96).

72 Ganong, *Champlain's Island*, 42.

73 Ibid., 148–50.

74 If marginalizing the events at Île Ste-Croix was Longley's intent, this goal was facilitated by the fact that the final stop on the tercentenary tour took place only hours after the Saint John events had finished, thus probably making it difficult for some to attend. While it was important to stage the Champlain re-enactment on the day that he had named the St John River (24 June), it did not seem to matter if the Île Ste-Croix events were staged two days later to coincide with the landing of Dugua and his men in 1604. Most likely, however, the events could not be held on the 26th because it was a Sunday.

75 Nova Scotia Archives and Records Management (NARM), Nova Scotia Historical Society Records, MG 20, vol. 687, Henry Burrage to Longley, 1 February 1904; Calais (Maine) Municipal Archives, City Council Minutes, 8 February 1904.

76 *St Croix Courier*, 30 June 1904.

77 *Collections of the Maine Historical Society*, 3rd series, 1 (1904): 2.

78 NARM, Nova Scotia Historical Society Records, MG 20, vol. 687, Henry Burrage to Longley, 1 February 1904.

79 *St Croix Courier*, 30 June 1904.

80 'Tercentenary of the Landing of De Monts at St Croix Island,' *Collections of The Maine Historical Society*, 3rd ser., 2 (1906): 112.

81 Ibid., 80.

82 *Souvenir de la visite de Son Excellence Mgr Sbarretti délégué apostolique en Acadie* (Shediac: Moniteur Acadien, 1904), 11–12.

83 Cited in Pichette, *Le pays appelé l'Acadie*, 68.

84 *Souvenir de la visite de Son Excellence Mgr Sbarretti*, 8.

85 Pichette, 66.

86 Estimates of the pre-deportation population very wildly, but rarely exceed 20,000. The figure of 14,000, based on sound archival research (not always the case in some other estimates), came from Stephen White, 'The True Number of the Acadians,' in *Du Grand Dérangement à la Déportation: Nouvelles perspectives historiques,* ed. Ronnie-Gilles LeBlanc (Moncton: Chaire d'études acadiennes, 2005), 21–56.

87 Antonine Maillet, *Cent ans dans les bois* (Montreal: Leméac, 1981). For an overview of nineteenth century demographic trends, see Muriel Roy, 'Settlement and Population Growth," in *The Acadians of the Maritimes*, ed. Jean Daigle (Moncton: Centre d'études acadiennes, 1982), 166–72.

88 On the emergence of this elite, see Sheila M. Andrew, *The Development of Elites in Acadian New Brunswick, 1861–1881* (Montreal: McGill-Queen's University Press, 1997).

89 Jean-Roch Cyr, 'Pierre-Amand Landry,' in *Dictionary of Canadian Biography*, http://www.biographi.ca/EN/ShowBio.asp?BioId=41628&query=. Also, see

Della Margaret M. Stanley, *Au service de deux peuples: Pierre-Amand Landry* (Moncton: Éditions de l'Acadie, 1977).

90 Cyr, 'Pierre-Amand Landry.'

91 Michel Roy, *Acadie des origines à nos jours* (Montreal: Québec/Amérique, 1981), 198.

92 Philippe Doucet, 'Politics and the Acadians,' in Daigle, ed., *Acadia of the Maritimes*, 308.

93 Léon Thériault, 'Acadians from 1763 to 1990,' ibid., 75.

94 Doucet, 'Politics and the Acadians,' 307.

95 Archives du Centre d'études acadiennes, Université de Moncton (hereafter CEA), 41.23-1, Meeting of executive committee of Société nationale l'Assomption, 20 January 1950. The situation of the SNA at the time of the bicentenary is discussed in Maurice Basque, *La Société Nationale de l'Acadie: Au coeur de la réussite d'un peuple* (Moncton: Éditions de la Francophonie, 2006), chap. 5.

96 CEA, 77.206, 'Mémoire présenté à l'Honorable Maurice Duplessis,' 16 November 1954.

97 Jules-Paul Hautecoeur, *L'Acadie du discours* (Ste-Foy: Presses de l'Université Laval, 1975), 97.

98 CEA, 41.3-2, Meeting of executive committee of Société nationale l'Assomption, 8 February 1950. The bicentenary, discussed at length in chapter 5, was a complex event precisely because of the mixed messages that were communicated.

99 *Welcome to Annapolis Royal's 350th Anniversary* (Annapolis Royal: n.p., 1955), 3.

100 *Halifax Chronicle-Herald*, 2 August 1955.

101 *Annapolis Spectator*, 4 August 1955,

102 Library and Archives Canada, V1 9006-0041, *Siege of Port-Royal*, silent film produced by television station CHSJ, 1955.

103 Caroline-Isabelle Caron, 'Se souvenir de l'Acadie d'antan: Représentation du passé historique dans le cadre de célébrations commémoratives locales en Nouvelle-Écosse au milieu du 20e siècle,' *Acadiensis* 36, 1 (Spring 2007): 62.

104 *L'Évangéline*, 17 August 1955.

105 *Halifax Chronicle-Herald*, 17 August 1955.

106 NBM, New Brunswick Historical Society, Minutes of 21 January and 23 February 1954; *Evening Times-Globe*, 24 February 1954.

107 *Evening Time-Globe*, 12 June 1954.

108 *The Loyalist*, 19 June 1954.

109 Ibid., 3 April 1954.

110 *Evening Times-Globe*, 21 June 1954.

111 Ibid., 31 May 1954.

112 Ibid., 24 June 1954.

113 The Acadian emphasis on Champlain was similarly reflected in the pages of *L'Évangéline*, which did not so much as mention Dugua's name in noting the festivities to mark 'the 350th anniversary of the St John River by Champlain' (14 June 1954).

114 *Calais Advertiser*, 13 November 1946. The emphasis is in the original.

115 *Dedication of the Establishment of Saint Croix Island as a National Monument: June 30, 1968* (Calais: n.p., 1968), 21–3.

116 Ibid.

117 'St Croix Island National Monument, Maine Interpretive Prospectus,' 1970. (Document secured from U.S. Department of Interior, National Park Service, Acadia National Park via Freedom of Information Act [FOIA] request.)

118 *L'Évangéline*, 10 December 1980; Memo by Steve Ridlington, Public Participation Meetings at Moncton, Halifax, Bangor, Boston, 18 December 1980. (Document secured from Parks Canada via Access to Information Program [ATIP] request.)

119 Memo by Steve Ridlington, 8 December 1980.

120 St Croix Island Project Team, *St Croix Island Open Houses: Summary of Public Comments and Suggestions*, June 1981.

121 Ibid.

122 *Memorandum of Understanding for Saint Croix Island International Historic Site*, 9 September 1982. Following up on this memorandum, the U.S. government passed a law in 1984 declaring that the island was an International Historic Site (Public Law 98-422, 25 September 1984). On this occasion, the specific Acadian reference was pushed to the side for a more *québécois* view that the expedition of 1604 was the starting point 'from which the French embarked to establish the settlement which became Québec.' This was not the first, nor would it be the last occasion on which an Acadian perspective was marginalized to make room for one from Quebec.

123 CEA, Fonds SNA, 41.43.282, 'Planification ... Fêtes du 375e anniversaire de la fondation de l'Acadie en Nouvelle-Ecosse.'

124 On the occasion of the 375th anniversary of the founding of Port-Royal, the National Film Board of Canada produced the documentary *J'avions 375 ans* (Montreal: NFB, 1982). The point is constantly made in the film that this was a celebration 'for the Acadians of Nova Scotia'; there was no longer the illusion that Port-Royal was the site of the start of Acadian history.

125 *Halifax Chronicle-Herald*, 16 May 1980. Mathieu Da Costa was a man of African origins who some believe accompanied Champlain. This issue is discussed in chapter 3.

126 *L'Évangéline*, 16 August 1980.
127 *Cahiers de la Société historique acadienne* 3, 8 (July–September 1970): 330.
128 CEA, Fonds Société historique acadienne, 60.106; submission from SHA '[sur]l'occasion de la journée d'accueil sur le futur de l'Île Ste-Croix,' 9 December 1980. While unattributed comments from these open houses were published (see above), this is the only signed submission that I could find.
129 CEA, Fonds SNA, 41.43.282, Yvon Fontaine to Raymond David (Radio-Canada), 11 December 1978.
130 Société des Acadiens du Nouveau-Brunswick, *Rapport annuel*, 1979, at http://collections.ic.gc.ca/saanb/rapports/rap79_01.html.
131 CEA, 41.43.282, Allocution prononcée le 13 mars 1979.
132 Centre de documentation et d'études madawaskayennes (Université de Moncton, Campus d'Edmundston; hereafter CDEM), Fonds SANB, 12.28.5, 'Document explicative: Fêtes du 375e anniversaire de la fondation de l'Acadie.'
133 For more detail regarding the linguistic situation in New Brunswick, see Roy, 'Demography and Demolinguistics in Acadia, 1871–1971.' On the issue of assimilation, the situation was even more dire for Acadians in the other Atlantic provinces, where the smaller populations (both numerically and as a percentage of the provincial totals) experienced even more rapid decline.
134 Andrée Peltier was hired by the Quebec Ministry of Intergovernmental Affairs to work for three months to organize a publicity campaign in advance of the 375th anniversaries. CEA, Fonds SANB, 42.204, Andrée Peltier, 'Rapport du Consultant en publicité pour les fêtes du 375e anniversaire de la fondation de l'Acadie,' 4 May 1979.
135 CEA, Fonds SANB, 42.204: Georges Bourdages to Richard Hatfield, 16 July 1979; Hatfield to Paul LeBlanc, 7 August 1979; Jean-Luc Bélanger to George Bourdages, 18 June 1980. In 1969 the lands of over 200 Acadian families were expropriated by the federal government in order to create a national park. This expropriation was viewed by many as a further expulsion of the Acadians, and so became a rallying cry for Acadian rights. The leader of the *expropriés*, Jackie Vautour, became a symbol to some of the aggression still being committed against the Acadian people.
136 CEA, Fonds SANB, 42.204, SANB, Communiqué de presse, 6 June 1979.
137 On the subject of CONA, see Jean-Guy Finn, Harley d'Entremont, and Philippe Doucet, 'Le nationalisme acadien vu à travers la convention d'orientation nationale de 1979,' *Revue de l'Université de Moncton* 13 (1980): 45–74.

138 See Ronald Labelle, 'Le tintamarre en Acadie: Une tradition inventée ou réinventée,' *Cahiers de la Société historique acadienne* 36 (2005): 109–21. For an idea of what an early-twenty-first century *tintamarre* looks and sounds like, see Andre Gladu's excellent documentary *Tintamarre*, DVD (Montreal: National Film Board of Canada, 2004).

139 *L'Évangéline*, 25 June and 16 August 1979. There was also no specific reference to the events of 1604 in the song 'Pour rester' that was written for the occasion by the Acadian singer-songwriter Calixte Duguay. The lyrics can be found at www.tu-dresden.de/sulcifra/quebec/calixte.pdf.

140 CEA, Fonds SANB, 42.204: Activités-jeunesse (Moncton), communiqué de presse, 22 March 1979; R.A. Ouellette, Superintendent of Conseil Scolaire 4-1, Bathurst, 11 April 1979; CDEM, Fonds SANB, 12-28-5, Rapport du secrétaire de la réunion du comité d'organisation des fêtes du 375e anniversaire, 29 April 1979.

141 *L'Évangéline*, 6 June 1979. The lack of respect on the 375th anniversary for both Dugua and Île Ste-Croix was evident when the New Brunswick government decided that some commemorative gesture was in order. It commissioned two plaques to be struck to mark the occasion. One was placed on the wall of the French town of Brouage, where Champlain (and not Dugua) was born. The other was apparently destined for Île Ste-Croix, but never made it to the site, ending up instead in a provincial warehouse, before being transferred (where I saw it) to the offices of the committee in St Stephen, New Brunswick, responsible for the 2004 commemorative events. (Comité de coordination Ste-Croix 2004, '2004: Célébration et commémoration du quatrième centenaire de l'établissement permanent des Français en Amérique du Nord,' October 1998. Document secured from Acadia National Park via FOIA request.)

142 CEA, Fonds SANB, 42.204, SANB, Communiqué de presse, 20 April 1979.

Chapter 2

1 Greg Allain, 'La "nouvelle capitale acadienne"? Les entrepreneurs acadiens et la croissance récente du Grand Moncton,' *Francophonies d'Amérique* 19 (Spring 2005): 19–43; Benoît Aubin, '400 ans plus tard dans les Maritimes,' *L'Actualité*, 1 September 2004. Assomption Vie began its existence in 1903 as 'la Société l'Assomption,' one of the institutions created during the turn-of-the-twentieth-century Acadian renaissance. Over time, it evolved, much like the Caisses populaires in Quebec, to become a major economic force.

2 Benedict Anderson, *Imagined Communities: Reflections on the Origin and Spread of Nationalism*, 2nd rev. ed. (London: Verson, 1991), 6.

3 As a sign of how much had changed since the 375th anniversary, in 1979 Maurice Léger claimed that both the cartographer and Dugua had received the charter in 1603, even though Champlain had not been on hand. (CEA, 41.43.282, Maurice Léger, 'L'origine du mot "Acadie. "')

4 Interview with Maurice Basque, 26 May 2004.

5 In chapter 1 we saw the evolution of the Société nationale l'Assomption, which became in 1957 the Société nationale des Acadiens. In 1992 the organization was renamed the Société nationale de l'Acadie. The initials SNA were retained throughout these changes.

6 Greg Allain, 'Le Congrès mondial acadien de 1994: Réseaux, Conflits, Réalisations,' *Revue de l'Université de Moncton* 30, 2 (1997): 147.

7 Chedly Belkhodja, 'L'Acadie confrontée au temps mondial,' *Francophonies d'Amérique* no. 11 (2001): 156.

8 *L'Acadie Nouvelle*, 3 August 2004.

9 Ibid.; Caron has made reference to the Basque 'affair' at the CMA in her 'Pour une nouvelle vision de l'Acadie,' in *Balises et références: Acadies, francophonies*, ed. Martin Pâquet and Stéphane Savard (Ste-Foy: Presses de l'Université Laval, 2007), 455–6. For a more positive view of this moment, see James Laxer, *The Acadians: In Search of a Homeland* (Toronto: Doubleday, 2006). As Laxer put it, Basque 'made a forceful, albeit gracious, case' (285). Basque is also defended in Marie-Linda Lord, 'L'incidence de l'exiguïté du milieu sur notre manière de vivre la liberté universitaire,' *Égalité* 52 (2005): 186–7.

10 *Le Devoir*, 14 August 2004. Thériault had distanced himself from the diaspora nearly a decade before the commemorative events of 2004 when he noted: 'It was already the case in the nineteenth century that the majority of French speakers in the Maritime provinces were not descendants of "deportees having managed to return." They were descendants of the former settlers of *Acadie française* who had managed to avoid deportation by fleeing to the territories that continued to belong to France; others – more numerous than usually believed – were descendants of relative newcomers who had come to Acadie to avoid the fall of the French empire in North America; still others were "French" settlers who were brought by Jersey merchants who took over from the French the fisheries of the St Lawrence valley' (*Identité à l'épreuve de la modernité* [Moncton: Éditions d'Acadie, 1995], 222–3).

11 *Les Mots de la Fête*, no. 7 (May 2004): 2. This publication was issued by the SNA as its 'bulletin d'information du 400e anniversaire de l'Acadie.'

12 Euclide Chiasson used these words at Fontainebleau on 8 November 2003; by 26 June 2004 he had relinquished leadership of the SNA to Michel Cyr, who used precisely the same words.

13 Interview with Euclide Chiasson, 8 November 2003.

14 'Rapport final de la Convention 2004 de la Société acadienne du Nouveau-Brunswick,' *Égalité* 51 (Spring 2005): 137.

15 Pierre Foucher, 'L'Égalité linguistique,' *Égalité* 51 (2005): 123.

16 Gilles Grenier, 'Linguistic and Economic Characteristics of Francophone Minorities in Canada: A Comparison of Ontario and Quebec,' *Journal of Multilingual and Multicultural Development* 18 (1997): 297; *Census of Canada,* 1996; 2001.

17 Pierre-Marcel Desjardins, 'L'Acadie des Maritimes: En périphérie de la périphérie,' *Francophonies d'Amérique* 19 (2005): 107–24.

18 In an action that anticipated further differences of opinion between Acadiens and Québécois about how to remember the past, at the start of the Moncton summit, the president of Quebec's Société St-Jean-Baptiste (SSJB) wondered how such a summit could take place in a city called Moncton. The SNA observed that this was a matter that did not overly concern Acadians and that the SSJB should mind its own business. (Radio-Canada, Nouvelles, 24 August 1999, http://www.radio-canada.ca/ nouvelles/29/29593.htm.)

19 Acadian Construction Ltd., 'Place 1604–Centre urbain d'Acadie,' http://www.acadianconstruction.com/place_1604.html#facts.

20 *L'Acadie Nouvelle,* 26 July 2005.

21 I have made this point in terms of Quebec in *Making History in Twentieth-Century Quebec* (Toronto: University of Toronto Press, 1997).

22 SNA, *Les actes du Forum 1986: Pour une Acadie de l'an 2000* (Moncton: Michel Henry Éditeur, 1987), 8.

23 SNA Archives, Conseil d'Administration, 26 January 1995.

24 Ibid., 17–18 October 1997.

25 SNA Archives, Letter to SNA, 29 October 1998, presented to meeting of Conseil d'Administration, 27–28 February 1998. The name of the author has been withheld for reasons of confidentiality.

26 Ibid. The emphasis is the author's.

27 SNA Archives, Conseil d'Administration, 17–18 October 1997.

28 SNA, '400e anniversaire de la présence française en Amérique (Acadie), Rencontre tenue à Dieppe, 12 Sept 2000' (document secured from Canadian Heritage via Access to Information Program [ATIP] request).

29 SNA, 'Rapport du comité central pour les fêtes, 2004–5 (préparé par Consultation Frenette), présenté au conseil d'administration de la SNA, 25 Mars 2000'; emphasis provided by the consultants (document secured from Parks Canada via ATIP request).

30 SNA, 'Rencontre d'historiens, 3 October 2000' (document secured from Canadian Heritage via ATIP request). In addition to Basque, this committee

also included Daniel LeBlanc (whom we shall see in chapter 6 as the leader of the Commission de l'Odyssée acadienne, a key player in 2005 events to mark the 250th anniversary of the deportation); Ronnie-Gilles LeBlanc (the archivist of the Centre d'études acadiennes); Père Maurice Léger (quoted above in regard to his work for the Société historique acadienne); and Fidèle Thériault (who worked in the Heritage Branch of the New Brunswick government and was involved with the organizing committee for the events at Île Ste-Croix). Also in attendance was Valérie Roy, who served as 'coordonnatrice.'

31 SNA, 'Rencontre d'historiens, 3 October 2000.'

32 SNA, 'Célébrations du 400e anniversaire de l'Acadie, Novembre 2000' (document secured from Canadian Heritage via ATIP request).

33 'Plan stratégique pour préparer et souligner le 400e anniversaire de la Nouvelle-France en terre d'Amérique, Ébauche – 24 mai 2000' (document secured from Canadian Heritage via ATIP request). The emphasis here is mine.

34 SNA, 'Le 400e anniversaire de l'Acadie, 17 novembre 2000,' 4 (document secured from Canadian Heritage via ATIP request).

35 Canadian Heritage, memo in response to 'Plan stratégique pour préparer et souligner le 400e anniversaire de la Nouvelle-France en terre d'Amérique,' 12 July 2000 (document secured from Canadian Heritage via ATIP request).

36 Rapport de Chantal Abord-Hugon au conseil d'administration de la SNA, 19–20 October 2001 (document secured from Canadian Heritage via ATIP request). The controversy over motion M-241 is discussed at length in chapter 6.

37 Chantal Abord-Hugon, email message to listserv, 30 October 2001 (document secured from Canadian Heritage via ATIP request).

38 Euclide Chiasson, letter to Norman Moyer, 21 December 2001 (document secured from Canadian Heritage via ATIP request).

39 Chantal Abord-Hugon, email message to listserv, 20 November 2001 (document secured from Canadian Heritage via ATIP request).

40 *L'Acadie Nouvelle*, 16 November 2001.

41 In response to a question posted on the website Capacadie.com at the time that motion M-241 was being debated, roughly two-thirds of respondents felt that they deserved such an apology (*L'Acadie Nouvelle*, 4 December 2001).

42 'Memorandum of Agreement between ACOA and PCH Concerning the Establishment of the "Atlantic Canada Cultural and Economic Partnership,"' 28 January 2002 (document secured from Canadian Heritage via ATIP request).

43 SNA, 'Compte rendu de la réunion du Comité d'Harmonisation, Halifax, le 14 mars 2002' (document secured from Canadian Heritage via ATIP request; emphasis in original document).

44 SNA, 'Compte rendu de la réunion du Comité d'Harmonisation, Halifax, le 23 mai 2002' (document secured from Canadian Heritage via ATIP request).

45 Claude DeGrâce, email message to Lucie LeBouthillier, 13 June 2002 (document secured from Canadian Heritage via ATIP request).

46 Canadian Heritage, press release, 15 August 2002, http://www .patrimoinecanadien.gc.ca/pc-ch/news-comm/cc020712_f.htm.

47 *L'Acadie Nouvelle*, 16 August 2002. The reference to 'an apology' pertained to the debate over motion M-241 (described briefly above) regarding an apology from the Crown for the deportation. The minister obviously held a grudge.

48 Ibid., 17 July 2003.

49 SAANB, Comité 2004, 12 September 2004. This committee was chaired by Théo Gagnon, who provided me with the committee's minutes, for which I am most grateful.

50 *L'Acadie Nouvelle*, 25 July 2003.

51 Atlantic Canada Opportunities Agency, *Summative Evaluation of Atlantic Canada Cultural and Economic Partnership (ACCEP)*, March 2006, 7; iv; 27. Available via pdf file at http://www.acoa.ca/e/library/evaluation/accep .shtml. The funding details of specific projects are presented in an appendix to the 'summative evaluation' that is available on demand from ACOA.

52 Historica, *Champlain in Acadia*, at http://www.histori.ca/champlain/index. do. Historica removed the material about Champlain in Quebec in August 2006.

53 *National Post*, 9 June 2003; Association for Canadian Studies, at http://www .acs-aec.ca/Polls/Poll42.pdf.

54 Downeast Heritage Museum, St Croix 2004 Coordinating Committee Archives, email message from Louise Fiset (Canadian Heritage) to Norma Stewart, 9 June 2004. The committee's files are housed in Calais, Maine, at the Downeast Heritage Museum (itself discussed in chapter 3), whose executive director, Jim Thompson, put them at my disposal. This process was facilitated when Gayle Moholland, director of the Calais Center of the University of Maine at Machias, arranged to have the files digitized. I am most grateful to both Jim and Gayle.

55 'Discours à l'occasion de l'inauguration de la Chaire d'études canadiennes de l'Université de Paris III Sorbonne Nouvelle,' 23 June 2000, at www .pco-bcp.gc.ca/default.asp?Language=F&Page=archivechretien&Sub= Speeches&Doc=sorbonne.20000623_f.htm.

56 Terrence Lonergan, email message to Jean-François Bergeron, 23 November
   2001. Attached to this message was the presentation '2004: 400e anniversaire du Canada: Programme Canada-France,' in which these goals were
   cited (document secured from Department of Foreign Affairs and International Trade [DFAIT] via ATIP request).
57 SNA archives, Meeting of conseil d'administration, 8 November 2002.
58 Interview with Terrence Lonergan, 5 November 2003; text prepared for
   Symposium Diderot, Langres (France), 14–17 April 2003. This document
   was secured from the embassy's Canada-France files by a research assistant,
   whose salary was paid from Canada-France funds and who was given free
   rein to secure documents for this project, with no strings attached.
59 More information about the major projects can be found at Canada-France,
   1604–2004, http://www.canada-2004.org/menu.php?langue=EN.
60 Interview with Pierre Duconseille and Perrine Wyplosz, 6 November 2003.
   Duconseille and Wyplosz were responsible for the project at the Cité
   des sciences.
61 In addition to the funding for these large projects, another $3.5 million was
   set aside for smaller, but by no means insignificant ones that might reinforce
   the overall aims of the program. In line with the goal of promoting the
   image of Canada as a modern nation, a project to allow a First Nation band
   from Newfoundland to construct a birch bark canoe and sail it to St Pierre
   and Miquelon, where they would build a traditional village, was rejected
   because 'the committee gave preference to projects that showed the
   modernity of Canada rather than to those which highlighted knowledge
   passed down through the generations' (Programme France-Canada, 2004,
   Deuxiéme appel à projets, 15 April 2003, p. 13; document secured from
   Canada-France files). More in line with the program's goals was the project
   most generously supported among these smaller ones. Roughly $200,000
   went to support 'Le forum international de jeunes défavorisés en insertion,'
   which consisted of two conferences (one in northern New Brunswick and
   one in France) to deal with integrating underprivileged children into
   society. Among the projects that appeared more closely connected with the
   events of 2004, $78,450 was provided to Les Éditions du Septentrion for a
   collection of essays dealing with Champlain. A further $175,000 went to
   support a project advanced by the SNA to allow Acadie to be the 'région à
   l'honneur' at the Festival Interceltique de Lorient, in France (Programme
   France-Canada, 2004, Inventaires des projets, distributed at Réunion du comité
   Canada-France, Paris, 10 November 2003). This level of funding only
   became available, however, after the cancellation of another large project
   that would have seen Canada feted on 1 July 2004 on Paris's Jardins du

Trocadéro (Programme France-Canada, 2004, 'Bilan du 30 juin 2003'; document secured from DFAIT via ATIP request).

62 Interview with Nathalie Fiquet (Curator of the Brouage site), 22 July 2004.

63 'Maison de l'Émigration française au Canada: Nouvelle-France, nouvelle vie ...' On a panel inside the museum, the same sentence from the pamphlet was reproduced, this time with the addition of the word '*Acadie*' to the list of places in Canada settled by the French.

64 Lysiane Gagnon, 'Retour à Tourouvre,' *La Presse*, 2 June 2001.

65 Terrence Lonergan, email message to Mirelle Cyr, 11 May 2001 (document secured from DFAIT via ATIP request); CBC, New Brunswick, 'France Scores Millions for Champlain Bash,' 21 July 2003.

66 Raymond Chrétien to Bruno Delaye (Ministère des Affaires étrangères, France), 24 November 2000 (document secured from internal files of Canada-France program).

67 Raymond Chrétien, email message to Sheila Copps et al. (listserv), 18 May 2001 (document secured from DFAIT via ATIP request).

68 Treasury Board of Canada, 'List of projects and initiatives approved from the Unity Reserve,' 29 April 2004, at http://www.tbs-sct.gc.ca/report/orp/ur-ru/pl-lp_e.asp.

69 *L'Acadie Nouvelle*, 17 July 2003.

70 CBC, New Brunswick, 'France Scores Millions for Champlain Bash,' 21 July 2003.

71 Chantal Abord-Hugon, email message to Lucie LeBouthillier, 15 January 2004 (document secured from Canadian Heritage via ATIP request).

72 Interview with Norma Stewart, 17 October 2003. In the files that I received via an ATIP request, there were also several letters of criticism from ordinary citizens, one of whom wrote anonymously to Prime Minister Chrétien: 'You present the impression that you are a moth eaten, non-sensible, inept, really stupid group of out of touch (with us) politicians. Gawd, you have upset me!' (letter to Jean Chrétien, 29 July 2003; document secured from Canadian Heritage via ATIP request). All the letters from individual citizens (and not from representatives of groups connected with the 400th anniversary) were in English. The absence of letters in French reflected the distance of the 400th anniversary from ordinary Acadians, a matter discussed at length below.

73 Canadian Press Wire Service, 23 July 2003.

74 The Congrès mondial acadien, staged in Nova Scotia, was part of an on-going series of reunions of the clans, and not a 400th anniversary event per se.

75 *New Brunswick Telegraph Journal*, 9 May 2002.

76 New Brunswick, Ministry of Intergovernmental Affairs, '2004: Une année de commémoration, l'Initiative 2004 du Nouveau-Brunswick,' 31 March 2005 (document secured via the New Brunswick Right to Information Act).

77 SNA, Press release, 3 July 2002.

78 New Brunswick, Interdepartmental Committee, 'Célébrations liées au 400e anniversaire de l'arrivée de de Mons et Champlain à l'Île Sainte-Croix,' Presentation to meeting, 23 February 2001 (document secured via the New Brunswick Right to Information Act).

79 New Brunswick, Ministry of Intergovernmental Affairs, '2004 Initiative,' 6 November 2002 (document secured via the New Brunswick Right to Information Act).

80 Downeast Heritage Museum, St Croix 2004 Coordinating Committee Archives, Letter from Fidèle Thériault interfiled in minutes of St Croix Co-ordinating Committee, 21 October 2002. The letter is cited here with the permission of its author.

81 Lieutenant Governor, New Brunswick, gnb.ca/lg/2004-e.htm. The lieutenant governor since August 2003 was Herménégilde Chiasson, a prominent Acadian in the arts in his own right. Ironically, elements of the new Acadian founding myth were not being easily communicated at a time when both the premier and lieutenant governor were Acadian.

82 Ministry of Intergovernmental Affairs, '2004: Une année de commémoration.'

83 In the document 'Initiatives 2004 du Nouveau-Brunswick: Projets financés sous le programme de l'Initiative 2004 du N.-B.' (secured via the province's Right to Information Act) 156 projects are listed that secured roughly $1,375,000 in funding. The remaining funds from the $2 million budget went to defray administrative costs ($200,000), to support a number of 'special projects,' or ones connected with education and the francophonie. Most of the projects under these last three rubrics did not show up in the list of 156, although some are referred to in '2004: Une année de commémoration,' a document from the Ministry of Intergovernmental Affairs.

84 'Initiatives 2004 du Nouveau-Brunswick: Projets financés.'

85 St Croix 2004 Coordinating Committee, '2004 Budget Details' (document secured via the New Brunswick Right to Information Act); *New Brunswick Telegraph Journal*, 15 March 2003.

86 Claude DeGrâce, Notes on conversations with New Brunswickers with a connection to 2004 commemorative events, 7–8 February 2002 (document secured from Parks Canada via ATIP request). This document was not

signed, so I appreciate Claude DeGrâce informing me that he was the author.

87 Letter from Facal to Copps, 3 October 2001 (document secured from Canadian Heritage via ATIP request).

88 *Le Soleil*, 20 February 2003.

89 Radio-Canada Atlantique, 7 August 2003 (http://www.radio-canada.ca/regions/atlantique/nouvelles/200308/07/002-doute-qc-2004.shtml).

90 *Le Soleil*, 20 February 2003.

91 *Le Devoir*, 27 November 2004.

92 *L'Acadie Nouvelle*, 29 November 2004.

93 Quebec, Ministre de la Culture et des Communications, *Communiqué*, 24 May 2003, at http://www.mcc.gouv.qc.ca/index.php?id=2328&tx_ttnews[swords]=champlain&tx_ttnews[periode]=y&tx_ttnews[year]=2003&tx_ttnews[posted]=1&tx_ttnews[tt_news]=1690&tx_ttnews[backPid]=2408&cHash=ff371f2d16.

94 The conference, 'Quatre siècles de francophonie en Amérique et d'échanges Europe-Afrique-Amérique,' was held from 26–29 May 2003.

95 Michel Tétu, *Sur les traces de Champlain, le visionnaire* (Quebec: Faculté des lettres, Université Laval, 2003), 15.

96 *Le Soleil*, 25 May 2003.

97 Basque was speaking to the conference 'Anniversaries That Work,' Amherst, Nova Scotia, 9–10 May 2003.

98 Historica, *Champlain in Acadia*, http://www.histori.ca/champlain/index.do (Historica removed the material about Champlain in Quebec in August 2006); CBC News, *Champlain Anniversary*, http://www.cbc.ca/news/background/champlainanniversary.

99 *L'Acadie Nouvelle*, 25 June 2004.

100 Ibid., 26 June 2004.

101 Transcript of interview on RDI, *L'Atlantique en direct*, 4 July 2001 (document secured from Canadian Heritage via ATIP request).

102 As if to underscore this point, the only picture on the front page of the first edition of the New Brunswick Telegraph-Journal to be published after 26 June showed members of 'Les Jeunes Chanteurs d'Acadie swoon[ing] over Wilfred Le Bouthillier' (28 June 2004).

103 Interview with Jay Reamer, 24 June 2004. I was quietly reading a newspaper at a St Andrews café when someone approached me, speaking with an Acadian accent, something not often heard in St Andrews, not even during the festive weekend marking the 400th anniversary in late June 2004. I looked up to see Chantal Abord-Hugon

of the SNA, whose presence underscored the relative absence of ordinary Acadians.

104 CapAcadie.com, 'Votre opinion,' 22 November 2003, at http://www .capacadie.com/poll/index.cfm?m=11&yy=2003. If it were not for the fact that there is other evidence that also shows the lack of recognition among Acadians for the Île Ste-Croix adventure, this evidence would be suspect. After all, in the same source there was a poll conducted only a few days later (on 26 November) that asked who was responsible for the assassination of President Kennedy. Over 21% of respondents said there had been a conspiracy directed by the vice-president, Lyndon Johnson.

105 *L'Acadie Nouvelle*, 16 August 2004.

106 Interview with Chantal Abord-Hugon, 26 May 2004.

107 In his homily, the auxiliary bishop of Halifax, Claude Champagne, referred to the presence of Huguenots in early *Acadie* only in passing.

108 The family-based nature of the CMA was underscored by the creation of the Fédération des Associations de Familles Acadiennes in 1995, as an outgrowth of the first CMA the previous year.

109 The campaign to secure this proclamation is discussed at length in chapter 6.

110 There were 203 Nova Scotians and 89 New Brunswickers. The information regarding the homes of the participants in the Melanson/Breau clans was provided in an email message from Lillian Stewart of Annapolis Royal, an organizer of the Melanson/Breau reunion, 10 August 2006.

111 Interview with Herménégilde Chiasson, 12 May 2005.

112 Caron, 'Pour une nouvelle vision de l'Acadie,' 443. She also made this point in *Se créer des ancêtres: Un parcours généalogique nord-américain XIXe–XXe siecles* (Sillery: Septentrion, 2006), 212–13.

113 While the Historic Sites and Monuments Board of Canada recommended that this site be declared of national historic significance in 1986, it was only in 2004 that a plaque was unveiled to give this recommendation public recognition (interview with Theresa Bunbury, Parks Canada, 13 July 2006). As for the plaque itself, some of the Melansons were quite appropriately agitated by its reference to the fact that the Melansons had 'abandoned' the settlement in 1755, as if they had had a choice.

114 Interviews conducted at official opening of the Melanson Settlement site, 3 August 2004.

115 ACOA, *Partnering for Success*, Fall 2002, 5.

116 *L'Acadie Nouvelle*, 14 August 2004.

117 Marie-Claude Bouchet and Michel Gemon, *Sur les pas de Pierre Dugua de Mons*, DVD (2002). I had the good fortune to spend a day in Royan with

Madame Bouchet and others from the city who were trying to keep the memory of Dugua alive. The activities of the Comité Dugua de Mons de Royan are described at http://www.comitedugua-royan.com.

118 Tour Pierre Dugua de Mons, 1604–2004, *Bulletin d'un voyage dans l'histoire*, at http://www.dugas.info/LeTour/Bulletin.asp; *L'Acadie Nouvelle*, 17 July 2004. I did not see their application for funding, and so pass no judgment on their unhappiness about being turned down.

119 *L'Actualité*, 1 September 2004.

120 Interview, 12 May 2005; Chiasson, 'Le festif en Acadie,' *Port Acadie* 8–9 (Fall 2006): 20.

121 Chiasson, 'Le festif en Acadie,' 18.

122 For the classic statement in this regard, see Hobsbawm, 'Mass-Producing Traditions,' in *The Invention of Tradition*, ed. Hobsbawm and Eric Ranger (Cambridge: Cambridge University Press, 1983), 263–307.

123 Guy Beiner, *Remembering the Year of the French: Irish Folk History and Social Memory* (Madison: University of Wisconsin Press, 2007), 272–3.

124 Jocelyn Létourneau has made this point in various publications, including 'L'imaginaire historique des jeunes Québécois,' *Revue d'histoire de l'Amérique française* 41, 4 (Spring 1989): 553–74; and, with Sabrina Moisan, 'Mémoire et récit de l'aventure historique du Québec chez les jeunes Québécois d'héritage canadien français: Coup de sonde, amorce d'analyse des résultats, questionnements,' *Canadian Historical Review* 85, 2 (June 2004): 325–56.

Chapter 3

1 Interview with Norma Stewart, 28 May 2004.

2 Interview with Maurice Basque, 26 May 2004.

3 Such questions have become ever more frequent with the explosion of public presentations of the past, not only via commemorative events, but also by such means as museum exhibits and documentary films. In Canada there have been heated debates, for instance, prompted by veterans groups which questioned the authority of others to interpret the bombing campaign against German cities in the Second World War. The issue emerged in terms of the documentary film *The Valour and the Horror*, and is discussed by Graham Carr in 'Rules of Engagement: Public History and the Drama of Legitimation,' *Canadian Historical Review* 86, 2 (June 2005): 317–54. Veterans groups also challenged the Canadian War Museum's interpretation of the same events, and succeeded in having it recast (CBC, News, 'Canadian War Museum Changes Controversial Wording on WWII Bombing,' http://web02.nm.cbc.ca/arts/artdesign/story/2007/10/11/

war-museum.html). For a similar example in the American context, see the debate over the Smithsonian exhibit regarding the *Enola Gay*, the aircraft from which the first nuclear bomb was dropped on Japan: *History Wars: The Enola Gay and Other Battles for the American Past*, ed. Edward T. Linenthal and Tom Engelhardt (New York: Henry Holt, 1996).

4 The 2000 U.S. Census indicates that the median household income for the country as a whole was $50,046, for Maine $37,240, for Washington County $25,869, and for Calais $24,623. Other criteria could be employed with the same results. Moreover, the status of Washington County as the poorest of Maine counties stretched back for decades.

5 Letter from Lee Sochasky, 29 March 1999 (document secured from U.S. Department of Interior, National Park Service, Acadia National Park, via FOIA request; the name of the recipient of the letter was obliterated before the document was released).

6 The 2001 Canadian census shows that the median income for New Brunswick was $18,257, for Charlotte County $18,500, for St Andrews $22,307 and for St Stephen $17,988.

7 St Croix International Waterway Commission, 'Proposal for Development of a Ste-Croix 2004 Celebration and Legacy Master Plan,' 30 October 1998 (document secured from Parks Canada via ATIP request).

8 Interview with Keith Guttormsen, 28 May 2004.

9 Interview with Allan Gillmor, 17 October 2003.

10 Interview with Allan Gillmor, 24 June 2004.

11 St Croix International Waterway Commission, 'Overview of a Celebration 2004 Workshop, July 18, 1995.'

12 Downeast Heritage Museum, St Croix 2004 Coordinating Committee Archives, Minutes (hereafter St Croix Minutes), 30 April 1998.

13 St Croix Minutes, 27 October 1998. This text was the result of editing that was visible from changes recorded in the minutes. An earlier version recognized that Dugua and Champlain had been French, but this reference to their nationality was crossed out.

14 Ibid., 27 October 1998.

15 Ibid., 24 November 1998.

16 Ibid., 28 May 1998.

17 Ibid., 23 February 1999. Alongside the French version, the minutes also reprinted the English version agreed upon in the fall. However, the typed version did not include the word 'French,' which had to be scribbled in the margins. Was this a Freudian slip? In any event, at the subsequent meeting of the committee (23 March), the lapse was noted as an 'inadvertent omission' and was corrected.

18 Ibid., 26 January 1999.

19 Ibid., 21 May 1998.

20 Ibid., 7 July 2004.

21 Ibid., 12 May 2003.

22 Ibid., 13 February 2004.

23 Chantal Abord-Hugon, email message to Lucie LeBouthillier, 15 January 2004 (document secured from Canadian Heritage via ATIP request).

24 SNA, 'Rencontre d'historiens, 3 October 2000' (document secured from Canadian Heritage via ATIP request). The role of this committee of historians was also discussed in chapter 2.

25 St Croix Minutes, 11 June 2001.

26 Société des Acadiens et Acadiennes du Nouveau-Brunswick (SAANB), Comité 2004 Minutes, 25 November 2002. I am grateful to Théo Gagnon, who held the SAANB seat on the St Croix Coordinating Committee, in addition to chairing this committee, for making these minutes available.

27 Interviews, 17 October 2003.

28 Interview with Norma Stewart, 31 May 2004.

29 Interview with Maria Kulcher, 31 May 2004. Kulcher made this point with much conviction. These lines were included in *Life After Île Ste-Croix*.

30 Basque was speaking to the conference, 'Anniversaries That Work,' Amherst, Nova Scotia, 9–10 May 2003.

31 Interview with Maurice Basque, 26 May 2004.

32 Interview with Euclide Chiasson, 26 May 2004.

33 SNA archives, Minutes, Comité d'harmonisation, 20 February 2004.

34 St Croix Minutes, 26 May 2004.

35 Downeast Heritage Museum, St Croix 2004 Coordinating Committee Archives, Memo from Agenda Managers to Ste-Croix 2004 Coordinating Committee, 21 May 2004.

36 Ibid., email message from Canadian Heritage to Norma Stewart, 9 June 2004.

37 Memo from Agenda Managers to Norma Stewart, 15 April 2004 (document secured from Canadian Heritage via ATIP request).

38 Downeast Heritage Museum, St Croix 2004 Coordinating Committee Archives, Memo from fund-raisers to Norma Stewart, 7 May 2004; St Croix 2004 Coordinating Committee, 2004 Annual Report.

39 Interview with Norma Stewart, 30 September 2004.

40 This point is discussed at length in chapter 2.

41 These Acadian stars had also appeared, albeit briefly, during the official ceremonies earlier in the day.

42 Downeast Heritage Museum, St Croix 2004 Coordinating Committee Archives, 'St-Croix 2004, Schedule of Events, Attendance Summary.' For its part, the *Bangor Daily News* estimated that 2500 people were in attendance, spending 'five or more hours in the mist and rain' (28 June 2004).

43 Daniel K. Glenn Ltd (Landscape Architects and Park Planners), 'Ste-Croix Island Historic Settlement, Event and Legacy Master Plan,' November 2000 (document secured from Parks Canada via ATIP request). Although the Passamaquoddy had been on hand in 1604, the architect referred to the aboriginal space as a 'Mi'kmaq area.' The Passamaquoddy were frequently ignored in the run-up to the quadricentenary, as we shall see in chapter 4.

44 Parks Canada, '400th Anniversary Saint Croix Island International Historic Site of Canada,' March 2002 (document secured from Parks Canada via ATIP request).

45 St-Croix 2004 Organizing Committee, 'Revised Proposal for Development at Bayside,' September 2002 (document secured from Parks Canada via ATIP request).

46 Downeast Heritage Museum, St Croix 2004 Coordinating Committee Archives, 'Ste-Croix 2004 Feasibility Study,' 30 June 2003.

47 St Croix Minutes, 5 May 2003; 4 December 2003.

48 Ibid., 4 December 2004.

49 Interview with Allan Gillmor, 17 October 2003.

50 St-Croix 2004 Coordinating Committee to Sheila Copps, 21 December 2001 (document secured from Parks Canada via ATIP request).

51 Parks Canada, Call for Artists' Entries for Commemorative Monument: St Croix Island International Historic Site, Bayside, New Brunswick, 15 December 2003.

52 Interview with Norma Stewart, 17 October 2003.

53 Letter from Lee Sochasky, 29 March 1999 (document secured from U.S. Department of Interior, National Park Service, Acadia National Park via FOIA request; the name of the recipient of the letter was obliterated before the document was released).

54 United States, Congress, Senate, *Saint Croix Island Heritage Act*, S.2485, 106th Congress, 2nd session, 2000.

55 National Park Service, *Media Alert*, 13 June 2003 (document secured from U.S. Department of Interior, National Park Service, Acadia National Park via FOIA request).

56 Wade and Soctomah also teamed up to create a number of trunks, each of which was filled with replicas of items relating to the winter of 1604–5. The trunks were made available to schools (on both sides of the border) so that the story might be better known.

57 Deb Wade, email message to Chuck Smythe, 24 September 2002 (document secured from U.S. Department of Interior, National Park Service, Acadia National Park via FOIA request). The Red Beach Trail, a wonderful example of bringing the past to life, is discussed again in the Epilogue.

58 Nathalie Gagnon and Donald Soctomah, *Tihtiyas and Jean* (Moncton: Bouton d'or Acadie, 2004). The book was recognized as an iParenting Media Award winner for one of the Best Products of 2005. (http://iparentingmediaawards.com/winners/6/802-2-338.php).

59 *Moncton Times and Transcript*, 20 April 2002.

60 Port Royal 400th Anniversary Society, 'Strategic Planning Report for Port Royal 400th Anniversary Society,' September 1999, 9. This document, as well as the minutes and newsletter of the Society, were provided to me by Linda Brown, the group's president at the time of the quadricentenary, to whom I am most appreciative.

61 Port Royal 400th Anniversary Society, *Newsletter*, March 2001.

62 Ibid., Summer 2000.

63 All income data are from the 2001 Census of Canada.

64 See http://www.annapolisroyal.com/downloads/niagarapresentation.pdf.

65 Port Royal 400th Anniversary Society, 'Strategic Planning Report,' 36.

66 Port Royal 400th Anniversary Society, First Annual General Meeting, 17 October 1996.

67 Port Royal 400th Anniversary Society, 'Strategic Planning Report,' Appendix I.

68 Ibid., 4.

69 DaCosta '400, at http://www.dacosta400.ca/cavalcade/mathieudacosta .shtml. The difficulties with corroborating the Da Costa story are presented in A.J.B. Johnston, *Mathieu Da Costa and Early Canada: Possibilities and Probabilities* (Halifax: Parks Canada, n.d.), 20 (http://www.pc.gc.ca/lhn-nhs/ns/portroyal/natcul/dacosta_e.pdf).

70 Ken Pinto, '400 years/Matthew de Costa, 2004/2005, Proposal,' 15 July 2001 (document secured from Canadian Heritage via ATIP request). Regarding 'Da Costa 400,' see http://www.dacosta400.ca.

71 Letter from Thériault to DeGrâce, 1 June 1998 (document secured from Parks Canada via ATIP request).

72 Port Royal 400th Anniversary Society, 'Forum 400: A Port Royal Community Think Tank,' 27 October 1998, 13.

73 As with the Passamaquoddy, chapter 4 will deal with these issues from aboriginal perspectives. Greater attention will be paid there to the history of the Bear River Mi'kmaq, but for an introduction, readers should consult Darlene A. Ricker, *L'sitkuk: The Story of the Bear River Mi'kmaw Community* (Lockeport, NS: Roseway Publishing, 1997).

74 The first proposal for setting aside land for such a reserve came in 1801, but the Mi'kmaq were not living at Bear River until the 1820s (Ricker, *L'sitkuk*, 80–4).

75 Interview with David Kern Jr, 18 July 2003.

76 One of the interesting aspects of this performance was the involvement of Elsie Basque who played an elderly Mi'kmaq but in 1934 had played the role of Membertou's daughter in another re-enactment staged at the habitation. In an interview in 1995 Basque reflected the spirit of 'The People's Story' when she talked about growing up in the mostly Acadian region of Clare, where she observed, 'One is accepted for who and what one is - not one's ethnic background. The bonds of friendship and understanding that began with Chief Membertou, Champlain, De Monts, Poutrincourt, have never faltered; their legacy lives on.' (Daniel Paul, *We Were Not Savages*, at http://www.danielnpaul.com/Col/1995/ElsieBasque-MicmacPioneer.html).

77 Federation of Nova Scotian Heritage, *News Bulletin*, March 2006.

78 Ironically, there was much better evidence of an African presence only a few kilometres from the Port-Royal habitation, at another Parks Canada facility. The site of the Melanson settlement was opened to the public in 2004 in conjunction with the Melanson family reunion during the Congrès mondial acadien. One of the interpretive plaques indicates that there were six households in this small 'village' in 1710, one of which was headed by Jean Roy. 'One document suggests that Jean Roy dit La Liberté was a person of African descent. He was married to Marie Aubois, an aboriginal woman who was possibly from Québec.' The official opening of the site of the settlement was discussed at length in chapter 2.

79 Acadie 2003–5, Marketing Plan, June 2002. This document was kindly provided by Lillian Stewart, the marketing coordinator of Acadie 2003–5.

80 Acadie 2003–5, Meeting of 22 August 2000 (document secured from Canadian Heritage via ATIP request).

81 Port Royal 400th Society, Minutes, 26 November 2001; 4 February 2002.

82 Ibid., 6 May 2002. The issue resurfaced in early 2003: a motion of support for Acadie 2003–5 was rejected on 6 January, and was reversed by a 4–3 vote on 27 January.

83 Ibid., 26 August 2002.

84 *The Spectator*, 19 August 2003. Kern also figured prominently in articles on 5 and 26 August, and 2 September 2003.

85 By the terms of the program, these funds had to be matched by monies raised from other sources.

86 *Le drapeau acadien*, words (in both French and English) and music by Jeanne (Doucet) Currie.

87 This same conceit had also been on display in 1904, when the inscription on the monument to Dugua at Annapolis Royal referred to Port-Royal as 'the first settlement of Europeans north of the Gulf of Mexico.' In this conception, not only was the Île Ste-Croix settlement ignored, but so too was the Spanish settlement at St Augustine, established in 1565.

88 Armstrong's treatment of the deportation paralleled that in other public performances of the history of the Annapolis Valley that were staged in the early twentieth century. See Caroline-Isabelle Caron, 'Se souvenir de l'Acadie d'antan: Représentation du passé historique dans le cadre de célébrations commémoratives locales en Nouvelle-Écosse au milieu du 20e siècle,' *Acadiensis* 36, 1 (Spring 2007): 55–71.

89 As for the real-life Marie, she was described as an enthusiastic British subject in the journals of the officer John Knox, who observed in 1757: 'I am also assured that this good lady has actually presided at councils of war in the fort, when measures have been concerting to distress the common enemy, her good kindred and countrymen' (John Knox, *An historical journal of the campaigns in North America for the years 1757, 1758, 1759, and 1760*, 3 vols. [Toronto: The Champlain Society, 1914–16], 1: 95.)

90 Earlier in 'Connections' there had been a brief appearance by one character described as Mi'kmaq, who was identified only as La Tour's daughter.

91 Interview with Maurice Basque, 26 May 2004.

92 Port Royal 400th Anniversary Society, Minutes, 28 January and 11 March 2006.

93 Having separated from Champlain on the voyage across the Atlantic, Dugua was not on hand on this occasion, although he joined up with the cartographer a few days later. Accordingly, the emphasis upon Champlain, which might have seemed out of place in the year of Dugua, was appropriate.

94 Interview with John Joe Sark, 8 May 2004.

95 Greg Allain and Maurice Basque, *De la survivance à l'effervescence: Portrait historique et sociologique de la communauté acadienne et francophone de Saint-Jean, Nouveau-Brunswick* (Saint John: Association régionale de la communauté francophone de Saint-Jean, 2001), 36.

96 This text by George MacBeath, read at the unveiling of the Dugua monument, was kindly provided by Elaine Geary, who was active in Saint John's 400th anniversary events.

97 *Le Saint-Jeannois*, 10 July 2004. For his part, the French consul general told me that he thought it had been inconsiderate of the St Croix

organizers to stage their events to conflict with the appearance of the
Comédie-Française (interview with Michel Freymuth, 25 May 2004).

98 Paul-Emile Chiasson, 'The Significance of the Francophone Community in
Greater Saint John' (The Industrial City in Transition, at http://www.unbsj
.ca/cura/projects/ Francophonecommunityinsaintjohn.htm).

99 Acadie 2003–5, Meeting of 22 August 2000 (document secured from
Canadian Heritage via ATIP request).

Chapter 4

1 E.M. Slader, *From the Victorian Era to the Space Age*, Collections of the New
Brunswick Historical Society no. 21 (n.p., 1973), 35. For the role of aboriginal
people at Quebec City in 1908, see Nelles, The *Art of Nation-Building*, chap. 8.

2 Stephen Summerhill and John Alexander Williams, *Sinking Columbus:
Contested History, Cultural Politics and Mythmaking during the Quincentenary*
(Gainesville: University Press of Florida, 2000), 117. In its exploration of the
construction of a series of commemorative events, *Sinking Columbus* bears
some similarity to this book, although the dynamics were a bit different for
Summerhill and Williams, the latter having at one point been involved with
the quincentenary commission.

3 Ibid., 119.

4 Theodore Walker, Jr, 'Native American Protests against 1992 Celebrations of
1492: A Sage-like Meaning of Solidarity,' at http://faculty.smu.edu/twalker/
protest4.htm.

5 Summerhill and Williams, *Sinking Columbus*, 124.

6 *Les Mots de la fête* no. 6 (May 2004): 6.

7 *La Croix*, August 2004.

8 *Les Mots de la fête* no. 6 (May 2004): 2.

9 Interview with Frank Meuse, Jr, 15 July 2005.

10 Interview with Donald Soctomah, 17 October 2003.

11 Interview with Norma Stewart, 31 May 2004.

12 The details of this case are taken from *St. Andrews (Town of) v. Lecky*, [1993]
133 N.B.R. (2d) 14 (N.B.Q.B.). Accessed via Lexis-Nexis.

13 Mary Caldbick, 'Locke's Doctrine of Property and the Dispossession of the
Passamaquoddy,' MA thesis, University of New Brunswick, 1997, 122. An
excellent summary of the Indian Point issue can also be found in Bonnie
Huskins and Michael Boudreau, '*Life After Île Ste-Croix*,' *Acadiensis* 35, 2
(Spring 2006): 180–7.

14 The Passamaquoddy role in the treaties legitimized by the Marshall
ruling is discussed in William Wicken, *Mi'kmaq Treaties on Trial: History,*

Land, and Donald Marshall Junior (Toronto: University of Toronto Press, 2002). Also, see Wicken, 'Passamaquoddy Identity and the Marshall Decision,' in *New England and the Maritime Provinces: Connections and Comparisons*, ed. Stephen J. Hornsby and John G. Reid (Montreal: MQUP, 2006), 50–9.

15 Paul Brodeur, *Restitution: The Land Claims of the Mashpee, Passamaquoddy, and Penobscot Indians of New England* (Boston: Northeastern University Press, 1985), 126. The 1980 Maine Indian Claims Settlement is also described in a report of the same title by Diane Scully, at www.abbemuseum.org/d_scully_landclaims.pdf.

16 Caldbick, 'Locke's Doctrine,' 101.

17 Cited in W.O. Raymond, 'The Indians after the Coming of the English,' *Saint Croix Courier*, 16 June 1892, at http://members.shaw.ca/caren.secord/locations/NewBrunswick/Glimpses/XXI.html.

18 Petition tabled by New Brunswick House of Assembly, 1 February 1854. Reproduced in James Wherry, *Documents Relating to the History of the Passamaquoddy Indian Presence in Charlotte County, New Brunswick* (Fredericton: n.p., 1981), Special Collections and Archives, Harriet Irving Library, University of New Brunswick, Fredericton. The Wherry collection is crucial to understanding the claims of the New Brunswick Passamaquoddy.

19 Interview with Donald Soctomah, 17 October 2003.

20 A. Reade to Revd. A. Campbell, 19 April 1842 (document secured from Department of Indian Affairs and Northern Development [DIAND] via ATIP request).

21 A reserve was also established nearby in York County in 1881. However, it does not appear that the 200-acre St Croix reserve was created solely for the benefit of the Passamaquoddy. James Wherry found that St Croix was 'set aside for the use of Indians whose modern descendants demonstrate an orientation, in unknown ratios, to the modern sociological and political units known as the Passamaquoddy and Maliseet Tribes' (35). In 1944 the federal government returned the land to the province 'free from any Indian trust' (Wherry, *Documents*, 160).

22 A.E. Hanson, Surveyor, to Frank Pedley, Supt. Indian Affairs, 23 July 1903 (document secured from DIAND via ATIP request).

23 New Brunswick Crown Lands Department to Frank Pedley, 10 November 1909 (document secured from DIAND via ATIP request).

24 James Farrell, Indian Agent, to Secretary, Indian Department, Ottawa, 6 July 1904; document reproduced in Wherry, *Documents*, 66. In regard to St Andrews at roughly the same time, Ganong noted at Indian Point 'two or three families of Passamaquoddies live near the railroad station, though

not upon a reservation.' (W.F. Ganong, 'A Monograph of Historic Sites in New Brunswick,' *Transactions of the Royal Society of Canada*, sect. 2, 5[1899]: 223.)

25 Grimmer to B.J. Griffith, Indian Agent, 20 February 1922 (document secured from DIAND via ATIP request).

26 Grimmer to Griffith, 25 May 1925 (document secured from DIAND via ATIP request). It is curious that this letter did not figure in the various government reports on the Canoose reserve that I secured via an access-to-information request. For instance, a manager of Indian lands for the federal government conveniently did not refer to this document, so that he could conclude in 1975 that 'although Mr Nicholas appeared willing to sign, he died before a surrender was obtained' (H.T. Vergette to Christine Jackson, 20 January 1975). This telling of the tale removed Nicholas's defence of his people's interests from the story. By contrast, the Nicholas story remains a part of the collective memory of the Passamaquoddy. In May 2004 Donald Soctomah explained how the government secured Canoose and other reserve land: 'They even tried to get some Passamaquoddy elders who were living in St Andrews to sign the parcels away. But they refused. So, the land ... they just did it, just converted it over, on their own, illegally, and sold the timber, the timbering rights on that land' (Interview, 31 May 2004).

27 Claim by Union of New Brunswick Indians, Canoose Indian Reserve, November 1974. Claims registry file 1/3-11-68 (document secured from DIAND via ATIP request).

28 H.T. Vergette to Anthony Francis (UNBI), n.d. (document secured from DIAND via ATIP request).

29 St Croix Schoodic Band of the Passamaquoddy Nation at Quanasquamcook, Band Council Resolution, 21 July 1999 (document secured from DIAND via ATIP request).

30 *Bangor Daily News*, 7 June 1995.

31 Ibid., 9 May 1997; 2 July 1997.

32 *New Brunswick Telegraph Journal*, 20 May 2002.

33 *Bangor Daily News*, 15 July 1997.

34 Ibid., 8 June 1998.

35 Ibid., 6 October 1999; *New Brunswick Telegraph Journal*, 20 May 2002.

36 CBC News, 'Development Dilemma,' 27 August 2001, at http://www.cbc.ca/news/story/2001/08/27/nb_mhsta_010827.html; WQDY Radio News, 2 October 2001, at http://www.wqdy.fm/2001_10_01_archive.html; Atlantic Policy Congress, Media Release, 28 September 2001.

37 *Bangor Daily News*, 6 February 2002.

38 CBC News, 'Land Battle Underway in St. Andrews,' 8 February 2002, at http://www.cbc.ca/canada/new-brunswick/story/2002/02/08/mh _zone020802.html.

39 St Croix Minutes, 24 November 1998.

40 Ibid., 26 January 1999.

41 Ibid., 24 January 2000.

42 Daniel K. Glenn Ltd (Landscape Architects and Park Planners), 'Ste-Croix Island Historic Settlement, Event and Legacy Master Plan,' November 2000 (document secured from Parks Canada via ATIP request). In an interview on 18 October 2003, Akagi remarked: 'I remember when they were first preparing a presentation and they were going around the area presenting this and I did notice that on one of the maps, they were talking about a Mi'kmaq encampment and I found that kind of interesting.'

43 St Croix Minutes, 6 February 2003.

44 Nathalie Gagnon, email message to Esma Taylor and Allan Gillmor, 8 April 2003 (document secured from Parks Canada via ATIP request).

45 Interview, 17 October 2003. This individual eventually ended up with a very supportive view of the role of the Passamaquoddy in the quadricentenary. I see no reason to cause embarrassment by disclosing the individual's name.

46 John Joe Sark, email message to Chantal Abord-Hugon, 11 December 2003 (document secured from Parks Canada via ATIP request).

47 Interview with Allan Gillmor, 17 October 2003.

48 Interview with Norma Stewart, 17 October 2003.

49 Interview with Donald Soctomah, 17 October 2003.

50 St Croix Minutes, 22 July 2003. Stewart made the same point publicly: *New Brunswick Telegraph Journal*, 26 June 2003.

51 St Croix Minutes, 22 July, 25 July, and 3 September 2003.

52 Interview with Hugh Akagi by Ed Bassett, August 2006. This interview, which formed part of a program that Bassett produced for broadcast on the closed-circuit network on the Pleasant Point Reservation, is reproduced here with Bassett's consent.

53 Interview with Donald Soctomah, 31 May 2004.

54 Interview with Hugh Akagi, 18 October 2003.

55 Interview with Hugh Akagi, 2 October 2004; interview with Norma Stewart, 1 October 2004.

56 Interview with Hugh Akagi, 24 June 2004. Minutes after this interview I had my fateful encounter with the pavement.

57 *Bangor Daily News*, 28 June 2004; United Church of Canada, 'Commemoration of the 400th Anniversary of Acadie,' Press Release, 28 June 2004.

It was ironic that there were apologies for the deportation at the time that the founding (and not destruction) of *Acadie* was being marked. The apologies in this regard might have been more appropriate a year later.

58 In terms of the attention paid to the role of First Nations people, there was a striking difference between the *St Croix Island Suite* and the *Annapolis Royal Suite*, discussed in the previous chapter.

59 Interview with Alasdair MacLean, 27 June 2004.

60 Interview with Norma Stewart, 1 October 2004.

61 Interview with Rita Fraser, 2 October 2004.

62 Ibid.; interview with Hugh Akagi by Ed Bassett, August 2006.

63 Ricker, *L'sitkuk*, 94.

64 Ibid., 163–5.

65 'Frank Meuse: Chief Author of Bear River Success Story,' *Halifax Herald*, 20 October, 1995, at http://www.danielnpaul.com/Col/1995/ ChiefFrankMeuse-SuccessStory.html.

66 Kenneth Coates, *The Marshall Decision and Native Rights* (Montreal: McGill-Queen's University Press, 2000), 139–41.

67 Scott Milsom, 'Fishing for Community Benefit,' *Coastal Communities Network, Rural Reports*, 15 March 2007, at http://www.coastalcommunities.ns.ca/ magazine/rural_report.php#bear_river.

68 Andi Rierden, 'Longard Award Winner,' *Gulf of Maine Times* 6, 1 (Spring 2002): http://www.gulfofmaine.org/times/spring2002/longard.html.

69 John F. Kearney, 'Community-Based Fisheries Management in the Bay of Fundy: Sustaining Communities through Resistance and Hope,' in *Natural Resources as Community Assets: Lessons from Two Continents*, ed. B. Child and M.W. Lyman (Washington: Aspen Institute and Sand County Foundation, 2005); also available at www.ecotrust.org/cbfm/CBFM_in _Bay_of_Fundy.pdf.

70 Milsom, 'Fishing for Community Benefit.'

71 Martha Stiegman, 'United We Fish,' *Alternatives Journal* 29 (Fall 2003): 40.

72 Milsom, 'Fishing for Community Benefit.'

73 Ibid.

74 Sherry Pictou, 'Community Learning Approach to Fishery Access and Management,' presentation to Coastal Zone Canada 2006 Conference and Youth Forum, at http://www.czc06.ca/text_e/db/summaryDetail.asp?id=70.

75 Atlantic Canada Opportunities Agency, *News Release*, 19 May 2004, at http:// www.acoa.ca/e/media/press/press.shtml?2969.

76 Interview with Frank Meuse, 15 July 2005.

77 Ibid., 5 August 2004.

78 These quotations are from the script of 'The People's Story,' provided by Hal Theriault, who was most generous in supporting this project.

79 Interview with Frank Meuse, 5 August 2004.

80 Interview with Hal Theriault, 15 July 2005.

81 The methodology behind the Community Wellbeing Index is explained at http://www.ainc-inac.gc.ca/pr/ra/pub4_e.html; the Bear River score can be found at http://sdiprod2.inac.gc.ca/FNProfiles/FNProfiles_Wellbeing_e .asp?BAND_NUMBER=21&BAND_NAME=Bear+River.

Chapter 5

1 Peter Novick, *The Holocaust in American Life* (Boston: Houghton Mifflin, 1999), 103.

2 Ibid., 110.

3 Ibid., 114.

4 Ibid., 7–8.

5 Ibid., 109. There is an imposing list of traumatic moments from various national histories that were long repressed. To take only one further example, public commemoration of the Irish Potato Famine of the 1840s was insignificant in Ireland until fairly recently. There was really no full-length study of this traumatic moment until the 1950s. (See Cormac Ó Gráda, 'Making History in Ireland in the 1940s and 1950s: The Saga of "The Great Famine,"' in *Interpreting Irish History: The Debate on Historical Revisionism, 1938–1994,* ed. Ciarán Brady [Dublin: Irish Academic Press, 1994], 269–87.) During the years of the Troubles in Northern Ireland, some were reluctant to speak too openly about the famine, fearful of adding fuel to the fire. However, with the noticeable reduction of tensions in the North and the emergence of the Celtic Tiger in the Republic, it was possible to stage large-scale state-funded commemorative events on the 150th anniversary of the Famine in 1997.

6 Novick, *The Holocaust in American Life,* 103; Robert Viau, *Les grands dérangements: La déportation des acadiens en littératures acadienne, québécoise et française* (Beauport: Publications MNH, 1997), 8.

7 *Du Grand-Dérangement à la Déportation: Nouvelles perspectives historiques,* ed. Ronnie-Gilles LeBlanc (Moncton: Chaire d'études acadiennes, 2005), 7.

8 There were frequent comparisons between the experiences of Jews and Acadians in texts prepared to mark commemorations of the deportation. The point was often made that both people had suffered for having insisted on being true to their faith, and that both were chosen people who were constantly being challenged to see if they warranted their special status. As we will see, such a view, the dominant Acadian perspective on the deporta-

tion until after the bicentenary in 1955, minimized the significance of British geo-political concerns, in a sense freeing them from responsibility. For an example, see the statement of the archbishop of Moncton at the kickoff for organizing the bicentenary: *L'Évangéline*, 26 April 1954.

9 Faragher, *A Great and Noble Scheme*, 469. Some may contest the use of a late-twentieth-century term to describe an event from the eighteenth century. Nevertheless, we need to have the ability to call past events by names that we understand if the same conditions are applied to those past events as we would apply to modern ones. For instance, in cases of premeditated murder of specific groups in the past, the use of the term 'genocide' is accepted by scholars in the field, if certain conditions can be found to have been met. The Balkan analogy proposed by Faragher is apt. In each case, the goal was to remove a people from its lands.

10 CEA, Fonds François G.J. Comeau, Lettre pastorale de l'archevêque de Halifax, Mgr Guillaume Walsh, aux Acadiens, 1855.

11 *Le Moniteur Acadien*, 17 August 1905.

12 Ibid., 7 September 1905.

13 Ibid., 31 August 1905

14 Ibid., 7 September 1905.

15 CEA, Fonds Placide Gaudet 1.62-6, Conférence de Placide Gaudet, cinquième Convention nationale acadienne, 1905; Placide Gaudet, *Le Grand Dérangement: Sur qui retombe la responsabilité de l'Expulsion des Acadiens* (Ottawa: Ottawa Printing Co, 1922). In this work Gaudet made the point that there was no euphemism in referring to the deportation by another term. As he noted, at the outset: 'Our forebears referred to their expulsion from *Acadie* as a *Grand Dérangement* and their descendants simply continued to follow the practice' (v). As for who was responsible for the deportation, Gaudet tried to erase any notions that the Acadians themselves had somehow been at fault. As he put it, 'Was the deportation ordered either by the King or by some of his ministers?' Based upon the available evidence, Gaudet concluded that 'we have to respond in the affirmative' (1).

16 For a discussion of the impact of Longfellow's poem, see Robert Viau, *Les visages d'Évangeline: Du poème au mythe* (Beauport: MNH, 1998). For an interesting, and at the same time amusing, look at the power of Evangeline, see the documentary film *Evangeline's Quest*, DVD (Montreal: NFB, 1996), which includes a terrific performance by Maurice Basque, who appears on various occasions in this book.

17 Robert Viau, *Grand-Pré: Lieu de mémoire, lieu d'appartenance* (Longueuil: MNH, 2005), 89.

18 Barbara Le Blanc, *Postcards from Acadie: Grand-Pré, Evangeline and Acadian Identity* (Kentville: Gaspereau Press, 2003), 116.

19 Viau, *Grand-Pré*, 90.

20 *L'Évangéline*, 2 August 1920. Cited in Viau, *Grand-Pré*, 101.

21 We will see, in the following chapter, the relocation of this cross in 2005 as part of the events to mark the 250th anniversary of the deportation.

22 Viau, *Grand-Pré*, 115.

23 Ernest Martin, *L'Évangéline de Longfellow et la suite merveilleuse d'un poème* (Paris: Hachette, 1936), 234. Cited in Viau, *Grand-Pré*, 103.

24 CEA, Fonds François G.J. Comeau: 12.1-2, Allard to Comeau, 5 March 1930.

25 Ibid., 12.1-2 Comeau to Allard, 26 March 1930.

26 Ibid., 12.1-7, Comeau to Landry, 2 August 1930; 12.1-8, Landry to Comeau, 6 August 1930; 12.1–8, Comeau to Landry, 11 August 1930.

27 Ibid., 12.1-8, Comeau to Milton Lufkin, 12 August 1930.

28 Ibid., 12.1-8, George Matthew Adams to George Graham, 18 August 1930.

29 In his *American Historical Pageantry: The Uses of Tradition in the Early Twentieth Century* (Chapel Hill: University of North Carolina Press, 1990), David Glassberg has made the point that during the 1920s, just as Grand-Pré was being developed, outdoor museums such as Greenfield Village, presented history as frozen in the past, 'far removed from the complexities of life in the present' (269). Greenfield Village's presentation of the past is also considered by Mike Wallace in his *Mickey Mouse History and Other Essays on American Memory* (Philadelphia: Temple University Press, 1996).

30 Much the same could be said about the pilgrimages organized by *Le Devoir* in the 1920s, particularly the first one, in 1924, which saw the enthusiastic reception of the québécois pilgrims by 5000 Acadians in Moncton. While this provided recognition for *la nouvelle Acadie*, it was significant that the people in the streets were visitors, not people who lived in *Acadie*. (The 1924 pilgrimage is described in Viau, *Grand-Pré*, 122.) A similar scene, described below, would be repeated during the 175th anniversary events.

31 *L'Évangéline*, 17 July 1930.

32 CEA, Fonds Comité de l'église-souvenir de Grand-Pré, 'Programme de la célébration du 175e anniversaire de la Déportation des Acadiens.'

33 *L'Évangéline*, 28 August 1930. While LeBlanc spoke these words in English, the only report of his remarks was this one in French. And so, I cannot be certain that my translation has recreated exactly the words he would have used.

34 Ibid.

35 CEA, Fonds François G.J. Comeau, 12.1-11, Comeau to Père Fidèle Chiasson, 14 September 1930.

36 *L'Évangéline*, 24 July 1930.

37 Ibid., 24 July 30; 21 August 1930.

38 Ibid., 21 August 1930.

39 Ibid., 28 August 1930.

40 Ibid. According to the 1931 census, 6848 of the 20,689 residents of Moncton were French speakers.

41 Le Blanc, *Postcards from Acadie*, 128–9.

42 CEA, Fonds François G.J. Comeau, 12.1-14, Fortier to Comeau, 24 June 1930. While this attack had been declared an event of national historic significance by the Historic Sites and Monuments Board of Canada in 1924, a plaque to mark the event was only put up at a site near (but not on) the Grand-Pré grounds in 1938. The controversy surrounding commemoration of the Battle of Grand-Pré is discussed at length in Roger Marsters, '"The Battle of Grand-Pré": The Historic Sites and Monuments Board of Canada and the Commemoration of Acadian History,' *Acadiensis* 36 (2006): 29–50.

43 *L'Évangéline*, 28 August 1930.

44 Viau, *Grand-Pré*, 134.

45 Sacha Richard, 'Commémoration et idéologie nationale en Acadie: Les fêtes du bicentenaire de la Déportation acadienne,' *Mens* 3 (2002): 41.

46 LeBlanc, *Postcards from Acadie*, 136; Richard, 'Commémoration et idéologie nationale en Acadie,' 41; Viau, *Grand-Pré*, 158.

47 *L'Évangéline*, 16 August 1955; CEA, Fonds Bicentenaire, 133.12, Meeting with military officials, 7 June 1955.

48 CEA, Fonds Bicentenaire, 41.27-11, Savoie to Leo Charlton, 20 December 1955. For his part, Savoie thought that there had been 7000 in attendance at Grand-Pré.

49 Ibid. The emphasis was in the original.

50 *L'Évangéline*, 16 August 1955; 21 August 1930. The changing role of the automobile was reflected in the recurring practice at bicentenary events for 'the blessing of cars.' (*L'Évangéline*, 22 June 1955).

51 CEA, Fonds Bicentenaire, 41.27-11, Savoie to Leo Charlton, 20 December 1955.

52 In spite of its unprecedented nature, the bicentenary has received remarkably scant attention by historians. Aside from the article by Sacha Richard cited above, little effort has been made to focus on this major public event.

53 *L'Évangéline*, 26 April 1954.

54 Ibid., 11 July 1955.

55 The figure of sixty for the local celebrations is a rough estimate based upon a listing of the sites of such events in an index of *L'Évangéline* prepared by

the Centre d'études acadiennes at the Université de Moncton. (http://www
.umoncton.ca/etudeacadiennes/centre/evangeline/eva-tab.html).

56 CEA, Fonds SNA, 41.23-1, Adélard Savoie, 'En marge des fêtes de 1755.'

57 Ibid., 41.3–2, SNA, Executive Committee, 8 February 1950. The imagined
unfolding of the events was sketched at this meeting by Père Clément
Cormier, who represented the Acadians at the events at Saint John in 1954
to mark the 350th anniversary of the passage of the Dugua expedition and
who would be a major figure in staging the bicentenary.

58 L'Évangéline, 24 August 1955. The sense that the fetes ended on 15 August in
Grand-Pré was reinforced by the instructions from the bicentenary organizers, who asked Acadians to fly their flag from their homes, but only 'until
the evening of 15 August' ('Prière et instructions pour l'ouverture des fetes
du bicentenaire acadien, 10 août 1955,' at http://www.cyberacadie.com/
acadie_tintamarre.htm). Port-Royal spoke to a moment of founding that was
a bit out of place in 1955. The 350th anniversary of Port-Royal can best be
understood in the context of other such commemorations of the sites of
Acadian beginnings, and so is discussed in chapter 1.

59 CEA, Fonds SNA, 41.3-2, SNA, Executive Committee, 28 October 1953.

60 Savoie, 'Les Acadiens hier et aujourd'hui,' speech to Société historique de
la Vallée du Richelieu, 26 September 1954; cited in Jean-Paul Hautecoeur,
L'Acadie du discours: Pour une sociologie de la culture acadienne (Sainte-Foy:
Presses de l'Université Laval, 1975), 93–4.

61 In this regard, see my In Whose Interest?: Quebec's Caisses Populaires, 1900–45
(Montreal and Kingston: McGill-Queen's University Press, 1990).

62 L'Évangéline, 21 September 1954. New Brunswick and Prince Edward Island
did their fund-raising on 31 October, with Nova Scotia following in February. Savoie had wanted everyone to go forward on the same day, but in this
as in other contexts, he could not impose his will.

63 CEA, Fonds SNA, 41.25-9, A.J. Saulnier to Savoie, 15 July 1954.

64 L'Évangéline, 21 September 1954.

65 Given the difficulties of this grassroots fund-raising, organizers were continu-
ally strapped for cash. The bicentenary only took place thanks to contributions from the New Brunswick, Nova Scotia, and Quebec governments.
Nevertheless, four months after the fetes had ended, Savoie wrote, 'Despite
our best efforts to balance the budget, we ran a small deficit; and we are
trying to find the means for paying off that debt at the moment' (CEA,
Fonds, SNA, 41.27-11, Savoie to Alphonse Courchesne, 16 December 1955).

66 In terms of the form of their events, local organizers received unsolicited
advice from Père Laurent Tremblay, a well-known author of French Canadian
historical pageants, who was responsible for several that would be staged

during the *bicentenaire* and who was in close collaboration with Savoie and his colleagues in Moncton. In early 1955, as the various local and regional committees were moving forward, Tremblay observed through the pages of *L'Évangéline*: 'The program for these fetes ought, by and large, to follow this outline: a religious ceremony, with a solemn mass in the morning; outdoor activities with a parish picnic in the afternoon; in the evening, a brief dramatization of a page from history, followed by dancing and folkloric activities' (17 February 1955).

67 *L'Évangéline*, 5 May 1955. I have discussed the Fête-Dieu and its place in Quebec society in my *Founding Fathers*, 33–9.

68 The list of community events that were focused on local (and not Acadian-wide) themes would be lengthy. To give only one further example, on the same weekend that the celebration took place in Haute-Aboujagane, there was one in St-Louis-de-Kent, just north of Moncton, a community best known in Acadian lore as the birthplace of Mgr Marcel-François Richard. A leader of the Acadian renaissance, Mgr Richard argued during the *conventions nationales* of the 1880s for symbols that were truly Acadian. In this regard, he came up with the design for the Acadian flag, and to this day St-Louis-de-Kent sees itself as the 'birthplace of the Acadian flag.' Given the connection of Richard with the history of the town, its bicentenary events focused on his works, with much less attention paid to the bicentenary of the deportation. Caroline-Isabelle Caron has made much the same point about the 'resolutely community nature' of local bicentenary events in Nova Scotia in 'Se souvenir de l'Acadie d'antan: Représentation du passé historique dans le cadre de célébrations commémoratives locales en Nouvelle-Écosse au milieu du 20e siècle.' *Acadiensis* 36, 1 (spring 2007): 57.

69 *L'Évangéline*, 2 July 1955. There are various theories as to why residents of the region are called 'Brayons.' One theory holds that early settlers of the region cultivated flax and ground the plants so that they could be used to make clothing. The people who ground (broyer) the plant were called 'brayeux,' which was generalized to the population as 'Brayons.' Yet another theory claims that some early settlers came from the Pays de Bray in France. Whatever the origin of the term, this region's location on the border with Quebec encouraged its cultivation of an identity separate from that of other Acadian regions in New Brunswick.

70 Jacques Paul Couturier, 'La République du Madawaska et l'Acadie: La construction identitaire d'une région néo-brunswickoise au XXe siècle,' *RHAF* 56 (2002): 170.

71 *L'Évangéline*, 7 July 1955; *Le Madawaska*, 16 June 1955.

72 Martin-J. Légère, *Parmi ceux qui vivent: Un demi-siècle au service de l'Acadie: Mémoires* (Moncton: Éditions d'Acadie, 1996), 216. As for the pageant staged at Caraquet, while it did include deportation-related scenes, there were also some of much more local interest, such as the one dedicated to the memory of the 'Caraquet school riots.' This riot in 1875 was provoked by a change in New Brunswick school laws that challenged the continued existence of Catholic education in the province.

73 *L'Évangéline*, 19 August 1955.

74 *Le Madawaska*, 18 August 1955.

75 CEA, Fonds SNA, 41.27-11, Adélard Savoie to Leo Charlton, 20 December 1955.

76 *L'Évangéline*, 13 August 1955; 12 August 1955.

77 CEA, Fonds SNA, 41.3-2, Executive Committee, 8 February 1950.

78 Ibid., 41.3-3, Executive Committee, 28 October 1953.

79 Ibid., Fonds Bicentenaire, 133.06, Bullock to Savoie, 21 September 1955; Fonds SNA, 41.23-13, 'Brief to Federal Minister of Labour in relation to the Acadian Celebrations of 1955,' 22 March 1955. In the official program for the bicentenary, it was noted that 'Col. T.L. Bullock, Department of External Affairs, Ottawa, has been of much assistance to our Bicentennial Publicity Committee' (31). However, it is not clear how an official from Ottawa ended up providing advice, on a range of issues that went far beyond publicity, to the Acadians.

80 CEA, Fonds Bicentenaire, 133.07, Bullock to Massey, 11 June 1955.

81 CEA, Fonds SNA, 41.23-1; emphasis in the original. The use of the word 'épreuve' can also be found in the initial conception for the bicentenary by Père Cormier in 1950 (CEA, Fonds SNA, 41.3-2). Also, see *L'Évangéline*, 26 July 1955.

82 *L'Évangéline*, 11 August 1955.

83 CEA, Fonds Bicentenaire, 133.27: Cormier to Carmen Roy, 4 July 1955.

84 Ibid., 133.36, text prepared by Cormier for the *Maritime Advocate*, nd.

85 Ibid., 133.07, Bullock to Cormier, 25 June 1955; emphasis in the original.

86 Ibid., 133.27, Cormier to Carmen Roy, 4 July 1955.

87 Ibid., 133.37, Program, Festival de Folklore, 9–12 August 1955.

88 Ibid., Fonds SNA, 41.26-12: Tremblay to Savoie, 29 May 1955. There were echoes here of the role of community theatre in staging 'The People's Story' at the Bear River Heritage and Cultural Centre in 2005, a matter discussed in chapter 4.

89 Archives du théâtre francophone de Trois-Rivières, Séminaire Saint-Joseph, Fonds Laurent-Tremblay, 111/1a, 8a (Scenario, 8 April 1955, *Pageant de l'Acadie*); 111/1a, 8 (Final scenario, *Pageant de l'Acadie*). All references to the

two versions of Tremblay's scenario come from these documents. I am very grateful to Raymond Pagé for securing my access to this rich collection of documents pertaining to the tradition of pageantry in French Canada. An inventory can be found in Rémi Tourangeau, *Collection des fonds sur le théâtre populaire au Canada français* (Trois-Rivières: Groupe de recherche en théâtre populaire, 1991). The two versions of Tremblay's text are also discussed in Judith Perron, 'Théâtres, fêtes et célébrations en Acadie (1880–1980),' PhD diss., Université de Moncton, 1995, 121.

90 As for the role of Hopson, who is often pushed into the shadows of narratives of the deportation because of the actions of such figures as Lawrence, John Mack Faragher has observed that while his time as governor was brief, it was important 'if only as a demonstration that there was nothing inevitable about the subsequent course of events' (*A Great and Noble Scheme*, 276). Just as Père Tremblay used Hopson as a device to underscore Lawrence's genocidal instincts, so too did Faragher see Hopson's course as an alternative to the policy of 'ethnic cleansing' (his term) that was implemented.

91 The full text of Frégault's speech was reprinted in *Le Madawaska*, 5 May 1955. I have written about Frégault and his place in Quebec historical writing in *Making History in Twentieth-Century Quebec* (Toronto: University of Toronto, 1997), chap. 3. Frégault and his colleagues of the time were self-conscious about the fact that they constituted the first professionally trained historians in French-speaking Quebec. Accordingly, at the start of this speech, presented to a Kiwanis Club in Montreal, he began by casting doubt on the 'large number of words' that would be produced by amateurs, in contrast with his own status as a 'professional man.'

92 CEA, Fonds SNA, 41.26-10, Savoie to Ephrem Boudreau, 3 May 1955. In this context, in his description of the pageants for which he was responsible in Caraquet in July 1955, Martin-J. Légère seemed to take a certain pride in breaking the code when he depicted 'the barbarity of our enemies, the English. Some English speakers who came to the fetes thought that I had gone a bit too far! ... Some of my observations were far from Christian charity, or so I was told the next day by a kindly nun!' (Légère, *Parmi ceux qui vivent*, 215).

93 CEA, Fonds SNA, 41.27-2, Savoie to Joseph Ponton, 15 July 1955.

94 Viau, *Grand-Pré*, 159; Richard, 'Commémoration et idéologie nationale en Acadie,' 30, 45; Caron, 'Se souvenir de l'Acadie d'antan,' 62.

95 Michael Gauvreau, *The Catholic Origins of Quebec's Quiet Revolution, 1931–1970* (Montreal and Kingston: McGill-Queen's University Press, 2005), 5.

96 *L'Évangéline*, 26 April 1954.

97 While opened in 1940, the cathedral was only entirely finished on the eve of the bicentenary.

98 Archives of Archdiocese of Moncton, R583, 5b, 'Sermon du bicentenaire'; *L'Évangéline*, 14 August 1954. In a similar manner, St-Jean-Baptiste was officially proclaimed as the patron saint of French Canadians (read Québécois) in 1908 as part of celebrations marking the bicentenary of the death of Mgr de Laval, the first bishop of Quebec. In Quebec, on that occasion, as in Acadie in 1938, there was an opportunity to give visibility to a specific people within the Catholic Church. I discussed this matter in *Founding Fathers*, 153.

99 Herménégilde Chiasson has quipped that 'some people are disappointed when they can't find a historical basis [for the tintamarre]. It's much like when people try too hard to find an Acadian connection for people who don't have one.' ('Oublier Évangéline,' in *Aspects de la nouvelle francophonie canadienne*, ed. Simon Langlois and Jocelyn Létourneau [Sainte-Foy: Presses de l'Université Laval, 2004], 150.) That said, it is commonly believed that the word came to North America when Acadians applied the term to the noise made by the large number of migratory birds who would stop at marshes near today's border between Nova Scotia and New Brunswick. The Acadians called the marsh 'tintamarre' to denote the immense noise that was created, and to be sure, the modern day *tintamarre* is noisy. As for why they selected this word to attribute to that noise, there is a connection to medieval France, where workers in vineyards would hit rocks with their *marre* (a spade of sorts) to send a message to others. So to 'tinte ta marre' would be to make noise towards some particular end. ('L'Abécédaire de la Vigne,' at http://www.yonne-89.net/abecedaire_de_la_vigne.htm.)

100 CEA, Fonds SNA, 41.3-2, Executive committee, 8 February 1950; *L'Évangéline*, 9 July 1954, 11 March 1955.

101 CEA, Fonds Bicentenaire, 133.37, 'Prière et instructions pour l'ouverture des fêtes du bicentenaire acadien, 10 août 1955.'

102 *L'Évangéline*, 12 August 1955.

103 CEA, Fonds Bicentenaire, 133.37, 'Prière et instructions pour l'ouverture des fêtes'; Calixte-F. Savoie, *Mémoires d'un nationaliste acadien* (Moncton: Éditions d'Acadie, 1980), 324–7.

104 *L'Évangéline*, 12 August 1955.

105 Library and Archives Canada, RG41, vol. 749, file 18-16-2-120, W.E.S. Briggs to Assistant Director of Programs, 17 March 1955; Briggs to General Manager, Ottawa, 21 June 1955. I would never have found this file without a lead from Mary Vipond, my colleague and expert on matters dealing with the history of the CBC.

106 'Le tintamarre (CBAF),' 10 August 1955. Les Archives de Radio-Canada, at http://archives.radio-canada.ca/IDC-0-104-1567-10569/annees50/1955/clip1.

107 This point was also made by Ronald Labelle, 'Le tintamarre en Acadie: Une tradition inventée ou réinventée,' *Cahiers de la société historique acadienne* 36 (2005): 119.

108 There is a massive literature on the origins of these festivals, some of which I refer to in *Founding Fathers*, chaps. 1–2.

109 *Programme et renseignements, 1755–1955* (Moncton: n.p., 1955), 25.

110 Christine Sheito, 'Une fête contestée: La procession de la Fête-Dieu à Montréal au XIXe siècle,' MA thesis (anthropology), Université de Montréal, 1983, 127.

111 *L'Évangéline*, 10 August 1955. In the same journal, 2 August 1955, the locations of the four arches 'at the main entry points to Moncton' were identified. In spite of evidence published on the day that the bicentenary began that these arches were in fact constructed, I could not find images of any of them in place over an entrance to Moncton.

112 For one of many references to Grand-Pré as 'l'apogée,' see *L'Évangéline*, 9 July 1954; Tremblay's remarks were part of an interview in *L'Évangéline*, 24 February 1955.

113 CEA, Fonds SNA, 41.3-2, Executive Committee, 8 February 1950.

114 Le Blanc, *Postcards from Acadie*, 154.

115 *L'Évangéline*, 15 August 1980.

116 Labelle, 'Le tintamarre en Acadie,' 114.

117 *L'Évangéline*, 15 August 1980. The celebrations to mark the 375th anniversary of the founding of Port-Royal are discussed in chapter 1.

118 Le Blanc, *Postcards from Acadie*, 157–8. The sites in question are Le Village historique acadien (located near Caraquet and opened in 1976); Le Pays de la Sagouine (Bouctouche, 1992); and Le Lieu historique national du Monument-Lefebvre (Memramcook, 1994). The first provides a glimpse of Acadian life from 1780 to 1880, while the second provides a stage for characters out of Antonine Maillet's iconic play based on the life of a women she knew. The last site is 'the only national historic site commemorating events that took place after the Deportation. It is also the only site situated in an Acadian community' (Village de Memramcook, at http://www.memramcook.com/culture_heritage.cfm).

Chapter 6

1 Interview with Jean Gaudet, 10 May 2005. When the federal government was weighing its options for the date that should be selected for an annual day

of deportation remembrance, an issue discussed in detail below, it reflected on whether it should not opt for 5 September, deciding in the end on the less provocative date of 28 July.

2 *L'Évangéline*, 16 August 1955. The Caraquet bicentenary events are referred to in chapter 5. In 2007 the Commission de l'Odyssée acadienne erected one of its monuments on this site. The work of the commission is discussed in the next section of this chapter.

3 A monument of the Commission de l'Odyssée acadienne was erected to mark the Camp d'Espérance in 2006.

4 Interview with Jean Gaudet, 10 May 2005.

5 SNA Archives, Conseil d'Administration, 17–18 October 1997.

6 'Rapport du comité central pour les fêtes 2004–5,' presented to meeting of Conseil d'Administration, SNA, 25 March 2000; emphasis in the original (document secured from Parks Canada via ATIP request).

7 *Telegraph-Journal*, 27 July 2005.

8 That initial meeting was chaired by Daniel LeBlanc, well known as leader of the group Petitcodiac Riverkeeper, which had the mission 'to restore and protect the ecological integrity of the Petitcodiac River system' (http://www.petitcodiac.org/riverkeeper/english/WhoWeAre/whoWeAre.htm). In addition, there was Muriel K. Roy (professor at the Université de Moncton); Père Maurice Léger (Société historique acadienne); Claude DeGrâce (Parcs Canada); Bernard Poirier (a former journalist and bureaucrat in Fredericton); and René Légère (the secrétaire-général of the SNA). Over the years, the committee was joined by Ronnie-Gilles LeBlanc (archivist of the Centre d'études acadienne at the Université de Moncton); Paul Delaney (a professor at the same university); Denis Laplante (directeur général of the SNA) and Jean Gaudet (discussed at length above).

9 Commission de l'Odyssée acadienne, Minutes, 25 November 1998. These minutes were kindly provided to me by Bernard Poirier, the commission's secretary from the start. I originally met him in his capacity as a member of a choir (Le Choeur Neil-Michaud) that was scheduled to sing on the stage at Bayside on the evening of 26 June 2004 – that is, before the rains came and the performance was cancelled.

10 For the history of the term *grand dérangement*, see Ronnie-Gilles LeBlanc, 'Du "dérangement des guerres" au Grand Dérangement: La longue évolution d'un concept,' in his *Du Grand Dérangement à la Déportation: Nouvelles perspectives historiques* (Moncton: Chaire d'études acadiennes, 2005), 11–20.

11 Minutes of the Historic Sites and Monuments Board of Canada, 6 February 1991. The Acadian Consultative Committee was co-chaired by Muriel Roy, who would be a founding member of the Commission de l'Odyssée acadienne.

12 Commission de l'Odyssée acadienne, Minutes, 1 October 1998; 21 October 1998. In 1999 they produced a document signed by the 'Comité pour la commémoration internationale de l'Odyssée acadienne,' but two years later were referring to themselves as the 'Commission pour la commémoration internationale de l'Odyssée acadienne et du Grand Dérangement' (Minutes, 13 September 2001). The saga ended when they came to the final formulation: They were to be known as the 'Commission de l'Odyssée Acadienne,' which was engaged with the 'commémoration internationale du grand dérangement.'

13 'Commémoration internationale de l'Odyssée acadienne,' March 1999. This strategic planning document was included in the files of the Commission provided by Bernard Poirier.

14 Commission de l'Odyssée acadienne, 13 April 2000.

15 Novick, *Holocaust in American Life*, 9.

16 Novick, *That Noble Dream: The 'Objectivity Question' and the American Historical Profession* (Cambridge: Cambridge University Press, 1988), 486.

17 Edward Linenthal, *Preserving Memory: The Struggle to Create America's Holocaust Museum* (New York: Columbia University Press, 2001), 191.

18 Commission de l'Odyssée acadienne, Minutes, 27 September 2000.

19 A press release from the Ville de Dieppe (29 July 2005) indicated: 'The monument is a joint project of the City of Dieppe, the government of Canada, with a contribution of $15 000 from the Atlantic Canada Opportunities Agency, the government of New Brunswick, the SNA and the SAANB' (http://www.dieppe.ca/news_wire.cfm?id=139). As for 250th anniversary funding more generally, while the SNA sought roughly $120,000 from Ottawa (Conseil d'Administration, 4 December 2004), it received only $65,000 (http://pch.gc.ca/newsroom/index_e.cfm?fuseaction=displayDocument& DocIDCd=3N0412). For its part, the New Brunswick government provided $90,000 for the monument project, and another $25,000 for the commemorative events in late July 2005 (http://www.gnb.ca/cnb/newsf/iga/ 2005f0944ig.htm).

20 In a publication outlining its project, the commission produced a text for this face of the monument that was dated 18 July 2005 and which did not have the reference to the resistance. Thus it would appear that the reference had been included at the last minute.

21 In addition to this reference on the text specific to the Dieppe monument, the commission also showed its admiration for Broussard by asking the Historic Sites and Monuments Board of Canada to recognize him as 'a person of national historical importance' (Commission de l'Odyssée acadienne, Minutes, 8 May 2002).

22 Paul Surette, 'L'esprit du Chignecto, ou comment déjouer une expulsion,' *Égalité* no. 52 (Fall 2005): 82, 87.

23 The details of the life of Beausoleil Broussard can be found in the biography by C.J. d'Entremont in the *Dictionary of Canadian Biography*, at http://www.biographi.ca/EN/ShowBio.asp?BioId=35349&query=broussard. For his part, Robert Viau has observed that in contemporary *Acadie* 'there is a preference for Beausoleil Broussard over Evangeline' (*Les grands dérangements: La déportation des acadiens en littératures acadienne, québécoise et française* [Beauport: Publications MNH, 1997], 303).

24 Warren Perrin, *Acadian Redemption: From Beausoleil Broussard to the Queen's Royal Proclamation* (Erath, LA: Acadian Heritage and Cultural Foundation, 2004), 24. In the same book, Perrin drew a parallel between British actions in regard to *Acadie* and that of American troops in terms of the 'abuse of prisoners ... in Afghanistan and at the Abu Ghraib prison in Iraq' (120).

25 Commission de l'Odyssée acadienne, Minutes, 15 July 1999; 8 May 2002.

26 By the start of 2008, aside from the two monuments unveiled in 2005, monuments have been erected, in 2006, at the site of the Camp d'Espérance (discussed above) and at St-Basile, in the Madawaska region (discussed in regard to the bicentenary in chapter 5). In 2007 new monuments were unveiled at Caraquet (see the discussion above regarding Ste-Anne-du-Bocage) and on the French island of Miquelon.

27 Commission de l'Odyssée acadienne, Minutes, 23 September 2004.

28 SNA Archives, letter from Parks Canada to SNA, 26 January 2005.

29 SNA, *Commémoration du 250e anniversaire du Grand Dérangement, Bulletin d'information* no. 1, 25 April 2005. This same expression was employed by Michel Cyr, the president of the SNA, in launching the logo (*Le Moniteur Acadien*, 17 June 2005). All subsequent references to the logo are from the *Bulletin*.

30 Cited in Robert Pichette, *Le pays appelé l'Acadie: Réflexions sur des commémorations* (Moncton: CEA, 2006), 158. Pichette felt that those proponents of an apology on the occasion of the 250th anniversary were misguided, since the Crown had already been forgiven fifty years earlier. Of course, Savoie's speech hardly constituted an 'official' act of forgiveness, but these details did not matter to Pichette, who spared no invective in belittling the advocates of the campaign for an apology.

31 *When Sorry Isn't Enough: The Controversy over Apologies and Reparations for Human Injustice*, ed. Roy Brooks (New York: NYU Press, 1999), 3.

32 Aaron Lazare, *On Apology* (Oxford: Oxford University Press, 2004), 6.

33 In 2005 the Liberal government established a $25 million 'grievance fund' to compensate 'ethnocultural groups' that had been wronged by the actions

of the federal government. The Ukrainian community secured $2.5 million from this fund in recognition of the internment, disenfranchisement, and loss of assets by its members during the First World War. The fund ceased to exist when the Conservatives took power in 2006. Nevertheless, later that year, the Harper government apologized to Chinese Canadians for the head tax and offered a small symbolic payment to individuals (or their surviving spouses) who had paid the tax. The same government then offered both a further apology and a financial settlement in regard to residential schools in 2008.

34 Michael Cunningham, 'Apologies in Irish Politics: A Commentary and a Critique,' *Contemporary British History* 18 (2004): 82.

35 *Taking Wrongs Seriously: Apologies and Reconciliation*, ed. Elazar Barkan and Alexander Karn (Stanford: Stanford University Press, 2006), 10.

36 Charles Maier, 'A Surfeit of Memory: Reflections on History, Melancholy and Denial,' *History and Memory* 5 (1993): 136–51. A very similar perspective on the emergence of the apology movement can be found in Michael R. Marrus, *Official Apologies and the Quest for Historical Justice* (Toronto: Munk Centre for International Studies, University of Toronto, 2006).

37 Robert Weyeneth, 'The Power of Apology and the Process of Historical Reconciliation,' *The Public Historian* 23 (2001): 25–9.

38 Canada, Parliament, House of Commons, *Debates*, 32nd Parl., 2nd session, 2 April 1984, p. 2623.

39 *L'Acadie Nouvelle*, 28 September 1988. The agreement for redress for Japanese Canadians was signed on 22 September.

40 Warren A. Perrin et al. versus Great Britain et al., 'Petition to Obtain an Apology for the Acadian Deportation,' at http://ahcn.ca/1755/perrin/perrin.htm#.

41 Perrin, *Acadian Redemption*, 111, 105.

42 This motion and the one introduced in 2001 (M-241) were identical. They read: 'That a humble Address be presented to Her Excellency (the Governor General) praying that she will intercede with Her Majesty to cause the British Crown to present an official apology to the Acadian people for the wrongs done to them in its name between 1755 and 1763.'

43 Interview with Stéphane Bergeron, 22 October 2007.

44 Canada, Parliament, House of Commons, *Debates*, 37th Parl., 1st session, 27 March 2001, letter from Chiasson to Bergeron, entered into the record by MP John Herron. The translation of the French original was in the English version of Hansard.

45 Ibid., 27 March 2001. In his documentary film *Tintamarre* (DVD, Montreal: National Film Board of Canada, 2004), André Gladu makes the

point (much like Bergeron) that 'history remains a taboo subject for the Acadian people.' Writing in *L'Acadie Nouvelle*, Stéphane LeBlanc questioned Gladu's choice of words, observing that 'the film shows very clearly that we have no difficulty in talking about our history' (1 March 2005). On the issue of the deportation, however, there are various interviewees in Gladu's film, such as Donatien Gaudet, one of the authors of the *Manifeste Beaubassin* (discussed below), who express concern about the reluctance of Acadians to face up to what the deportation really was.

46 Canada, Parliament, House of Commons, *Debates*, 37th Parl., 1st session, 27 March 2001.

47 Ibid., 22 November 2001.

48 Michel Vastel, 'Les grands dérangés du Parlement,' *Le Soleil*, 29 November 2001.

49 *L'Acadie Nouvelle*, 4 December 2001.

50 Stéphane Savard, 'Les Acadiens et la reconnaissance des torts pour la déportation. Interprétation des discours, 1999–2003,' in *Faute et réparation au Canada et au Québec contemporains*, ed. Martin Pâquet (Quebec: Éditions Nota Bene, 2006), 137, 135.

51 SNA Archives, Conseil exécutif, 11 April 2001.

52 Commission de l'Odyssée acadienne, Minutes, 13 September 2001.

53 SNA Archives, Conseil d'administration, 1 June 2001.

54 My efforts to find these submissions, which were aided by Maurice Basque and the SNA, were futile. No trace seems to remain of these documents.

55 SNA, 'Éléments tirés du rapport du comité consultatif sur la reconnaissance des torts causés aux Acadiens et Acadiennes,' 1 October 2001, at http://www.snacadie.org/SNA/index.cfm?id=1363.

56 Rapport du comité consultatif sur la motion M-241, at http://ahcn.ca/1755/comite/rapport.htm.

57 SNA Archives, Conseil d'Administration, 20 November 2001.

58 Ibid., 15–16 February 2002.

59 Ibid., 3 May 2002.

60 Ibid., 28 August 2003. Letter from Euclide Chiasson to Stéphane Dion, 26 August 2003.

61 Ibid., 17–18 October 2003: *Ébauche (draft of royal proclamation)*, 2 October 2003.

62 *Proclamation Designating July 28 of Every Year as 'A Day of Commemoration of the Great Upheaval,' Commencing on July 28, 2005*, 10 December 2003, SI/2003.188, *Canada Gazette*, part II, vol. 137, no. 27, 31 December 2003 at http://gazetteducanada.gc.ca/partII/2003/20031231/html/si188-e.html. While

the proclamation was signed on 10 December 2003, the cabinet had approved the text on 2 December.

63 Canadian Heritage News Release, 10 December 2003, 'La ministre Copps annonce la journée de commémoration du Grand Dérangement'; *L'Acadie Nouvelle*, 11 December 2003. Lest the reader think that this formulation was a product of my translation, here is the original: 'La proclamation permettra aux Acadiens de tourner la page et permettra finalement, après presque 250 ans, une réconciliation.'

64 *Proclamation.*

65 *L'Acadie Nouvelle*, 10 December 2003.

66 SNA, Discours de Euclide Chiasson, le 10 décembre 2003, at http://www .snacadie.org/SNA/index.cfm?id=1363.

67 *L'Acadie Nouvelle*, 11 December 2003.

68 Weyeneth, 'The Power of Apology,' 31.

69 Interview with Michel Cyr, 10 May 2005.

70 Radio-Canada, *La déportation des Acadiens*, Première Chaine, March 2005, episode 8. This series was prepared by Marc Poirier, who kindly provided me with the transcript of this episode.

71 *L'Acadie Nouvelle*, 16 May 2005.

72 Ibid., 25 October 2002. The text of the *Manifeste Beaubassin* can also be found at http://www.ahcn.ca/1755/beaubassin/manifest.htm.

73 Achille Hubert, 'À propos de la Proclamation royale canadienne publiée le 9 décembre 2003,' *La petite souvenance* no. 19 (July 2005): 10.

74 *L'Acadie Nouvelle*, 3 December 2003. This reference was to a site of pilgrimage at the top of a site overlooking Montreal, where 100 stairs are reserved to allow worshippers to climb on their knees to reach the sanctuary.

75 Jean-François Thibault, 'Pourquoi des excuses sont-elles nécessaires? Mémoire de la déportation acadienne et la justice historique,' *Égalité* no. 52 (Fall 2005): 59–60.

76 *L'Acadie Nouvelle*, 27 August 2005.

77 Renée Blanchar, *Le souvenir nécessaire*, DVD (Moncton: Productions Phare-Est, 2005). Blanchar travelled with the writer Serge Patrice Thibodeau, with whom she also met with the psychologist Déogratias Bagilishya, who provided much the same advice about the importance of facing up to such a trauma.

78 Claude Le Bouthillier, *Complices du silence?* (Montreal: XYZ éditeur, 2004), 93. This brief description does not do justice to the range of psychological and identity issues in the novel. There is also an English heir to the throne who, like Poséidon, hates his life, but finds some meaning when he starts to explore the story of the deportation. Undercover, he ends up in Nova

Scotia, and falls in love with Evangeline (who else), a young women who is
unaware of her own Acadian roots, but has also become engaged by the
deportation story through her studies in archaeology. In the end, the two
marry so that if the prince were to become king, it could happen that 'an
Acadian could ascend to the British throne!' (210).

79 Ibid., 212.
80 *L'Acadie Nouvelle*, 3 September 2005. Writing in similar terms, Robert Viau
   asked: 'Can Acadians really "turn the page" when they have not read all of
   it, as they are lacking pieces of information about what really happened in
   1755?' ('Les commémorations du 250e anniversaire de la déportation,'
   Égalité no. 52 [Fall 2005]: 39).
81 Robert Viau, '*Complices du silence?* de Claude Le Bouthillier et les "excuses"
   de la reine,' *Port-Acadie* nos. 8–9 (Fall 2005–Spring 2006): 93. The proclamation's full, official title was *Proclamation Designating July 28 of Every Year as 'A
   Day of Commemoration of the Great Upheaval.'*
82 Advice to the Minister of Canadian Heritage, 8 October 2003 (document
   secured from Canadian Heritage via ATIP request).
83 Hélène Lacroix, email message to Julie Francoeur, 4 December 2003
   (document secured from Canadian Heritage via ATIP request). In the draft
   invitation, there is explicit reference to the insertion of 'célébrant la vitalité
   de la communauté acadienne au lieu d'insérer "La journée de la commémoration du grand dérangement."'
84 *L'Acadie Nouvelle*, 29 July 2005.
85 During 2005 there were other cases of individuals involved in genuine acts
   of reconciliation. In early September, one such event took place in the town
   of Hillsborough, New Brunswick, to mark the 250th anniversary of the
   victory of Acadian resistance fighters over British soldiers. Hillsborough
   is now an almost entirely English-speaking town, and so the event was
   designed to achieve some '*rapprochement* with today's Acadians' (*L'Acadie
   Nouvelle*, 30 August 2005). I might have attended that event, but I was busy
   getting ready to be 'le seul pèlerin de Caraquet,' as described at the start of
   this chapter.
86 *L'Acadie Nouvelle*, 8 June 2005.
87 Ibid. Gallant's views can be found at length in his 'Lettre à Sa Majesté la
   Reine pour des excuses et non une simple reconnaissance des torts,' *La
   petite souvenance*, No. 19 (July 2005), 42–4.
88 Antonine Maillet, *Pélagie-la-Charette* (Montreal: Leméac, 1979). Maillet won
   the French Prix Goncourt for this work, thus becoming the first foreigner to
   be so honoured. This achievement is often cited as a mark of the emergence
   of the Acadians as a force to be reckoned with.

89 By contrast, in his various processions from Horton Landing to Grand-Pré, Jean Gaudet always made a point of signalling the role played by the Mi'kmaq, who took great risks in befriending the Acadians during the deportation. Reflecting the relatively marginal role of the Mi'kmaq in events marking the 250th anniversary of the deportation, the minutes of the Commission de l'Odyssée acadienne do not make reference to aboriginal issues until the eve of the formal events in 2005. In June 2005 the commission recognized that it had run out of time to deal adequately with such matters, and hoped that 'there will be an aboriginal presence for the ceremomies at Grand-Pré' (23 June 2005).

90 *L'Acadie Nouvelle*, 3 September 2005. Letter from Paul-Pierre Bourgeois.

91 The production *Odyssée 1604–2004* is discussed in chapter 2.

92 The text of Castonguay's spectacle was found in SNA Archives, Conseil d'Administration, 3 June 2005, 'Le 28 juillet 2005 – Journée de commémoration du Grand Dérangement.' My account of this spectacle is also based upon notes that I took (in the dark) at the performance and on a video of the show kindly provided to me by Bellefeuille Production, for which I am most appreciative.

93 Canada was represented by Mauril Bélanger, an MP from Ontario and the minister for internal trade.

94 SNA, 'Allocution du président de la Société Nationale de l'Acadie à l'occasion de la commémoration du Grand Dérangement: Grand-Pré, 28 juillet 2005.'

95 For an account of those smaller events, see Viau, 'Les commémorations du 250e anniversaire de la déportation.'

96 Capacadie.com, 6 December 2003.

97 *L'Acadie Nouvelle*, 11 December 2003.

98 Robert Proulx, 'Grand Dérangement: De la "terre à mon père" à la terre entière,' *Port-Acadie* nos. 8–9 (Fall 2005–Spring 2006): 240–1.

99 Michel Thibault, email message to author, 9 November 2007.

Epilogue

1 Canada-France, 1604–2004, 'Backgrounder,' at http://www.dfait-maeci .gc.ca/canada-europa/france/canada2004/initiative-en.asp.

2 *Globe and Mail*, 7 June 2003. The series ran in twelve instalments between this date and 1 July 2003.

3 Cité des sciences et de l'industrie, *Le Canada vraiment*, at http://www .cite-sciences.fr/cgi/canada?vref=c99f4bd79d6b25d9d8c91c0e8309ccc9& expoid=6&q=visite&langue=fr. The object that I am holding is the minisat.

4 Interview with Pierre Duconseille and Perrine Wyplosz (Cité des sciences et de l'industrie), 6 November 2003.

5 Office of the Inspector General, Department of Foreign Affairs and International Trade, 'Evaluation of the Canada-France Program (October 2005),' at http://www.international.gc.ca/department/auditreports/ evaluation/evalCanadaFrance05-en.asp#N_5_.

6 Ibid.

7 Ibid.

8 The *livre d'or* was made available to me by my hosts at the Cité des sciences, Pierre Duconseille and Perrine Wyplosz, who had worked on the development of *Canada vraiment*, to whom I am most grateful.

9 'Evaluation of the Canada-France Program.'

10 Interview with Pierre Duconseille and Perrine Wyplosz, 6 November 2003.

11 Rosenzweig and Thelen, *Presence of the Past*, 106.

12 Interview with Nathalie Fiquet, 22 July 2004.

13 Charles-Antoine Rouyer, 'La Maison Champlain,' *Le Devoir*, 13 August 2005.

14 Canadian Museum of Civilization, Press release, 10 June 2004, http://www .civilization.ca/media/show_pr_e.asp?ID=465.

15 David Glassberg, 'History and the Public: Legacies of the Progressive Era,' *Journal of American History* 73 (1984): 974.

16 There is obviously nothing scientific about this collection of reactions that I gathered on 27 June 2004. In the end, even though historians are always eager to know what the audience thought, it was not easy in the course of my travels to collect the perspectives of spectators. Talking to people in front of sculptures, because there was a shared object for discussion, worked much better than efforts to gauge reactions to commemorative events. People out for a good time were not too eager to answer questions, no matter how nicely phrased. At one such event, when I had some graduate students fan out to sample popular opinion, the idea that the crowd was being subjected to interrogation led one youngster to yell to his grandmother, 'Run Granny' when she was about to be approached.

17 James E. Young, 'The Biography of a Memorial Icon: Nathan Rapoport's Warsaw Ghetto Monument,' *Representations* 26 (Spring 1989): 101.

18 Meg Scheid, email message to the author, 27 November 2007.

19 Maurice Agulhon, 'La "statuomanie"' en l'histoire,' *Ethnologie française* nos. 2–3 (1978): 145–72.

20 Young, 'Biography of a Memorial Icon,' 101.

21 W.F. Ganong, 'A Visitor's Impression of the Champlain Tercentenary,' *Acadiensis* 5 (1905): 21.

22 Nelles, *Art of Nation-Building*, 163.

23 Rosenzweig and Thelen, *Presence of the Past*, 106.

24 Interview with Norma Stewart, 1 October 2004.

25 Interview with Hugh Akagi, 2 October 2004.

26 Since the close of the commemorative events to mark the 250th anniversary of the deportation, a sculpture has been unveiled on the Grand-Pré grounds. *Déportation*, by the artists Jules Lasalle and André Fournelle, shows a family that appears to be on the run, and yet the life-size characters (in the spirit of the bronzes at Red Beach discussed above) do not appear overly distressed, thus keeping with the general tone of the Grand-Pré site. The official text produced in connection with the unveiling of the sculpture on the 251st anniversary of Winslow's reading of the deportation order, in September 2006, noted: 'The close proximity of the characters speaks to their hope of being together again in better days. The fact that the family is in motion suggests the forcible removal from their ancestral lands, and at the same time suggests their arrival in a new land.' A photo of the sculpture and the complete text from the unveiling are at http://www.grand-pre .com/Archives/Sculptureen.html.

27 Throughout the book, I have attributed comments to those responsible for them. In this case, I saw no reason to hold individuals up to ridicule, particularly since – in the case of the St Croix organizing committee – these views, which threw the existence of the Passamaquoddy into doubt, were later recanted.

28 Interview with Norma Stewart, 1 October 2004.

29 *New Brunswick Telegraph-Journal*, 30 December 2004.

30 Interview with Hugh Akagi, 2 October 2004.

31 Interview with Hugh Akagi by Ed Bassett, August 2006. This interview formed part of a program that Bassett produced for broadcast on the closed-circuit network on the Pleasant Point Reservation, and is reproduced here with Bassett's consent.

32 The same line ended the film *Life After Île Ste-Croix.* I guess this repetition shows a certain lack of imagination on my part, but it also pays tribute to someone using the past as a tool for making gains for his people while at the same time showing generosity towards others.

Bibliography

Primary Sources

1. Manuscript Collections

Annapolis Royal, Nova Scotia. Municipal Archives. Minutes of Town Council, 1902–4.

Archdiocese of Moncton. Documents Relating to *Bicentenaire*.

Centre de documentation et d'études madawaskayennes. Université de Moncton, Campus d'Edmundston. Fonds Société des Acadiens du Nouveau-Brunswick.

Centre d'études acadiennes (CEA), Université de Moncton, Campus de Moncton.
– Fonds Bicentenaire
– Fonds Comité de l'église-souvenir de Grand-Pré
– Fonds François G.J. Comeau
– Fonds Placide Gaudet
– Fonds Société des Acadiens du Nouveau-Brunswick
– Fonds Société historique acadienne
– Fonds Société nationale de l'Acadie
– Fonds Société nationale l'Assomption

Centre d'études acadiennes, Université de Moncton, Campus de Moncton. '1755: L'histoire et les histoires.' http://www2.umoncton.ca/cfdocs/ etudacad/1755/entree.cfm?&lang=fr&style=J&admin=false&linking=.

Centre d'études acadiennes, Université de Moncton, Campus de Moncton. 400 ans de présence française au Canada, 1604–2004. http://www2.umoncton .ca/cfdocs/cea/index.cfm.

Cité des sciences et de l'industrie (Paris). *Livre d'or de l'Exposition Canada Vraiment.*

Commission de l'Odyssée acadienne. Documents in the possession of Bernard
    Poirier, Dieppe, New Brunswick.
Downeast Heritage Museum (Calais, Maine). St Croix 2004 Coordinating
    Committee Archives.
Library and Archives Canada
– Canadian Broadcasting Corporation Fonds
– Laurier Papers
– Ministère des affaires étrangères, France, Correspondance consulaire avec le
    consulat de Québec
New Brunswick Museum
– Alice Fairweather Fonds, Minutes of the Loyalist Society
– Champlain Tercentenary Fonds
– New Brunswick Historical Society Fonds.
Nova Scotia Archives and Records Management. Nova Scotia Historical Society
    Records.
Port Royal 400th Anniversary Society. Documents in the possession of Linda
    Brown, Annapolis Royal, Nova Scotia.
Séminaire Saint-Joseph (Trois-Rivières). Archives du théâtre francophone de
    Trois-Rivières. Fonds Laurent Tremblay.
Société nationale de l'Acadie (Dieppe, New Brunswick). Minutes of Conseil
    d'Administration.
Société des Acadiens et Acadiennes du Nouveau-Brunswick (SAANB). Comité
    2004. Documents in the possession of Théo Gagnon, Saint John, New Brunswick.

2. Printed Primary Material

Champlain, Samuel de. *The Works of Samuel de Champlain.* 3 vols. Toronto:
    Champlain Society, 1922–36.
*Dedication of the Establishment of Saint Croix Island as a National Monument: June 30,
    1968.* Calais, ME: n.p, 1968.
Ganong, W.F. *Champlain's Island.* Saint John: New Brunswick Museum, 2003.
    First published 1902 in *Transactions* of the Royal Society of Canada.
– 'A Monograph of Historic Sites in New Brunswick.' *Transactions of the Royal
    Society of Canada,* section 2, 5 (1899): 213–357.
– 'A Visitor's Impression of the Champlain Tercentenary.' *Acadiensis* 5 (1905):
    15–23.
Gaudet, Placide. *Le Grand Dérangement: Sur qui retombe la responsabilité de l'Expul-
    sion des Acadiens.* Ottawa: Ottawa Printing Co., 1922.
Langelier, Charles. *Le Trois-Centième Anniversaire de l'Arrivée de M. DeMonts à
    Port-Royal: Discours prononcé par l'Honorable Chs. Langelier, le 21 juin 1904.*
    Quebec, n.p., 1904.

Le Bouthillier, Claude. *Complices du silence?* Montreal: XYZ éditeur, 2004.

Légère, Martin-J. *Parmi ceux qui vivent: Un demi-siècle au service de l'Acadie. Mémoires.* Moncton: Éditions d'Acadie, 1996.

Longfellow, Henry Wadsworth. *Evangeline: A Tale of Acadie* (1847). In *Poems and Other Writings,* 57–115. New York: Library of America, 2000.

Longley, J.W. 'Demonts Tercentenary at Annapolis, 1604–1904.' *Collections of the Nova Scotia Historical Society* 14 (1910): 107–29.

Parker, Barrett. *Saint Croix Island, 1604–1942.* Cambridge, MA: Crimson Printing Co., 1942.

Savoie, Calixte-F. *Mémoires d'un nationaliste acadien.* Moncton: Éditions d'Acadie, 1980.

Société nationale des Acadiens. *Les actes du Forum 1986: Pour une Acadie de l'an 2000.* Moncton: Michel Henry Éditeur, 1987.

Souvenir de la visite de Son Excellence Mgr Sbarretti délégué apostolique en Acadie. Shediac: Moniteur Acadien, 1904.

St. Andrews (Town of) v. Lecky, [1993] 133 N.B.R. (2d) 14 (N.B.Q.B.).

'Tercentenary of the Landing of De Monts at St. Croix Island.' *Collections of the Maire Historical Society,* 3rd ser., 2 (1906): 74–151.

U.S. National Park Service. *Île Ste-Croix / Saint Croix Island International Historic Site.* Boston: Support Office, National Park Service, 1968.

Welcome to Annapolis Royal's 350th Anniversary. Annapolis Royal: n.p., 1955.

Wherry, James. *Documents Relating to the History of the Passamaquoddy Indian Presence in Charlotte County, New Brunswick.* Fredericton: n.p., 1981.

3. Access to Information Requests from Government Agencies

Canada (Access to Information Program)
– Canadian Heritage. Documents Relating to the 250th Anniversary of the Acadian Deportation. File: 232-ATI-05/06-100.
– Canadian Heritage. Documents Relating to the 400th Anniversary of French Settlement. Files: 232-ATI-03/04-093; 232-ATI-04/05-105.
– Foreign Affairs and International Trade. Documents Relating to Canada-France, 1604–2004. File: A-2004-00059/fa.
– Indian and Northern Affairs. Documents Relating to Claims on the St Croix and Canoose [*sic*] Indian Reserves. File: A-2006/00114/mg.
– Parks Canada. Documents Relating to Île Ste-Croix. File: AP-2006-0007.
New Brunswick (Right to Information Program). Department of Intergovernmental Affairs. Documents Relating to the 400th Anniversary of Acadie.
United States (Freedom of Information Act). Department of Interior, National Park Service. Documents Relating to St Croix Island. File: A7221 (NER).

4. Interviews with Author (Place of interview)

Abord-Hugon, Chantal (Dieppe, New Brunswick).
Akagi, Hugh (St Andrews, New Brunswick).
Basque, Maurice (Moncton, New Brunswick).
Bergeron, Stéphane (Varennes, Québec).
Chiasson, Euclide (Dieppe, New Brunswick; Fontainebleau, France).
Chiasson, Herménégilde (Fredericton, New Brunswick).
Cyr, Michel (Dieppe, New Brunswick).
Duconseille, Pierre (Paris, France).
Fraser, Rita (St Andrews, New Brunswick).
Gaudet, Jean (Dieppe, New Brunswick).
Gillmor, Allan (St Stephen, New Brunswick).
Guttormsen, Keith (St Stephen, New Brunswick).
Kern, David (Annapolis Royal, Nova Scotia).
Kulcher, Maria (St Stephen, New Brunswick).
Laplante, Denis (Dieppe, New Brunswick).
Lonergan, Terrence (Paris, France).
Meuse, Frank (Bear River First Nation Reserve, Nova Scotia).
Soctomah, Donald (Indian Township, Maine).
Stewart, Norma (St Stephen, New Brunswick).
Theriault, Hal (Bear River First Nation Reserve, Nova Scotia).
Wyplosz, Perrine (Paris, France).

Secondary Sources

1. Print Sources

Acheson, T.W. 'The National Policy and the Industrialization of the Maritimes, 1880–1910.' *Acadiensis* 1 (1972): 3–29.
'Actes de la Convention 2004 de la Société acadienne du Nouveau-Brunswick.' Special issue, *Égalité* 51 (2005).
Agulhon, Maurice. 'La "statuomanie" en l'histoire.' *Ethnologie française* nos. 2–3 (1978): 145–72.
Allain, Greg. 'Le Congrés mondial acadien de 1994: Réseaux, Conflits, Réalisations.' *Revue de l'Université de Moncton* 30, 2 (1997): 141–59.
– 'La "nouvelle capitale acadienne"? Les entrepreneurs acadiens et la croissance récente du Grand Moncton.' *Francophonies d'Amérique* 19 (Spring 2005): 19–43.

Allain, Greg, and Maurice Basque. *De la survivance à l'effervescence: Portrait historique et sociologique de la communauté acadienne et francophone de Saint-Jean, Nouveau-Brunswick.* Saint John: Association régionale de la communauté francophone de Saint-Jean, 2001.

Anderson, Benedict. *Imagined Communities: Reflections on the Origin and Spread of Nationalism.* 2nd ed. revised. London: Verson, 1991.

Andrew, Sheila M. *The Development of Elites in Acadian New Brunswick, 1861–1881.* Montreal and Kingston: McGill-Queen's University Press, 1997.

Barkan, Elazar, and Alexander Karn, eds. *Taking Wrongs Seriously: Apologies and Reconciliation.* Stanford: Stanford University Press, 2006.

Basque, Maurice. *La Société Nationale de l'Acadie: Au coeur de la réussite d'un peuple.* Moncton: Éditions de la Francophonie, 2006.

Beiner, Guy. *Remembering the Year of the French: Irish Folk History and Social Memory.* Madison: University of Wisconsin Press, 2007.

Belkhodja, Chedly. 'L'Acadie confrontée au temps mondial.' *Francophonies d'Amérique* no. 11 (2001): 151–8.

Brodeur, Paul. *Restitution: The Land Claims of the Mashpee, Passamaquoddy, and Penobscot Indians of New England.* Boston: Northeastern University Press, 1985.

Brooks, Roy, ed. *When Sorry Isn't Enough: The Controversy over Apologies and Reparations for Human Injustice.* New York: NYU Press, 1999.

Caldbick, Mary. 'Locke's Doctrine of Property and the Dispossession of the Passamaquoddy.' MA thesis, University of New Brunswick, 1997.

Caron, Caroline-Isabelle. *Se créer des ancêtres: Un parcours généalogique nord-américain XIXe–XXe siecles.* Sillery: Septentrion, 2006.

– 'Se souvenir de l'Acadie d'antan: Représentation du passé historique dans le cadre de célébrations commémoratives locales en Nouvelle-Écosse au milieu du 20e siècle.' *Acadiensis* 36, 1 (Spring 2007): 55–71.

Chiasson, Herménégilde. 'Le festif en Acadie.' *Port Acadie* 8–9 (Fall 2006): 15–21.

Coates, Kenneth. *The Marshall Decision and Native Rights.* Montreal and Kingston: McGill-Queen's University Press, 2000.

Couturier, Jacques Paul. 'La République du Madawaska et l'Acadie: La construction identitaire d'une région néo-brunswickoise au XXe siècle.' *Revue d'histoire de l'Amérique française* 56 (2002): 153–84.

Cunningham, Michael. 'Apologies in Irish Politics: A Commentary and a Critique.' *Contemporary British History* 18 (2004): 80–92.

Daigle, Jean, ed. *Acadia of the Maritimes.* Moncton: Chaire d'études acadiennes, 1995.

– *Acadians of the Maritimes.* Moncton: Chaire d'études acadiennes, 1982.

Davis, Harold. *An International Community on the St Croix (1604–1930)*. Orono, ME: University Press, 1950.

Desjardins, Pierre-Marcel. 'L'Acadie des Maritimes: En périphérie de la périphérie.' *Francophonies d'Amérique* 19 (2005): 107–24.

Eagan, Bill. *Woven in Time: An Oral History of the Milltown (St Croix) Cotton Mill*. Bayside, NB: Kolby Publishing, 2004.

Faragher, John Mack. *A Great and Noble Scheme: The Tragic Story of the Expulsion of the French Acadians from their American Homeland*. New York: W.W. Norton, 2005.

Finn, Jean-Guy, Harley d'Entremont, and Philippe Doucet. 'Le nationalisme acadien vu à travers la convention d'orientation nationale de 1979.' *Revue de l'Université de Moncton* 13 (1980): 45–74.

Foner, Eric. *Who Owns History? Rethinking the Past in a Changing World*. New York: Hill and Wang, 2002.

Gagnon, Nathalie, and Donald Soctomah. *Tihtiyas and Jean*. Moncton: Bouton d'or Acadie, 2004.

Glassberg, David. *American Historical Pageantry: The Uses of Tradition in the Early Twentieth Century*. Chapel Hill: University of North Carolina Press, 1990.

– 'History and the Public: Legacies of the Progressive Era.' *Journal of American History* 73 (1984): 957–80.

Griffiths, Naomi. *From Migrant to Acadian: A North American Border People, 1604–1755*. Montreal: McGill-Queen's University Press, 2005.

Hautecoeur, Jules-Paul. *L'Acadie du discours*. Sainte-Foy: Presses de l'Université Laval, 1975.

Hobsbawm, Eric, and Eric Ranger, eds. *The Invention of Tradition*. Cambridge: Cambridge University Press, 1983.

Huskins, Bonnie, and Michael Boudreau. '*Life After Île Ste-Croix*.' *Acadiensis* 35, 2 (Spring 2006): 180–7.

Johnston, A.J.B. *Mathieu Da Costa and Early Canada: Possibilities and Probabilities*. Halifax: Parks Canada, n.d. http://www.pc.gc.ca/lhn-nhs/ns/portroyal/natcul/dacosta_e.pdf.

Kaplan, Stephen Laurence. *Farewell Revolution, Disputed Legacies: France, 1789/1989*. Ithaca: Cornell University Press, 1995.

Labelle, Ronald. 'Le tintamarre en Acadie: Une tradition inventée ou réinventée.' *Cahiers de la Société historique acadienne* 36 (2005): 109–21.

Langlois, Simon, and Jocelyn Létourneau, eds. *Aspects de la nouvelle francophonie canadienne*. Sainte-Foy: Presses de l'Université Laval, 2004.

Laxer, James. *The Acadians: In Search of a Homeland*. Toronto: Doubleday, 2006.

Lazare, Aaron. *On Apology*. Oxford: Oxford University Press, 2004.

Le Blanc, Barbara. *Postcards from Acadie: Grand-Pré, Evangeline and Acadian Identity*. Kentville: Gaspereau Press, 2003.

LeBlanc, Ronnie-Gilles, ed. *Du Grand Dérangement à la Déportation: Nouvelles perspectives historiques.* Moncton: Chaire d'études acadiennes, 2005.

Linenthal, Edward. *Preserving Memory: The Struggle to Create America's Holocaust Museum.* New York: Columbia University Press, 2001.

Lowenthal, David. *The Heritage Crusade and the Spoils of History.* Cambridge: Cambridge University Press, 1998.

Maier, Charles. 'A Surfeit of Memory: Reflections on History, Melancholy and Denial.' *History and Memory* 5 (1993): 136–51.

Marquis, Greg. 'Celebrating Champlain in the Loyalist City: Saint John, 1904–10.' *Acadiensis* 32 (2004): 27–43.

Marrus, Michael R. *Official Apologies and the Quest for Historical Justice.* Toronto: Munk Centre for International Studies, University of Toronto, 2006.

Marsters, Roger. '"The Battle of Grand-Pré": The Historic Sites and Monuments Board of Canada and the Commemoration of Acadian History.' *Acadiensis* 36 (2006): 29–50.

Nelles, H.V. *The Art of Nation-Building.* Toronto: University of Toronto Press, 1998.

Novick, Peter. *The Holocaust in American Life.* Boston: Houghton Mifflin, 1999.

Pâquet, Martin, ed. *Faute et réparation au Canada et au Québec contemporains.* Quebec: Éditions Nota Bene, 2006.

Pâquet, Martin, and Stéphane Savard, eds. *Balises et références: Acadies, francophonies.* Sainte-Foy: Presses de l'Université Laval, 2007.

Perrin, Warren. *Acadian Redemption: From Beausoleil Broussard to the Queen's Royal Proclamation.* Erath, LA: Acadian Heritage and Cultural Foundation, 2004.

Perron, Judith. 'Théâtres, fêtes et célébrations en Acadie (1880–1980).' PhD diss., Université de Moncton, 1995.

Pichette, Robert . *Le pays appelé l'Acadie: Réflexions sur des commémorations.* Moncton: Centre d'études acadiennes, 2006.

Proulx, Robert. 'Grand Dérangement: De la "terre à mon père" à la terre entière.' *Port-Acadie* nos. 8–9 (Fall 2005–Spring 2006): 239–53.

Reid, John G. *Acadia, Maine and New Scotland: Marginal Colonies in the Seventeenth Century.* Toronto: University of Toronto Press, 1981.

Reid, John G., Maurice Basque, Elizabeth Mencke, Barry Moody, Geoffrey Plank, and William Wicken. *The 'Conquest' of Acadia: Imperial, Colonial, and Aboriginal Constructions.* Toronto: University of Toronto Press, 2004.

Richard, Sacha. 'Commémoration et idéologie nationale en Acadie: Les fêtes du bicentenaire de la Déportation acadienne.' *Mens* 3 (2002): 27–60.

Ricker, Darleen. *L'sitkuk: The Story of the Bear River Mi'kmaw Community.* Lockeport, NS: Roseway Publishing, 1997.

Rosenzweig, Roy, and David Thelen. *The Presence of the Past: Popular Uses of History in American Life.* New York: Columbia University Press, 1993.

Rudin, Ronald. 'The Champlain-DeMonts Tercentenary: Voices from Nova Scotia, New Brunswick and Maine, June 1904.' *Acadiensis* 32 (2004): 3–26.

– *Founding Fathers: Champlain and Laval in the Streets of Quebec.* Toronto: University of Toronto Press, 2003.

Summerhill, Stephen, and John Alexander Williams. *Sinking Columbus: Contested History, Cultural Politics and Mythmaking during the Quincentenary.* Gainesville: University Press of Florida, 2000.

Surette, Paul. 'L'esprit de Chignecto, ou comment déjouer une expulsion.' *Égalité* no. 52 (Fall 2005): 81–90.

Tétu, Michel. *Sur les traces de Champlain, le visionnaire.* Quebec: Faculté des lettres, Université Laval, 2003.

Thériault, Joseph Yvon. *Identité à l'épreuve de la modernité.* Moncton: Éditions d'Acadie, 1995.

Thibault, Jean-François. 'Pourquoi des excuses sont-elles nécessaires? Mémoire de la déportation acadienne et la justice historique.' *Égalité* no. 52 (Fall 2005): 59–60.

Viau, Robert. 'Les commémorations du 250e anniversaire de la déportation.' *Égalité* no. 52 (Fall 2005): 13–56.

– '*Complices du silence?* De Claude Le Bouthillier et les "excuses" de la reine.' *Port-Acadie* nos. 8–9 (Fall 2005–Spring 2006): 75–98.

– *Grand-Pré: Lieu de mémoire, lieu d'appartenance.* Longueuil: MNH, 2005.

– *Les grands dérangements: La déportation des acadiens en littératures acadienne, québécoise et française.* Beauport: Publications MNH, 1997.

– *Les visages d'Évangeline: Du poème au mythe.* Beauport: MNH, 1998.

Wallace, Mike. *Mickey Mouse History and Other Essays on American Memory.* Philadelphia: Temple University Press, 1996.

Weyeneth, Robert. 'The Power of Apology and the Process of Historical Reconciliation.' *The Public Historian* 23 (2001): 25–9.

Wicken, William. *Mi'kmaq Treaties on Trial: History, Land, and Donald Marshall Junior.* Toronto: University of Toronto Press, 2002.

Young, James E. 'The Biography of a Memorial Icon: Nathan Rapoport's Warsaw Ghetto Monument.' *Representations* 26 (Spring 1989): 69–106.

2. Video Sources

Aristimuño, Leo, and Ronald Rudin. *Life After Île Ste-Croix.* DVD. Montreal: National Film Board of Canada, 2006.

Blanchar, Renée. *Le souvenir nécessaire.* DVD. Moncton: Productions Phare-Est, 2005.

Bouchet, Marie-Claude, and Michel Gemon. *Sur les pas de Pierre Dugua de Mons.* VHS. N.p.: Micro-Média, 2002.

Comeau, Phil, Rhéal Drisdelle, and Raymond Gauthier. *J'avions 375 ans.* VHS. Montreal: National Film Board of Canada, 1982.

Gladu, André. *Tintamarre.* DVD. Montreal: National Film Board of Canada, 2004.

Index